Contemporary Issues in Breast Cancer: A Nursing Perspective

Second Edition

Contemporary Issues in Breast Cancer: A Nursing Perspective

Second Edition

Karen Hassey Dow
PHD, RN, FAAN

Professor, School of Nursing
College of Health and Public Affairs
University of Central Florida
Orlando, Florida

JONES AND BARTLETT PUBLISHERS
Sudbury, Massachusetts
BOSTON   TORONTO   LONDON   SINGAPORE

World Headquarters
Jones and Bartlett Publishers
40 Tall Pine Drive
Sudbury, MA 01776
978-443-5000
info@jbpub.com
www.jbpub.com

Jones and Bartlett Publishers Canada
2406 Nikanna Road
Mississauga, ON L5C 2W6
CANADA

Jones and Bartlett Publishers International
Barb House, Barb Mews
London W6 7PA
UK

Production Credits
Chief Executive Officer: Clayton Jones
Chief Operating Officer: Don W. Jones, Jr.
Executive V.P. and Publisher: Robert W. Holland, Jr.
V.P., Sales and Marketing: William J. Kane
V.P., Design and Production: Anne Spencer
V.P., Manufacturing and Inventory Control: Therese Bräuer
Acquisitions Editor: Penny M. Glynn
Associate Production Editor: Scarlett L. Stoppa
Associate Editor: Karen Zuck
Manufacturing and Inventory Coordinator: Amy Bacus
Composition and Text Design: GEX, Inc.
Cover Design: Philip Regan
Printing and Binding: Malloy, Inc.
Cover Printing: Malloy, Inc.

Library of Congress Cataloging-in-Publication Data
Contemporary issues in breast cancer / edited by Karen Hassey Dow.—2nd ed.
        p. ; cm.
    Includes bibliographical references and index.
    ISBN 0-7637-1482-8 (hard cover : alk. paper)
        1. Breast—Cancer. I. Dow, Karen Hassey.
    [DNLM: 1. Breast Neoplasms. WP 870 C761 2003]
RC280.B8639 2003
616.99'449—dc21

                                    2003040076

Notice: The indications and dosages of all drugs in this book have been recommended in the medical literature and conform to the practices of the general community. The medications described do not necessarily have specific approval by the Food and Drug Administration for use in the diseases and dosages for which they are recommended. The package insert for each drug should be consulted for use and dosage as approved by the FDA. Because standards for usage change, it is advisable to keep abreast of revised recommendations, particularly those concerning new drugs.

Printed in the United States of America
07 06 05 04 03   10 9 8 7 6 5 4 3 2 1

∾

For my mother, Leonina, and my daughter, Lauren—

three generations of caring nurses

∾

Contents

Preface

Six years have passed since the publication of the first edition of *Contemporary Issues in Breast Cancer*. With the first edition my aim was to focus specifically on new and emerging issues in breast cancer treatment, acute symptom management, and the larger family, cultural, and community issues. Little did I know at the time that the first edition would become the first in a series of books dedicated to contemporary issues involved in prostate, lung, and colorectal cancers.

In the past six years we have witnessed enormous and significant changes in our understanding of early and advanced breast cancer with the introduction of new hormonal therapies, targeted therapy, and different combinations of chemotherapy and radiation therapy. In addition, new reconstructive and surgical techniques continue to improve cosmetic outcomes. Knowledge about long-term survivorship, recurrence, advanced disease, and end of life has likewise improved.

Given these changes, in this second edition I have reorganized the major topics into six sections: epidemiology, treatment of primary breast cancer, treatment of recurrent and metastatic breast cancer, symptom management, culture and ethnicity, and survivorship and end of life. All chapters have been updated and revised. New chapters appearing in this edition include information on targeted therapy and hormonal treatment of recurrent and metastatic disease. Chapters focusing on acute symptoms, persistent symptoms, and late effects of treatment include the most recent evidence and research interventions.

The second edition continues to be the result of tremendous work of many professionals and I would like to thank them for their contributions to our endeavors. First, to our contributing authors who generously shared their time and expertise and have enriched our knowledge and understanding of breast cancer. Second, to my colleagues and support staff in the School of Nursing at the University of Central Florida, particularly Sharon Austin and Thalia Basora who have diligently prepared, read, and re-read the edited manuscripts. Thanks also to Penny Glynn, Scarlett Stoppa, and Karen Zuck of Jones and Bartlett Publishers for their perseverance. And finally, to my lovely and talented daughter, Lauren Hassey, for her love and support.

Contributors

Jane Armer, PhD, RN; Associate Professor and Director of Nursing Research; Sinclair School of Nursing, University of Missouri Columbia, Columbia, Missouri

Roberta Baron, RN, MSN, AOCN; Clinical Nurse Specialist; Memorial Sloan-Kettering Cancer Center, New York, New York

Jennifer Bucholtz, RN, MS, CRNP, OCN®; Nurse Practitioner; The Sidney Kimmel Comprehensive Cancer Center at Johns Hopkins, Baltimore, Maryland

Janet S. Carpenter, PhD, RN, AOCN; Assistant Professor, School of Nursing; Vanderbilt University, Nashville, Tennessee

Patricia M. Clark, MSN, APRN, BC, AOCN; Practitioner and Research Nurse, Comprehensive Cancer Care; University of Michigan, Ann Arbor, Michigan

M. Joyce Dienger, DNSc, RN; Assistant Professor; College of Nursing, University of Cincinnati, Cincinnati, Ohio

Julie L. Elam, RN, MSN; Clinical Research Nurse; School of Nursing, Vanderbilt University, Nashville, Tennessee

Teresa Fraker, RN, BSN, OCN®; Charge Nurse; Center for Breast Health, Genesis Medical Center, Davenport, Iowa

Patricia I. Geddie, RN, MS, AOCN; Education Specialist II; M.D. Anderson Cancer Center Orlando, Orlando, Florida

Karen Hassey Dow, PhD, RN, FAAN; Professor, School of Nursing; University of Central Florida, Orlando, Florida

Kyle-Anne Hoyer, RN, MSN, AOCN; Clinical Nurse Specialist; Deaconess Billings Clinic, Billings, Montana

Dianne Ishida, PhD, APRN, CMC; Associate Professor; School of Nursing, University of Hawaii at Manoa, Honolulu, Hawaii

Victoria Wochna Loerzel, RN, MSN, AOCN; Project Director; School of Nursing, University of Central Florida, Orlando, Florida

Jean Lynn, MPH, RN, OCN®; Program Director; Breast Care Center and Mobile Mammography, George Washington University, Washington, D.C.

Joelle Machia, RN, BSN, BA; Clinical Research Nurse and Program Coordinator; Fred Hutchinson Cancer Research Center, Seattle, Washington

Jana Perun, MSN, ARNP; Advance Registered Nurse Practitioner; Radiation Oncology, M.D. Anderson Cancer Center Orlando, Orlando, Florida

Janice Phillips, PhD, RN, FAAN; Program Director; National Institute of Nursing Research, Bethesda, Maryland

Eva Smith, PhD, RN; Associate Professor; College of Nursing, University of Illinois Chicago, Chicago, Illinois

Nasrin Vaziri, RN, CPSN; Plastic Surgical Nurse; Plastic and Reconstructive Surgery, Memorial Sloan-Kettering Cancer Center, New York, New York

Gloria Velez-Barone, ARNP, MSN, AOCN; Clinical Coordinator; Oncology and Pain Management, Parrish Medical Center, Titusville, Florida

Section I

BREAST CANCER EPIDEMIOLOGY

INCIDENCE, EPIDEMIOLOGY, AND SURVIVAL

KAREN HASSEY DOW, PHD, RN, FAAN

INTRODUCTION

Breast cancer is the most common cancer in American women, accounting for 31% of new cancer cases (American Cancer Society, 2002). Breast cancer is the second leading cause of cancer deaths in American women after lung cancer, and it accounts for 15% of all cancer deaths in American women. Incidence rates of invasive breast cancer in the United States remained constant during the 1990s. However, with the use of mammographic screening, the incidence of noninvasive breast cancer increased. The purpose of this chapter is to review trends in the incidence and survival of breast cancer; variations in incidence and survival by age, histology, race, and ethnicity; and social factors such as insurance and access to care; and to provide a perspective on promising areas for predicting survival in the future.

INCIDENCE TRENDS IN THE UNITED STATES

Several federal and national organizations, including the American Cancer Society, the National Cancer Institute (NCI), the North American Association of Central Cancer Registries, the Centers for Disease Control and Prevention, and the National Center for Health Statistics (NCHS), collaborate to provide an annual update on cancer occurrence and trends in the United States. Howe *et al.* (2001) used the data to evaluate age-adjusted rates and annual percent changes from 1992 to 1998 and death rates for 1994–1998 for the major cancers, including breast cancer. From 1992 through 1998, the cancer incidence rates in females increased slightly. Howe *et al.* posited that this was due to an increase in breast cancer in some older age groups, possibly as a result of increased early detection. Deaths from lung cancer for females continued to increase but more slowly than in earlier years.

Breast cancer death rates declined an average of 1.8% per year between 1990 and 1996. Five-year relative survival for all women with localized invasive breast cancer is 96.5% based on the National Cancer Institute's Surveillance, Epidemiology, and End Results (SEER) program. The five-year survival rate for all stages is 85%. Survival is markedly decreased with an advanced stage of disease at diagnosis.

WORLDWIDE BREAST CANCER TRENDS

Worldwide, the incidence of breast cancer increased 0.5% annually, with 1.35 to 1.45 million new cases projected by 2010 (Mettlin, 1999). Breast cancer mortality is declining in the United States and in other industrialized countries such as Canada, Austria, Germany, and the United Kingdom. The decline may be a result of increased use of mammographic screening, early detection of disease, and newer improved treatments (Mettlin, 1999). Some of the decline may also result from higher fertility rates among the cohort of women born between 1924 and 1938 who had children after World War II. In contrast, European countries, including Spain, Portugal, Greece, Hungary, Poland, and Italy, have not reported favorable mortality trends. Asian regions report the lowest breast cancer mortality rates, which may be related to dietary, cultural, and/or environmental factors (Mettlin, 1999).

AGE

The incidence of breast cancer increases with age. Breast cancer is extremely rare in women in their early 20s. The incidence gradually increases with age; a large increase is seen in women after the age of menopause, generally considered to be age 50 years. The incidence continues to climb as women age into their 60s and 70s. The lifetime risk of developing breast cancer is one in eight.

Among minority women, there are differences in the incidence of breast cancer in women younger than the age of 45 years. There is a long-term pattern of higher incidence and mortality and poorer survival seen in African American (Swanson *et al.,* 2003) and Hispanic women (Biffl *et al.,* 2001; Shavers *et al.,* 2003).

HISTOLOGY

The incidence and patterns of invasive and noninvasive breast cancers have changed, most likely related to the increased use of mammographic screening. Today, about half of all breast cancers diagnosed are localized, with the majority being noninvasive breast cancer such as ductal carcinoma in situ (DCIS) (Ganz, 2002). (See Chapter 5 for further discussion on DCIS.) Women express some confusion about DCIS and its treatment. Findings showed that a diagnosis of DCIS has a significant psychological impact on women. De Morgan *et al.* (2002) explored women's experiences of being diagnosed with DCIS using focus group techniques. Five focus group interviews were conducted in New

South Wales, Australia, with 26 women diagnosed with DCIS. They found that women were confused about whether or not they had cancer that could result in death. Women's confusion was compounded by using the term "carcinoma" and by the recommendation of treatments such as mastectomy. Women's confusion was not alleviated by appropriate information, with most women reporting dissatisfaction with the information they received about DCIS specifically.

RACIAL AND ETHNIC DIFFERENCES

Racial and ethnic differences in incidence, treatment, and survival are seen across many studies. Clegg *et al.* (2002) analyzed cancer-specific survival rates for more than 1.78 million patients in the SEER Program geographic areas who were diagnosed between 1975 and 1997 as having invasive cancer, based on six racial or ethnic group categories (non-Hispanic whites, Hispanic whites, African Americans, Asian Americans, Hawaiian natives, and American Indians and Alaskan natives). They found that survival rates improved between 1988 and 1997 for all racial or ethnic groups. However, racial or ethnic differences in relative risks of cancer death persisted after controlling for age for all cancers combined and for age and stage for specific cancer sites ($p < .01$). African American, American Indian and Alaskan native, and Hawaiian native patients had higher relative risks of cancer death compared with the other minority groups. American Indians and Alaskan natives had the highest relative risks of cancer death, with the exception of colorectal cancer in males.

Breast cancer incidence is higher in Caucasian women than minority women. However, a disproportionate number of cancer deaths occur among racial/ethnic minorities. Disease characteristics such as larger tumor size, greater nodal involvement, estrogen receptor (ER) negative tumors, and shorter time to recurrence are related to differences in survival. Limited access to breast cancer screening, less than adequate treatment, and social and economic factors may also contribute to racial disparities in mortality.

AFRICAN AMERICAN WOMEN

African American women have a disproportionately higher risk of dying from breast cancer, 33%, compared to Caucasians. African American and white women differ in terms of age at menarche, menstrual cycle pattern, birth rates, lactation histories, patterns of oral contraceptive use, levels of obesity, frequency of hormone use, physical activity pattern, and alcohol intake (Bernstein *et al.*, 2003). This risk factor profile of African American women differs from white women and may partially explain the higher incidence rates for African Americans before age 45 years and the lower incidence rates at older ages.

Shavers and Brown (2002) evaluated racial/ethnic disparities with respect to receiving cancer treatment. The investigators found evidence of racial disparities in surgery, conservative therapy, and adjuvant therapy for breast cancer. Treatment differences could not be explained by racial/ethnic variation in clinical factors. Treatment differences were associated with an adverse impact on the health outcomes of racial/ethnic minorities, including more frequent recurrence, shorter disease-free survival, and higher mortality. Reducing the influence of social factors that impact delay in treatment may provide an important means of reducing racial/ethnic disparities in health. (See Chapter 18 for further discussion on African American women and breast cancer.)

Shavers *et al.* (2003), in a separate review using SEER Program data for 1990–1998 and SEER Patterns of Care data for 1990, 1991, and 1995, found that the age-specific breast cancer incidence rate for African American women younger than age 35 years was more than twice the rate for white women of similar age, and the mortality rate was more than three times higher. The investigators found further racial/ethnic variation in clinical presentation and treatment, which influenced survival. African American and Hispanic women presented with advanced disease had higher prevalence of adverse prognostic indicators compared to whites. African American and Hispanic women received cancer-directed surgery and radiation less frequently after undergoing breast-conserving surgery.

HISPANIC WOMEN

Biffl *et al.* (2001), using institutional and state cancer registry data, found that Latinas presented at a younger age, with more advanced stage III/IV disease, higher bilateral breast cancer, and poor five-year survival. Latinas comprise a disproportionate share of the young breast cancer population and may suffer more aggressive disease than other young women. Young Latinas may benefit from more vigilant and culturally appropriate screening and early detection.

ASIAN WOMEN

Asian American women are generally considered at lower risk for breast cancer than other ethnic groups. However, incidence and survival rates are typically based on aggregated data, which may obscure specific ethnic variations. Deapen *et al.* (2002) examined trends in invasive female breast cancer incidence using data from the Los Angeles Cancer Surveillance Program, which has a diverse multiethnic Asian American population. Overall breast cancer incidence rates among Asian American women remained stable in the late 1980s and early 1990s. Data from 1993 to 1997 suggest that incidence may be increasing for Asian American and non-Hispanic white women older than age 50 (estimated annual percent change [EAPC] = 6.3%, $p < 0.05$ and 1.5%, $p < 0.05$, respectively).

Deapen *et al.* also found that invasive breast cancer rates for Japanese American women increased rapidly since 1988 and are now approaching rates for non-Hispanic white women. Rates among Filipinas, who have historically had higher rates than their other Asian American counterparts, are not increasing as rapidly as rates for Japanese women, but they are still relatively high. Breast cancer risk among women of Japanese and Filipino ancestry is twice that of Chinese and Korean women. Asian women, who commonly have low breast cancer rates in their native countries, typically experience increasing breast cancer incidence after immigrating to the United States. Ethnic-specific incidence rates show that Japanese Americans, the first Asian population to immigrate to Los Angeles County in large numbers and the most acculturated, experienced a higher increase in breast cancer incidence. (See Chapter 19 for further discussion of Asian women and breast cancer.)

SOCIOCULTURAL FACTORS

SOCIOCULTURAL STATUS

Elevated rates of breast cancer in affluent Marin County, California, were first reported in the early 1990s. These rates have since been related to higher regional prevalence of known breast cancer risk factors, including low parity, education, and income. Close surveillance of Marin County breast cancer trends has continued, because distinctive breast cancer patterns in well-defined populations may help improve our understanding of breast cancer etiology.

Prehn *et al.* (2002) evaluated breast cancer incidence trends in the San Francisco Bay area, where breast cancer rates are higher compared to other communities across the country. The investigators included all white women diagnosed with invasive breast cancer between 1988 and 1997 in the five-county Bay Area (N = 19,807) and calculated annual age-specific incidence rates and estimated annual percent changes (EAPCs) for women in three age groups: younger than 45, 45–64, and 65 or older. They found that women aged 45–64 years from Marin County experienced a marked increase in breast cancer rates between 1991 and 1997 (EAPC = 8%, p = 0.02), controlling for disease stage or tumor histology. For the youngest and oldest women, they observed no rate differences. They found that the regional difference in trend by age was not the result of screening mammography or environmental exposures. Rather, the use of oral contraceptives and/or hormone replacement therapy may have contributed to the rate increase.

In a related study, Clarke *et al.* (2002) used recent incidence and mortality data available from the California Cancer Registry to examine rates and trends for 1990–1999 for invasive breast cancer among non-Hispanic white women in Marin County, in other San Francisco Bay Area counties, and in other urban California counties. They found that Marin County breast cancer incidence rates between 1990 and 1999 increased 3.6% per year, six times more rapidly than in comparison areas. The increase was limited to women aged 45–64 years, in whom rates increased at 6.7% per year (95% confidence interval, 3.8–9.6). Mortality rates did not change significantly in Marin County, despite 3–5% yearly declines elsewhere.

INSURANCE AND ACCESS TO CARE

Roetzheim *et al.* (2000) examined insurance issues and their influence on care and outcomes for patients with breast cancer. They evaluated treatments and adjusted risk of death using state tumor registry data for breast cancers in Florida in 1994 (N = 11,113). They found that patients lacking health insurance were less likely to receive breast-conserving surgery (BCS) compared to patients with private health insurance. Patients insured by a health maintenance organization (HMO) or Medicare were more likely to receive BCS but less likely to receive radiation therapy after BCS.

Non-Hispanic African Americans had higher mortality rates even when stage at diagnosis, insurance payer, and treatment modalities used were adjusted in multivariate models. Patients who had HMO insurance had similar survival rates compared to those with fee-for-service (FFS) insurance. Among non-Medicare patients, mortality rates were higher for patients who had Medicaid insurance and those who lacked health insurance, compared to patients who had FFS insurance. There were no insurance-related differences in survival rates, however, once stage at diagnosis was controlled. As a result of later stage at diagnosis, breast cancer patients who were uninsured, or were insured by Medicaid, had higher mortality rates. Mortality rates were also higher among non-Hispanic African Americans.

THE FUTURE

Recent advances in our knowledge of the human genome and the development of new high-performance screening techniques have revolutionized the ways in which researchers can study the pathogenesis of disease. Analysis of the levels of expression of thousands of genes with the use of DNA microarrays has shown distinct patterns in different kinds of tumors. These patterns may be used to classify histologically similar tumors into specific subtypes, a process that provides clinically relevant information.

Van 't Veer *et al.* (2002) identified a specific gene-expression profile that provides prognostic information about breast cancer. They analyzed gene expression patterns of 98 primary tumors from young patients with lymph-node-negative breast cancer using oligonucleotide microarrays. They used this information to identify a set of 70 genes with an expression pattern that allowed highly accurate classification of the patients into those with a poor prognosis (N = 180) and those with a good prognosis (N = 115). The prognostic profile did not depend on lymph node status, since patients with node-negative disease and those with node-positive disease had similar distribution in the two prognostic categories. Evaluation of other clinical characteristics indicated that the molecular prognosis profile was associated with age, histologic grade of the tumor, and estrogen receptor status—three of the currently accepted prognostic factors in breast cancer.

In a follow-up study using microarray analysis, the investigators used their previously established 70-gene prognosis profile to categorize 295 younger patients (less than 53 years of age) with stage I or II breast cancers with gene-expression signatures as having either a poor or a good prognosis. Of this group, 151 had lymph-node-negative disease, and 144 had lymph-node-positive disease. They evaluated the predictive power of the prognosis profile and found that the molecular signature of a poor prognosis was associated with an increased risk of distant metastases. The probability of remaining free of distant metastases at 10 years was 85.2% in the group of patients with a good prognosis and 50.6% in the group with a poor prognosis. They used the prognosis profile to also predict survival. The overall 10-year survival rate was 94.5% in the good prognosis group and 54.6% in the poor prognosis group.

Van de Vijver and colleagues (2002) showed that the gene-expression profile may be a better predictor of clinical outcome than current prognostic criteria, particularly because the gene expression profile accurately identified patients with positive nodes as having a good prognosis (Kallioniemi, 2002). While their findings are confined to a group of younger women with early-stage disease, they still provide an interesting window of opportunities for the clinical management of breast cancer in the future (Kallioniemi, 2002).

REFERENCES

American Cancer Society. (2002). Facts & Figures. Atlanta, Ga.: Author.

Bernstein, L., Teal, C.R., Joslyn, S., & Wilson, J. (2003). Ethnicity-related variation in breast cancer risk factors. *Cancer, 97*(1 Suppl), 222–229.

Biffl, W.L., Myers, A., Franciose, R.J., Gonzalez, R.J., & Darnell, D. (2001). Is breast cancer in young Latinas a different disease? *American Journal of Surgery, 182,* 596–600.

Clarke, C.A., Glaser, S.L., West, D.W., Ereman, R.R., Erdmann, C.A., Barlow, J.M., & Wrensch, M.R. (2002). Breast cancer incidence and mortality trends in an affluent population: Marin County, California, USA, 1990–1999. *Breast Cancer Research, 4,* R13.

Clegg, L.X., Li, F.P., Hankey, B.F., Chu, K., & Edwards, B.K. (2002). Cancer survival among U.S. whites and minorities: a SEER (Surveillance, Epidemiology, and End Results) Program population-based study. *Archives of Internal Medicine, 162,* 1985–1993.

Deapen, D., Liu, L., Perkins, C., Bernstein, L., & Ross, R.K. (2002). Rapidly rising breast cancer incidence rates among Asian-American women. *International Journal of Cancer, 99,* 747–770.

De Morgan, S., Redman, S., White, K.J., Cakir, B., & Boyages, J. (2002). "Well, have I got cancer or haven't I?" The psycho-social issues for women diagnosed with ductal carcinoma in situ. *Health Expectations, 4,* 310–318.

Ganz, P. (2002). Breast cancer 2002—where do we stand? *CA—A Cancer Journal for Clinicians, 52,* 253–255.

Howe, H.L., Wingo, P.A., Thun, M.J., Ries, L.A., Rosenberg, H.M., Feigal, E.G., & Edwards, B.K. (2001). Annual report to the nation on the status of cancer (1973 through 1998), featuring cancers with recent increasing trends. *Journal of the National Cancer Institute, 93,* 1656.

Kallioniemi, A. (2002). Molecular signatures of breast cancer—predicting the future. *New England Journal of Medicine, 347,* 2067–2068.

Mettlin, C. (1999). Global breast cancer mortality statistics. *CA—A Cancer Journal for Clinicians, 49,* 138–144.

Prehn, A., Clarke, C., Topol, B., Glaser, S., & West, D. (2002). Increase in breast cancer incidence in middle-aged women during the 1990s. *Annals of Epidemiology, 12,* 476–481.

Roetzheim, R.G., Gonzalez, E.C., Ferrante, J.M., Pal, N., Van Durme, D.J., & Krischer, J.P. (2000). Effects of health insurance and race on breast carcinoma treatments and outcomes. *Cancer, 89,* 2202–2213.

Shavers, V.L., & Brown, M.L. (2002). Racial and ethnic disparities in the receipt of cancer treatment. *Journal of the National Cancer Institute, 94,* 334–357.

Shavers, V.L., Harlan, L.C., & Stevens, J.L. (2003). Racial/ethnic variation in clinical presentation, treatment, and survival among breast cancer patients under age 35. *Cancer, 97,* 134–147.

Swanson, G.M., Haslam, S.Z., & Azzouz, F. (2003). Breast cancer among young African-American women. *Cancer, 97*(1 Suppl), 273–279.

van de Vijver, M., He, Y., van 't Veer, L., Dai, H., Hart, A., Voskuil, D., Schreiber, G., *et al.* (2002). A gene-expression signature as a predictor of survival in breast cancer. *New England Journal of Medicine, 347,* 1999–2009.

van 't Veer, L., Dai, H., van de Vijver, M., He, Y., Hart, A., *et al.* (2002). Gene expression profiling predicts clinical outcome of breast cancer. *Nature, 415,* 530–536.

Chapter 2

NONGENETIC AND HERITABLE RISK FACTORS

PATRICIA M. CLARK, MSN, APRN, BC, AOCN

INTRODUCTION

With an annual incidence in the United States of over 200,000 women, debates about screening, public interest in preventive medicine, discovery of breast cancer specific genes, and the rise of chemoprevention as part of the cancer continuum have combined to fuel interest in risk assessment for breast cancer. Risk for breast cancer is generally divided into nonheritable and heritable risks. This division is somewhat artificial, as most theories of cancer genesis involve both types of risk. The advantage of this distinction is in considering which factors may be more likely to be affected by lifestyle changes and which may dictate more stringent surveillance. The purpose of this chapter is to discuss the risk factors for breast cancer, risk assessment tools, issues relating to genetic testing, and the oncology nursing role.

NONHERITABLE RISK FACTORS

Many clinicians, upon giving a diagnosis of breast cancer, have heard a woman say, "But no one in my family has cancer!" Indeed, the etiology of most breast cancers is not genetic but is likely related to environmental and lifestyle factors leading to somatic mutations that result in malignancy. For those with a genetic predisposition to breast cancer determined by genetic testing or by compelling family history, modification of nonheritable risk factors may facilitate a greater sense of control. Whether or not lifestyle changes in those with a strong family history will decrease their risk of breast cancer is not fully known (Greco, 2000). Unfortunately, many nonheritable risk factors cannot be modified. Those factors that can be modified may not only decrease risk for breast cancer but may also contribute to improvement of overall health. The role of lifestyle modification in decreasing the risk of breast cancer has at times been controversial and merits further rigorous investigation.

GENDER

Gender is the most obvious risk factor for developing breast cancer, with 99% of breast cancers occurring in women.

AGE

The strongest risk factor for developing breast cancer is age (Key, Allen, *et al.*, 2002). The chance of a woman in North America developing breast cancer by the age of 90 is 1 in 8 or approximately 12.5%. This statistic has often been misinterpreted by the public to mean that every woman has a 1 in 8 chance of developing breast cancer, when in reality the majority of risk occurs after the age of 50 years. Table 2.1 shows a breakdown of the risk by decade of life, which may be useful in explaining this risk to patients and family members.

CHILDBEARING

Risk of breast cancer initially increases after childbearing, because of acute hormonal stimulation of occult tumors (Lambe *et al.*, 1994), but overall, the effect of childbearing confers an average 25% decrease in the risk of developing breast cancer compared with nulliparous women (Ewertz *et al.*, 1990). Risk decreases by 50% for women who have five or more live births (Layde *et al.*, 1989; Ewertz *et al.*, 1990). Young age at first live birth decreases the risk of breast cancer, and it appears that the younger the age, the greater the protection (Kelsey *et al.*, 1993).

Birth of a first child after the age of 35 years seems to confer a higher risk than nulliparity. Conflicting data exists regarding the role of gender of offspring in increasing risk of breast cancer. Data obtained from three Swedish registries showed an inverse association between male offspring and breast cancer occurrence in women under age 40 years, but no evidence was found to indicate that gender changes the long-term protective effect of pregnancy (Hsieh *et al.*, 1999). A Norwegian study supported this hypothesis in part, but found that the protective effect was observed in women with three children only (Albrektsen & Kvale, 2000).

Table 2.1 Probability of Developing Breast Cancer in Next 10 Years

Current age	Probability
20 years	1 in 2044
30 years	1 in 249
40 years	1 in 67
50 years	1 in 36
60 years	1 in 29
70 years	1 in 24

Adapted from: American Cancer Society. (2002). *Breast Cancer Facts and Figures 2001–2002*. Atlanta, Ga.: Author.

ABORTION: INDUCED AND SPONTANEOUS

The topic of abortion and breast cancer risk has been argued in medical, lay, and political literature. The theory behind the association between abortion and breast cancer hypothesizes that high concentrations of estrogen released into the circulatory system by the corpus luteum in early pregnancy stimulates undifferentiated breast cells. In a full-term pregnancy, the stimulated cells achieve full differentiation, but in the setting of induced abortion, they do not. The theory is that this proliferation of partially undifferentiated cells is more susceptible to carcinogens later in life.

In animal models, interrupted pregnancy resulted in a risk of breast cancer that equaled that of a nulliparous animal (Russo & Russo, 1980). A variety of epidemiologic studies have been performed to answer this question, and a variety of criticisms have been leveled at them, including recall bias of subjects and "wish" bias, or the belief of the investigator that the hypothesis is true to the exclusion of objectivity in research (Weed & Kramer, 1996). The largest cohort studied, 1.5 million women in the Danish Cancer Registry, showed that induced abortions have no overall effect on the risk of breast cancer (Melbye *et al.*, 1997). In contrast, there is little disagreement that spontaneous abortions are not associated with increased breast cancer risk, as they are often characterized by low circulating maternal estrogen, suggesting a low risk of later breast cancer (Davidson, 2001).

BREAST-FEEDING

While childbearing is known to be protective against breast cancer, the relationship between breast cancer and breast-feeding is less clear. Until recently, no one study has been large enough to accurately associate breast-feeding with risk of breast cancer. Two meta-analyses have recently looked at this phenomenon. Bernier and colleagues (2000) in France reviewed the literature using ever/never breast-feeding and duration of breast-feeding as primary variables with menopausal status as a potential effect modifier. They found that the decrease in breast cancer risk was most prominent in premenopausal women and in women who breast-fed for more than 12 months. Duration of breast-feeding was also noted to significantly affect breast cancer risk in studies performed by Zheng *et al.* (2000) in China, Chang-Claude *et al.* (2000) in Germany, and Coogan *et al.* (1999) in South Africa.

The Collaborative Group on Hormonal Factors in Breast Cancer more recently published a reanalysis of 47 epidemiological studies from 30 countries involving more than 50,000 women with breast cancer and more than 96,000 women without breast cancer. They found that the relative risk of breast cancer decreased by 4.3% for every 12 months of breast-feeding, in addition to a reduction of 7.0% for every birth. This relationship did not differ by age, ethnic origin, childbearing pattern, or other personal characteristics (Collaborative Group, 2002). This contradicts earlier findings that the effect of breast-feeding on breast cancer risk was stronger in premenopausal women (Newcomb, 1997; Bernier *et al.*, 2000; Lipworth *et al.*, 2000). The Collaborative Group also noted that the cumulative incidence of breast cancer in developed countries would be reduced by more than 50% by age 70 years if the average number of births and number of months breast-feeding were equivalent to women in developing countries. Incidence could be decreased by 42% if duration of breast-feeding alone was increased (Collaborative Group, 2002). Although an increase in childbearing or length of breast-feeding may be impractical, especially in Western countries, the same effect might be achieved if a way could be established to mimic the effect of breast-feeding.

ORAL CONTRACEPTIVES

The contribution of oral contraceptives, defined as combination contraceptives (containing both estrogen and progestin in each cycle in monophasic, multiphasic, or sequential formulation) and progestin-only contraceptives, to the risk of breast cancer was studied by Marchbanks *et al.* (2002). In 4575 women between the ages of 35 and 64 years, there was no significant increase in breast cancer risk that could be attributed to oral contraceptive use in present or past. This confirms the findings of the Cancer and Steroid Hormone (CASH) study conducted by Sattin *et al.* (1986) and refutes the findings of a meta-analysis of 54 epidemiologic studies that showed that taking oral contraceptives caused an increased risk of breast cancer, compared with nonusers, that decreased steadily after cessation (Collaborative Group, 1996).

DIET

Doll and Peto (1981) estimated that dietary factors accounted for nearly a third of cancers in western countries in 1981. This made diet second only to tobacco as a potentially preventable cause of cancer in developed countries. A report by the World Health Organization states that this may be an overestimate, but agrees that dietary factors may play an important role in cancer prevention (Key, Schatzkin, *et al.,* 2002). Evidence that dietary fat contributes significantly to the risk of breast cancer has been incongruous. Hunter and colleagues (1996) pooled prospective data and showed no positive association between dietary fat intake and breast cancer.

Use of dietary phytoestrogens has shown some influence in reducing breast cancer risk, probably because of their antiestrogenic effect (Shu *et al.,* 2001). However, phytoestrogens also have estrogenic effects on breast tissue, and current evidence does not support their use in breast cancer prevention. The Diet and Androgens (DIANA) randomized trial showed that women who dramatically altered their diet to one that was low in animal fat and refined carbohydrates and high in low-glycemic-index foods, monounsaturated and n-3 polyunsaturated fatty acids, and phytoestrogens had increased sex hormone-binding globulin, decreased serum testosterone and serum estradiol levels, and significant decrease in body weight—all of which are favorable changes in hormonal indicators of breast cancer risk (Berrino *et al.,* 2001). Further studies are needed to assess the ability to sustain this type of diet and to determine whether these changes are actually linked to breast cancer risk reduction. While no dietary protective factors have been firmly established to prevent breast cancer (Key, Allen, *et al.,* 2002), alcohol consumption and obesity, two controllable risk factors, are thought to play a part in breast cancer risk.

ALCOHOL CONSUMPTION

The relationship of alcohol consumption to breast cancer risk has been reviewed in several meta-analyses (Longnecker *et al.,* 1988; Howe *et al.,* 1991; Longnecker, 1994; D'Arcy *et al.,* 1996; Smith-Warner *et al.,* 1998; Carrao *et al.,* 1999; Ellison *et al.,* 2001; Singletary & Gapstur, 2001), confirming the dose–response relationship between alcohol and breast cancer. This effect is present at moderate consumption of one to two drinks per day and includes various types of alcohol, including wine, beer, and spirits. Relative risk seems to rise approximately 9% for each 10-gram increase in alcohol consumed (Smith-Warner *et al.,* 1998). The reported protective effect of resveratrol and other components of wine in suppression of human cancer cell growth has not been seen in these studies (Ellison *et al.,* 2001). Both premenopausal and postmenopausal breast cancer risk increase with greater alcohol intake (Singletary & Gapstur, 2001). Potential mechanisms for the effect of ethanol on breast tissue include increased estrogen and androgen levels, increased breast tissue susceptibility to carcinogenesis with ethanol consumption, increased mammary carcinogen DNA damage, and greater potential for metastasis of breast cancer cells (Singletary & Gapstur, 2001).

OBESITY

The effect of weight, weight gain, and obesity on breast cancer risk has been well studied. In the Women's Health Initiative Observational Study (Morimoto *et al.,* 2002), over 85,000 women aged 50–79 years were enrolled in 50 clinics in the United States. Upon entry into the study, height, weight, and waist and hip circumference were measured. Over 1000 women developed invasive breast cancer. Women who had never used hormone replacement therapy (HRT) and who had a body mass index (BMI) greater than 31.1 had an elevated risk of postmenopausal breast cancer (relative risk 2.52; 95% confidence interval 1.62–3.93) compared to women with a BMI less than 22.6. In this study, risk was most evident in younger postmenopausal women. Other weight-related risk factors for breast cancer in this group included change in BMI since age 18, maximum BMI, and weight. Ratio of waist to hip circumference—a measure of fat distribution—was not associated with increased breast cancer risk (Morimoto *et al.,* 2002).

A second large study, the American Cancer Society's Cancer Prevention Study II (Petrelli *et al.,* 2002), looked at BMI and height in 424,168 postmenopausal women who did not have cancer at the time of their interview. Fourteen years into the study, 2852 breast cancer deaths had been observed. Breast cancer mortality was directly proportional to increasing BMI and was higher in women with increasing height up to 66 inches compared to those less than 60 inches (Petrelli *et al.,* 2002).

The mechanism by which obesity increases the risk of breast cancer is probably by increasing serum concentrations of free estradiol (Key, Allen, *et al.,* 2002). Estradiol production is increased by conversion of androstenedione (produced in the adrenal gland) into estrone by aromatase. The rate of estradiol production is related to the amount of adipose tissue—usually greater in postmenopausal women (Bray, 2002). Other studies have looked at the type of obesity in relationship to risk of breast cancer. Stoll (2002) hypothesizes that higher breast cancer risk related to increased abdominal fat may be related to abnormal insulin signaling through the insulin receptor substrate 1 pathway, leading to insulin resistance, hyperinsulinemia, and increased concentrations of endogenous estrogen and androgen. This relationship between insulin regulation and cancer promotion may help explain the relationship between breast cancer risk and age at menarche, pregnancy, and onset of obesity (Stoll, 2002). Effects of obesity on breast cancer risk in ethnic populations have been studied. Wenten and colleagues studied Hispanic white women, the group with the highest rate of obesity in the United States. Weight change from age 18 years to usual adult weight was associated with increased risk of breast cancer. For the Hispanic women in this study, the increased risk was independent of menopausal status (Wenten *et al.*, 2002).

HERITABLE RISK FACTORS

While familial cancers have been recognized by clinicians for more than a century, only recently has the molecular basis for inherited cancer been recognized (Marsh & Zori, 2002). Alfred Knudson (2001) explained the development of retinoblastoma with his "two-hit" hypothesis. This theory states that the first "hit" is a mutation in the germline tissue, and the second "hit" occurs in the somatic allele of the same gene. Most genes linked with familial cancer syndromes seem to function as tumor suppressor genes. Tumor suppressor genes in colon cancer may act as "gatekeepers" to prevent unregulated growth, as "caretakers" to repair DNA proteins, or as "landscapers"—genes that indirectly affect cancer development by influencing the stromal environment (Kinzler & Vogelstein, 1998). Mutations in these genes prevent them from carrying on their prescribed functions. In breast cancer, both BRCA1 and BRCA2 genes appear to have a caretaker function, and mutation seems to prevent DNA repair (Pellegrini *et al.*, 2002; Thompson & Schild, 2002). Table 2.2 describes a variety of genes associated with breast cancer.

GENETIC SYNDROMES ASSOCIATED WITH INCREASED RISK FOR BREAST CANCER

BRCA1 Mutation Syndrome. Individuals with BRCA1 mutations are likely to develop premenopausal breast and/or ovarian cancers and may have close family members with like diagnoses. These tumors are often estrogen receptor-negative with a high mitotic index, and they may have TP53 mutation. All of these are characteristics of aggressive tumors (Marsh & Zori, 2002). BRCA1 mutation carriers have a greater than 80% risk of developing breast cancer and a 40% risk of developing ovarian cancer by age 70 years (Marsh & Zori, 2002). Founder mutations are present in isolated ethnic groups with limited parent gene pools. BRCA1 founder mutations are present among Ashkenazi Jews. The most common is 185delAG; BRCA1 5382insC and BRCA2 6174delT are examples of other founder mutations in this population. One of the three mutations can be found in more than 2% of Ashkenazi Jewish breast or ovarian cancer patients without a family history

Table 2.2 Genes Associated with Breast Cancer

Gene	Syndrome	Other cancers	Location	Function/classification
BRCA1	Breast/ovarian	Ovarian cancer	17q21	DNA repair
BRCA2	Breast/ovarian	Male breast cancer Prostate cancer	13q12.3	DNA repair
PTEN/MMAC/TEP1	Cowden syndrome	Thyroid (follicular adenoma, follicular carcinoma, papillary carcinoma), endometrial carcinoma	10q23.3	Protein tyrosine phosphatase
PT53	Li-Fraumeni syndrome	Soft tissue sarcoma, brain tumors, adrenocortical tumors, leukemia	17q13	Transcription factor, cell cycle regulation, apoptosis
STK11/LKB1	Peutz-Jeghers syndrome	GI tract carcinoma, testicular cancer, gynecological cancers	19p13.3	Serine-threonine kinase
ATM	Ataxia-telangiectasia	Cerebellar ataxia, occulocutaneous telangiectasia, immunodeficiency, radiation sensitivity and predisposition to malignancy/leukemia, lymphoma, breast cancer	11q22-33	DNA damage recognition

Reference: Marsh, D.J. & Zori, R.T. (2002). Genetic insights into familial cancers—update and recent discoveries. *Cancer Letters, 181,* 125–164.

(Arver *et al.,* 2000). BRCA1 founder mutations are also seen in the Netherlands, Sweden, Norway, Germany, and Latvia and in African American families (Arver *et al.,* 2000).

BRCA2 Mutation Syndrome. Both males and females with this mutation are at increased risk of developing breast cancer. Other cancers that are overrepresented in these families include prostate cancer, pancreatic cancer, malignant melanoma, colon cancer, and ovarian cancer (Marsh & Zori, 2002). BRCA2 mutation carriers have an 84% risk of developing breast cancer by age 70 years and a 76% risk of developing ovarian cancer by the same age. Founder mutations are also common in this gene; 3–8% of breast cancers in the Ashkenazi Jewish population are ascribed to BRCA2 mutations. Specific founder mutations represent a wide variance in cancer susceptibility. For example, the BRCA2 999del5 has a prevalence of 0.5% in the general Icelandic population and accounts for nearly one quarter of breast cancers diagnosed before the age of 40 years. Another mutation, BRCA2 6174delT, is present in 1.5% of the general Ashkenazi population but accounts for only 4% of breast cancers diagnosed before age 40 years. (Arver *et al.,* 2000). Founder mutations of BRCA2 are in Iceland, Belgium, Spain, Wales, and Hungary. In Iceland and Hungary, 35–40% of male breast cancers are attributable to BRCA2 mutations (Arver *et al.*, 2000). The risk of breast cancer in founder populations varies by the method used to study the mutation. An example is that population-based studies of 5318 Ashkenazi volunteers estimated the risk of breast cancer in BRCA2 carriers to be 56%, but family-based studies have estimated the risk to be 84% (Levy-Lahad *et al.*, 1997; Ford *et al.*, 1998).

Cowden Syndrome (CS). Cowden syndrome is most often seen in women in their twenties, but this may vary between and within families. This syndrome is characterized by development of hamartomas that are not malignant but are tumorlike tissue overgrowths that may occur in the breast, thyroid, skin, GI tract, and CNS. Breast fibroadenomas are present in 70% and malignant breast cancer develops in 25–50% of women with Cowden syndrome. Other clinical signs of Cowden syndrome include macrocephaly, genitourinary abnormalities, and Lhermitte-Duclos disease (Marsh & Zori, 2002).

Peutz-Jeghers Syndrome (PJS). Overall rate of malignancy in this syndrome is 20–50% and gastrointestinal malignancy is the most common (Marsh & Zori, 2002). There is a five-fold increase in early-onset breast cancer in individuals with this syndrome (Arver *et al.*, 2000). Clinical signs include pigmented freckling of lips, buccal mucosa, face, fingers, and hands (Marsh & Zori, 2002).

Li-Fraumeni Syndrome. This syndrome first described family clusters of cancers, including premenopausal breast cancer, sarcomas, brain tumors, adrenocortical carcinomas, and leukemia, occurring at uncommonly young ages (Li & Fraumeni, 1969). Although most p53 mutations are somatic in nature, this syndrome is characterized by germline p53 mutations in 50% of those families with syndrome characteristics. Individuals with germline p53 mutations have a 50% risk of developing cancer by age 30 years and 90% by age 70 years. A second gene, hCHK2, has been identified in Li-Fraumeni families (Bell *et al.*, 1999).

Ataxia-telangiectasia (A-T). The ATM gene is located at 11q22-23 and encodes a protein that plays a role in DNA damage recognition systems. Clinically, A-T manifests itself as progressive cerebellar ataxia, oculomotor apraxia, oculocutaneous telangiectasia, immunodeficiency, sensitivity to radiation, premature aging, and increased incidence of leukemia and lymphoma, as well as increased risk of breast cancer reported as a relative risk of 6.8 (Arver *et al.*, 2000; Marsh & Zori, 2002).

RISK ASSESSMENT

Who should undergo risk assessment for breast cancer? What sort of assessment should be completed? There are generally two types of assessment for breast cancer risk: nonmedical, consisting of use of risk assessment tools, and medical, consisting of genetic and cellular testing.

NONMEDICAL RISK ASSESSMENT

Initial screening for breast cancer may occur with the primary care provider in the form of a breast exam performed at the time of the annual Pap test. Formal breast cancer risk assessment is based on evaluation of personal history, heredity, lifestyle (dietary, reproductive), hormonal, environmental, and other factors (Greco, 2000). The primary care provider needs to know when to refer a patient and family for in-depth risk analysis. Table 2.3 provides key points found on history that may trigger a referral for genetic assessment.

Assessment of personal history includes an in-depth medical history with confirmation of cancer diagnoses by pathology report. Hereditary factors may be assessed by obtaining at least three generations of family history and attempting to obtain pathology reports from first- and second-degree family members (Greco, 2000). Because genetic testing is expensive and may carry social, legal, and insurance liabilities, use of risk assessment tools can determine degree of risk or probability of carrying a gene mutation.

Risk Assessment Tools.   Two risk assessment tools are most often used by health care providers for determining breast cancer risk: the Gail model and the Claus model. The Gail model is used most often. This model was based on Caucasian women participating in the Breast Cancer Detection Demonstration Project (BCDDP). A nested case-control study in the BCDDP was implemented to estimate risks based on age at menarche, age at first live birth, number of first-degree relatives with breast cancer, number of breast biopsies, and presence or absence of atypical hyperplasia on any biopsy specimen (Gail *et al.,* 1989).

This model has been updated using data from the Surveillance, Epidemiology, and End Results (SEER) Program of the National Cancer Institute, and it provides separate estimates for white and black women (Costantino *et al.,* 1999). Limitations of this model include underestimating risk in women with a history of in situ and invasive breast cancers. It may also underestimate risk for women with mutations in the BRCA1 or BRCA2 genes, and those with Cowden syndrome or Li-Fraumeni syndrome. It may overestimate risk for recent immigrants from rural China or Japan. Data for this model has not been strongly validated

---

Table 2.3 Guidelines for Referral to Cancer Genetics Services—Breast Cancer Risk

- Two or more family members (first- or second-degree relatives) on same side of family (maternal or paternal)
- Bilateral breast cancer or bilateral ovarian cancer
- Multiple primary cancers in one person
- Early-age breast or ovarian cancer
- Pattern of breast and/or ovarian cancer in family (any age onset)
- Family member with known genetic mutation predisposing to breast or ovarian cancer
- Male breast cancer in family
- Ashkenazi Jewish ethnicity

Reference: Greco, K.E. (2000). Cancer genetics: impact of the double helix. *Oncology Nursing Forum, 27*(9), 29–36.

in women of African American, Hispanic, or other ethnicities. Because of these inadequacies, the Gail model is probably best used by a knowledgeable risk counselor (Gail & Costantino, 2001).

The Claus model was developed using data from the Cancer and Steroid Hormone (CASH) study. This was a population-based, case-control study conducted by the Centers for Disease Control and Prevention. Data was used to provide age-specific risk estimates of breast cancer for women with a family history of breast cancer. This model differs from the Gail model primarily by emphasizing family history of breast cancer.

A third model estimates the probability that an individual carries a genetic mutation based on specific family history. BRCAPRO is based on age-specific and cumulative breast and ovarian cancer incidence rates for BRCA gene mutation carriers, compared with the same rates for noncarriers. This model, unlike the previous two models discussed, accounts for Ashkenazi Jewish heritage and male breast cancer (Euhus *et al.,* 2002).

GENETIC TESTING

Prior to genetic testing, a thorough discussion about genetic testing must take place. Table 2.3 describes the critical pieces of this discussion. Testing should only be done when the primary care provider, oncologist, genetic counselor, nurse, or medical geneticist is able to address these issues prior to testing and is available to discuss results of testing in detail (American Society of Clinical Oncology, 1996).

Post-testing discussion should include individualized options for breast cancer screening, including possible increased frequency of mammography and/or ultrasound, clinical breast exams, or serial ductal lavage. Discussion of prophylactic mastectomy and oophorectomy should be offered to those with a known breast cancer susceptibility gene mutation, and these discussions should take into account the specifics of the carrier. Post-testing discussion should also stress the need for definitive research to confirm the efficacy of increased surveillance and risk reduction strategies in those with breast cancer susceptibility mutations (American Society of Clinical Oncology, 1996).

CELLULAR ASSESSMENT OF BREAST CANCER RISK

In addition to the use of mathematical models and genetic testing, assessment of breast cancer risk at the cellular level may help women choose appropriate risk reduction strategies. Cytological examination of nipple aspirate fluid, fine-needle aspirate of normal breast tissue, and ductal lavage are three ways that cellular assessment of breast cancer risk may be accomplished.

Nipple Aspiration. Nipple aspiration is a noninvasive, simple procedure used to obtain nipple aspiration fluid (NAF) from the breast. NAF is obtained by using a modified suction cup adapted to fit a syringe and applying gentle suction to the nipple to elicit fluid. The aspirate may be examined for cytology as well as a variety of biomarkers, including carcinoembryonic antigen (CEA) (Foretova *et al.,* 1998), prostate-specific antigen (PSA)

(Sauter *et al.*, 1996), and proteomic signatures (Paweletz *et al.*, 2001). Cellular atypia found in cytologic evaluation of NAF is correlated with increased risk for breast cancer (Wrensch *et al.*, 1992; Sauter *et al.*, 1997; Wrensch *et al.*, 2001).

Fine-Needle Aspiration (FNA). Periareolar fine-needle aspirates have been used to obtain tissue for cytology and biomarkers as a way of identifying women at high short-term risk for breast cancer. Local anesthetic is injected prior to multiple FNAs performed in the periareolar region. Biomarkers done on FNA specimens obtained in this fashion include epidermal growth factor receptor, estrogen receptor, p53, and HER-2/neu (Fabian *et al.*, 2000).

Ductal Lavage. Ductal lavage is a newer technique that consists of cannulating fluid-producing ducts with a microcatheter and using retrograde lavage to obtain cellular contents from the duct. Both topical anesthesia and intraductal anesthetic are used for this procedure. One advantage of this procedure over nipple aspiration and fine needle aspiration is the theoretical ability to serially cannulate the duct of interest. In addition, higher cell counts allow for additional biomarker studies to be performed. Ductal lavage also seems to be more sensitive than nipple aspiration. In one large study, ductal lavage detected abnormal intraductal breast cells 3.2 times more often than nipple aspiration (Dooley *et al.*, 2001). Disadvantages common to this technique and to nipple aspiration are that only ducts that are secretory have been studied for atypia. Issues of sensitivity, specificity, and localization require further study using this technique.

ONCOLOGY NURSING AND RISK ASSESSMENT

The role of the oncology nurse in risk assessment begins with each new patient encounter. A thorough medical history will include past environmental and occupational exposures, dietary and social habits, reproductive history, and family history. Using these key parts of the history, along with current age, a preliminary evaluation of breast cancer risk can be made. Once this preliminary assessment has taken place, a discussion with the patient about the need for referral to a specialty high-risk clinic should ensue. Often overlooked is updating this risk assessment. Aging as well as changes in family and personal history should be noted when updating the risk assessment at regular intervals. Surveillance frequency for women at high risk for developing breast cancer is controversial.

Regular breast self-exam and mammography in all women has recently been called into question, as neither seems to benefit survival (Duffy *et al.*, 2002; Thomas *et al.*, 2002). For women considered at high risk for breast cancer, there are no specific guidelines for surveillance, apart from general guidelines in place for all women, unless cellular atypia has been found on exam. This leaves the woman who has been labeled "high risk" by virtue of age or reproductive or family history to wonder how often and even if she should undergo more frequent mammography, clinical breast exams, or perhaps serial ductal lavage. Further research is needed to help define appropriate surveillance and to determine the effect of increased surveillance on quality of life in women at high risk for breast cancer.

REFERENCES

Albrektsen, G., & Kvale, G. (2000). Does gender of offspring modify the time-related effects of a pregnancy on breast cancer risk? *International Journal of Cancer, 86,* 595–597.

American Society of Clinical Oncology. (1996). Policy statement: genetic testing for cancer susceptibility. *Journal of Clinical Oncology.* Alexandria, Va.: Author.

Arver, B., Du, Q., Chen, J., Luo, L., & Lindblom, A. (2000). Hereditary breast cancer: a review. *Seminars in Cancer Biology, 10,* 271–288.

Bell, D.W., Varley, J.M., Szydlo, T.E., Kang, D.H., Wahrer, D.C., Shannon, K.E., Lubratovich, M., Verselis, S.J., Isselbacher, K.J., Fraumeni, J.F., Birch, J.M., Li, F.P., Garber, J.E., & Haber, D.A. (1999). Heterozygous germ line hCHK2 mutations in Li-Fraumeni syndrome. *Science, 286*(5449), 2433–2434.

Bernier, M.O., Plu-Bureau, G., Bossard, N., Ayzac, L., & Thalabard, J.C. (2000). Breastfeeding and risk of breast cancer: a meta-analysis of published studies. *Human Reproductive Update, 6*(4), 374–386.

Berrino, F., Bellati, C., Secreto, G., Camerini, E., Pala, V., Panico, S., Allegro, G., & Kaaks, R. (2001). Reducing bioavailable sex hormones through a comprehensive change in diet: the diet and androgens (DIANA) randomized trial. *Cancer Epidemiology, Biomarkers and Prevention, 10,* 25–33.

Bray, G. (2002). The underlying basis of obesity: relationship to cancer. *Journal of Nutrition, 132,* 3451–3455.

Carrao. G., Bagnardi, V., *et al.* (1999). Exploring the dose-response relationship between alcohol consumption and the risk of several alcohol-related conditions: a meta-analysis. *Addiction, 94,* 1551–1573.

Chang-Claude, J., Eby, N., Kiechle, M., Bastert, G., & Becher, H. (2000). Breastfeeding and breast cancer risk by age 50 among women in Germany. *Cancer Causes Control, 11*(8), 687–695.

The Collaborative Group on Hormonal Factors in Breast Cancer. (1996). Breast cancer and hormonal contraceptives: collaborative reanalysis of individual data on 53,297 women with breast cancer and 100,239 women without breast cancer from 54 epidemiological studies. *Lancet, 347*(9017), 1713–1727.

The Collaborative Group on Hormonal Factors in Breast Cancer. (2002). Breast cancer and breast feeding: collaborative reanalysis of individual data from 47 epidemiological studies in 30 countries, including 50,302 women with breast cancer and 96,973 women without the disease. *Lancet, 360,* 187–195.

Coogan, P.F., Rosenberg, L., Shapiro, S., & Hoffman, M. (1999). Lactation and breast carcinoma risk in a South African population. *Cancer, 86*(6), 982–989.

Costantino, J.P., Gail, M.H., Pee, D., Anderson, S., Redmond, C.K., Benichou, J., & Wieand, H.S. (1999). Validation studies for models projecting the risk of invasive and total breast cancer incidence. *Journal of the National Cancer Institute, 91*(18), 1541–1548.

D'Arcy, C., Holman, C., *et al.* (1996). Meta-analysis of alcohol and all-cause mortality: a validation of NHMRC recommendations. *Medical Journal of Australia, 164,* 141–145.

Davidson, T. (2001). Abortion and breast cancer: a hard decision made harder. *Lancet Oncology, 2,* 756–758.

Doll, R., & Peto, R. (1981). The causes of cancer: quantitative estimates of avoidable risks of cancer in the United States today. *Journal of the National Cancer Institute, 66,* 1191–1308.

Dooley, W.C., Ljung, B.M., Veronesi, U., Cazzaniga, M., Elledge, R.M., O'Shaughnessy, J.A., Kuerer, H.M., Hung, D.T., Khan, S.A., Phillips, R.F., Ganz, P.A., Euhus, D.M., Esserman, L.J., Haffty, B.G., King, B.L., Kelley, M.C., Anderson, M.M., Schmit, P.J., Clark, R.R., Kass, F.C., Anderson, B.O., Troyan, S.L., Arias, R.D., Quiring, J.N., Love, S.M., Page, D.L., & King, E.B. (2001). Ductal lavage for detection of cellular atypia in women at high risk for breast cancer. *Journal of the National Cancer Institute, 93*(21), 1624–1632.

Duffy, S.W., Tabar, L., Chen, H.H., Holmqvist, M., Yen, M.F., Abdsalah, S., Epstein, B., Frodis, E., Ljungberg, E., Hedborg-Melander, C., Sundbom, A., Tholin, M., Wiege, M., Akerlund, A., Wu, H.M., Tung, T.S., Chiu, Y.H., Chiu, C.P., Huang, C.C., Smith, R.A., Rosen, M., Stenbeck, M., & Holmberg, L. (2002). The impact of organized mammography service screening on breast carcinoma mortality in seven Swedish counties. *Cancer, 95*(3), 458–469.

Ellison, R.C., Zhang, Y., McLennan, C.E., & Rothman, K.J. (2001). Exploring the relation of alcohol consumption to risk of breast cancer. *American Journal of Epidemiology, 154*(8), 740–748.

Euhus, D.M., Smith, K.C., Robinson, L., Stucky, A., Olopade, O.I., Cummings, S., Garber, J.E.,

Chittenden, A., Mills, G.B., Rieger, P., Esserman, L., Crawford, B., Hughes, K.S., Roche, C.A., Ganz, P.A., Seldon, J., Fabian, C.J., Klemp, J., & Tomlinson, G. (2002). Pretest prediction of BRCA1 or BRCA2 mutation by risk counselors and the computer model BRCAPRO. *Journal of the National Cancer Institute, 94*(11), 844–851.

Ewertz, M., Duffy, S.W., Adami, H.O., Kvale, G., Lund, E., Meirik, O., Mellemgaard, A., Soini, I., & Tulinius, H. (1990). The independent associations of parity, age at first full term pregnancy, and duration of breast feeding with the risk of breast cancer. *International Journal on Cancer, 46*, 597–603.

Fabian, C.J., Kimler, B.F., Zalles, C.M., Klemp, J.R., Kamel, S., Zeiger, S., & Mayo, M.S. (2000). Short-term breast cancer prediction by random periareolar fine-needle aspiration cytology and the Gail risk model. *Journal of the National Cancer Institute, 92*(15), 1217–1227.

Ford, D., Easton, D.F., Stratton, M., Narod, S., Goldgar, D., Devilee, P., Bishop, D.T., Weber, B., Lenoir, G., Chang-Claude, J., Sobol, H., Teare, M.D., Struewing, J., Arason, A., Scherneck, S., Peto, J., Rebbeck, T.R., Tonin, P., Neuhausen, S., Barkardottir, R., Eyfjord, J., Lynch, H., Ponder, B.A., Gayther, S.A., Zelada-Hedman, M., *et al.* (1998). Genetic heterogeneity and penetrance analysis of the BRCA1 and BRCA2 genes in breast cancer families. The Breast Cancer Linkage Consortium. *American Journal of Human Genetics, 62*(3), 676–689.

Foretova, L., Garber, J.E., Sadowsky, N.L., Verselis, S.J., Joseph, D.M., Andrade, A.F., Gudrais, P.G., Fairclough, D., & Li, F.P. (1998). Carcinoembryonic antigen in breast nipple aspirate fluid. *Cancer Epidemiology, Biomarkers and Prevention, 7*(3), 195–198.

Gail, M.H., Brinton, L.A., Byar, D.P., Corle, D.K., Green, S.B., Schairer, C., & Mulvihill, J.J. (1989). Projecting individualized probabilities of developing breast cancer for white females who are being examined annually. *Journal of the National Cancer Institute, 81*(24), 1879–1886.

Gail, M., & Costantino, J. (2001). Validating and improving models for projecting the absolute risk of breast cancer. *Journal of the National Cancer Institute, 93*(5), 358–366.

Greco, K. (2000). Cancer genetics nursing: impact of the double helix. *Oncology Nursing Forum, 27*(9), 29–36.

Howe, G., Rohan, T., Decarli, A., Iscovich, J., Kaldor, J., Katsouyanni, K., Marubini, E., Miller, A., Riboli, E., Toniolo, P., *et al.* (1991). The association between alcohol and breast cancer risk: evidence from the combined analysis of six dietary case-control studies. *International Journal of Cancer, 47,* 707–710.

Hsieh, C., Wuu, J., Trichopoulos, D., Adami, H.O., & Ekbom, A. (1999). Gender of offspring and maternal breast cancer risk. *International Journal of Cancer, 81,* 335–338.

Hunter, D.J., Spiegelman, D., Adami, H.O., Beeson, L., van den Brandt, P.A., Folsom, A.R., Fraser, G.E., Goldbohm, R.A., Graham, S., Howe, G.R., *et al.* (1996). Cohort studies of fat intake and the risk of breast cancer—a pooled analysis. *New England Journal of Medicine, 334*(6), 356–361.

Kelsey, J., Gammon, M., & John, E.M. (1993). Reproductive factors and breast cancer. *Epidemiology Review, 15,* 36–47.

Key, T.J., Allen, N.E., Spencer, E.A., & Travis, R.C. (2002). The effect of diet on risk of cancer. *Lancet, 360,* 861–868.

Key, T., Schatzkin, A., *et al.* (2002). The scientific basis for diet, nutrition and the prevention of cancer. Geneva: World Health Organization.

Kinzler, K.W., & Vogelstein, B. (1998). ONCOGENESIS: landscaping the cancer terrain. *Science, 280*(5366), 1036–1037.

Knudson, A. (2001). Two genetic hits (more or less) to cancer. *Nature Review Cancer, 1,* 157–162.

Lambe, M., Hsieh, C., Trichopoulos, D., Ekbom, A., Pavia, M., & Adami, H.O. (1994). Transient increase in the risk of breast cancer after giving birth. *New England Journal of Medicine, 331*(1), 5–9.

Layde, P.M., Webster, L.A., Baughman, A.L., Wingo, P.A., Rubin, G.L., & Ory, H.W. (1989). The independent associations of parity, age at first full term pregnancy, and duration of breast feeding with the risk of breast cancer. *Journal of Clinical Epidemiology, 42,* 963–973.

Levy-Lahad, E., Catane, R., Eisenberg, S., Kaufman, B., Hornreich, G., Lishinsky, E., Shohat, M., Weber, B.L., Beller, U., Lahad, A., & Halle, D. (1997). Founder BRCA1 and BRCA2 mutations in Ashkenazi Jews in Israel: frequency and differential penetrance in ovarian cancer and in breast-ovarian cancer families. *American Journal of Human Genetics, 60*(5), 1059–1067.

Li, F.P., & Fraumeni, J.F., Jr. (1969). Soft-tissue sarcomas, breast cancer, and other neoplasms. A familial syndrome? *Annals of Internal Medicine, 71*(4), 747–752.

Lipworth, L., Bailey, L.R., & Trichopoulos, D. (2000). History of breast-feeding in relation to breast cancer risk: a review of the epidemiologic literature. *Journal of the National Cancer Institute, 92*(4), 302–312.

Longnecker, M. (1994). Alcoholic beverage consumption in relation to risk of breast cancer: meta-analysis and review. *Cancer Causes Control, 5,* 73–82.

Longnecker, M.P., Berlin, J.A., Orza, M.J., & Chalmers, T.C. (1988). A meta-analysis of alcohol consumption in relation to risk of breast cancer. *Journal of the American Medical Association, 260*(5), 652–656.

Marchbanks, P.A., McDonald, J.A., Wilson, H.G., Folger, S.G., Mandel, M.G., Daling, J.R., Bernstein, L., Malone, K.E., Ursin, G., Strom, B.L., Norman, S.A., Wingo, P.A., Burkman, R.T., Berlin, J.A., Simon, M.S., Spirtas, R., & Weiss, L.K. (2002). Oral contraceptives and the risk of breast cancer. *New England Journal of Medicine, 346*(26), 2025–2032.

Marsh, D. & Zori, R. (2002). Genetic insights into familial cancers—update and recent discoveries. *Cancer Letters, 181,* 125–164.

Melbye, M., Wohlfahrt, J., Olsen, J.H., Frisch, M., Westergaard, T., Helweg-Larsen, K., & Andersen, P.K. (1997). Induced abortion and the risk of breast cancer. *New England Journal of Medicine, 336,* 81–85.

Morimoto, L.M., White, E., Chen, Z., Chlebowski, R.T., Hays, J., Kuller, L., Lopez, A.M., Manson, J., Margolis, K.L., Muti, P.C., Stefanick, M.L., & McTiernan, A. (2002). Obesity, body size, and risk of postmenopausal breast cancer: the Women's Health Initiative (United States). *Cancer Causes Control, 13*(8), 741–751.

Newcomb, P. (1997). Lactation and breast cancer risk. *Journal of Mammary Gland Biological Neoplasia, 2*(3), 311–318.

Paweletz, C.P., Trock, B., Pennanen, M., Tsangaris, T., Magnant, C., Liotta, L.A., & Petricoin, E.F., 3rd. (2001). Proteomic patterns of nipple aspirate fluids obtained by SELDI-TOF: potential for new biomarkers to aid in the diagnosis of breast cancer. *Disease Markers, 17*(4), 301–307.

Pellegrini, L., Yu, D.S., Lo, T., Anand, S., Lee, M., Blundell, T.L., & Venkitaraman, A.R. (2002). Insights into DNA recombination from the structure of a RAD51–BRCA2 complex. *Nature, 420,* 287–293.

Petrelli, J.M., Calle, E.E., Rodriguez, C., & Thun, M.J. (2002). Body mass index, height, and postmenopausal breast cancer mortality in a prospective cohort of US women. *Cancer Causes Control, 13*(4), 325–332.

Russo, J., & Russo, I. (1980). Susceptibility of the mammary gland to carcinogenesis. II. Pregnancy interruption as a risk factor in tumor incidence. *American Journal of Pathology, 100,* 497–512.

Sattin, R., Rubin, G., *et al.* (1986). Oral contraceptive use and the risk of breast cancer. The Cancer and Steroid Hormone Study of the Centers for Disease Control and the National Institute of Child Health and Human Development. *New England Journal of Medicine, 315*(7), 405–411.

Sauter, E.R., Daly, M., Linahan, K., Ehya, H., Engstrom, P.F., Bonney, G., Ross, E.A., Yu, H., & Diamandis, E. (1996). Prostate-specific antigen levels in nipple aspirate fluid correlate with breast cancer risk. *Cancer Epidemiology, Biomarkers and Prevention, 5*(12), 967–970.

Sauter, E.R., Ross, E., Daly, M., Klein-Szanto, A., Engstrom, P.F., Sorling, A., Malick, J., & Ehya, H. (1997). Nipple aspirate fluid: a promising non-invasive method to identify cellular markers of breast cancer risk. *British Journal of Cancer, 76*(4), 494–501.

Shu, X.O., Jin, F., Dai, Q., Wen, W., Potter, J.D., Kushi, L.H., Ruan, Z., Gao, Y.T., & Zheng, W. (2001). Soyfood intake during adolescence and subsequent risk of breast cancer among Chinese women. *Cancer Epidemiology, Biomarkers and Prevention, 10,* 483–488.

Singletary, K., & Gapstur, S. (2001). Alcohol and breast cancer. Review of epidemiologic and experimental evidence and potential mechanisms. *Journal of the American Medical Association, 286*(17), 2143–2151.

Smith-Warner, S.A., Spiegelman, D., Yaun, S.S., van den Brandt, P.A., Folsom, A.R., Goldbohm, R.A., Graham, S., Holmberg, L., Howe, G.R., Marshall, J.R., Miller, A.B., Potter, J.D., Speizer, F.E., Willett, W.C., Wolk, A., & Hunter, D.J. (1998). Alcohol and breast cancer in women. A pooled analysis of cohort studies. *Journal of the American Medical Association, 279,* 535–540.

Stoll, B. (2002). Upper abdominal obesity, insulin resistance and breast cancer risk. *International Journal of Obesity & Related Metabolic Disorders, 26*(6), 747–753.

Thomas, D.B., Gao, D.L., Ray, R.M., Wang, W.W., Allison, C.J., Chen, F.L., Porter, P., Hu, Y.W., Zhao, G.L., Pan, L.D., Li, W., Wu, C., Coriaty, Z., Evans, I., Lin, M.G., Stalsberg, H., & Self, S.G. (2002). Randomized trial of breast self-examination in Shanghai: final results. *Journal of the National Cancer Institute, 94*(19), 1445–1457.

Thompson, L., & Schild, D. (2002). Recombinational DNA repair and human disease. *Mutation Research, 509*, 49–78.

Weed, D., & Kramer, B. (1996). Induced abortion, bias, and breast cancer: why epidemiology hasn't reached its limit. *Journal of the National Cancer Institute, 88*(23), 698–700.

Wenten, M., Gilliland, F.D., Baumgartner, K., & Samet, J.M. (2002). Associations of weight, weight change, and body mass with breast cancer risk in Hispanic and non-Hispanic white women. *Annals of Epidemiology, 12*(6), 435–444.

Wrensch, M.R., Petrakis, N.L., King, E.B., Miike, R., Mason, L., Chew, K.L., Lee, M.M., Ernster, V.L., Hilton, J.F., Schweitzer, R., *et al.* (1992). Breast cancer incidence in women with abnormal cytology in nipple aspirates of breast fluid. *American Journal of Epidemiology, 135*(2), 130–141.

Wrensch, M.R., Petrakis, N.L., Miike, R., King, E.B., Chew, K., Neuhaus, J., Lee, M.M., & Rhys, M. (2001). Breast cancer risk in women with abnormal cytology in nipple aspirates of breast fluid. *Journal of the National Cancer Institute, 93*(23), 1791–1798.

Zheng, T., Duan, L., Liu, Y., Zhang, B., Wang, Y., Chen, Y., Zhang, Y., & Owens, P.H. (2000). Lactation reduces breast cancer risk in Shandong Province, China. *American Journal of Epidemiology, 152*(12), 1129–1135.

PREVENTION STRATEGIES

JENNIFER BUCHOLTZ, RN, MS, CRNP, OCN®

INTRODUCTION

Can breast cancer be prevented? The search for the answer to this question began a century ago but has been gathering momentum in the last two decades. Several factors have fueled this heightened search, including an increased rate of breast cancer, validated breast cancer risk factors, and the identification of rare genetic mutations that lead to a high rate of this disease. In addition, research concerning the molecular, environmental, and lifestyle determinants of breast cancer is now routinely available in the media and pursued by breast cancer advocacy groups. Deluged with an increasing amount of information on breast cancer, women turn to health care providers to seek practical advice on ways to prevent this disease. What guidelines exist to help women make choices on breast cancer prevention? What scientific evidence guides health care providers' current recommendations for breast cancer prevention strategies? How should individual women, as well as the general population of women, be counseled with this information?

This chapter will present the current state of knowledge about primary breast cancer prevention and issues involved in the search for prevention solutions. It will also highlight clinical breast cancer prevention strategies for individual women at increased risk and identify those women most likely to benefit from these strategies. Practical pointers in counseling women on issues involved in prevention strategies will be described. Future potential strategies for breast cancer prevention in both individuals and in populations of women will be presented.

SCIENTIFIC BELIEFS INVOLVED IN PRIMARY BREAST CANCER PREVENTION

What is currently known about breast cancer prevention? Numerous basic scientific inquiries, epidemiological data, and recent clinical studies suggest that breast cancer can be prevented. Although a huge amount of data has been obtained in these studies, there is no one specific, proven method of preventing breast cancer (Vogel, 2000). A large amount of unknown science concerning breast cancer prevention remains. Table 3.1 summarizes some of the scientific tenets of known and unknown factors.

As is true of other diseases, more scientific evidence exists to guide secondary breast cancer prevention than primary prevention. Improved treatments documented in large, randomized prospective trials have reduced breast cancer morbidity and mortality. Research on specific primary prevention strategies, such as chemoprevention with tamoxifen and bilateral preventive mastectomy, have only surfaced in the past decade for women at an increased risk.

True primary prevention involves measures to prevent the development and occurrence of a particular disease. When exact causes of a disease are unknown, prevention strategies are often aimed at modifying risk factors implicated in the disease. Because the exact sequence of molecular events and host interactions that leads to breast cancer in a given person is unknown, current primary breast cancer prevention strategies focus on reducing risk factors (Love *et al.,* 2002). Breast cancer development is most likely a result of interaction of inherited factors, environmental exposures, and lifestyle factors (Martin & Weber, 2000). Before mutations in BRCA1 and BRCA2 and other rare

Table 3.1 Scientific Beliefs of Known and Unknown Factors in Breast Cancer Prevention

Concept	Unknown
1. Cancer development likely due to molecular step-by-step progression of changes to breast cells leading to breast cancer	Exact biologic mechanisms
2. Cancer development from carcinogenic exposures can take years to develop	All environmental factors that may promote breast cancer
3. Wide range international variation in breast cancer rates suggests breast cancer may be preventable by modifying lifestyle and environmental determinants	Mechanisms of interaction of genetic, environmental and lifestyle factors
4. Cancer development can be reversible	Timing and interventions to reverse breast cancer development
5. Deleterious mutations in certain genes can lead to a high risk of breast cancer	All possible genetic mutations that lead to an increased risk
6. Cancer development likely due to interaction of genetic, hormonal, lifestyle, and environmental factors	Interaction and timing of factors

genes were known, environmental and lifestyle factors were the focus of many breast cancer prevention studies. A wide international variation in breast cancer rates was the basis for many of these studies, suggesting that breast cancer may be preventable by modifying lifestyle and environmental determinants (NCI, 2002). Epidemiological studies have identified numerous risk factors for breast cancer (see Chapters 1 and 2 for a thorough discussion of the topic), but studies of environmental and lifestyle factors have not been able to explain all risk factors for breast cancer or the interdependence of factors that lead to this disease.

Table 3.2 lists factors in breast cancer development and possible preventive actions. In the future, when the molecular step-by-step model of breast carcinogenesis is unraveled, prevention strategies will likely be aimed at interrupting the molecular pathway changes taking place in breast cells. A more thorough study of how and when individual hormonal influences and lifestyle factors affect this pathway will likely help in understanding breast cancer development (Love *et al.*, 2002). To truly evaluate the interaction of all factors involved in breast cancer development, individuals would need to be studied throughout the life span, taking into consideration their genetic heritage, environmental exposures, hormonal factors, and other lifestyle behaviors. These types of studies are extremely difficult to carry out. In the absence of cause and effect documentation, clinical guidelines are often based upon suggestive data.

GENERAL GUIDELINES FOR BREAST CANCER PREVENTION

In the general population and in increased-risk women, primary prevention strategies aim to reduce the incidence of clinically recognized invasive breast cancers and in situ breast cancers. Although scientific data on breast cancer prevention is incomplete, some general guidelines for breast cancer prevention have emerged in clinical practice (Chlebowski *et al.*, 2002; Gail *et al.*, 1999; NCI, 2002). Figure 3.1 offers a suggested approach to prevention guidelines for women of average risk and those at increased risk for breast cancer.

All women should first obtain an assessment of their breast cancer risk. The woman's perceived breast cancer risk also needs to be ascertained. In the past few years, breast cancer risk assessment has become a routine part of a woman's overall health assessment (Vogel, 2000). Several breast cancer risk prediction models are helpful in identifying women who are at an increased risk for breast cancer. Nurses are and can be intimately involved in this risk assessment process and need to be familiar with and choose the appropriate risk assessment tool for an individual woman. These risk models are now widely used in not only selecting women for breast cancer prevention clinical trials, but also in helping clinicians counsel women in genetic testing and breast cancer prevention options. The applicable risk model needs to be chosen based on the woman's personal and family health history. The nurse needs to be familiar with the components, the clinical

Table 3.2 Summary of Factors Implicated in Breast Cancer Development and Possible Preventive Actions

Factor	Possible preventive actions
Environmental	
Irradiation exposure causing germline and/or somatic breast cell mutations in developing fetus and individuals	Avoidance of irradiation, particularly in utero and between menarche and first full-term pregnancy
	Early screening of women who had mantle radiation for Hodgkin's Disease
Genetic	
Germline mutations in BRCA1/2; p53; pTEN	Genetic screening/counseling and current breast cancer prevention options of increased surveillance, chemoprevention, preventive surgery
Limited repair of acquired breast epithelial cell DNA damage (ATM)	Limit exposure to irradiation and cigarette smoke
Hormonal	
Increased estrogen exposure/prolonged duration of ovulation	Delay onset of menarche
	Initiate early menopause
	Oophorectomy; LHRH agonists
	Avoid delayed childbearing
	Reduce ovarian activity (prolonged lactation)
	Modify endogenous hormone levels
	Exercise, avoid weight gain; limit alcohol
	Low fat diet
	Aromatase inhibitors
	Avoid exogenous hormones
	Modify hormone receptor function
	Selective estrogen receptor modulators: tamoxifen, raloxifene, phytoestrogens
	Modify estrogen metabolism/breast growth factor action

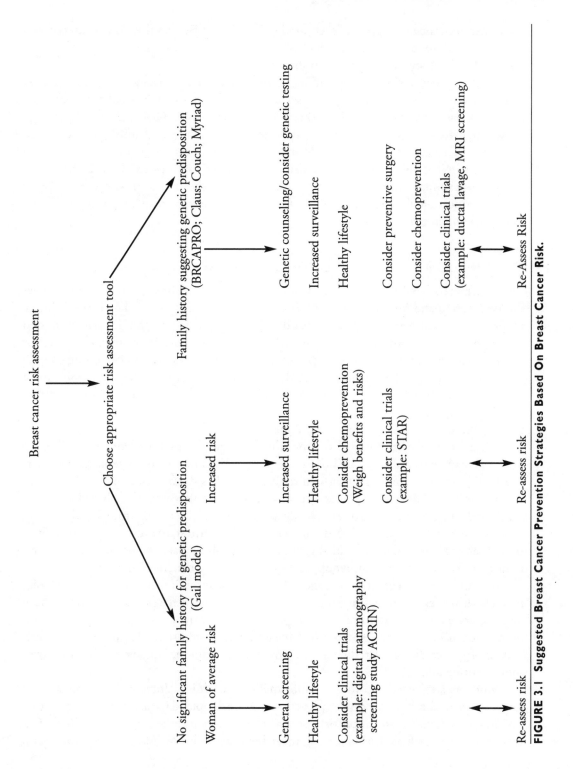

FIGURE 3.1 Suggested Breast Cancer Prevention Strategies Based On Breast Cancer Risk.

usefulness, and the limitations of each model (Table 3.3). Besides their breast cancer risk, women today also may want to know if they should have genetic testing for known mutations if they have any family history of breast cancer.

Genetic predisposition information is important to understand in order to steer women toward genetic counseling. Nurses have many of the skills needed for breast cancer risk assessment and counseling (Foltz & Mahon, 2000; Greco, 2000). Oncology nurses, in particular, have experience as educators, patient and family advocates, and counselors. They also have a good understanding of cancer, carcinogenesis, informed consent, and specifics about benefits and risks of prevention options (Mahon, 2000). With additional training, nurses and genetic counselors have been shown to provide equally effective education about genetic testing to women regarding breast cancer susceptibility testing (Bernhardt *et al.*, 2000).

PREVENTION GUIDELINES FOR WOMEN AT LOW/AVERAGE RISK

All women are advised to follow breast cancer screening guidelines so that breast changes can be detected and found before invasive breast cancer is diagnosed. The increase in the number of women being diagnosed with ductal carcinoma in situ (DCIS) has supported the importance of breast cancer screening. Prevention guidelines for women of average or low risk have mainly been aimed at promoting a healthy lifestyle and obtaining routine screening. Although the scientific data do not establish a cause–effect relationship of breast cancer to specific lifestyle practices, the data support limiting alcohol consumption, avoiding weight gain, engaging in routine exercise, and eating a diet rich in fruits and vegetables (Birkimer, 2002; Brinton *et al.*, 2002).

Recent research has focused on the different age groups for whom these lifestyle practices may be recommended (Love *et al.*, 2002). Data on hormone replacement therapy (HRT) in the Women's Health Initiative Study has confirmed avoiding long-term use of combined hormone replacement in women with a uterus to slightly reduce breast cancer risk (Rossouw *et al.*, 2002). The decision to use HRT for any individual woman, however, needs to be made based on her overall health status and symptoms. Even though any use of HRT may add slightly to breast cancer risk, the use of HRT for less than two years to relieve postmenopausal symptoms may benefit individual women.

In counseling women at an average risk for breast cancer, it is important to emphasize that a healthy lifestyle, consisting of good nutrition, proper exercise, and avoidance of both unnecessary radiation exposure and long-term hormone replacement, is important for overall health maintenance and not just breast cancer prevention. Because more women will die from cardiovascular disease than from breast cancer, this overall health advice should not be minimized.

Women also need up-to-date information regarding interpreting proven and unproven data about breast cancer prevention. For example, data has not yet shown that soy protein reduces breast cancer risk, or that antiperspirants increase risk. Credible information sources, such as the National Cancer Institute Web site (*http://www.cancer.gov*),

Table 3.3 Features of Breast Cancer Risk and Genetic Predisposition for Breast Cancer Models

Model	Usefulness	Limitations	Comments
Gail model (Costantino *et al.*, 1999)	Most women without genetic predisposition for breast cancer	Underestimates risk if genetic predisposition	Easy to use Readily available on disk from National Cancer Institute (*www.cancer.gov*) Accessible from *www.breastcancer.com*
		Uses only first-degree maternal family history, omits paternal family history	Hand held calculator tool available with Caucasian, African American and Hispanic modified Gail risk estimate
		Only assesses family history of breast cancer	
		Does not factor in age of family breast cancer diagnosis	
		Does not ask personal history of lobular cancer in situ	
Claus model (Claus *et al.*, 1994)	Validated risk assessment tool		
	Estimates breast cancer risk solely on family history of breast cancer	Only assesses family history of breast cancer, not ovarian cancer	Risk estimates are provided in 10-year increments, which can help younger women keep risk estimates in perspective
	Considers age of family member's breast cancer	Can underestimate breast cancer risk in an individual who does not carry a genetic predisposition	
	Considers both maternal and paternal family history of breast cancer	Can underestimate BRCA1/BRCA2 risk	
		Does not consider Ashkenazi Jewish heritage	

Table 3.3 (continued)

Model	Usefulness	Limitations	Comments
Couch model (Couch et al., 1997)	Predicts the probability of finding a BRCA1/2 mutation Considers average age of breast cancer in family	Can underestimate risk of an individual from a family with few members who have breast/ovarian cancer Does not identify individual breast cancer risk	Available on computer software package CancerGene through *www.swmed.edu* licensed through David Euhus, M.D.
BRCAPRO (Berry et al., 2002)	Predicts individual breast cancer risk based on probability that family carries BRCA mutation Considers family history of breast and ovarian cancer Considers age at onset of family member's breast cancer Validated risk assessment tool	Does not take into consideration nonfamily breast cancer risk factors Considers only first- and second-degree relatives	Useful tool in cancer genetics research studies
Myriad Genetics Model (Myriad Genetics™)	Predicts probability of individual in finding a BRCA mutation Considers premenopausal versus postmenopausal family history of breast cancer Considers family history of ovarian cancer Considers Ashkenazi Jewish heritage factor		Available on-line from *www.BRCAAnalysis.com* through Myriad Genetics Available in handheld prediction slide calculator Can be downloaded into PDA

are offered as resources for information seekers. Women should be counseled that all the information at a given time is not known, but that information based on well-conceived and well-conducted studies offers the best advice available.

In counseling women at average or low risk, it is also important to assess a woman's own predicted risk of breast cancer. Women often overestimate their risk and need an open mind from their health care providers so that they can voice their breast cancer fears. Use of the Gail model has served useful for many women to point out that their predicted risk may not be as high as they thought (Gail *et al.*, 1994). Since the majority of women who develop breast cancer do not have a family history or suggestions for a genetic predisposition, the Gail model will be the model used for most American women. It is important to point out to women that the model offers a *predicted* risk. Many women already diagnosed with breast cancer are amazed that they do not score at an increased risk when putting their data into the Gail model.

Models can be best used to determine if women are at an increased risk so that proven options for risk reduction can be recommended. Models use risk factors for predictors of breast cancer. To date, though, risk factors, other than being a woman and older than age 50 years, have not been able to explain the causes of the majority of breast cancers (Brinton *et al.*, 2002). Even for women with an average breast cancer risk score, it is imperative that they follow recommended breast cancer screening guidelines. There is no data to support that women of average or low risk consider tamoxifen or preventive mastectomy to reduce breast cancer risk.

BREAST CANCER PREVENTION OPTIONS FOR WOMEN AT INCREASED RISK

The three standard breast cancer prevention options for women at increased risk are increased surveillance, chemoprevention, and preventive or prophylactic surgery. Integral to counseling women about the choice among these options is a thorough understanding of the data that supports each option and the potential benefits and risks of each option. Only by maintaining current knowledge of known prevention data, unknown data, and current prevention studies can nurses best assist women in their decision-making.

Quite often scientific studies and breakthroughs occur before practical strategies for management are available and tested. BRCA1 and BRCA2 testing is an example (Helzlsouer, 1999). By 1996, a woman could be tested for mutations in BRCA1 and BRCA2, but no data existed to tell her by how much either tamoxifen or preventive mastectomy could reduce her breast cancer risk. Studies of breast cancer prevention strategies have emerged in the past six years for women at increased risk (Fisher *et al.*, 1998; Hartmann *et al.*, 1999; Eisen *et al.*, 2000; Cuzick *et al.*, 2002).

Increased Breast Cancer Surveillance. To date, increased surveillance practices in high-risk women have not been proven to reduce breast cancer risk (Allain *et al.*, 2002). These surveillance practices, however, have been encouraged by some organizations, based on literature pointing to a high risk of breast cancer in mutation carriers at earlier ages than seen in the general population. Recommendations for increased surveillance include monthly breast self-exam starting at age 18 years, yearly to twice yearly clinical breast exam starting at age 25 years, and earlier mammography in younger women at increased risk with a genetic predisposition.

A general guideline for an at-risk woman is to begin screening mammography at an age ten years earlier than the youngest diagnosed age of a close family member's breast cancer diagnosis. Since mammography may be less sensitive to detecting breast cancers in young women with more normal, dense breast tissue, bilateral screening ultrasound may be suggested to accompany mammography. Current research trials are investigating breast MRI to screen women at genetic predisposition for breast cancer. The earliest eligible age for breast MRI for these women is age 25 years.

Lifestyle modifications mentioned for women of average or low risk are also encouraged for women at increased risk. Health practices, such as weight control, routine exercise, and a diet rich in fruits and vegetables and low in fat, have not been proven to reduce breast cancer, but they are thought to interact with genetic factors. Data linking high alcohol consumption as a contributor to breast cancer risk is more convincing (Martin & Weber, 2001).

Chemoprevention. The interest in studying drugs to prevent breast cancer was sparked by results seen in adjuvant hormonal breast cancer trials. These trials showed that tamoxifen prevented second primary breast cancers in the contralateral breast by at least 40% and led to randomized tamoxifen/placebo chemoprevention trials in high-risk women (Pritchard, 2001).

The Breast Cancer Prevention Trial (BCPT), a randomized, double-blind clinical trial, conducted by the National Surgical Adjuvant Breast and Bowel Project (NSABP), demonstrated that taking tamoxifen 20 mg daily for five years, compared to placebo, reduced the incidence of breast cancer by 49% in healthy women at an increased risk for breast cancer (Fisher *et al.,* 1998). A Gail five-year predicted breast cancer risk of at least 1.66%, or that risk of a 60-year-old woman in the United States, was the definition of increased risk used in the BCPT. Women ages 35 years and older were enrolled in the BCPT. Side effect data on tamoxifen existed in premenopausal and postmenopausal women. The BCPT demonstrated statistically significant reductions in both invasive (49%) and noninvasive (50%) breast cancer. In addition, an 86% risk reduction was seen in a small subset of women in the BCPT who had atypical hyperplasia and a 56% risk reduction in women with lobular carcinoma in situ (LCIS). This risk reduction was exclusively seen in estrogen receptor-positive tumors. All of the 6681 participants who were randomized to tamoxifen have completed the prescribed five years of therapy, and data continue to show the persistence of breast cancer risk reduction. Table 3.4 lists the relative risks of tamoxifen versus placebo in the BCPT and the absolute numbers of events.

With the BCPT data, the Food and Drug Administration (FDA) approved tamoxifen for breast cancer risk reduction in high-risk women in October 1998. This was an historic first approval by the FDA of a cancer-preventive agent, even though the FDA declined to use the word "prevention" (Pritchard, 2001). Quickly after this approval, a working group

Table 3.4 Relative Risks Comparing the Tamoxifen Group with the Placebo Group in the Breast Cancer Prevention Trial

Type of event	Number of events		Average annual incidence rate per 1000		Relative risk	95% confidence interval
	Placebo	Tamoxifen	Placebo	Tamoxifen		
Life-threatening events						
1. Invasive breast cancer	175	89	6.76	3.43	0.51	0.39–0.66
2. Hip fracture	22	12	0.84	0.46	0.55	0.25–1.15
3. Endometrial cancer						
All women	15	36	0.91	2.30	2.53	1.35–4.97
Women age 50+ years at entry	7	27	0.76	3.05	4.01	1.70–10.90
4. Stroke	24	38	0.92	1.45	1.59	0.93–2.77
5. Pulmonary embolism	6	18	0.23	0.69	3.01	1.15–9.27
Other severe events						
6. In situ breast cancer	69	35	2.68	1.35	0.50	0.33–0.77
7. Deep vein thrombosis	22	35	0.84	1.34	1.60	0.91–2.86
Other events						
8. Colle's fracture	23	14	0.88	0.54	0.61	0.29–1.23
9. Spine fracture	31	23	1.18	0.88	0.74	0.41–1.32
10. Cataracts	507	574	21.72	24.82	1.14	1.01–1.29

Adapted from: Fisher, B., Costantino, J.P., Wickerham, D.L., et al. (1998). Tamoxifen for prevention of breast cancer: report of the National Surgical Adjuvant Breast and Bowel Project P-1 Study. *Journal of the National Cancer Institute, 90,* 1371–1388.

of breast cancer specialists, statisticians, and epidemiologists met to help determine which women would best benefit from tamoxifen (Gail *et al.*, 1999). This group analyzed not only breast cancer risk, but also the rates and risks of the potential serious side effects of tamoxifen (i.e., uterine cancer and thromboembolic events for Caucasian and African American women). Tables 3.5 and 3.6 list the net benefit and risk of tamoxifen in these women. Although other personal health factors often need to be considered, the risk data from this panel can offer guidelines for recommending tamoxifen to high-risk women for chemoprevention. In general, tamoxifen is best recommended for women who have high Gail scores, are under age 50 years, and have had a hysterectomy.

During the 1990s, two smaller international studies investigated the use of tamoxifen for chemoprevention of breast cancer. Unlike the BCPT, neither of these studies showed breast cancer reduction with tamoxifen, but they were criticized for their study designs and target populations. The study from Italy by the European Oncology Group included 5408 women of low to normal risk for breast cancer (Veronesi *et al.*, 1998). Forty-three percent of women may have been at low risk for breast cancer as a result of a history of bilateral oophorectomy. In the British study conducted by the Royal Marsden Hospital, 2471 women studied were at high risk for breast cancer because of strong family histories, with many suggestive of a genetic predisposition (Powles *et al.*, 1998). Both international studies included women who could be

Table 3.5 Net benefit/risk indices for tamoxifen treatment by level of five-year projected risk of invasive breast cancer (IBC), age group, and race for women *with* a uterus

Five-year predicted breast cancer risk (%)	Age groups for white women					Age groups for black women				
	35–39	40–49	50–59	60–69	70–79	35–39	40–49	50–59	60–69	70–79
1.5	77**	43**	-103	-260	-383	47**	-17	-215	-442	-513
2.0	107**	73**	-75	-232	-355	77**	14	-187	-414	-485
2.5	139**	105**	-46	-203	-326	109**	46*	-158	-385	-456
3.0	169**	135**	-18	-175	-298	139**	76*	-130	-358	-429
3.5	200**	166**	10	-147	-270	170**	107**	-102	-330	-401
4.0	230**	196**	38*	-119	-242	200**	137**	-74	-302	-373
4.5	261**	227**	66*	-92	-215	231**	168**	-46	-274	-345
5.0	292**	258**	94*	-64	-187	262**	199**	-19	-246	-317
5.5	322**	288**	122*	-36	-160	292**	229**	10	-219	-290
6.5	352**	318**	149**	-9	-132	322**	259**	37	-191	-262
7.0	383**	349**	176**	19	-104	353**	290**	64*	-164	-235
7.5	413**	379**	204**	47	-77	383**	320**	92*	-137	-208

*The probability that I (1, 0.5, 0) exceeds zero, taking random variation into account, is estimated to be in the range of 0.60–0.89.

**The probability that I (1, 0.5, 0) exceeds zero, taking random variation into account, is estimated to be in the range of .90–1.00.

From: Gail M.H., *et al.* (1999). Weighing the risks and benefits of tamoxifen treatment for preventing breast cancer. *Journal of the National Cancer Institute*, *91*, p. 1838.

Table 3.6 Net benefit/risk indices for tamoxifen treatment by level of five-year projected risk of invasive breast cancer (IBC), age group, and race for women *without* a uterus

Five-year predicted breast cancer risk (%)	Age groups for white women					Age groups for black women				
	35–39	40–49	50–59	60–69	70–79	35–39	40–49	50–59	60–69	70–79
1.5	79**	59**	18*	-54	-160	48**	-11	-163	-316	-394
2.0	109**	89**	46*	-26	-132	78**	20*	-135	-288	-366
2.5	141**	121**	75*	4	-103	110**	52*	-106	-259	-337
3.0	171**	151**	102**	31	-75	140**	82**	-78	-232	-310
3.5	202**	182**	130**	59*	-47	171**	113**	-50	-204	-282
4.0	232**	212**	158**	87*	-19	201**	143**	-22	-176	-254
4.5	263**	243**	186**	115**	9	232**	174**	6	-148	-226
5.0	294**	274**	214**	143**	37	263**	205**	34	-120	-189
5.5	324**	304**	242**	171**	64	293**	235**	62*	-93	-171
6.5	354**	334**	269**	198**	92*	323**	265**	89*	-65	-143
7.0	385**	365**	296**	225**	119*	354**	296**	116*	-38	-116
7.5	415**	395**	324**	253**	146*	384**	326**	144*	-11	-89

*The probability that I (1, 0.5, 0) exceeds zero, taking random variation into account, is estimated to be in the range of 0.60–0.89.
**The probability that I (1, 0.5, 0) exceeds zero, taking random variation into account, is estimated to be in the range of .90–1.00.
From: Gail M.H., et al. (1999). Weighing the risks and benefits of tamoxifen treatment for preventing breast cancer. *Journal of the National Cancer Institute, 91*, p. 1839.

on concurrent HRT with tamoxifen or placebo. The enrolled women in the Italian and British studies differed from the women in the BCPT, so comparisons could not be made directly.

A study with greater similarity to the BCPT study design, the International Breast Intervention Study (IBIS-I), reported a statistically significant reduction of breast cancer in high-risk women taking tamoxifen versus placebo (Cuzick *et al.*, 2002). IBIS-I analyzed 7139 women ages 35–70 years at an increased risk for breast cancer randomized to tamoxifen 20 mg daily or placebo for five years (tamoxifen N = 3573; placebo N = 3566). An overall 32% reduction in invasive breast cancer and DCIS was found in the tamoxifen group after median follow-up of 50 months (101 breast cancers in placebo group; 69 in tamoxifen group). There was a 39% reduction in estrogen receptor-positive tumors and a 69% reduction in DCIS seen in the tamoxifen versus placebo groups.

A nonstatistical increased risk of endometrial cancer was seen in the tamoxifen group (11 in tamoxifen group; 5 in placebo group). A statistically significant increased rate of thromboembolic events was also seen in the tamoxifen group (43 in tamoxifen group versus 17 in placebo group). Notably, the increased risk of thromboembolic events was especially seen in tamoxifen participants after surgery or long periods of immobilization. Of concern is that there was a significant excess of deaths in the tamoxifen group (25 in tamoxifen group versus 11 in placebo group), but this may have been a chance finding resulting from a range of causes of death. In IBIS-I, women could also be taking HRT with tamoxifen or placebo. Age and use of HRT, however, did not significantly affect breast cancer risk reduction.

In general, tamoxifen used for chemoprevention of breast cancer is generally well tolerated by most women (Chlebowski, 2000). Despite being relatively new for the use of chemoprevention, it has been used for over 30 years and has a well-known side effect profile. Women should be counseled in the potential benefits and risks of tamoxifen before choosing this prevention option. The most common acute side effects include hot flashes and vaginal drainage. Treatments for nonhormonal management of hot flashes are now available and can be prescribed based on their potential benefits and risks (Barton *et al.,* 2002). Rare but serious side effects include blood clots that cause deep vein thrombosis, pulmonary embolism, or stroke. Tamoxifen also confers an increased risk of endometrial cancer, especially in postmenopausal women. In the BCPT, a small but statistically significant increase in the incidence of cataracts was also seen in women on tamoxifen, especially in older women.

Additional benefits of tamoxifen seen in the BCPT were the reduction of hip, wrist, and spine fractures. Tamoxifen is also known to reduce serum cholesterol and C-reactive protein. Important for women considering tamoxifen for chemoprevention of breast cancer is the finding that no increase in weight gain, depression, or altered quality of life factors were seen with tamoxifen versus placebo in the BCPT.

Tamoxifen for chemoprevention of breast cancer is contraindicated in women who are pregnant or have a history of blood clots. Women who have risk factors for blood clots, such as uncontrolled hypertension, uncontrolled diabetes, atrial fibrillation, or abnormal clotting factors, may not be good candidates for tamoxifen. In addition, premenopausal women with endometriosis and an intact uterus and ovaries, or extrapelvic endometriosis, may wish to avoid the potential endometrial effects of tamoxifen.

Premenopausal women need to use a nonhormonal birth control method to avoid pregnancy while taking tamoxifen, as this drug can harm a fetus. Recommended follow-up on tamoxifen includes a yearly gynecologic exam, if a woman has an intact uterus and/or one or both ovaries, a routine eye exam every one to two years, depending on a woman's age, and a periodic health examination with special attention to signs and symptoms of blood clots. Routine endometrial biopsies or pelvic ultrasounds are not recommended on tamoxifen, as the majority of women will not have endometrial problems.

Women should stop tamoxifen with any signs of abnormal vaginal bleeding or blood clots and have these symptoms immediately assessed. Women on tamoxifen for chemoprevention also need to engage in a healthy lifestyle, including routine exercise. This may help prevent blood clots. Prolonged immobility or surgical procedures that place women at an increased risk for blood clots can warrant a temporary period of stopping tamoxifen. The drug can be resumed once a woman has recovered from her surgery or is back to her normal mobility. Women should be encouraged to move their extremities periodically during long-distance flights and car travel. Women also need to know the cost of taking tamoxifen for five years. Since tamoxifen is approved by the FDA for breast cancer risk reduction, it is generally covered by a woman's prescription plan, should she have this with her health insurance. A co-payment amount is based on the individual plan. The monthly out-of-pocket expense for those without prescription coverage is approximately $100.00.

In addition to a discussion of the potential benefits, risks, and costs of tamoxifen for chemoprevention, women should be counseled to continue with their increased surveillance strategies for breast cancer.

Preventive Mastectomy. Retrospective studies have shown the benefit of bilateral preventive mastectomy in breast cancer risk reduction in women at an increased risk (Hartmann *et al.,* 1999; Eisen *et al.,* 2000). Before these studies, no data existed to counsel women at an increased risk regarding exactly how much their breast cancer risk would be reduced. The landmark study by Hartmann and colleagues showed a greater than 90% breast cancer reduction in women with a strong family history of breast cancer who had bilateral prophylactic mastectomy. This retrospective cohort study compared breast cancer occurrence in 215 women at high risk and 425 women at moderate risk. Results showed that bilateral mastectomy reduced breast cancer risk by 89% in moderate-risk women and 90–94% in high-risk women. The median follow-up after surgery was 14 years.

Another study at Erasmus University Medical Center in the Netherlands reported the benefits of bilateral prophylactic mastectomy in high-risk women (Meijers-Heijboer *et al.,* 2001). This prospective study of 139 BRCA1 or BRCA2 carriers compared prophylactic mastectomy (N = 76 women) versus surveillance (N = 63 women). No invasive breast cancers were found in women with prophylactic mastectomy, but eight breast cancers were found in women in the routine surveillance group within a follow-up period of three years.

Women considering prophylactic mastectomy need to be fully aware of the issues involved, the recommended procedure, and possible outcomes (Houshmand *et al.,* 2000). A total mastectomy, which removes the breast tissue and the nipple and areola, is recommended instead of a subcutaneous mastectomy, which preserves the nipple, as this minimizes residual at-risk tissue. Nipple reconstruction and areola tattoos are later performed. Women having prophylactic mastectomy may not need to undergo axillary lymph node sampling or dissection. Any woman considering this option should consult with both a breast surgeon and plastic surgeon to learn specific, individual benefits and risks for bilateral preventive mastectomy. The types of reconstruction recommendations vary among women based on the amount of tissue able to be transplanted in an autologous reconstructed breast, or on the potential dangers and length of anesthesia required based on the chosen reconstruction method used.

Preventive mastectomy may cause chest numbness and absent nipple sensation. Other potential complications include seromas, hematomas, pain, skin necrosis, dissatisfaction with cosmetic results, and psychologic distress (Eisen *et al.,* 2000; Houshmand *et al.,* 2000). Despite these sequelae, the majority of women who have elected preventive mastectomy have reported satisfaction with their decision (Frost *et al.,* 2000).

Although specific selection guidelines for prophylactic mastectomy do not exist, Love *et al.,* (2002) suggest four potential groups of women to consider this breast cancer prevention option. These include women with atypical hyperplasia; women with noninvasive breast cancer; women with a strong family history of breast cancer; and women with invasive breast cancer who want to remove their contralateral breast. For women with suspected genetic predisposition of rare mutations implicated in breast cancer, genetic testing may be very useful in a decision for prophylactic mastectomy. Women with DCIS and invasive breast cancer may wish to pursue testing before having a mastectomy, especially if considering bilateral mastectomy with transverse rectus abdominis myocutaneous (TRAM) reconstruction.

Preventive Oophorectomy. Data obtained retrospectively has suggested that women who have early surgical menopause with a bilateral oophorectomy also lower their risk for breast cancer (Colditz & Rosner, 2000). More recent data from preventive oophorectomy in BRCA mutation carriers points to a 50% reduction in breast cancer in these women (Rebbeck *et al.,* 1999, 2002). Mutation carriers primarily select bilateral oophorectomy to prevent ovarian cancer, a malignancy that is more difficult to screen for and diagnose compared to breast cancer. The potential benefit of breast cancer risk reduction with this surgery may offer mutation carriers more support for this choice.

The potential risks of preventive oophorectomy include risks of the surgical procedure and resultant early menopausal symptoms. With modern surgical techniques and improvements in anesthesia, the risks of this surgery have been minimized but nonetheless need to be considered. Side effects of premature menopause, including hot flashes, vaginal dryness, and early osteoporosis, need to be addressed with each woman. Low doses of hormones are often prescribed in the postoperative period for a short time to lessen the abrupt changes in the production of hormones and resultant early menopausal symptoms.

Bilateral oophorectomy performed in increased-risk women who are nonmutation carriers may also decrease breast cancer risk if performed particularly in premenopausal women (NCI, 2002). No prospective data is available to define the magnitude of the reduction of breast cancer risk. In addition, no data is available to know how much tamoxifen increases breast cancer risk reduction after a prophylactic oophorectomy.

CURRENT CHEMOPREVENTION STUDIES

The Study of Tamoxifen and Raloxifene (STAR) Breast Cancer Prevention Trial NSABP P-2 (Vogel, 2001), the second largest US breast cancer prevention trial, began in July 1999. This large, randomized, double-blind placebo-controlled trial plans to enroll 19,000 postmenopausal women at a five-year Gail risk of 1.66% or greater, or with history of LCIS, and compare tamoxifen 20 mg daily to raloxifene 60 mg daily for breast cancer prevention. To date, over 14,700 women have enrolled. (The total enrollment goal was changed to 19,000 from the original 22,000 in November 2001 by the NSABP.)

Study endpoints include invasive and noninvasive breast cancer, endometrial cancer, vascular events, cardiovascular disease, and bone fractures. The basis for STAR stemmed from the 74% invasive breast cancer reduction seen in women taking raloxifene versus placebo in the Multiple Outcomes of Raloxifene Evaluation (MORE) trial (Cummings *et al.,* 1999; Bevers, 2001). Raloxifene is approved by the FDA for the prevention and treatment of osteoporosis. STAR is the first prevention trial to include a proven drug, tamoxifen, as the standard of care. Since raloxifene does not have studied side effect data in premenopausal women, STAR is limited to postmenopausal women. Although many community physicians began prescribing raloxifene to women for the intent of breast cancer prevention after the MORE trial results were published, major organizations do not recommend raloxifene for breast cancer risk reduction in high-risk women outside of a clinical trial (Chlebowski *et al.,* 2002). Table 3.7 provides a comparison of hormones to selective estrogen receptor modulators.

OTHER POTENTIAL CHEMOPREVENTION AGENTS

Several other drugs are in beginning clinical trials and may hold promise for chemoprevention of breast cancer. These include aromatase inhibitors, fenretinide and goserelin (Chlebowski, 2002). Aromatase inhibitors have been shown to reduce new primary contralateral breast cancers in postmenopausal women treated to prevent breast cancer recurrence (Lonning *et al.,* 2001).

CONSIDERATIONS IN PREVENTION OPTIONS

By explaining complex issues in breast cancer risk assessment, genetic testing, and the pros and cons of each breast cancer prevention option, nurses and advanced practice nurses can facilitate a woman's informed decision-making process with regard to breast cancer prevention options. All women can be advised to pursue a healthy lifestyle and obtain breast cancer screening. Counseling women in potential selection of chemoprevention/preventive surgery options involves an open dialogue of assessing a woman's main concerns regarding breast cancer and the consequences of the choices available for prevention.

Understanding a woman's current health status is also important. A woman who is experiencing severe vasomotor symptoms and is considering tamoxifen should first have

Table 3.7 Comparison of Hormones to Selective Estrogen Receptor Modulators

	ERT	HRT	Tamoxifen	Raloxifene
Breast Cancer Risk	↑	↑	↓	?
Blood Clot Risk	↑	↑	↑	↑
Uterine Cancer Risk	↑	-	↑	?
Cataracts			↑	
Bone Density	↑	↑	↑	↑
Total Cholesterol	↓	↓	↓	↓
Menopausal Symptoms	↓	↓	↑	↑

these symptoms addressed before taking a drug that may exacerbate them. It is also important not to limit a discussion of risks and benefits solely to breast cancer issues. Breast cancer is not the only health concern that a woman should have. Heart disease, osteoporosis, and other diseases and personal issues need to be considered in each individual woman's situation. Women who have vaginal dryness and cannot take hormone replacement can greatly benefit from the use of vaginal lubricants and low-dose vaginal estrogen products, such as Estring™ and Vagifem™.

Providing a framework for the various actions of the medication choices women are often faced with can help a woman highlight her individual health needs. Offering tools for a woman to navigate the abundance of health information she uses to make decisions is also important. A thorough handout on tamoxifen for chemoprevention is available at the NCI website, *http://www.cancer.gov*. It is also important to understand that a woman's choice in the diseases that she wants most to prevent is often affected by her own personal experiences with family and friends and an understanding of her own health issues. For example, a woman with a strong family history of postmenopausal breast cancer who cared for a mother who died from metastatic breast cancer may opt to choose a preventive mastectomy if she is not confident that breast cancer screening methods will diagnose breast cancer, and if she feels she could not tolerate chemotherapy.

Women at increased risk who have faced multiple breast biopsies/lumpectomies may wish to pursue preventive mastectomy if every mammogram seems to result in another biopsy. There are many women who are adverse to taking medications and do not wish to pursue tamoxifen for that reason. Only an open dialogue and assessment of a woman's health concerns can guide the complex discussion of the choices in breast cancer prevention from which a woman can now select. Many women may also benefit from the perspective of another woman who has also faced similar decisions regarding breast cancer prevention (Prouser, 2000).

As with any other aspect of health care, the basic philosophy of "do no harm" needs to be kept in consideration. With prevention options, women need to understand that not all women will benefit from prevention options regarding breast cancer reduction. The majority of women at increased risk not resulting from known genetic mutations who select either tamoxifen or preventive mastectomy may never have progressed to having invasive breast cancer.

SUMMARY

Nurses can offer women at an increased risk for breast cancer both up-to-date information on breast cancer risk reduction options and strategies to ensure a woman's understanding of what each potential option offers and requires. Much progress has been made in identifying risk factors for breast cancer and in proven methods to reduce risk in certain at-risk women. Further cancer research, especially in the molecular and biologic mechanisms of breast cancer development, may identify the women who are most likely to personally benefit from prevention strategies.

REFERENCES

Allain, D., Gilligan, M.A., & Redlich, P.N. (2002). Genetics and genetic counseling for breast cancer. In W.L. Donegan & J.S. Spratt (Eds.), *Cancer of the breast, 5th ed.,* pp. 249–268. Philadelphia: W.B. Saunders.

Barton, D., La, V.B., Loprinzi, C., Novotny, P., Wilwerding, M.B., & Sloan, J. (2002). Venlaflaxine for the control of hot flashes: results of a longitudinal continuation study. *Oncology Nursing Forum, 29*(1), 33–40.

Bernhardt, B.A., Geller, G., Doksum, T., & Metz, S.A. (2000). Evaluation of nurses and genetic counselors as providers of education about breast cancer susceptibility testing. *Oncology Nursing Forum, 27,* 33–39.

Berry, D.A., Iverson, E.S., Gudbjartsson, D.F., *et al.* (2002). BRCAPRO validation, sensitivity of genetic testing of BRCA1/BRCA2, and prevalence of other breast cancer susceptibility genes. *Journal of Clinical Oncology, 20,* 2701–2708.

Bevers, T.B. (2001). Breast cancer chemoprevention. *Biomedical Pharmacotherapy, 55*(9–10), 559–564.

Birkimir, S.J. (2002). Nutrition and breast disease. In W.L. Donegan & J.S. Spratt (Eds.), *Cancer of the breast, 5th ed.,* pp. 145–168. Philadelphia: W.B. Saunders.

Brinton, L., Lacey, J., & Devesa, S.S. (2002). Epidemiology of breast cancer. In W.L. Donegan & J.S. Spratt (Eds.), *Cancer of the breast, 5th ed.,* pp. 111–132. Philadelphia: W.B. Saunders.

Chlebowski, R.T. (2000). Reducing the risk of breast cancer. *New England Journal of Medicine, 343*(3), 191–198.

Chlebowski, R.T. (2002). Breast cancer risk reduction: strategies for women at increased risk. *Annual Review of Medicine, 53,* 519–540.

Chlebowski, R.T., Col., N., Winer, E.P., Collyar, D.E., Cummings, S.R., Vogel, V.G. 3rd, Burstein, H.J., Eisen, A., Lipkus, I., & Pfister, D.G. (2002). American Society of Clinical Oncology technology assessment of pharmacologic interventions for breast cancer risk reduction including tamoxifen, raloxifene and aromatase inhibition. *Journal of Clinical Oncology, 20*(15), 3328–3343.

Claus, E.B., Risch, N., & Thompson, W.D. (1994). Autosomal dominant inheritance of early onset breast cancer. *Cancer, 73,* 643–651.

Colditz, G.A., & Rosner, B. (2000). Cumulative risk of breast cancer to age 70 years according to risk factor status: data from the Nurses' Health Study. *American Journal of Epidemiology, 152*(10), 950–964.

Costantino, J.P., Gail, M.H., Pee, D., Anderson, S., Redmond, C.K., Benichou, J., & Wieand, H.S. (1999). Validation studies for models projecting the risk of invasive and total breast cancer incidence. *Journal of the National Cancer Institute, 91,* 1541–1548.

Couch, F.J., DeShano, M.D., & Blackwood, M.A. (1997). BRCA1 mutations in women attending clinics that evaluate the risk of breast cancer. *New England Journal of Medicine, 336,* 1409–1415.

Cummings, S.R., Eckert, S., Krueger, K.A., Grady, D., Powles, T.J., Cauley, J.A., Norton, L., Nickelsen, T., Bjarnason, N.H., Morrow, M., Lippman, M.E., Black, D., Glusman, J.E., Costa, A., & Jordan, V.C. (1999). The effect of raloxifene on risk of breast cancer in postmenopausal women: results from the MORE randomized trial. Multiple Outcomes of Raloxifene Evaluation. *Journal of the American Medical Association, 281*(23), 2189–2197.

Cuzick, J., Forbes, J., Edwards, R., *et al.* (2002). First results from the International Breast Cancer Intervention Study (IBIS-I): a randomized prevention trial. *Lancet, 360,* 817–824.

Eisen, A., Rebbeck, T.R., Wood, W.C., & Weber, B.L. (2000). Prophylactic surgery in women with a hereditary predisposition to breast and ovarian cancer. *Journal of Clinical Oncology, 18*(19), 3454–3455.

Fisher, B., Costantino, J.P., Wickerham, D.L., Redmond, C.K., Kavanah, M., Cronin, W.M., Vogel, V., Robidoux, A., Dimitrov, N., Atkins, J., Daly, M., Wieand, S., Tan-Chiu, E., Ford, L., & Wolmark, N. (1998). Tamoxifen for prevention of breast cancer: report of the National Surgical Adjuvant Breast and Bowel Project P-1 Study. *Journal of the National Cancer Institute, 90,* 1371–1388.

Foltz, A.T., & Mahon, S.M. (2000). Application of carcinogenesis theory to prevention [supplement]. *Oncology Nursing Forum, 27,* 5–11.

Frost, M.H., Schaid, D.J., Sellers, T.A., Slezak, J.M., Arnold, P.G., Woods, J.E., Petty, P.M., Johnson, J.L., Sitta, D.L., McDonnell, S.K., Rummans, T.A., Jenkins, R.B., Sloan J.A., & Hartmann, L.C. (2000). Long-term satisfaction and psychological and social function following bilateral prophylactic mastectomy. *Journal of the American Medical Association, 284*(3), 319–324.

Gail, M.H., Brinton, L.A., Byar, D.P., Corle, D.K., Green, S.B., Scairer, C., & Mulvihill, J.J. (1994). Projecting individualized probabilities of developing breast cancer for white females who are being examined annually. *Journal of the National Cancer Institute, 86,* 620–625.

Gail, M.H., Costantino, J.P., Bryant, J., Croyle, R., Freedman, L., Helzlsouer, K., & Vogel, V. (1999). Weighing the risks and benefits of tamoxifen treatment for preventing breast cancer. *Journal of the National Cancer Institute, 91,* 1829–1846.

Greco, K.E. (2000). Cancer genetics nursing: impact of the double helix [supplement]. *Oncology Nursing Forum, 27,* 29–36.

Hartmann, L.C., Schaid, D.J., Woods, J.E., Crotty, T.P., Myers, J.L., Arnold, P.G., Petty, P.M., Sellers, T.A., Johnson, J.L., & McDonnell, S.K. (1999). Efficacy of bilateral prophylactic mastectomy in women with a family history of breast cancer. *New England Journal of Medicine, 340*(2), 77–84.

Helzlsouer, K.J. (1999). Bad news/good news: information about breast cancer risk following prophylactic oophorectomy. *Journal of the National Cancer Institute, 91,* 1442–1443.

Houshmand, S.L., Campbell, C.T., Briggs, S.E., McFadden, A.W., & Al-Tweigeri, T. (2000). Prophylactic mastectomy and genetic testing: an update. *Oncology Nursing Forum, 27,* 1537–1547.

Lonning, P.E., Kragh, L.E., Erikstein, B., Hagen, A., Risberg, T., Schlichting, E., & Geisler, J. (2001). The potential for aromatase inhibition in breast cancer prevention. *Clinical Cancer Research, 7*(12), 4423s–4428s.

Love, R.R., Newcomb, P.A., & Trentham-Deitz, A. (2002). Prevention of breast cancer. In W.L. Donegan & J.S. Spratt (Eds.), *Cancer of the breast, 5th ed.,* pp. 199–223. Philadelphia: W.B. Saunders.

Mahon, S.M. (2000). Principles of cancer prevention and early detection. *Clinical Journal of Oncology Nursing, 4*(4), 169–176.

Martin, A.M., & Weber, B. (2001). Genetic and hormonal risk factors in breast cancer. *Journal of the National Cancer Institute, 92,* 1126–1135.

Meijers-Heijboer, H., van Geel, B., van Putten, W.L., Henzen-Logmans, S.C., Seynaeve, C., Menke-Pluymers, M.B., Bartels, C.C., Verhoog, L.C., van den Ouweland, A.M., Niermeijer, M.F., Brekelmans, C.T., & Klijn, J.G. (2001). Breast cancer after prophylactic bilateral mastectomy in women with a BRCA1 or BRCA2 mutation. *New England Journal of Medicine, 345*(3), 159–164.

National Cancer Institute. (December 2002). Breast cancer prevention (PDQ®): health professional version. Available at *www.cancer.gov.*

Powles, T., Eeles, R., Ashley, S., Easton, D., Chang, J., Dowsett, M., Tidy, A., Viggers, J., & Davey, J. (1998). Interim analysis of the incidence of breast cancer in the Royal Marsden Hospital tamoxifen randomised chemoprevention trial. *Lancet, 352*(9122), 98–101.

Pritchard, K.I. (2001). Breast cancer prevention in selective estrogen receptor modulators: a perspective. *Annals of the New York Academy of Science, 949,* 89–98.

Prouser, N. (2000). Case report: genetic susceptibility testing for breast and ovarian cancer: a patient's perspective. *Journal of Genetic Counseling, 9*(2), 153–159.

Rebbeck, T.R., Levin, A.M., Eisen, A., Snyder, C., Watson, P., Cannon-Albright, L., Isaacs, C., Olopade, O., Garber, J.E., Godwin A.K., Daly, M.B., Narod, S.A., Neuhausen, S.L., Lynch, H.T., & Weber, B.L. (1999). Breast cancer risk after bilateral oophorectomy in BRCA1 mutation carriers. *Journal of the National Cancer Institute, 91*(17), 1475–1479.

Rebbeck, T.R., Lynch, H.T., Neuhausen, S.L., Narod, S.A., Van 't Veer, L., Garber, J.E., Evans, G., Isaacs, C., Daly, M.B., Matloff, E., Olopade, O.I., & Weber, B.L. (2002). Prophylactic oophorectomy in carriers of BRCA1 or BRCA2 mutations. *New England Journal of Medicine, 346,* 1616–1622.

Rossouw, J., & Writing Group for the Women's Health Initiative Investigators. (2002). Risks and benefits of estrogen plus progestin in healthy postmenopausal women. Principal results from the Women's Health Initiative randomized controlled trial. *Journal of the American Medical Association, 288*(3), 321–333.

Veronesi, U., Maisonneuve, P., Costa, A., Sacchini, V., Maltoni, C., Robertson, C., Rotmensz, N., & Boyle, P. (1998). Prevention of breast cancer with tamoxifen: preliminary findings from the Italian randomised trial among hysterectomised women [on behalf of the Italian tamoxifen prevention study]. *Lancet, 352*(9122), 93–97.

Vogel, V. (2000). Breast cancer prevention: a review of current evidence. *CA—A Cancer Journal for Clinicians, 50,* 156–170.

Vogel, V.G. (2001). Follow-up of the breast cancer prevention trial and the future of breast cancer prevention efforts [supplement]. *Clinical Cancer Research, 7*(12), 4413s–4418s.

4 SCREENING AND EARLY DETECTION

JOELLE MACHIA, RN, BSN, BA

INTRODUCTION

As the incidence of breast cancer continues to rise, the mortality rate has decreased 3.5% annually since 1999 (National Breast Cancer Coalition, 2002). Decreased mortality is most likely due in part to increased utilization of mammography and overall awareness of the importance of a strong early detection program. Through media and scientific debate, women have recognized that breast cancer is a survivable disease if detected in its earliest stages. Through the directives and initiatives from agencies such as the National Cancer Institute (NCI), the American Cancer Society (ACS) and the United States Preventive Services Task Force (USPSTF), women are learning the importance of screening all women for breast cancer. Only through education and understanding will women take control of their own breast health.

Even though the mortality trends are encouraging, many women still needlessly die from breast cancer. Many women do not have a clear understanding of breast cancer risk or how diagnostic screening mitigates that risk. Inaccurate media coverage and a subsequent inadvertent public health message come with most new scientific discoveries. The world of science is not exact, and new research findings often contradict each other. Women who are faced with confusing and contradicting information may choose not to practice early detection out of the belief that no screening tool is truly effective. The recent mammography debate, even confounding among the experts, has brought forth new uncertainty. Complicating the situation further is the belief that most women who develop breast cancer are at high risk, when in reality most women diagnosed have no identifiable risk factors other than age (ACS, 2002).

This chapter will review the current screening and early detection programs that are currently the standard of care. The chapter will also discuss some of the newer screening and detection methods on the horizon. Nurses have a unique opportunity both professionally and personally to help women realistically assess their risks and recognize the benefit of appropriate screening. The overall goal is to empower nurses to become effective health messengers who play a vital role in decreasing the mortality and morbidity from breast cancer.

THE GOLD STANDARD FOR BREAST CANCER SCREENING

The goal of screening is to intervene in the progression of the disease after biological onset but before it is symptomatic. The decision to screen women for breast cancer is based on the importance of the disease as a public health problem and the demonstrated ability of screening tests to meet acceptable levels of performance and to reduce morbidity and mortality (Harris *et al.*, 2000).

Three methods are used to screen for breast cancer: mammography, clinical breast exam, (CBE), and breast self-exam (BSE). These should be viewed as a triad of methods (Figure 4.1). No single method is perfect in itself, but each is complementary to the others in portraying a complete clinical picture. Given the known variation in the quality of mammography, CBE, and BSE, and the fact that the relative sensitivity of any of these tests differs according to the tissue characteristics of a woman's breasts, it is prudent that all women older than age 40 years should be screened by all of these methods (Marchant, 1997). Current recommended guidelines for breast cancer screening vary slightly among various organizations, as noted in Tables 4.1 & 4.2. Variations are particularly noted in the timing of mammography; however, all three methods are always included. Of the three, mammography has been shown to be the most efficacious, offering the greatest potential for decreasing mortality from breast cancer.

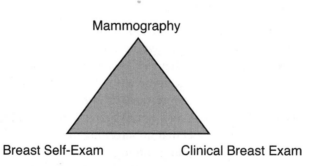

All components complement each other, and no component is independent of the others.

FIGURE 4.1 Triad of Early Detection.

Table 4.1 American Cancer Society (ACS) Guidelines for Breast Screening in Average-Risk Asymptomatic Women

Breast self-examination	Monthly starting at age 20 years
Clinical breast examination	Every three years from age 20 years to age 39 years; annually thereafter
Mammogram	Annually starting at age 40 years

All three components must be present to ensure a strong early detection.

MAMMOGRAPHY

Screening mammography is used to detect breast changes in women who are asymptomatic. It is the best tool available for detection of breast cancer. Scientific evidence clearly shows that it saves lives. Breast cancer screening in women age 50 years and older reduces the death rate by 30%. In women age 40 to 50 years, the results become a bit more uncertain, but nonetheless it is still believed to provide a 17% reduction (Dixon, 2000). The use of mammography is accepted by virtually all organizations that provide guidelines for the early detection of breast cancer. Exact guidelines may differ, but few argue the overall merit of mammography. Though a strong tool, it still has limitations. Up to 15–20% of cancers are missed on mammograms. Women with dense breast tissue are more likely to have their cancers missed. Dense breasts appear white on a mammogram film, as does breast cancer. Thus, the cancer is difficult to visualize in women with dense breast tissue as opposed to fatty breast tissue.

Mammography uses ionizing radiation to image breast tissue. The examination is performed by compressing the breast firmly between a plastic plate and an X-ray cassette that contains the film. For routine screening two views are taken: mediolateral oblique and craniocaudal. Sensitivity ranges from 85% to 90%. Lesions can present as a soft tissue mass, an architectural distortion, microcalcifications, a focal asymmetry, or a new and

Table 4.2 U.S. Preventive Services Task Forces (USPSTF) Screening Recommendations, 2002

Screening mammography, with or without clinical breast examination:

Every 1–2 years for women age 40 or older

Clinical breast exam:

Evidence is insufficient to recommend for or against routine CBE alone to screen for breast cancer.

Breast self-exam:

Evidence is insufficient to recommend for or against teaching or performing routine BSE.

Women who are at higher than average risk for breast cancer should seek medical advice about whether they should begin screening before or after the age of 40 years and also about the frequency of screening.

[These guidelines have been adopted by The National Cancer Institute (NCI) and Health and Human Services (HHS).]

developing density. Microcalcifications may be the only sign of early breast cancer and are associated with 30% of invasive cancers (Vogel, 2001).

The fear of radiation exposure from screening mammography can be a deterrent to women. The thought of exposing oneself to radiation for screening for a disease that one is unlikely to have is frightening to some. Women need to receive the message that the amount of radiation is negligible and that the benefit far outweighs the risk. Another deterrent to screening mammography is the discomfort from the breast compression. Women should be prepared that they can expect discomfort during the procedure and told why the compression is necessary. With understanding comes greater compliance to a regular screening program. If breast tenderness is a problem, advising the woman to take an analgesic one half hour prior to the procedure may make the discomfort more tolerable (Gorenwalk, 1997).

Because of inconsistent quality and safety issues in mammography centers in the early years of mammography use, Congress enacted the Mammography Quality Standards Act (MQSA) in 1992. MQSA requires the FDA to certify all facilities that perform mammography. This statute establishes requirements for the accreditation, certification, and inspection of facilities to ensure that a woman in the United States receives a high-quality mammogram. This has resulted in improved mammography technique, lower radiation exposure, and extensive training of personnel. The list of FDA-certified mammography facilities is updated weekly on the FDA Web site at *www.fda.gov* (Food and Drug Administration, 2002).

The usefulness of mammography is highly dependent on the proper use of dedicated equipment and the diagnostic skills of the radiologist. A mammography center should have a strong quality assurance (QA) system in place. There should be a set of minimum and expected standards, a plan to monitor performance, and a focus on overall excellence. Failure to meet the standards should lead to prompt corrective action followed by reevaluation. A good QA program should include all facets of the screening process, such as equipment, radiography, radiology, and surgery (Dixon, 2000). A physician's competence in reading mammograms should be continuously evaluated, as well. Sickles *et al.* (2002) found that specialist radiologists detected more total cancers and more early-stage cancers, recommended more biopsies, and had lower recall rates than general radiologists. Thus, women should seek out a facility that has a dedicated mammography radiologist for the most optimal care possible.

Screening versus Diagnostic Mammography. There are important differences between screening and diagnostic mammography. Screening mammography is performed on asymptomatic women. Diagnostic mammography is performed on women with signs or symptoms of breast disease. In screening mammography, two standard views of each breast are taken. The technologist performs the mammogram and checks the film for image quality. To keep costs down and to improve efficiency, the patient is usually sent home to receive word of the results later, after the radiologist has read the films. The radiologist usually reads films in a "batch format," with pertinent clinical data and previous mammograms in hand for comparison. Some centers perform a "double reading," that is, two separate radiologists read the same film. Double reading has been shown to improve the breast cancer detection rate by 5% to 15% (Harris *et al.*, 2000). Double reading does increase the cost of screening and may make it cost-prohibitive.

Using screening mammography, the incidence of breast cancer detection is between 3 and 7 cancers per 1000 women screened. In most cases, if the two views taken during screening mammography are not sufficient to fully assess the areas of concern, the woman will be called back for further workup. The recall rate is less than 10% when an experienced breast imaging radiologist is doing the interpretation (Vogel, 2001).

In diagnostic mammography, the radiologist is present to review the films immediately after they are taken. The radiologist is able to correlate the patient's clinical findings with the mammogram findings. If any additional diagnostic procedures are required, such as ultrasound or percutaneous image-guided biopsies, the radiologist is prepared to perform them immediately. The cost of a diagnostic mammogram is substantially higher than a screening mammogram.

The Mammography Debate. Because mammography has been under intense scrutiny by the media, patients now realize that many factors contribute to whether a breast cancer will be detected by mammography. These include the technique and the equipment used, the skill of the radiologist reading the films, and even the characteristics of the woman herself (Taplin & Lehman, 2002).

It is important for health professionals not to let these controversial and confounding headlines discourage women from getting a potentially lifesaving mammogram. The limitations of mammography are balanced by their benefit. The role of the nurse in education and support is an extremely valuable one. One avenue is to encourage women who are frustrated with a lack of strong research to become part of the answer. Offer them a chance to support and take part in breast cancer screening research. Only through women participating in screening research will we make improvements in the screening and early detection of breast cancer.

CLINICAL BREAST EXAM

Clinical breast exam (CBE) remains an important component of routine physical examinations. CBE should be done by a trained and licensed health care provider screening for palpable or visual abnormalities. The practitioner can be a physician, a nurse-practitioner, physician's assistant, or nurse who has specialized training in CBE. At some mammographic facilities, a radiological technician performs CBE prior to mammography.

Although mammography is an excellent tool for detection of breast cancer, it may still miss up to 15% of cancers (Harris *et al.*, 2000). CBE, along with mammography, provides a more complete picture of a woman's breast health. Areas of palpable concern found with CBE can be more closely assessed at the time of mammography and can also indicate the need for other diagnostic procedures such as ultrasound.

With the advent of fast and clinically validated tools for breast cancer risk assessment, many practitioners are routinely completing a personal breast cancer risk assessment of their patients at their annual exams (Machia, 2001). The NCI Risk Disk, a CD available free from the NCI, now makes it possible for any practitioner to provide this service. If the patient is at an increased risk for breast cancer, this tool offers an excellent opportunity to discuss screening guidelines based on her specific history. The NCI Breast Cancer Risk Tool can be accessed at *http://www.radiotherapy.com/BrCaRiskTool/BCRT.htm.*

Examiners vary in their approach to performing CBE. The practitioner should develop a standardized, systematic approach to CBE and use it during each exam. CBE should always begin with a thorough medical history, evaluation of risk factors, and a discussion of any breast complaints. The patient should be asked specifically if there have been any changes in her breasts. The entire anatomic region of the breast and lymph nodes needs to be visually inspected and palpated. The examination must be detailed and unhurried. In a study of the physician's ability to detect breast lumps in silicon breast models, a strong correlation existed between the time spent on the exam and the detection of abnormalities (Bassett *et al.,* 1997). While performing the exam, the practitioner should take this opportunity to discuss an appropriate breast cancer screening program. Finally, documentation of the findings is essential. The best method is a combination of a written description and a diagram of the breasts.

It is imperative to communicate any findings with the patient after the exam. Delay in diagnosis is one of the most common reasons for medical malpractice claims in the United States. If any clinically significant findings appear on exam, even with a negative mammogram, further evaluation is required. (See Chapter 5 for additional details about clinically positive mammograms.)

BREAST SELF-EXAM

Since neither CBE nor mammography is 100% sensitive, breast self-exam (BSE) is an important part of any woman's screening and early detection program. BSE is the systematic visual inspection and palpation of the breast tissue. Lack of proficiency is one of the most common barriers to BSE. An education process using verbal, visual, and hands-on demonstration can provide the needed proficiency. Many women find practicing BSE on breast models to be very useful in breaking down barriers and instilling confidence in their ability to detect any changes or abnormalities. The breast models simulate both normal and abnormal tissue.

The recommended age for women to begin monthly breast self-exam is 20 years old. Starting BSE at this early age gives the woman a chance of developing strong, consistent health screening behavior. The principal goal of these early breast exams is to help the woman determine what her "normal tissue" is so that a change or abnormality can be detected. What is normal for one woman is not necessarily normal for another; a woman should become familiar with what her "norm" is. Many women still feel apprehensive in their ability to detect changes. In teaching BSE, it is helpful to advise women to search for asymmetry. If a woman finds that one breast feels different from the other, follow-up is indicated. This seems a simple and obvious recommendation, but it is a strong tool in getting women to practice BSE. There are three styles of BSE: circular, vertical, and wedge patterns. No matter which the woman is the most comfortable with, all exams should have the following two steps:

1. Visual inspection using a mirror (a good time is before taking a shower while fully unclothed); and
2. Palpation in a supine position or in the shower.

In premenopausal women, monthly exam should be done after the end of the menstrual period. In postmenopausal women, monthly exam is ideally done on a day of the month that is easy to remember. Women must be made aware that once a month is the goal. Examinations made more than once a month may decrease a woman's ability to detect subtle changes. In today's busy world, women have difficulty finding privacy and time to care for themselves. This should be recognized, and the practitioner should work with the woman to structure a plan for BSE without instilling guilt.

Monthly breast self-exam is strongly advocated, but evidence for its effectiveness is weak. Even though many women find their own cancers with BSE, clinical trials have not shown that BSE is effective in decreasing cancer deaths (Thomas *et al.,* 2002). Observational trials evaluating BSE and breast cancer stage at diagnosis or death have shown mixed results (USPSTF, 2002a, b, c, d). Despite the lack of scientific evidence, it is known that women who practice regular BSE find smaller lumps, and the earlier the breast cancer is detected, the better the chance of survival. BSE remains immediately available and inexpensive, and it is a noninvasive method of evaluation (Bassett *et al.,* 1997). BSE increases breast health awareness. Anytime a woman is more aware of her body and takes an active role in her own health care, she is empowered.

OTHER SCREENING AND EARLY DETECTION METHODS

DIGITAL MAMMOGRAPHY

Digital mammography is a technique for recording X-ray images on a computer instead of on film as with conventional mammography. The images are displayed on a computer monitor and can be enhanced before they are printed on film. Images can be easily manipulated, offering the radiologist the ability to zoom in or out on any area of concern. The radiologist then has the ability to pick up subtle differences between tissues.

The FDA approved the first digital mammography system in 2000. From the patient's viewpoint, the mammogram procedure is identical to conventional mammography. Women who are interested in digital mammography should speak with their primary care physician or contact a local FDA-approved and certified mammography center to determine availability in their area. The FDA must certify facilities before they can offer digital mammography.

One of the advantages of digital mammography over conventional mammography is that images can be stored and retrieved electronically. This facilitates consultation with other specialists. With the improved accuracy of digital mammography, fewer unnecessary follow-up procedures may be needed. Fewer exposures further reduce the (already low) level of radiation exposure. Despite these early positive results, studies have not yet shown that digital mammography is more effective than conventional mammography in finding cancer. One disadvantage is that a digital mammography unit is more expensive than a conventional mammography system. The additional costs must be weighed against the potential advantages that have yet to be proven.

BREAST SONOGRAPHY (ULTRASOUND)

Wild and Neal first used ultrasound in the examination of the breast in 1951. Early on, there was hope that ultrasound would allow early detection of breast cancer and that it would eventually replace mammography. Ultrasound has not replaced mammography, although ultrasound's role in screening women with dense breast tissue is still being evaluated. Ultrasound is considered complementary to CBE and mammography. It cannot be used for screening of asymptomatic women, because it does not detect microcalcifications, which may be the only sign of a malignancy (Vogel, 2001). Its most important role is the determination of the cystic or solid nature of a circumscribed noncalcified occult mass, either palpable on physical exam or seen on mammography. In fact, ultrasound can diagnose a cyst with 96% to 100% accuracy (Jellins *et al.,* 1977).

Breast ultrasound equipment has greatly improved, with high-resolution transducers that better characterize the shape, borders, and acoustic properties of breast masses. The improved definition allows for better understanding of benign and malignant masses. With real-time ultrasound, the entire breast, including skin, subcutaneous tissue, glandular tissue, chest wall, and axilla, can be scanned (Vogel, 2001). Ultrasound is frequently used as part of diagnostic procedures such as fine-needle aspiration or biopsy of a suspected mass, cyst aspiration, or wire localization.

Ultrasound uses high-frequency sound waves that bounce off of tissues and internal organs. An image is then formed from the echoes. To aid in conduction, during the exam the technician spreads a thin coating of lubricating jelly over the area to be imaged. The transducer, a handheld device, directs the sound waves through the skin toward the area of concern. The sound waves reflected back form a two-dimensional image on a computer screen.

Other indications for ultrasound include evaluation of patients with symptoms of breast infections and symptomatic patients with breast implants (Gordon, 2002). It is the most operator dependent of all screening modalities. Because of a substantial false positive rate in asymptomatic women, the routine use of ultrasound has been mostly abandoned. Only areas of mammographic or palpable abnormality are typically studied with ultrasound (Bassett *et al.,* 1997).

PET SCANNING

Positron emission tomography (PET) is a computerized imaging modality that can be used to measure tumor metabolism, blood flow, and estrogen and progesterone receptor density (Dixon, 2000). PET has the ability to image primary, axillary, and systemic breast carcinoma. Computerized images of the chemical changes that take place in tissue are created. Breast cancer tumors typically show elevated metabolic activity and increased consumption of sugar. Fluorine-18-labeled glucose [(18)F=fluorodeoxyglucose, or FDG], a substance consisting of sugar and a small amount of radioactive material, is injected. Because cancer cells absorb sugar faster than other tissues in the body, the radioactive sugar concentrates in the tumor (NCI, 2002a).

The patient must fast for four hours prior to the procedure to lower insulin and blood glucose levels. After receiving the FDG, the patient remains still for up to two hours while the drug is absorbed. The patient then lies supine on a table while the PET scanner gradually moves up and down the whole body six to seven times. The PET scanner resembles a CT scanner. There are no known adverse reactions to the FDG.

It is doubtful that PET scanning will ever be used as a screening tool for breast cancer. Rather, it may be an adjunct to mammography and ultrasonography in select patients (Vogel, 2001). At present, PET scanning is approved by the FDA for breast cancer imaging. It is still being evaluated as a breast cancer diagnostic tool (Czernin & Phelps, 2002). One limitation is that PET scanners are more accurate in detecting larger, more aggressive tumors than they are in locating tumors that are smaller than 8 mm or are less aggressive (NCI, 2002a).

MAGNETIC RESONANCE IMAGING (MRI) OF THE BREAST

Mammograms have demonstrated that mammography screening can reduce mortality from breast cancer. Although advances in mammography have greatly improved image quality, the technique is still fraught with shortcomings resulting in limitations in sensitivity and specificity of the breast image. Mammography is well known for its lack of sensitivity in the dense breast tissue common in younger women. There is now considerable interest in breast MRI. Extensive research in this modality has arisen from its superb sensitivity and its potential role in screening for breast cancer in high-risk patients with dense breast tissue (Vogel, 2001). Other potential uses have been identified, such as identifying recurrences in women with breast cancer treated by lumpectomy or radiation, and examining responses to chemotherapy (Harris *et al.*, 2000).

In MRI technology, a magnet is linked to a computer that creates detailed images of the breast without exposure to radiation. The MRI produces hundreds of images. With three-dimensional technology, it is possible to reformat images of soft tissue in fine sections and in various planes. Numerous studies have estimated the MRI sensitivity rates for detecting breast cancer at 95% to 100%. Specificity has been an obstacle, however, varying from 37% to 97% depending on the technique and setting used (Tillam *et al.*, 2002). MRI imaging works on the premise that malignant lesions require vascular supplies. Contrast-enhanced imaging can determine vascularity and vessel permeability, differentiating between benign and malignant lesions. MRI also allows the removal of fat from the image, which improves the conspicuity of the tumor (Vogel, 2001).

During the procedure, the patient lies on her stomach on the scanning table. The breast is placed through a depression in the table that contains coils that generate the magnetic signal. The table then moves into a tubelike machine that contains a magnet. After initial images are taken, a contrast agent is given intravenously to improve the visibility of the tumor. As the contrast agent is absorbed, additional images are taken over the course of the one-hour procedure.

Breast MRI is not indicated in routine breast cancer screening. Clinical trials are ongoing to determine which select populations may benefit (Warren, 2001). MRI should be considered an ancillary test to be used in selected patients in addition to standard mammography. To date, breast MRI has proven most useful to assess patients with proven breast cancer for multifocal/multicentric or diffuse masses (Morris, 2002). It is sensitive in detecting small lesions less than 1 cm in size. MRI is able to detect breast abnormalities that can be felt but not imaged by mammography or ultrasound (Warner *et al.,* 2001). Another potential role is screening of patients with dense breasts or implants.

Some of the disadvantages are cost and the inability of some patients to tolerate the enclosed space. MRI cannot always accurately distinguish between cancer and benign breast conditions. MRI is also unable to detect microcalcifications.

COMPUTER-AIDED DETECTION (CAD)

In 1998, the FDA approved a breast-imaging device that uses CAD technology. CAD involves the use of computers to bring suspicious areas on a mammogram to the radiologist's attention. It is used after the radiologist has done the initial review of the mammogram. CAD technology may improve the accuracy of the screening mammogram. This device scans the mammogram with a laser beam and converts it into a digital signal that is processed by a computer. The image is then displayed on a video monitor, and the radiologist can highlight a suspicious area for review. The image can be compared with the original mammogram film to see if the suspicious area was missed on the initial review. Incorporation of CAD technology into digital mammography is under evaluation (NCI, 2002a).

DETECTION OF BREAST CANCER

STEREOTACTIC BIOPSY

As a direct result of women following screening mammography guidelines and the greatly improved sensitivity of mammograms, an increasing number of suspicious, nonpalpable lesions have been found. Historically, these were assessed with needle localization and excisional biopsy. As with any surgery, there is a significant cost and morbidity involved. This is especially troubling because 80% of these lesions were benign (Vogel, 2001).

Stereotactic biopsy was introduced in 1988 and is considered a highly accurate, less invasive, and less costly alternative to surgical biopsy. Sensitivity is generally reported to be approximately 98% with specificity of 100%. The stereotactic biopsy device includes a computer, a needle holder, a biopsy device, and a method of obtaining stereotactic mammograms, that is, two projections separated by 30° from one another (Vogel, 2001). The precise locations within the suspicious area(s) are determined, a needle is inserted into the breast, and a tissue sample is obtained by moving the needle within the abnormal area(s). The patient can be in a seated or prone position on a dedicated table with the breast placed within an opening in the table.

MAMMOTOME®

Mammotome®, a vacuum-assisted biopsy device, is used for nonpalpable, mammographically detected lesions. Nonpalpable breast lesions can present diagnostic challenges. Ultrasound-guided fine-needle aspiration is a popular method used to attain tissue for diagnosis, but this procedure can be inconclusive and inaccurate (Ancona *et al.*, 2001). Mammotome® obtains multiple tissue cores in a circumferential manner around the biopsy probe inserted under stereotactic guidance. Multiple core biopsies can be collected with a single needle insertion. It provides more complete sampling of lesions than the conventional 14-gauge stereotactic core biopsy, thus reducing the number of unsatisfactory biopsies. It reduces the need for open biopsy without compromising diagnostic accuracy. It can be performed in an outpatient setting and is very well tolerated by most patients (Hung *et al.*, 2001).

DUCTAL LAVAGE

Ductal lavage is an investigational technique for collecting samples of cells from breast ducts for pathological analysis. A saline solution is introduced into the milk ducts through a catheter that is inserted into the opening of the duct on the surface of the nipple. Fluid, which contains cells from the duct, is withdrawn back through the catheter. The cells are examined by a pathologist to determine if they indicate breast cancer or an increased risk for breast cancer. This procedure is still considered experimental and is still under study (NCI, 2002a).

ELECTRICAL IMPEDANCE SCANNING

Electrical impedance scanning is the measurement of how fast an electrical signal travels through a given material. Various types of tissues have different levels of impedance. Breast tissue that is cancerous has a much lower impedance (that is, it conducts electricity better) than normal breast tissue. Electrical impedance scanning devices are used as an adjunct to mammography to diagnose breast cancer. This device can confirm the location of abnormal areas found on a mammogram.

The electrical impedance scanning device, a handheld scanning probe that displays two-dimensional images of the breast on a computer screen, does not emit any radiation.

An electrode patch is placed on the patient's arm, and a small amount of electrical current is transmitted through the patch into the body. The current travels to the breast, where the probe measures the electrical impedance of the tissue. An image is then displayed on the computer monitor. Tumors may appear as bright white spots, because the breast cancer cells are better able to conduct electricity. (NCI, 2002a).

The electrical impedance scanner does not have a role in screening and is only used when mammography and other findings clearly indicate the need for biopsy. Its safety has not been studied with patients who have implanted electronic devices.

SUMMARY

A strong screening and early detection program is still a woman's best defense against breast cancer. Despite all the new diagnostic and screening technology, no program has been proven more effective than the triad of early detection: mammography, CBE, and BSE.

As nurses, we need to help our patients decipher relevant information and guide them in forming a strong and consistent screening plan. We cannot allow women to become complacent. We need to engage women to make sure that the important facts are being heard and understood. Time must be spent explaining new findings and providing balanced commentary to help women put all the information into proper perspective. A more educated woman will be an empowered one who will take responsibility for her own breast health.

The field of breast screening and early detection is one of excitement and endless possibilities, but there is much work yet to be done. Decreasing the morbidity and mortality from this disease is a work in progress. Through research and evidence-based practice this goal will be achieved.

REFERENCES

Ancona, A., Caiffa, L., & Fazio, V. (2001). Digital stereotactic breast microbiopsy with the mammotome: study of 122 cases. *Radiological Medicine, 101*(5), 341–347.

American Cancer Society. (2001). *Cancer statistics.* Atlanta, Ga.: Author.

American Cancer Society. (2002). *Prevention and early detection—can breast cancer be found early?* Atlanta, Ga.: Author.

Bassett, L., Jackson, V., Jahan, R., Fu, Y., & Gold, R. (1997). *Diagnosis of diseases of the breast.* Philadelphia: W.B. Saunders.

Burbank, F., & Fogarty, T.J. (1996). Stereotactic breast biopsy: improved tissue harvesting with the mammotome. *American Surgery, 62*(9), 738–744.

Czernin, J., & Phelps, M. (2002). Positron emission tomography scanning: current and future applications. *Annual Review of Medicine, 53,* 89–112.

Dixon, J.M. (2000). Breast cancer: diagnosis and management. Amsterdam, New York: Elsevier Science B.V.

Food and Drug Administration. (2002). *Mammography-certified facilities.* Rockville, Md.: Author.

Gail, M.H., Brinton, L.A., Byar, D.P., Corle, D.K., Green, S.B., Scairer, C., & Mulvihill, J.J. (1994). Projecting individualized probabilities of developing breast cancer for white females who are being examined annually. *Journal of the National Cancer Institute, 86,* 620–625.

Gordon, P.B. (2002). Ultrasound for breast cancer screening and staging. *Radiologic Clinics of North America, 40*(3), 431–441.

Gorenwalk, S., Goodman, M., Frogge, M., & Yarbo, C. (1997). *Cancer nursing principles and practice* (4th ed.). Sudbury, Mass.: Jones & Bartlett.

Harris, J., Lippman, M., Morrow, M., & Hellman, S. (1996, 2000). *Diseases of the breast.* Philadelphia: Lippincott-Raven.

Hung, W.K., Lam, H.S., Lau, Y., Chan, C.M., & Yip, A.W. (2001). Diagnostic accuracy of vacuum-assisted biopsy device for image-detected breast lesions. *ANZ Journal of Surgery, 71*(8), 457–460.

Jellins, J., Kossoff, G., & Reeve, T.S. (1977). Detection and classification of liquid-filled masses in the breast by gray scale echography. *Radiology, 125*(1), 205–212.

Machia, J. (2001). Breast cancer: risk, prevention and tamoxifen. *American Journal of Nursing, 101*(4), 26–35.

Marchant, D. (1997). *Breast disease.* Philadelphia: W.B. Saunders.

Morris, E.A. (2002). Breast cancer imaging with MRI. *Radiologic Clinics of North America, 40*(3), 443–466.

National Breast Cancer Coalition. (2002). *Facts about breast cancer in the United States.* Washington, D.C.: Author.

National Cancer Institute. (2002a). *Cancer facts: improving methods for breast cancer detection and diagnosis.* Bethesda, Md.: Author.

National Cancer Institute. (2002b). *Cancer facts: screening mammograms: questions and answers.* Bethesda, Md.: Author.

Sickles, E.A., Wolverton, D.E., & Dee, K.E. (2002). Performance parameters for screening and diagnostic mammography: specialist and general radiologists. *Radiology, 224*(3), 861–869.

Taplin, S., & Lehman, C. (2002, August 8). Despite limitations, mammograms save lives. *Seattle Times:* Opinion.

Thomas, D.B., Gao, D.L., Ray, R.M., Wang, W.W., Allison, C.J., Chen, F.L., Porter, P., Hu, Y.W., Zhao, G.L., Pan, L.D., Li, W., Wu, C., Coriaty, Z., Evans, I., Lin, M.G., Stalsberg, H., & Self, S.G. (2002). Randomized trial of breast self-examination in Shanghai: final results. *Journal of the National Cancer Institute, 94*(19), 1445–1457

Tillam, G., Orel, S., Schnall, M., Schultz, D., Tan, J., & Solin, L. (2002). Effect of breast magnetic resonance imaging on the clinical management of women with early stage breast carcinoma. *Journal of Clinical Oncology, 20*(16), 3413–3423.

U.S. Preventive Services Task Force. (2002a). Breast cancer screening: a summary of the evidence for the U.S. Preventive Services Task Force. *Annals of Internal Medicine, 137*(5), 347–362.

U.S. Preventive Services Task Force. (2002b). The mammography dilemma: a crisis for evidence-based medicine. *Annals of Internal Medicine, 137*(5), 363–365.

U.S. Preventive Services Task Force. (2002c). Newspaper reporting of screening mammography. *Annals of Internal Medicine, 137*(5), 373–374.

U.S. Preventive Services Task Force. (2002d). Screening for breast cancer: recommendation and rationale. *Annals of Internal Medicine, 137*(5), 344–346.

Vogel, V. (2001). *Management of patients at high risk for breast cancer.* Malden, Mass.: Blackwell Science.

Warner, E., Plewes, D.B., Shumak, R.S., Catzavelos, G.C., Di Prospero, L.S., Yaffe, M.J., Goel, V., Ramsay, E., Chart, P.L., Cole, D.E., Taylor, G.A., Cutrara, M., Samuels, T.H., Murphy, J.P., Murphy, J.M. & Narod, S.A. (2001). Comparison of breast magnetic resonance imaging, mammography, and ultrasound for surveillance of women at high risk for hereditary breast cancer. *Journal of Clinical Oncology, 19*(15), 3524–3531.

Warren, R. (2001). Is breast MRI mature enough to be recommended for general use? *Lancet, 358*(9295), 1745–1746.

DIAGNOSIS AND STAGING

5

TERESA FRAKER, RN, BSN, OCN®

INTRODUCTION

A woman's best chance for surviving breast cancer is in screening and early detection. In addition, methods of breast cancer diagnosis and staging are also important. Although the previous chapter contained information about screening and early detection, the information is also contained here as an adjunct prior to a comprehensive review of the diagnosis and staging of breast cancer.

BREAST CANCER DETECTION

Breast cancer is detected in several ways: breast self-examination (BSE), clinical breast examination (CBE), and mammography. BSE has an important role. When women are encouraged to do monthly BSE, breast cancers can be found at an earlier stage, which is associated with better overall survival. A woman who practices regular BSE knows her own breast tissue well, and in all likelihood she will present to her health care provider when she notices a change in what she is feeling. If her statement is, "There is just something different," she is usually correct, even though breast changes may not ultimately yield a malignancy.

CBE includes both inspection and palpation of the breasts. First, the breasts are examined by palpation and visualization, with the patient's arms relaxed at her sides, her arms above her head, and her arms flexed and pushing against her hips. The patient should then be placed in the supine position for additional examination. The supine position allows greater distribution of the breast tissue across the chest wall area for more accurate assessment. The experienced examiner looks for any asymmetry between the breasts. It is normal to have one breast larger than the other. Changes in breast shape, however, may be a subtle sign of an abnormality. Changes in the nipple are important because the nipple may be flattened, or retracted inward, medially, or laterally with malignancy. Other nipple changes, such as scaling, peeling, cracking, or bleeding, and changes in the overall texture and color of the breast are also important in CBE. Palpation must include the breasts, chest, supraclavicular areas, and bilateral axilla. Fibrocystic-type variations that are lumpy and ropelike throughout breast tissue are generally benign. Breast cysts typically feel soft and mobile (similar to a water balloon), and can be easily aspirated. These, too, are benign.

In contrast to benign lesions, breast cancers have an irregular, stellate, firm consistency. They are usually solitary, nontender lesions that can be fixed to the skin or to deeper structures of the breast. Lesions with this clinical finding warrant further investigation by imaging and pathologic means, regardless of the patient's age.

Delay in diagnosis of breast cancer is the subject of much review in the literature, both in the medical and, oftentimes, legal communities. Strong evidence indicates that delayed presentation of symptomatic breast cancer is associated with lower survival rates (Ramirez *et al.,* 1999). Patients with total delays of three to six months have significantly worse survival rates than those with delays of less than three months. Denial also has a major role in delay of diagnosis, and future research should focus on psychosocial, emotional, and socioeconomic barriers to care. There is strong evidence to support the hypothesis that older age is associated with a longer delay by patients (Ramirez *et al.,* 1999). Counteracting this delay in diagnosis can be achieved by enhancing and augmenting the education of women and their health care providers. Up to 50% of patients present to a family physician within one month of developing symptoms, but 20–30% delay more than three months. Studies over the past 20 years have shown that when health care providers seek care for breast cancer their delays in diagnosis are roughly equal to those seen in other patients (Ramirez *et al.,* 1999).

MAMMOGRAPHY

Mammography is the use of radiographs to visualize breast tissue. It can detect cancers that are too small to be palpated on clinical exam (Judkins & Akins, 2001). Although it is not a perfect test, mammography will detect about 90% of breast cancers in women without symptoms. Unlike screening mammograms, diagnostic mammograms are indicated for women with symptoms such as masses, nipple discharge, and breast pain, or for women with a history of previous breast cancer. With diagnostic mammograms, generally more X rays are taken of the affected side where the woman reports symptoms. These mammograms often include a lateral-medial view or magnification views.

Mammographic detection is more accurate in postmenopausal women compared to premenopausal women (ACS, 2001). Young women have dense breast tissue that is more difficult to penetrate with X ray compared to fatty tissue. As women age, glandular tissue is replaced with fat, thus affording greater ease in the interpretation of the mammogram. Hormone replacement therapy can cause the breast tissue to appear denser on mammography. Women should inform the mammography technologist of their gynecologic history (including hormone use), any history of biopsy, and history (both family and personal) of breast cancer. All of this information is vital for the radiologist when interpreting the mammogram.

Digital Mammography. Digital mammography is increasingly used in some facilities. In digital mammography, the procedural part of the mammogram is identical to film-screen mammography, but it offers the radiologist the additional advantage of a computerized tool for capturing, enhancing, and storing mammographic images (Mautner *et al.,* 2000). Digital mammography incorporates the use of computer-aided digital displays, greatly reducing the time between image acquisition and display. Time of delivery is approximately five seconds with this method, versus five minutes with the standard film-screen approach. With all of the apparent advantages, the most significant hurdle with this system is cost. Digital mammography units cost about five times as much as conventional units, and some regulatory bodies require that the computer-generated photos be transferred to regular film.

Mammographic Abnormalities. An experienced radiologist looks for two subsets of mammographic findings: masses and calcifications. A third finding is architectural distortion, but for the purposes of this chapter, we will focus on masses and calcifications. The American College of Radiology (ACR) Breast Imaging Reporting and Data System (BI-RADS™) developed a lexicon for mammography designed to standardize reporting and reduce confusion in breast imaging interpretation. The lexicon categorizes mammographic findings as follows:

- Negative (N)
- Benign finding (B)
- Probably benign finding (P)
- Suspicious abnormality (S)
- Highly suggestive of malignancy (M)

Lesions in category three (P) usually indicate a need for a six-month follow-up mammogram, whereas those in category four (S) or five (M) indicate the need for biopsy (Norris, 2001).

Masses on Mammography. In examining nonpalpable masses or lesions on mammography, the radiologist looks for certain characteristics that are cause for concern. Typically, benign masses such as cysts, fibroadenomas, and lymph nodes are well defined, with sharp, well-circumscribed margins. Benign masses do not disrupt the surrounding breast architecture and are usually not as dense in appearance as that of a cancer.

In contrast, cancers appear as stellate, irregular, infiltrative masses or lesions on mammography (see Figure 5.1). Generally, cancers cause distortion of the surrounding tissue. When evaluating a mass or lesion, radiologists ask the following questions:

1. Is this really a mass? (It must be identified in more than one view, and special views may be required)
2. Where is the mass located?
3. Are there associated calcifications?
4. Is the mass solid or cystic? (Usually ultrasound is required to determine this)
5. Is the mass new since the last mammogram?

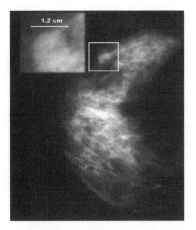

FIGURE 5.1 Craniocaudal view of a mammographically suspicious lesion. Note the irregular margins and the calcifications within the mass. (Courtesy of Robert W. Hartung, MD, Center for Breast Health, Genesis Medical Center, Davenport, Iowa).

Typically the mammographic abnormality having the highest rate of malignancy is a mass density on radiograph with associated calcification (Abeloff *et al.,* 2000).

Calcifications on Mammography. Calcifications on a mammogram are indicative of a change occurring in that particular area of the breast. It is theorized that as breast cancers grow in the ductal system, they leave behind calcium deposits, and these calcium deposits are what radiologists see on the mammogram. Calcifications are so small—often the size of a grain of sand—that they cannot be felt or palpated. About 20–25% of biopsied clustered calcifications are positive for cancer. The calcification pattern most characteristic of malignancy is one in which calcifications are typically linear, small (< 1 mm in diameter), non-uniform in size, and clustered (Abeloff *et al.,* 2000).

ADJUNCT DIAGNOSTIC IMAGING TOOLS

ULTRASOUND OR SONOGRAPHY

Diagnostic and interventional ultrasound for evaluation of breast abnormalities has experienced rapid growth in recent years. This method of examining the breast emits high frequency sound waves through breast structure. Ultrasound often works in conjunction with mammography, affording the best assessment of a lesion that is difficult to characterize. Ultrasound has many advantages. It continues to be the preferred method of evaluating the differences between cystic and solid lesions. It helps radiologists evaluate women with extremely dense breast tissue. It gives radiologists the ability to distinguish between benign and malignant nonpalpable lesions, and it also provides the same information about palpable lesions that are not detected on mammogram. Typically cancers appear on ultrasound by the irregularity in their shadowing pattern and their indistinct, jagged margins. Malignant lesions will also be anechoic or hypoechoic in their ability to allow sound to penetrate them (see Figure 5.2).

MAGNETIC RESONANCE IMAGING (MRI)

Breast MRI is being investigated as to its role in the evaluation of breast cancer, with cost as its major disadvantage. Breast MRI is sensitive in detecting small tumors (less than 1 cm) and in imaging dense breasts. The reported sensitivity of MR imaging for the visualization of invasive breast cancer approaches 100% (Orel & Schnall, 2001). In order for breast MRI to be performed, the patient must be able to lie in the prone position. The MRI unit must have dedicated breast coils, and a paramagnetic contrast agent is injected prior to the imaging component. Even with all of the advances that have been made with MRI, there is no "standard" or "optimal" technique for its performance. There are no standard interpretation criteria for evaluating breast MR imaging studies and no unifying definition of what constitutes potentially clinically important contrast enhancement (Orel & Schnall, 2001). Further investigation is needed to define the use of MRI as an adjuvant to conventional imaging methods and to demonstrate that MRI will add value and ultimately decrease the cost of care (Mautner *et al.,* 2000).

POSITRON EMISSION TOMOGRAPHY (PET) SCANNING

It has been widely known since the 1930s that malignant tumors tend to use glucose more than normal tissue, with glucose utilization greatest in rapidly growing tumors (Mautner *et al.,* 2000). PET scanning has been widely used in many malignant disorders, as an adjunct or

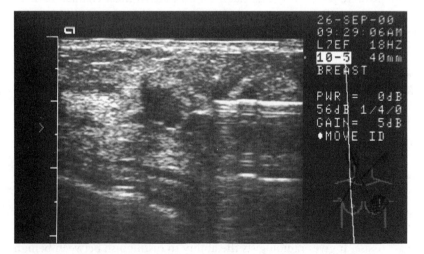

FIGURE 5.2 Hypoechoic, irregular, suspicious nodule on ultrasound undergoing ultrasound-guided core biopsy. Note the needle to the right of the nodule pre-fire. (Courtesy of Robert W. Hartung, MD, Center for Breast Health, Genesis Medical Center, Davenport, Iowa).

stand-alone test beside computerized tomography (CT) scanning. PET scanning of the breast and axilla is a highly specific test for malignancy, although its sensitivity is limited in patients with tumors smaller than 8 mm and/or less aggressive tumors, because of their lower glucose metabolic rate (Mautner *et al.*, 2000). Similar to MRI, PET scanning is not considered a screening tool, but it may have more applicability in the metastatic breast cancer setting.

PERCUTANEOUS BIOPSY OF PALPABLE LESIONS

Tissue may be obtained in one of several ways once a biopsy is recommended. There are different schools of thought regarding what type of biopsy should be done for palpable lesions; however, most physicians find it preferable to utilize the least invasive way of obtaining a diagnosis.

FINE-NEEDLE ASPIRATION AND NEEDLE CORE BIOPSY

Fine-needle aspiration biopsy (FNAB) and needle core biopsy are the most common forms of nonsurgical biopsy. Both biopsies can be done for either nonpalpable or palpable lesions, but for the purpose of discussion in this chapter, we will focus on the patient who presents with a palpable mass. The main differences between these biopsies are the size of the needle used, and the ability to obtain a confirmatory diagnosis, based upon the facility where the biopsy is performed.

Fine-Needle Aspiration Biopsy. FNAB is noninvasive and is generally well tolerated by most women. FNAB techniques are as follows (Foster, 2000): The skin is cleansed with an antiseptic solution. A 22-gauge needle is applied to a 10–20 cc syringe, and the needle is passed through the lesion in multiple directions, "shaving" multiple cells from the mass in question. The specimen is obtained in the hub of the needle, then the cells are purged onto a slide or placed in preservative for interpretation by the pathologist. In many tertiary care and teaching facilities, a cytopathologist is on staff to perform the FNAB and interpret its results while the patient is in the clinic. However, many facilities do not have such service available. In these cases the specimen is sent to the laboratory for analysis, and a diagnosis is rendered in about 48 hours. Usually, an FNAB pathology report will read, "Negative for Malignancy," "Indeterminate or Suspicious," or "Positive for Malignancy." Treatment decisions can then be based on these results.

Needle Core Biopsy. Needle core biopsy differs from FNAB in that a larger needle is used and a histologic diagnosis is obtained. Instead of rendering a report of "Positive for Malignancy," needle core biopsy allows for a definitive diagnosis of breast cancer and, in many cases, estrogen and progesterone receptor (ER/PR) status, as well. In a core needle biopsy, the skin is again cleansed with antiseptic solution, local anesthetic is instilled into the area of puncture, and pieces of tissue are removed from the mass via a spring-loaded, core-cutting needle device (Foster, 2000). A 14-gauge needle is typically used, which allows for better diagnostic sensitivity and specimen quality.

PERCUTANEOUS BIOPSY OF NONPALPABLE LESIONS

The following section will focus on a discussion of nonsurgical biopsy of nonpalpable, or mammographically detected, lesions. The surgeon cannot palpate the lesion, so assistance in direction for diagnosis is necessary. Both stereotactic and Mammotome® biopsy are excellent ways to sample calcifications found on a mammogram. FNAB can also be used in this setting, either with the use of ultrasound or stereotactic guidance.

STEREOTACTIC NEEDLE CORE BIOPSY

Stereotactic core biopsy combines high accuracy with low complication rates, allowing for tissue diagnosis of suspicious nonpalpable lesions and increased diagnosis of early (in situ, T1, or T2) tumors (Mautner *et al.*, 2000). This type of biopsy uses computerized needle core biopsy with mammographic guidance. In facilities with a dedicated stereotaxic unit, the procedure requires that the patient lie prone on a stereotactic table with the breast suspended through an opening in the table. Once the lesion is localized, the breast is cleaned with antiseptic solution, local anesthesia is used, and the computer calculates the exact area from which to obtain the tissue. For every specimen obtained, the needle "fires," the tissue is obtained, and the needle is removed to extract the tissue. Once the area has been adequately biopsied, postbiopsy films are taken to ensure that the lesion has been adequately sampled.

MAMMOTOME® BIOPSY

Mammotome® biopsy is a new method of sampling breast lesions that uses a vacuum-assisted system under local anesthesia. With Mammotome® biopsy, once the needle is in place, the vacuum-assisted system helps obtain the tissue, and the needle is not passed in and out of the breast during biopsy. Advantages of this biopsy method are the yield of larger and better tissue samples, less discomfort, and fewer complications (Mautner *et al.*, 2000).

ULTRASOUND-GUIDED NEEDLE CORE BIOPSY

Ultrasound-guided needle core biopsy uses the same principles as stereotactic biopsy, but the computer coordination and mammographic compression are not necessary. This type of biopsy uses local anesthesia with a 14-gauge core needle and the guidance of the ultrasound machine to locate the area in question. This type of biopsy offers better comfort for patients, because they do not have to undergo the prone positioning and compression with mammogram paddles.

EXCISIONAL AND INCISIONAL BIOPSY OF PALPABLE LESIONS

Excisional biopsy is a straightforward surgical procedure for the experienced surgeon, because the mass is palpable. The surgeon removes the entire mass by surgical means, frequently using intravenous sedation and local anesthesia. This is an outpatient procedure that usually takes about 30–40 minutes. The goal is to remove the mass and a surrounding margin of normal tissue. Excisional biopsy provides for complete evaluation of the tumor, including size and histology. Estrogen receptor (ER) and progesterone receptor (PR) assays and HER-2/neu assays can also be assessed.

In contrast, incisional biopsy removes a portion of the mass for pathologic evaluation. Incisional biopsy is done purely for diagnostic purposes. For example, it is used in situations where patients with locally advanced breast cancer might warrant neoadjuvant chemotherapy before definitive surgery. Because excellent pathologic information is easily obtained from needle core biopsy, incisional biopsy is used less commonly in many facilities.

EXCISIONAL BIOPSY OF NONPALPABLE LESIONS

The goal of excisional biopsy of nonpalpable lesions is to excise the abnormal area with a normal margin of breast tissue around it. In this procedure, a needle-localized or wire-localized biopsy is indicated. In this type of biopsy, a radiologist places a fine, thin wire through the breast tissue and lodges the wire adjacent to the mammographic abnormality (Kopans & Smith, 2000). The radiologist places the wire in a position similar to the one used to start an IV and anchors the wire with a 21-gauge needle. The needle is then removed and the wire remains in place. The wire has a hook on the end, similar to a fish hook. The surgeon makes the incision on the breast and follows the wire to the location where the hook is placed. The surgeon then excises the tissue around this questionable area and sends the tissue for pathologic evaluation. If calcifications were the target area on the mammogram, the radiologist will perform specimen radiography to ensure that the calcifications are within the specimen and correspond to those identified on the mammogram. Excisional biopsy of nonpalpable lesions is usually done under local anesthesia with intravenous sedation.

DIAGNOSIS

There are several types of breast cancer histologies. This section will review these individually, dividing breast cancers into three distinct groups: noninvasive, invasive, and a miscellaneous category.

NONINVASIVE CANCER

Ductal Carcinoma in Situ (DCIS). Prior to the advent of improved screening mammography, diagnoses of DCIS were relatively rare, comprising approximately 3% of all breast cancers. Today, it is estimated that DCIS accounts for 10–20% of all diagnosed breast cancers and up to 40% of breast cancers identified by mammography (Watson, 2001).

Also called intraductal carcinoma, DCIS is considered a preinvasive lesion for most women, but if left untreated, it will eventually progress to an invasive ductal carcinoma. DCIS particularly manifests itself on mammograms with the appearance of calcifications. As noted previously, as the carcinoma cells are forming in the ducts, they leave behind calcifications that are noted on the mammogram. Histologically, DCIS is described as malignant epithelial cells found inside the mammary ducts and lobules, showing no evidence of invasion through the basement membrane of the ducts or lobules into the surrounding breast tissue (Watson, 2001).

Lobular Carcinoma in Situ (LCIS). The use of the term "carcinoma" in LCIS is misleading, because LCIS is not viewed as a cancer. Rather, LCIS serves as a "marker" for subsequent development of invasive cancer. It has the ability to convert to the invasive ductal form of breast cancer, rather than the invasive lobular type. Women have an increased risk of developing this invasive cancer for approximately two decades after diagnosis of LCIS. LCIS tends to be multicentric and bilateral in its processes, and it perhaps can be more appropriately coined "lobular neoplasia." Whereas patients with DCIS often require radiation therapy with or without tamoxifen therapy, patients with LCIS do not require radiation therapy or chemotherapy. Patients can safely be followed with observation with or without tamoxifen.

INVASIVE BREAST CANCER

This section will review four different types of breast cancer: invasive ductal, invasive lobular, mucinous, and medullary cancers. All four are considered different in their types and abilities to metastasize.

Invasive Ductal Carcinoma. Invasive ductal carcinoma, sometimes called infiltrating ductal carcinoma, is the most common type of breast cancer, accounting for approximately 75–80% of all cases. These cancers arise from the duct system of the breast. It is usually theorized that these cancers started as DCIS but developed the capacity to invade and penetrate the basement membrane of the duct. Typically, invasive ductal carcinoma presents as a stellate, irregular mass on mammography, or as a fixed, irregular mass on clinical exam. These cancers are usually graded histologically into three categories: well differentiated (grade I), moderately differentiated (grade II), or poorly differentiated (grade III) (Watson, 2001). Poorly differentiated tumors are the most aggressive type of invasive ductal carcinoma. For example, stage I, grade I tumors have a five-year survival rate of greater than 90%, but five-year survival rates drop steadily with increasing grade and stage (Watson, 2001).

Invasive Lobular Carcinoma. Lobular carcinoma of the breast, otherwise called infiltrating lobular carcinoma, arises from the lobular and terminal duct epithelium and accounts for approximately 5–10% of all breast cancers (Watson, 2001). Among all types of breast cancer, it is the most often multicentric, representing multiple quadrants of the breast, and it can be bilateral. This cancer presents a challenge for radiologists, because it rarely manifests itself as a stellate mass on mammogram. Rather, it usually appears as an area of architectural distortion without mass. In women with dense breasts, invasive lobular carcinoma is often difficult to diagnose. The presentation of this cancer tends to be a diffuse infiltrative process that produces no clinically palpable or mammographically identifiable mass, making it difficult to diagnose in the early stages (Watson, 2001).

Mucinous Carcinoma. Another name for mucinous carcinoma is colloid carcinoma. Mucinous cancer is rare, accounting for only 5% of all invasive breast cancers. Mucinous carcinoma is characterized by islands or clumps of tumor cells floating in extracellular mucus, and it is considered to be a low-grade type of invasive ductal carcinoma (Watson, 2001). This cancer usually presents clinically as a discrete mass on clinical exam and/or mammography. Mucinous cancers are typically seen in the postmenopausal population, usually age 75 years and older. Prognosis for this cancer is considerably better than invasive ductal or lobular carcinoma, with reported survival rates between 86% and 100% at five years (Watson, 2001).

Medullary Carcinoma. Medullary carcinoma is extremely rare, accounting for fewer than 5% of all breast cancers. These cancers tend to be diagnosed more often in women younger than 50 years of age. Typically, women present with a palpable mass, but these can be mistaken for benign conditions such as cysts or fibroadenomas due to their often benign appearance on mammography and/or ultrasound. These tumors often present at a larger mass size than many of the other types of breast cancer; even so, the prognosis for medullary carcinoma is usually better than for other types of breast cancers (Watson, 2001).

MISCELLANEOUS BREAST CANCER DIAGNOSES

Inflammatory Breast Cancer. Inflammatory breast cancer is a rare and aggressive form of breast cancer, accounting for 1–4% of breast cancers. This cancer is not necessarily a histological subtype but rather a type of clinical change that occurs as a result of breast cancer cells blocking lymph channels in the breast (Watson, 2001). The clinical presentation is typically evidenced by thick, erythematous, edematous skin often called peau d'orange (similar to the skin of an orange). Many practitioners can confuse inflammatory breast cancer, a lethal disease, with mastitis, an infectious breast process. Unlike most breast cancers, whose initial primary therapy includes surgery, therapy for this type of breast cancer usually begins with chemotherapy and rarely involves surgery.

Paget's Disease. Paget's disease is also rare, and fortunately it does not tend to be as invasive or life threatening. This disease appears as a scaling, itching, or skin excoriation on or around the nipple and areola that does not heal with topical medication. It is almost never found as a bilateral phenomenon, and it is confirmed by punch biopsy of the involved skin area. Surgical management is used, depending upon the invasiveness of the disease.

SENTINEL LYMPH NODE (SLN) MAPPING AND DISSECTION

Nodal status is the single most important prognostic factor in breast carcinoma, and it has a major influence when decisions are made about adjuvant systemic treatment (Cserni, 2000). The role of axillary lymph node dissection (ALND) is threefold. First, there is an ill-defined, but probably small, therapeutic benefit. Second, ALND offers effective regional control of the disease. Third, ALND also ensures accurate staging (Whitworth, 2000). Histologic assessment of the axillary lymph nodes is important; a minimum of 10 nodes should be assessed for accurate axillary staging (Cserni, 2000). Because of the increasing risk of lymphedema and other complications such as paresthesia, seroma, infection, and limited shoulder mobility, it is thought that approximately 55–70% of patients undergoing SLN biopsy may be spared from having complication from axillary dissection (Kellar, 2001).

Morton and colleagues (1992) initially investigated SLN biopsy for use in patients with metastatic melanoma using isosulfan blue dye to visualize the path of lymph flow from the tumor site to regional lymphatic drainage basins. Alex and Krag (1993) expanded this work to include the use of radiotracers for lymphatic mapping and sentinel node identification. In 1994, Giuliano and colleagues first reported the application of the blue dye technique in patients with breast cancer. Because of this work, investigators felt that it might be feasible to incorporate this concept in patients with breast cancer as a means to apply a minimally invasive technique to identify and remove specific lymph nodes suspected of containing metastatic disease.

SLN is based on the concept that in breast cancer tumors smaller than 5 cm, the first lymph node in a lymph node bed to receive drainage from a tumor shows metastasis if there has been lymphatic tumor spread. When the SLN is tumor-free, there is 98% accuracy that the tumor has not spread beyond the lymphatics (Alazraki *et al.*, 2001). In general, the rate of sentinel node identification is greater than 90%, and the accuracy of SLN status as a predictor of axillary nodal status exceeds 95%. These figures are higher than the reported accuracy of any other noninvasive method (Hsueh *et al.*, 2000). The American Society of Breast Surgeons issued a consensus statement that suggests that the false-negative rate for breast cancer SLN biopsy should be 5% or less, recognizing that SLN biopsy is more accurate than axillary dissection, because SLN biopsy focuses the pathologist's attention on the node or nodes that most likely contain metastatic disease (Tafra *et al.*, 2000). Therefore, instead of performing one histological section through the center of 20 lymph nodes, the pathologist can perform 20 sections with immunohistochemical staining for one or two SLNs. The American Society of Breast Surgeons statement is contained in Table 5.1.

SLN METHODS

There are two primary methods of lymphatic mapping to identify the SLN: use of blue dye and use of a radiotracer. Although some facilities use either or both of these techniques, most facilities use both for increased accuracy of locating the SLN. With the combination technique, O'Hea and colleagues (1998) reported an SLN success rate of 93%, identifying a sentinel node in 55 of 59 breast cancer patients. The sentinel node status was 95% (52 of 55) in predicting axillary tumor involvement. For five other studies of 609 patients where preoperative lymphoscintigraphy, intraoperative gamma probe, and blue dye were used, the sensitivity of finding sentinel nodes ranged from 87% to 98%, with a weighted average of 93.81%. Statistically, these differences were highly significant (Alazraki *et al.*, 2001).

Table 5.1 American Society of Breast Surgeons Consensus Statement on Guidelines for Performance of Sentinel Lymphadenectomy for Breast Cancer

Original statement released November 1998; first revision released August 2000. Second revision approved and released by the Board of Directors on November 1, 2002.

Sentinel lymphadenectomy (SL) is a minimally invasive staging procedure for patients with breast cancer. SL, when performed in lieu of axillary dissection, is associated with potentially less morbidity and enhanced staging.

Multiple studies from single-institution and multi-center trials have validated the accuracy of SL when performed by experienced surgeons and SL is rapidly becoming the standard of practice. However, the degree of experience required to reliably and accurately perform the procedure, although becoming better understood, remains undefined.

In regard to SL for breast cancer, the American Society of Breast Surgeons has updated and revised our prior statement. As of November 2002, the American Society of Breast Surgeons acknowledges the following:

1. Indications and Contraindications:

In the following situations the published data are neither extensive nor supportive and SL should be performed as part of a research protocol or in conjunction with a full node dissection: the presence of suspicious palpable axillary lymph nodes, a history of prior breast radiation therapy, or a history of either extensive prior breast surgery or axillary surgery. Patients with invasive multifocal disease or patients receiving pre-operative chemotherapy represent a group for which data, although not extensive, thus far supports SL as accurate, and SL can be considered in the well informed patient. SL should be considered for patients with DCIS who are undergoing mastectomy. It is highly recommended that all patients who are candidates for SL have this procedure discussed as an option in their surgical management.

2. Axillary Management:

Axillary treatment for patients with metastatic disease found in sentinel nodes is currently under investigation in clinical trials. For patients not participating in a clinical trial, a complete level I and II lymph node dissection is recommended. Because the definition of a positive sentinel node is controversial, careful clinical judgment is encouraged in cases of micrometastatic disease.

3. Credentialing and Privileging:

The credentialing and privileging of SL, as with any surgical procedure, are to take place in accordance with the policies and processes of each local hospital. The accumulated data from many multi-center trials continues to support the need to perform 20 cases of SL in combination with axillary dissection, or to perform 20 SL procedures with mentoring, as being necessary to minimize the risk of false-negative results. We recommend this experience be obtained before the surgeon proceeds to performing sentinel node biopsy on his or her own. The false-negative rate (i.e. the ratio of the number of false-negative biopsy results to the number of patients with positive lymph nodes) is the most important factor regarding accurate sentinel lymph node staging. Fellows and residents who achieve similar experience with a credentialed sentinel node surgeon in 20 procedures of SL should be credentialed. The use of mentoring, proctored cases and formal training in accredited continuing medical education courses is thought to reduce the personal case experience necessary to achieve optimal results, but this effect has yet to be quantified.*

Table 5.1 (continued)

4. Technique:

The node-identification rate has been shown to be higher, and the false-negative rate lower, when a combination technique (both technetium sulfur colloid and blue dye) is used.

5. Axillary Recurrences:

Surgeons are encouraged to track their axillary recurrence rate. We also encourage surgeons to report their experience by contributing to national registries and by enrolling patients in clinical trials.

The Research and Education Committee of the American Society of Breast Surgeons:

Lorraine Tafra, Chair
Peter D. Beitsch, MD
Celia Chao, MD
Michael J. Edwards, MD
C. Alan Henry, MD
Donald Lannin, MD
Stephanie R. Moline, MD
Helen A. Pass, MD
Nancy D. Perrier, MD
Rachel Simmons, MD
S. Eva Singletary, MD
Pat Whitworth, MD
Shawn C. Willey, MD

*The ACS has organized a mentoring program to help surgeons become credentialed as well as to investigate the effect of mentoring on the learning curve of SL. To obtain more information on this program contact:

Lee G. Wilke, MD
Duke University Health System
4020 North Roxbury Rd.
Box 2013F
Durham, NC 27704
Phone: 919-620-5396 E-Mail: wilke031@mc.duke.edu

Approximately three hours before the scheduled surgery, the patient is injected either peritumorally or in the subareolar portion of the breast with a radiopharmaceutical. At many facilities, technetium (Tc) 99m–sulfur colloid is used, and 6 cc of this preparation is injected by a diagnostic radiologist in a clockwise fashion around the tumor site. The procedure is usually done in the nuclear medicine suite of the radiology department. In the case of a non-palpable tumor, the injection is done around the preoperative wire placement at the patient's skin surface. After injection, a dressing is put in place, and the patient is asked to massage the site every 10–15 minutes for 90 minutes. Massage encourages uptake into the lymphatics and allows for better visualization of the SLN on the lymphoscintigraphy pictures. SLN mapping and biopsy, as currently practiced, is quite safe from a radiation safety standpoint (Edwards *et al.*, 2000).

After 90 minutes, the patient is brought back to the nuclear medicine suite, where a series of anterior and lateral views produces a lymphoscintigraphic image (see Figure 5.3). If an SLN is identified, the radiologist will indicate this area on the patient's skin by marking the spot corresponding to the area of interest on the lymphoscintigraphy image. This image helps the surgeon in incision planning and assists in locating the SLN.

The patient is then taken to surgery, where isosulfan blue dye is injected around the tumor, and the breast is massaged vigorously to again encourage uptake of this material. After the patient is prepped and draped accordingly, the surgeon excises the primary tumor, ensuring negative surrounding margins. After the tumor has been excised, a hand-held gamma probe is used to assess the counts of radioactivity in the axillary area.

Conventional practice defines a node as radioactive or "hot" when it emits 10 times the amount of normal background radiation (Weinholz, 2000) (see Figure 5.4). The surgeon

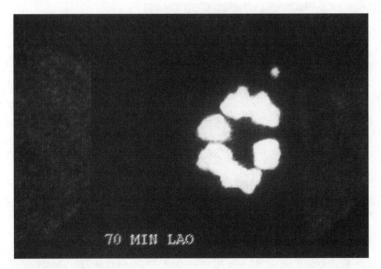

FIGURE 5.3 Lymphoscintigraphy image showing the series of injection sites, with the sentinel node located at the upper right portion of the photo. (Courtesy of Daniel P. Congreve, MD, Center for Breast Health, Genesis Medical Center, Davenport, Iowa).

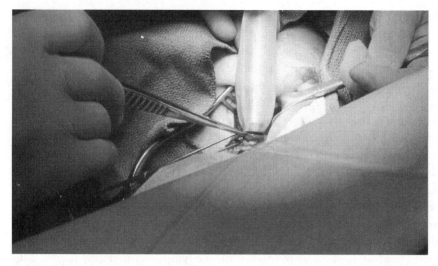

FIGURE 5.4 Using the Neoprobe™ to assess the radioactivity of the SLN in vivo. (Courtesy of Daniel P. Congreve, MD, Center for Breast Health, Genesis Medical Center, Davenport, Iowa).

will also watch for tracking of the blue dye into the presumed SLN (see Figure 5.5). The counts of the SLN are then measured again ex-vivo (see Figure 5.6) to ensure accuracy of the correct node sampled. Both of these parameters can be met, or they can be confirmed individually, that is, the node can be "hot" or blue, but it does not have to be "hot" and blue.

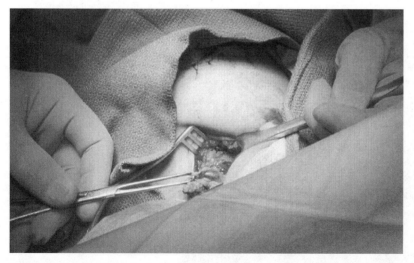

FIGURE 5.5 Sentinel node biopsy technique locating the blue lymph node during lymphatic mapping procedure in the OR. (Courtesy of Daniel P. Congreve, MD, Center for Breast Health, Genesis Medical Center, Davenport, Iowa).

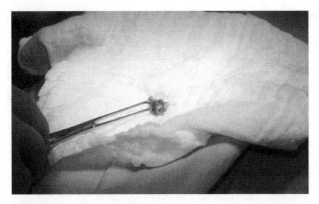

FIGURE 5.6 Sentinel lymph node ex vivo is blue stained and registers a radioactive count. (Courtesy of Daniel P. Congreve, MD, Center for Breast Health, Genesis Medical Center, Davenport, Iowa).

Pathologic analysis involves hematoxylin-eosin (H & E) staining, and the specimen is sectioned in 1-mm segments on the SLN. In many facilities, immunohistochemical (IHC) staining is done to further assess the presence of possible micrometastatic disease. If micrometastatic disease is found, clinicians generally agree that a follow-up ALND is necessary to avoid missing any other potential positive nodes in the axilla. If the SLN is found to be negative on the final pathologic analysis, then the patient's surgical therapy is complete.

Credentialing issues surrounding SLN biopsy are multifactorial. There is a significant learning curve associated with performing the procedure, and women should question their surgeon as to how many procedures he or she has done and what his or her false negative rate is. The primary reason for the current delay in universal acceptance of sentinel node staging for early breast cancer is that no consensus and no standardization of an optimum method for sentinel node identification exist. At different breast cancer centers, SLN identification using radiotracer is performed differently. The major variations are injection site, injection volume, injection activity, the radiopharmaceutical, and the use of imaging (Alazraki *et al.,* 2001).

STAGING OF BREAST CANCER

Staging of breast cancer is performed using the American Joint Committee on Cancer's (AJCC) TNM (i.e., tumor, nodes, and metastasis) Classification System (Table 5.2). Clinical staging involves the physical examination only. The primary goal of staging evaluation is to assess whether the patient is potentially curable by surgery with or without radiation therapy or has advanced disease beyond reasonable expectation of cure with

TABLE 5.2 TNM Classification and Staging of Breast Cancer

	Characteristics		
Stage	*Tumor (T)*	*Nodes (N)*	*Metastasis (M)*
Stage 0	Carcinoma in situ or Paget's disease of nipple with no tumor	No regional lymph node involvement	No distant metastasis
Stage 1	Tumor 2 cm or less	No axillary node involvement	No distant metastasis
Stage IIA			
T0 N1 M0	No tumor	Movable ipsilateral axillary node involvement	No distant metastasis
T1 N1 M0	Tumor 2 cm or less	Movable ipsilateral axillary node involvement	No distant metastasis
T2 N0 M0	Tumor 2–5 cm	No nodal involvement	No distant metastasis
Stage IIB			
T2 N1 M0	Tumor 2–5 cm	Movable ipsilateral axillary node involvement	No distant metastasis
T3 N0 M0	Tumor > 5 cm	No nodal involvement	No distant metastasis
Stage IIIA			
T0 N2 M0	No tumor	Ipsilateral axillary lymph node(s) fixed to one another or to other structures	No distant metastasis
T1 N2 M0	Tumor < 2 cm	Ipsilateral axillary nodes containing tumor growth and fixed to one another or other structures	No distant metastasis
T2 N2 M0	Tumor > 2 cm but < 5 cm	Ipsilateral axillary lymph nodes fixed to one another or to other structures	No distant metastasis
T3 N1 M0	Tumor > 5 cm	Movable ipsilateral axillary node involvement	No distant metastasis
T3 N2 M0	Tumor > 5 cm	Ipsilateral axillary lymph nodes fixed to one another or to other structures	No distant metastasis
Stage IIIB			
T4 any N M0	Tumor of any size with direct extension to chest wall, peau d'orange, or skin ulceration	With or without nodal involvement	No distant metastasis
Any T N4 M0	Tumor of any size	Metastasis to ipsilateral internal mammary lymph nodes	No distant metastasis
Stage IV	Tumor of any size with direct extension to chest wall or skin	Nodal involvement	Any metastasis

surgery or radiation therapy (Abeloff *et al.*, 2000). The *T* (Tumor) stands for pathologic tumor size and measures only the amount of invasive component of the lesion. The *N* (Nodes) refers to involvement of cancer in the regional lymph nodes. The *M* (Metastasis) refers to the presence of distant metastasis in other organs outside of the breast. In breast cancer, the usual sites for metastasis are the bones, liver, lungs, and brain. Use of TNM continues to have the greatest impact on decisions regarding the determination of operability and the utilization of surgery, radiation therapy, adjuvant chemotherapy, and hormone therapy in the management of primary breast cancer (Abeloff *et al.*, 2000).

SUMMARY

This chapter provided a review of the diagnosis and staging of breast cancer. Obviously, the overall goal in this phase of breast cancer care is to diagnose breast cancer when it offers the most treatment options and optimal survival for the patients. Axillary dissection is considered the current standard of care, whereas SLN biopsy is considered "state-of-the-art" (Whitworth *et al.*, 2000). Perhaps, in the near future, SLN biopsy may become the standard of care. As new technology unfolds with regard to diagnostic and assessment tools, the possibilities for practitioners and patients alike will be endless.

ACKNOWLEDGMENT

The author acknowledges a seven-year breast cancer survivor who helped inspire this chapter. Carol J. Kinney is the author's mentor and mom.

REFERENCES

Abeloff, M.D., Lichter, A.S., Niederhuber, J.E., Pierce, L.J., & Love, R.R. (2000). Breast. In M. Abeloff, J. Armitage, A. Lichter, & J. Niederhuber (Eds.), *Clinical oncology, 2nd ed.*, pp. 2064–2084. New York: Churchill Livingstone.

Alazraki, N.P., Styblo, T., Grant, S.F., Cohen, C., Larsen, T., Waldrop, S., & Aarsvold, J.N. (2001). Sentinel node staging of early breast cancer using lymphoscintigraphy and the intraoperative gamma detecting probe. *Radiologic Clinics of North America, 39*(5), 947–956, viii.

Alex, J.C., & Krag, D.N. (1993). Gamma probe guided localization of lymph nodes. *Surgical Oncology, 2,* 137–143.

American Cancer Society. (2001). *Breast cancer facts and figures 2001–2002.* Atlanta, Ga.: Author.

American Cancer Society. (2002). *Cancer facts and figures 2002.* Atlanta, Ga.: Author.

American Joint Committee on Cancer: Breast. (2002). *AJCC cancer staging manual* (6th ed., pp. 223–240). New York: Springer.

Cserni, G. (2000). Axillary staging of breast cancer and the sentinel node. *Journal of Clinical Pathology, 53,* 733–741.

Dauway, E.L., Giuliano, R., Haddad, F., Pendas, S., Costello, D., Cox, C.E., Berman, C., Ku, N.N., & Reintgen, D.S. (1999). Advances in breast cancer therapy. *Hematology Oncology Clinics of North America, 13*(2), 349–371.

Edwards, M.J., Whitworth, P., Tafra, L., & McMasters, K.M. (2000). The details of successful sentinel lymph node staging for breast cancer. *American Journal of Surgeons, 180,* 257–261.

Foster, R. (2000). Techniques of diagnosis of palpable breast masses. In J. Harris, M. Lippman, M. Morrow, & C. Osborne (Eds.), *Diseases of the breast, 2nd ed.*, pp. 95–100. Philadelphia: Lippincott Williams & Wilkins.

Giuliano, A.E., Kirgan, D.M., Guenther, J.M., & Morton, D.L. (1994). Lymphatic mapping and sentinel lymphadenectomy for breast cancer. *Annals of Surgery, 220;* 391–401.

Hart, D. (1999). Diagnosis and treatment of breast cancer. *Plastic Surgery in Nursing, 19*(3), 137–147.

Hsueh, E.C., Hansen, H., & Giuliano, A.E. (2000). Intraoperative lymphatic mapping and sentinel lymph node dissection in breast cancer. *CA—A Cancer Journal for Clinicians, 50,* 279–291.

Judkins, A.F., & Akins, J. (2001). Breast cancer: initial diagnosis and current treatment options. *Nursing Clinics of North America, 36*(3), 527–541.

Kellar, S.J. (2001). Sentinel lymph node biopsy for breast cancer. *AORN Journal, 74*(2), 197–201.

Kopans, D., & Smith, B. (2000). Preoperative imaging-guided needle localization and biopsy of nonpalpable breast lesions. In J. Harris, M. Lippman, M. Morrow, & C. Osborne (Eds.), *Diseases of the breast, 2nd ed.*, pp. 165–174. Philadelphia: Lippincott Williams & Wilkins.

Mautner, B.D., Schmidt, K.V., & Brennan, M.B. (2000). New diagnostic techniques and treatments for early breast cancer. *Seminars in Oncology Nursing, 16*(3), 185–196.

McCarthy, E.P., Burns, R.B., Freund, K.M., Ash, A.S., Shwartz, M., Marwill, S.L., & Moskowitz, M.A. (2000). Mammography use, breast cancer stage at diagnosis, and survival among older women. *Journal of the American Geriatric Society, 48*(10), 1226–1233.

Morton, D.L., Wen, D.R., Wong, J.H., Economou, J.S., Cagle, L.A., Storm, F.K., Foshag, L.J., & Cochran, A.J. (1992). Technical details of intraoperative lymphatic mapping for early state melanoma. *Archives of Surgery, 127;* 392–399.

Norris, T.G. (2001). Stereotactic breast biopsy. *Radiology Technology, 72*(5), 431–450.

O'Hea, B.J., Hill, A.D., El-Shirbiny, A.M., Yeh, S.D., Rosen, P.P., Coit, D.G., Borgen, P.I., & Cody, H.S. 3rd. (1998). Sentinel lymph node biopsy in breast cancer: initial experience at Memorial Sloan-Kettering Cancer Center. *Journal of American College of Surgeons, 186,* 423–427.

Orel, S.G., & Schnall, M.D. (2001). MR imaging of the breast for the detection, diagnosis, and staging of breast cancer. *Radiology, 220*(1), 13–30.

Ramirez, A.J., Westcombe, A.M., Burgess, C.C., Sutton, S., Littlejohns, P., & Richards, M.A. (1999). Factors predicting delayed presentation of symptomatic breast cancer: a systematic review. *Lancet, 353,* 1127–1131.

Tafra, L., McMasters, K.M., Whitworth, P., & Edwards, M.J. (2000). Credentialing issues with sentinel lymph node staging for breast cancer. *American Journal of Surgeons, 180,* 268–273.

Thomas, S., & Greifzu, S. (2000). Breast cancer. *RN, 63*(4), 40–45.

van der Ent, F.W., Kengen, R.A., van der Pol, H.A., Povel, J.A., Stroeken, H.J., & Hoofwijk, A.G. (2001). Halstead revisited: internal mammary sentinel lymph node biopsy in breast cancer. *Annals of Surgery, 234*(1), 79–84.

Velez, N., Earnest, D.E., & Staren, E.D. (2000). Diagnostic and interventional ultrasound for breast disease. *American Journal of Surgeons, 180,* 284–287.

Watson, L. (2001). Breast cancer: diagnosis, treatment and prognosis. *Radiology Technology, 73*(1), 45–61.

Weinholz, S., & Dean, S.F. (2000). Sentinel lymph node dissection as a means of managing breast cancer. *AORN Journal, 72*(4), 633–638.

Whitworth, P., McMasters, K.M., Tafra, L., & Edwards, M.J. (2000). State-of-the-art lymph node staging for breast cancer in the year 2000. *American Journal of Surgeons, 180,* 262–267.

Section II

TREATMENT OF PRIMARY BREAST CANCER

Chapter 6

SURGERY TECHNIQUES

JEAN LYNN, MPH, RN, OCN®

BREAST CANCER SURGERY

The surgical treatment of breast cancer dates back to 1750 with the surgical excision of the breast and palpable lymph nodes by Jean Louis Petit (Robinson, 1986). In the mid-1840s, general anesthesia became available, as well as antiseptic practice as proposed by Joseph Lister (Robinson, 1986), which led to an escalated effort to treat breast cancer surgically. The earliest procedures all advocated total removal of the breast and the axillary lymph nodes, as well as the fascia of the pectoralis muscle. In 1889, William Halstead, a surgeon at the Johns Hopkins University, believed that removal of the entire pectoralis major muscle, in addition to the breast and the axillary nodes, was the only "complete operation" for the treatment of breast cancer. This procedure later became known as the Halstead radical mastectomy (Robinson, 1986).

The Halstead radical mastectomy was not believed by all surgeons to be the only surgical procedure to treat breast cancer. D.H. Patey and W.H. Dyson were two of many surgeons who began to question the appropriateness of routine removal of the pectoralis major muscle, particularly in instances in which there was no discernible involvement by the tumor (Robinson, 1986). They proposed removing the breast and the pectoralis minor with a full axillary node dissection that also encompassed wide margins of the skin, as was done in the Halsteadian procedure. A subsequent analysis of the results of this procedure on 143 patients showed equivalent survival rates compared to those with Halstead radical mastectomies (Wagner, 1991).

Based on the work of Patey, Dyson, and several others, the Halstead approach had declined dramatically by the 1960s in the United States and Europe (Frykberg & Bland, 1982). Surgeons were opting to perform modified radical mastectomies (removal of the breast and level I and II lymph nodes), and surgical trials were beginning to be introduced to define other surgical options for the treatment of breast cancer. The first was the

National Surgical Adjuvant Breast and Bowel Project (NSABP) B-04 (Fisher *et al.,* 1985). Between 1971 and 1974, 1765 patients in 34 institutions were randomized to radical mastectomy, total mastectomy followed by chest wall and regional nodal radiation, or total mastectomy alone if the axillary nodes were clinically negative. Axillary dissection was performed for the last group if the nodes were found to be clinically positive. Women with clinically positive nodes were randomized to either radical mastectomy or total mastectomy and local–regional radiation. In the node-negative and node-positive groups, there was no difference in disease-free survival or overall survival in any of the treatment arms of the study. These results corroborated many surgeons' suspicions that radical mastectomy was more surgery than women needed to treat their breast cancers. It also provided further support for those who were skeptical about the therapeutic benefits of axillary dissection (Veronesi *et al.,* 1981).

Between 1973 and 1980, the National Cancer Institute of Milan conducted a trial with 701 patients who had clinically negative axilla. These patients, who were all stage I, were randomized to either radical mastectomy or partial mastectomy and axillary dissection followed by radiotherapy. Relapse-free and overall survival were the same for both groups (Roses, 2001). As a result of this trial, the NSABP launched the B-06 trial between 1976 and 1984. This trial randomized approximately 1843 patients with clinical stage I and II breast cancers with lesions up to 4 cm in diameter to mastectomy or partial mastectomy with or without radiation. The results concluded that total mastectomy or lumpectomy and radiation were equally effective and that overall survival was the same for all three groups. An analysis of this study in 2002 corroborated these findings (Fisher *et al.,* 2002).

SURGICAL TREATMENT OF STAGE 0 DUCTAL CARCINOMA IN SITU (DCIS) AND LOBULAR CARCINOMA IN SITU (LCIS)

With the increased use of mammography, the incidence of preinvasive cancers has risen more than 300% since the early 1980s. It is anticipated that in the year 2003, more than 50,000 preinvasive breast cancers will be diagnosed (ACS, 2002). The issue of surgical treatment of DCIS and LCIS generates several different opinions, because not all DCIS will develop into invasive breast cancer. Several factors must be considered when assessing how much surgery is necessary to treat these lesions appropriately. How did the DCIS present itself? Was it localized in one quadrant of the breast or was it a multicentric presentation (in various quadrants of the breast)? Is the lesion smaller or larger than 5 mm? Is the DCIS of a comedo or noncomedo type? All of these components of the presentation need to be carefully considered before deciding on which course to take.

If the preinvasive cancer presents with microcalcifications or with a nonpalpable density on a mammogram and the lesion is located in one quadrant of the breast, a diagnosis is established by either a stereotactic biopsy or by wire localization biopsy. Before the wire is placed, the radiologist determines which view, the cranial—caudal or the medial—lateral, best visualizes the calcifications or the nonpalpable lesion. Once that is determined, a pen is used to mark the skin near the point of the predicted entry into the breast. A needle is inserted into the breast, and the wire is advanced through the hub of the needle to the location of the nonpalpable density. An image is obtained to ensure proper placement of the wire. Once confirmed, the needle is withdrawn from the breast, and the wire is taped to the chest to ensure that the wire does not move prior to the surgery. At the time of surgery, the surgeon makes an incision into the breast based on the placement of the wire. The area with the density or calcifications is then excised with some surrounding normal tissue. Before the patient's incision is closed, the specimen is x-rayed to ensure that the area excised corresponds to the mammographic abnormality.

This procedure is done on an outpatient basis. Patients are sent home with a pressure dressing to remain in place for at least 24 hours. Pain associated with this procedure is usually minimal; extra-strength acetaminophen or ibuprofen plus or minus a mild opioid is usually sufficient to relieve the pain. The patient returns to see the surgeon within seven days to discuss the pathology and further treatment options. Most patients with DCIS receive external radiation therapy to the breast to decrease local recurrence. The NSABP B-24 study showed that the women who received tamoxifen with radiation therapy had a 44% reduction in the development of invasive breast cancer (Fisher *et al.,* 2001). Thus, women will also be offered tamoxifen 20 mg daily for 5 years (Wickerham, 2001).

If the lesion is multicentric (i.e., in different quadrants of the breast) or the surgeon cannot obtain clear margins, then a simple mastectomy is often recommended followed by immediate reconstruction. Women with this diagnosis often find it very difficult to accept. Although the disease is Stage 0 and highly treatable and curable when treated appropriately, the diagnosis puts them into a category where they know they should feel fortunate because their cancer does not need aggressive treatment. But at the same time, having a mastectomy for such an early-stage breast cancer is very overwhelming for many of these patients.

LCIS, on the other hand, is usually an incidental finding from a biopsy. No surgical treatment is necessary for this type of lesion, because it is not actually a cancer. It is a marker of increased risk of developing the disease. Patients with this diagnosis need close surveillance, including clinical breast exams biannually, annual mammography, and appropriate instruction in breast self-exam. They also may be offered tamoxifen. Tamoxifen demonstrated clinical benefit to women with this diagnosis based on the breast cancer prevention trial that showed a reduction of 47% for women with LCIS in developing invasive breast cancer (Fisher *et al.,* 1998).

INDICATIONS FOR BREAST-CONSERVING SURGERY VERSUS MASTECTOMY

Once a breast cancer is diagnosed, it is important that women are presented with all of the appropriate treatment options and provided with information so that they can make an informed decision. Breast cancer is not an emergency situation. It takes about 5–8 years for a breast cancer to be clinically diagnosed, either with a mammogram or clinical breast exam. Taking some extra time to discuss the options will not affect the patient's overall survival. The role of the nurse in this setting includes, but is not limited to, providing patient triage, patient family education, and psychosocial support, and serving as patient advocate and navigator through the system. Information should be given in amounts that can be understood by the patient and reinforced by the nurse. Having the patient and a family member return for preoperative teaching a couple of days before the surgery may be helpful for the patient who is overwhelmed by the diagnosis and the treatment that she will have to incorporate into her life for the next six months.

For women who are premenopausal, fertility issues may be a concern. The patient may have questions regarding the timing of her surgery in relation to her menstrual cycle. There have been reports that this may be an independent prognostic variable if surgery is performed during the luteal phase of menstruation (day 15–36) versus the follicular phase of the menstrual cycle. A study completed by the North Central Cancer Treatment Group (NCCTG) Protocol BI-65 addressed this very issue, but the results have not yet been released. If this is an important issue for the patient, every effort within reason should be made to accommodate her wishes with regard to the timing of surgery.

Women today have the opportunity and are encouraged to become empowered with information and to involve themselves in the decision-making process. When a breast cancer is diagnosed, there are usually several treatment options available. Surgical resection of the tumor is the first line of defense in treating a breast cancer. The size and location of the tumor will be considered when making a recommendation.

BREAST CONSERVATION

If the tumor is confined to one area, breast-conserving treatment (i.e., lumpectomy, quadrantectomy, partial mastectomy) is the preferred option. This, of course, is dependent on an acceptable cosmetic result. This surgery involves removing the breast tumor with clear margins (i.e., no tumor cells seen at the edge of the excised breast tissue) determined by pathologic examination. This surgery also includes a sentinel node mapping and/or axillary node dissection, which means that the lymph nodes closest to the breast tissue are removed to determine whether cancer cells have spread to the nodes. (See Chapter 5 for more information on sentinel node mapping.) This procedure has become an accepted standard of care in many institutions across the country for early-stage breast cancers in women with a clinically negative axilla.

Patients who have breast-conserving surgery with a negative sentinel node mapping generally go home within 2–4 hours after their surgery. The dressing stays intact for 24 hours, after which time the patient can shower and resume normal activity. Patients should be instructed not to actively exercise the affected arm and not to engage in any strenuous activity for a period of 10–14 days. Postoperative discomfort from this procedure is generally minimal and can be relieved with over-the-counter pain (OTC) relievers with or without a mild narcotic. Patients should be instructed not to drink alcohol or drive if they are taking any narcotics.

MODIFIED RADICAL MASTECTOMY

A modified radical mastectomy entails removing all of the breast tissue and the axillary lymph nodes under the arm. This procedure is recommended when breast-conserving surgery is not appropriate because the tumor is too extensive (multifocal) and/or is in different quadrants of the breast tissue (multicentric), or when a good cosmetic result is not attainable and there is a clinically positive axilla. Breast-conserving surgery versus modified radical mastectomy is a major and often difficult decision for all women. Women sometimes feel that their breast has "betrayed" them and they want to remove it. If the patient decides on a mastectomy or a mastectomy is recommended, a consultation with a plastic surgeon should be made prior to surgery so that all reconstructive options can be explored with the patient. Most often, breast reconstruction is performed at the time of mastectomy. If it is not feasible or recommended to have immediate reconstruction, this surgery can always be performed at a later date.

If a mastectomy is recommended, the patient may also be offered the sentinel node mapping at the time of surgery. If the sentinel node is negative, then a simple mastectomy will be performed. A drain may be placed on the chest wall to decrease the chances of developing a seroma. Patients will need to be instructed on how to empty the drain and record the drainage.

If the patient has a positive sentinel node, then she will need to have an axillary node dissection. The reasons that an axillary node dissection is performed are twofold: diagnostic and prognostic. If the patient has a clinically positive axilla either by palpation or PET scan, then sentinel node mapping is not indicated. The surgeon will remove Level I (i.e., nodes located below the axillary vein and between the lateral border of the pectoralis minor muscle and the anterior border of the latissimus dorsi muscle) and Level II (i.e, nodes that lie behind the pectoralis minor muscle) lymph nodes and possibly level III lymph nodes (i.e., nodes that lie below the axillary vein from the medial border of the pectoralis minor muscle to the submergence of the axillary vein below the subclavius muscle at the costoclavicular [Halstead's] ligament, if they are involved. The lymph nodes vary in size and amount, and each patient is different. More than 90% of the lymphatic fluid draining from the breast drains into the axilla.

Although special care is taken to prevent nerve damage to the affected arm, many patients experience numbness in their arm from the upper arm down to the fingertips. Sensation usually returns to the affected arm within several months, or at most up to a year. However, some patients indicate that the numbness never diminishes completely. When the numbness starts to dissipate, many patients experience a "pins and needles" sensation in the arm. This is quite common and reflects nerve regeneration.

The number of lymph nodes involved with tumor cells will be factored into the type of treatment that will be recommended. When a lymph node dissection is performed, the nurse will need to provide education regarding lymphedema management. Patients will usually stay in the hospital for 24 hours following an axillary node dissection because of the drain. The preoperative teaching should address drain care, and the hospital staff should reinforce the information after surgery. The drain usually stays in place for a period of 5–7 days. The requirement for removal of the drain is 30 cc over a 24-hour period. If the drain is removed too soon after surgery, the patient can develop seromas postoperatively, which will require aspiration in the outpatient setting. Pain management with the drain in place may require a narcotic prescription, in addition to OTC pain relievers that can be used with the narcotic. Nursing education should focus on pain management, lymphedema precautions, and wound management. Figure 6.1 provides useful patient information on lymphedema management after axillary node dissection.

PROPHYLACTIC MASTECTOMY

Some women may wish to explore the option of having a prophylactic mastectomy especially if they are considered to be at high risk because of personal or family history or they carry the BRCA1 and/or BRCA2 genes. Surgeons used to be more reluctant to perform a prophylactic mastectomy, but with the new genetic information available, it is not discouraged as an option as it once was. For many women, the peace of mind that comes with not having to worry about breast cancer returning is very comforting, but can be misleading. In many cases, only 95% of the breast glandular tissue is removed. Breast cancer may or may not occur or recur, but, in most cases, it does reduce the risk of local recurrence, or a second primary from occurring.

FIGURE 6.1 Patient Information on Lymphedema Management After Axillary Node Dissection.

The lymph nodes that are located in the axilla will be removed to determine whether the nodes have any cancer cells. Lymph nodes are located throughout the body. They filter fluids, proteins, and bacteria that are in our bodies. Occasionally, removal of the lymph nodes causes an ineffective filtering of this fluid, which sometimes results in edema (fluid accumulation) in the arm. The following guidelines have been established to prevent lymphedema from occurring. It is important to review these guidelines and incorporate them into your daily lifestyle.

1. Practice good skin hygiene; use lotion after bathing. When drying the arm, be gentle, but thorough.
2. Avoid having blood drawn, injections, and infusions in the affected arm.
3. Wear protective gloves when working outside or with cleaning products.
4. Wear sunscreen to protect against sunburn and use insect repellent to protect against bites and stings.
5. Do not cut hangnails or cut nails too short; do not push cuticles back to the nailbed.
6. Exercise and use the affected arm. Full range of motion and strength of the affected arm should return in a couple of months.

You can expect to resume all your activities of daily living (i.e., swimming, golfing, tennis) within a few months and without any compromise to the affected arm.

If you should experience a cut, scrape, or burn on the affected arm, clean the area thoroughly, use an antiseptic, and cover the area with a bandage. If you should notice any redness, swelling, or tenderness, contact your physician immediately. You may need to take an antibiotic.

CARING FOR SURGERY PATIENTS

PREOPERATIVE EVALUATION/TESTING/CONSULTATIONS

The nurse on the breast care team not only provides the appropriate information and education, but also is the one who can navigate the system for the patient during this period of time before surgery. If the patient is to have breast-conserving surgery, the radiation oncologist may prefer to see the patient preoperatively so that all of the risks and benefits of radiation therapy can be explained to the patient. This is also to ensure that the patient is an appropriate candidate for radiation therapy. If the patient has special concerns regarding anesthesia, a preoperative consultation with the anesthesiologist should be facilitated. Patients may request the use of a personal stereo with headphones to listen to their favorite music or imagery tapes during surgery. Every effort should be made to accommodate this request.

Preoperative assessment should also include measurement of the circumference of both arms. The arm is measured 5 and 10 cm above and below the olecranon process. This ensures accurate and consistent measurement on a consecutive basis. If there is a change in measurement of 1.0–1.5 cm compared with the unaffected extremity, it is classified as mild (less than 3 cm), moderate (3–5 cm), or severe (more than 5 cm) (Maxwell, 1997). These measurements should be done postoperatively on a regular basis to monitor for lymphedema.

Patients should also be instructed not to take any aspirin products for at least seven days prior to surgery. If the patient is taking vitamin E, this should also be discontinued seven days prior to surgery, as it can interfere with blood clotting. Any herbal medications that the patient is taking should be provided to the anesthesiologist. A good rule of thumb would be to have the patient discontinue taking any herbal medicines seven days prior to surgery. If the patient is having a mastectomy without reconstruction, a referral should be made to the Reach to Recovery program (offered through the American Cancer Society) so that the woman can receive a temporary prosthesis and/or a mastectomy bra.

DAY OF SURGERY

The day of surgery needs to be coordinated with nuclear medicine, the operating room, and radiology if the patient is having wire localization. The patient should be instructed to wear a loose-fitting blouse that buttons down the front in case an axillary node dissection needs to be performed. No solid food or drink should be ingested six hours prior to surgery. If the patient is on any heart or blood pressure medications, the anesthesia department will advise which medications to take on the day of surgery.

POSTOPERATIVE CARE

The patient is discharged within 4–23 hours after surgery, depending upon the type of procedure performed. The first postoperative visit usually takes place 5–7 days after surgery. If the patient had reconstruction, then the first postoperative visit may be sooner. At this time, the drain (if there is one) will be removed and the pathology will be discussed, as well as further treatment that may be necessary. Figure 6.2 provides a patient information sheet for drain care after surgery.

Referrals to an oncologist and/or radiation oncologist should be facilitated. Also, if the patient had an axillary node dissection, instructions in arm exercises need to be provided. The arms should be measured (as noted in the previous section) and the measurements documented. The patient should return to see the nurse within seven days to monitor range of motion with the arm.

For the patient who had a mastectomy without reconstruction, she should be fitted with a well-fitted breast prosthesis approximately four to six weeks after surgery. This is an important part of the physical and psychological recovery. The patient should also obtain a well-fitting mastectomy bra. The cost of these products varies but most insurance plans cover a portion of the expense. If the patient has financial concerns, a referral to the American Cancer Society may be appropriate for assistance with these expenses.

PSYCHOSOCIAL SUPPORT

Breast cancer can be a life-altering experience. The diagnosis not only affects the woman but also the many roles she has in her life. There are many groups for breast cancer patients. Finding the right groups can take some trial and error. This author's institution offers one support group specifically for women under age 40 years, a second group for women over age 40 years, and a third group for long-term survivors. These groups provide immeasurable insight into the coping strategies that are employed by women with breast cancer.

Nurses should be knowledgeable about the availability of these groups within their demographic area. If there are none available, there are groups conducted on-line by the

FIGURE 6.2 Patient Information Sheet for Drain Care After Surgery.

After surgery, you will have a bulblike reservoir connected to tubing coming from your incision. This device suctions and collects fluid from your incision area. The drain promotes healing and reduces the chance of infection. This drain will be in place for several days after surgery. When you go home with the drain, follow these care instructions:

1. Empty the drain every 8–12 hours. You will be provided with a small cup with measurement markings on the side. Empty the drain into the cup so that you can accurately record how much drainage you have.

2. Unpin the drainage bulb from your bra or shirt. Remove the rubber stopper from the drain. Turn the drain upside down, and squeeze the contents into the measuring cup. Completely empty the bulb.

   Keep a record of the amount of fluid in the measuring cup.

   Note: To prevent infection, don't let the rubber stopper or the top of the drain touch the measuring cup or any other surface.

3. Now, use one hand to squeeze all of the air from the drain. With the drain still compressed, use your other hand to replace the rubber stopper. Do this to ensure that the drain suction works well.

Wellness Community with a trained social worker (*www.thewellnesscommunity.org*). This type of group may also be appropriate for a woman who does not want face-to-face contact with other members of the group.

The nurse's role in the surgical setting is challenging but can be very rewarding. Roles continue to evolve as new treatment strategies become available. Promoting quality cancer care is the best gift we can provide to our patients. In addition to the Quality of Care Standards position by the Oncology Nursing Society, the National Breast Cancer Coalition Fund has released the Guide to Quality Breast Cancer Care (2002). This is a very comprehensive guide that provides excellent information for the breast cancer patient. This guide can be obtained free of charge by calling 1-866-624-5307.

REFERENCES

American Cancer Society. (2002). *Facts and figures.* Atlanta, Ga.: Author.

Fisher, B., Anderson, S., Bryant, J., Margolese, R.G., Deutsch, M., Fisher, E.R., Jeong, J.H., & Wolmark, N. (2002). Twenty-year follow-up of a randomized trial comparing total mastectomy, lumpectomy and lumpectomy plus irradiation for the treatment of invasive breast cancer. *New England Journal of Medicine, 347*(16), 1233–1241.

Fisher, B., Costantino, J.P., Wickerham, D.L., Redmond, C.K., Kavanah, M., Cronin, W.M., Vogel, V., Robidoux, A., Dimitrov, N., Atkins, J., Daly, M., Wieand, S., Tan-Chiu, E., Ford, L., & Wolmark, N. (1998). Tamoxifen for prevention of breast cancer: report of the National Surgical Adjuvant Breast and Bowel Project P-1 study. *Journal of the National Cancer Institute, 90*(18), 1371–1385.

Fisher, B., Land, S., Mamounas, E., Dignam, J., Fisher, E.R., & Wolmark, N. (2001). Prevention of invasive breast cancer in women with ductal carcinoma in situ: an update of the National Surgical Adjuvant Breast and Bowel Project experience. *Seminars in Oncology, 28*(4), 400–418.

Fisher, B., Redmond, C., Fisher, E.R., Bauer, M., Wolmark, N., Wickerham, D.L., Deutsch, M., Montague, E., Margolese, R., & Foster, R. (1985). Ten-year results of a randomized clinical trial comparing radical mastectomy and total mastectomy with or without radiation. *New England Journal of Medicine, 312,* 674–681.

Frykberg, E.R., & Bland, K.I. (1982). Evolution of surgical principles for the management of breast cancer. In K.I. Bland & E.M.Copeland, III (Eds.), *The Breast,* pp. 543–553. Philadelphia: W.B. Saunders.

Maxwell, M. (1997). Malignant effusions and edema. In C. Yarbro, M. Frogge, M. Goodman, & S. Groenwald (Eds). *Cancer nursing principles and practice, 4th ed.,* pp. 721–741. Sudbury, Mass.: Jones & Bartlett.

North Central Cancer Treatment Group. (1996, July). *Menstrual cycle and surgical treatment of breast cancer.* Rochester, Minn.: Author.

Robinson, J.O. (1986). Treatment of breast cancer through the ages. *American Journal of Surgeons, 151,* 317–333.

Roses, D. (2000). Development of modern breast cancer treatment. In D. Roses (Ed). *Breast Cancer,* pp. 289–308. New York: Churchill Livingstone.

Veronesi, U., Saccozzi, R., Del Vecchio, M., Banfi, A., Clemente, C., De Lena, M., Gallus, G., Greco, M., Luini, A., Marubini, E., Muscolino, G., Rilke, F., Salvadori, B., Zecchini, A., & Zucali, R. (1981). Comparing radical mastectomy with quadrantectomy, axillary dissection and radiotherapy in patients with small cancers of the breast. *New England Journal of Medicine, 305,* 6–11.

Wagner, F.B. (1991). History of breast disease and its treatment. In K.I. Bland, & E.M. Copeland (Eds.), *The Breast, 3rd ed.,* pp. 5–16. Philadelphia: W.B. Saunders.

Wickerham, D.L. (2001). Ductal carcinoma in situ. *Journal of Clinical Oncology, 19*(18), 985–1005.

RECONSTRUCTIVE SURGERY

ROBERTA BARON, RN, MSN, AOCN
NASRIN VAZIRI, RN, CPSN

INTRODUCTION

Breast reconstruction, once a rarely performed procedure, is recognized today as an integral component in the rehabilitation process following mastectomy. In 1952, Renneker and Cutler identified two psychological issues facing breast cancer patients: anxiety brought about by the diagnosis of a potentially deadly disease, and anxiety resulting from the mutilation caused by breast cancer surgery. Quality of life has since become an important consideration when determining a patient's treatment, and advances have been made in the development of less disfiguring procedures. Although breast-conservation therapy often provides a superior cosmetic outcome with an overall survival rate equivalent to mastectomy (Fisher *et al.,* 1989), a significant number of patients will still require or choose to undergo a mastectomy. Improvements in the quality and reliability of reconstructive techniques and the increased availability of plastic surgery expertise have made breast reconstruction a viable option for most women who desire it.

BREAST RECONSTRUCTION: A PERSONAL DECISION

Breast reconstruction is elective surgery that can enhance a woman's self-image and sense of well-being. As such, the decision to undergo a reconstructive procedure is highly personal. Although the ideal goal of breast reconstruction is to create a breast mound that is realistic in feel and appearance, drapes and moves naturally, and is symmetrical with the opposite breast, reconstruction is not an exact science, and no method will precisely duplicate a normal breast. Some reconstructive techniques have only limited ability to create a soft breast and to imitate the natural ptosis (sag) of a mature breast. Also, it is impossible to eliminate the mastectomy scar, although it can frequently be integrated into the reconstruction so that it is less obvious. Nerve injury routinely occurs during the mastectomy and causes loss of normal sensation, which reconstruction will not restore. Despite these shortcomings, many women still opt to undergo breast reconstruction and are pleased with the results. Many find that they can wear all types of clothing, including more revealing styles, with complete confidence. When the woman is dressed, it is usually difficult for anyone to tell which side has been reconstructed. Reconstruction also eliminates the need to wear an external prosthesis, which some women may find awkward and embarrassing should it shift or become dislodged.

Not all women who are candidates opt to have reconstruction. Historically, factors that led women to forego reconstruction included older age, significant medical problems, concern of undergoing additional elective surgery and anesthesia, uncertainty over the cosmetic outcome, and fear of additional discomfort or pain. Some women feared, unnecessarily, that reconstruction could trigger or hide a cancer recurrence or that other people would view the surgery as an act of vanity. Today, the majority of women slated to undergo mastectomy are candidates for some form of breast reconstruction.

TIMING OF BREAST RECONSTRUCTION

In the past, breast reconstruction was delayed for months or years after mastectomy. It was feared that the additional surgical procedure of immediate reconstruction (at the time of mastectomy) might increase the risk of postoperative complications, leading to a longer recovery period and a delay in the initiation of adjuvant therapy. There was further concern that it would mask a local recurrence in the breast. Studies have shown that there is little evidence to support these concerns.

In a retrospective review, Allweis *et al.* (2002) compared 49 patients who underwent mastectomy with immediate reconstruction with 308 patients who had mastectomy alone and found that immediate reconstruction did not delay the initiation of adjuvant chemotherapy. Yule *et al.* (1996) found that patients could safely receive chemotherapy after immediate reconstruction with a tissue expander and subsequent implant placement, with no increase in infection, capsular contracture, or delayed wound healing. One study, however, evaluated 326 patients who were recruited by 32 plastic surgeons from 12 centers and followed for complications for 2 years. They found that immediate reconstruction was associated with significantly higher complication rates than delayed procedures (Alderman *et al.* 2002). The investigators postulated that this higher complication rate may be attributable to the combination of surgical procedures. Adding the complication rate for mastectomy alone to that of delayed reconstruction alone yielded a complication rate equal to or greater than that of immediate reconstruction. Studies also found that immediate reconstruction does not interfere with the detection or treatment of a local recurrence in the breast (Noone *et al.*, 1994), nor does it adversely affect treatment in patients with locally advanced breast cancer (Newman *et al.*, 1999).

Immediate reconstruction has several advantages. In some cases the breast surgeon is able to preserve much larger areas of unaffected (i.e., cancer-free) skin, thus minimizing the size of the mastectomy scar. When immediate reconstruction is not being performed, all of the redundant skin must be removed, because it is unsightly and may be uncomfortable for the patient when trying to wear an external breast prosthesis. Immediate reconstruction also saves the patient from undergoing an additional general anesthesia and increases cost-effectiveness by eliminating the need for a subsequent hospitalization.

In selected patients, a skin-sparing mastectomy may be performed. In this technique, the breast, nipple–areolar complex, biopsy scars, and skin overlying superficial tumors are removed, while the remaining breast skin envelope is preserved (Carlson *et al.*, 2001). The breast surgeon will decide who is an appropriate candidate for this procedure based on factors such as size, type, and location of the tumor and its associated biopsy scar. Skin-sparing techniques have resulted in far superior cosmetic results compared to older, larger incisions, with comparable local recurrence rates (Foster *et al.*, 2002; Rubio *et al.*, 2000). This can have significant psychological benefit during the patient's convalescence.

Delayed reconstruction is indicated in certain situations. Some patients may be so overwhelmed by their cancer diagnosis and the accompanying maze of treatment options that they are unable to make a sound decision regarding their preferences for breast reconstruction at the time of mastectomy. It is far better for a patient to postpone the decision rather than elect a form of reconstruction that she may later regret. Delayed reconstruction may also be preferable in patients with inflammatory carcinoma or in those with large tumors involving the pectoralis muscle. These patients will likely require extensive treatment (chemotherapy and radiation), which should be administered without delay. Any potential delays in healing after immediate reconstruction may interfere with initiation of treatment.

METHODS OF BREAST RECONSTRUCTION

Modern breast reconstruction techniques have evolved steadily since the introduction in the 1960s of the silicone gel-filled implants. Today these techniques comprise the use of prosthetic material in the form of a silicone gel or saline implant (alloplastic), the patient's own tissue (autologous), or a combination of the two. Each method has its own advantages and disadvantages. The breast surgeon and plastic surgeon should discuss and plan the surgery as a team. The breast surgeon determines the orientation of the mastectomy and axillary incisions and determines the extent of tissue and skin to be removed, based on factors such as the size and location of the tumor and the shape of the breast. Ideally, the mastectomy flaps should be as thin as possible to achieve the optimal oncologic goal without compromising the vascular integrity of the flaps. These flaps must be handled gently to avoid complications during reconstruction. Factors that help the plastic surgeon decide which method will be best for an individual patient include the patient's preference, body habitus, and comorbid medical conditions, as well as her personal habits, such as smoking, and the size and shape of her contralateral breast.

ALLOPLASTIC RECONSTRUCTION: BREAST IMPLANTS

Breast reconstruction using implants is the simplest and most commonly performed procedure in the United States today. In this technique, the surgeon creates a breast mound by placing an implant through the mastectomy incision beneath the pectoralis muscle and anterior serratus muscle. The two types of implants available today have a hard silicone outer shell, with a smooth surface (rarely used today) or textured surface, and are filled with either silicone gel or sterile saline. The textured surface serves to hold the implant in position and decreases the incidence of implant firmness from capsular contracture (scar tissue that can form around the implant and can tighten and squeeze it, leading to varying degrees of pain and unnatural firmness of the reconstructed breast) (Hakelius & Ohlsen, 1997; Pollock, 1993).

Implant reconstruction has several advantages, including less time in the operating room and a shorter recuperation period compared with surgery using autologous tissue. There are no additional scars, because it does not involve the use of a donor site. For those patients unhappy with their implant reconstruction, autologous tissue reconstruction remains a viable option at a later date.

The main disadvantage of the implant reconstruction technique is that there is little natural ptosis, and the implant tends to feel firm and round. Although the majority of women remain satisfied with their results, several factors, including significant weight gain (10 to 15 pounds), which can increase the size of the unaffected breast, or formation of a capsular contracture, can result in asymmetry. In a five-year prospective study after immediate implant reconstruction, the cosmetic results of 334 women were evaluated at the time of their biannual exams. The cosmetic results deteriorated in an almost linear fashion over the five years. It was the investigators' opinion, after a retrospective photographic review, that the deterioration was due to late asymmetry from the failure of the reconstructed breast to achieve natural ptosis when compared with the contralateral breast (Clough *et al.*, 2001).

Candidates for Breast Implants. Ideal candidates for breast implants are women who have a small to medium contralateral (opposite) breast, with minimal ptosis and healthy mastectomy flaps. Large, ptotic breasts cannot be duplicated well with implants. Women with larger breasts usually require a reduction and/or mastopexy (breast lift) on the contralateral side to achieve symmetry.

Patients who are not good candidates for breast implant reconstruction include those who have severe connective-tissue disease such as advanced systemic sclerosis (i.e., scleroderma). In this situation, the inelasticity of the tissues significantly increases the chance of infection and/or extrusion of the implant (i.e., implant pushing through incision site). Patients with morbid obesity and those who smoke heavily are at higher risk for developing postoperative complications. Patients who received previous radiation to the breast or those who need radiation treatment after their mastectomy and reconstruction are not ideal candidates. Radiation can result in permanent skin changes such as dry, fragile skin with diminished elasticity, which can lead to delayed healing, skin breakdown, and flap ischemia resulting in infection and implant extrusion. For these patients, most plastic surgeons favor autologous reconstruction.

Vandeweyer and Deraemaecker (2000) found a 100% rate of severe capsular contractures and suboptimal breast symmetry in 6 patients who had mastectomy and reconstruction followed by radiation. Krueger *et al.* (2001) found a higher rate of complications (infection and contractures) and tissue expander/implant failure (removal of implant or expander) in irradiated patients (N = 19) compared to nonirradiated patients (N = 62). Of the 19 patients who received radiation, 9 of them received treatment after their reconstruction, and 10 of them before.

Conversely, some studies suggest that carefully selected patients may still be candidates for implant reconstruction in this setting (Krueger *et al.*, 2001; Bacilious *et al.*, 2002). Krueger *et al.* (2001) also found that patients' general satisfaction and aesthetic satisfaction one to two years after the procedure were not significantly different in those who had radiation compared with those who did not. Bacilious *et al.* (2002) examined the complication rate of seven patients who had received mantle radiation (i.e., radiation to the chest wall) for the treatment of Hodgkin's disease and subsequently underwent mastectomy with implant reconstruction. The only complication was cellulitis that resolved with intravenous antibiotics. These findings are important, as certain patients are not candidates for or choose not to undergo autologous tissue reconstruction, making implant reconstruction their only option.

Tissue Expansion. The amount of skin remaining after mastectomy is often insufficient for placement of a permanent implant. In addition, the implant is placed under the pectoralis muscle, which is initially very tight. In order to accommodate the appropriate size implant for the individual, the skin and pectoralis muscle must be stretched gradually by a process called tissue expansion. The tissue expander is a balloonlike device that is inserted under the pectoralis and serratus muscles either at the time of mastectomy or at a later date. Intraoperatively, a small amount of normal saline is introduced through a metal port in the expander to partially inflate it. The initial amount of saline inserted depends on the status of the mastectomy flaps. Less saline is used when the flaps are very thin or when a large amount of skin has been removed. In these cases, overfilling the expander could put excess pressure on the flaps and interfere with wound closure and healing.

The expansion process starts 10 to 15 days after surgery and is repeated at weekly intervals for about 6 to 8 weeks. The average amount of fluid instilled (about 50 to 150 cc at each visit) is determined by the patient's comfort level, the amount of tension on the breast mound, and the condition of the mastectomy flaps. The saline injections are carried out under sterile technique. The number of visits and the amount of saline instilled ultimately depends on the patient's desired breast size and the condition of her pectoralis muscle. A firm, overdeveloped muscle may not expand easily and quickly, as in the case of serious body builders. The expander is usually inflated about one third larger than the desired breast size to prevent shrinking around the permanent implant and to achieve a softer, more natural result. Full expansion is maintained for approximately 4 to 6 weeks, allowing the skin to stabilize and loosen.

Permanent Implant. The exchange of the tissue expander for a permanent implant is performed as outpatient surgery about three months following its initial insertion (Figure 7.1). If the patient is receiving chemotherapy, the procedure will be delayed until approximately one month after completion of treatment in order to allow blood counts to stabilize. If a patient requires postmastectomy radiation for maximum local control of disease, the first treatment will then begin about a month after the exchange of the temporary tissue expander for the permanent implant. The permanent implant may be filled with either saline or silicone gel. Although silicone gel implants tend to feel softer and more natural, in 1992 the Food and Drug Administration (FDA) issued a moratorium on the use of silicone gel for breast augmentation after concerns about its risk of causing autoimmune or connective-tissue diseases came to light. A recent extensive meta-analysis, however, found no evidence to support these concerns (Janowsky *et al.*, 2000). Today, patients who choose to have silicone gel implants must enroll in an FDA-approved study, in which information about implant safety is collected prospectively for five years.

Complications. The most common complication is capsular contracture, which can vary in degree from slight firmness of the implant to visible or painful distortion of the reconstructed breast. An open capsulotomy (cutting the scar tissue) or capsulectomy (removing the scar tissue) can be performed in the operating room to correct severe capsular contractures. Other complications include infection, which, if detected early, can be treated with intravenous antibiotics. Mastectomy flap necrosis is a common complication and can sometimes be corrected surgically by doing a revision of the mastectomy flaps. Severe infection, not responding to IV antibiotics, extensive mastectomy flap necrosis, and poor soft tissue coverage can lead to implant extrusion, which requires removal of the implant. Implants may rupture or deflate because of injury or normal wear over time. Saline implants usually deflate quickly, and the saline is absorbed by the surrounding tissues. If silicone gel implants rupture, the gel is usually contained by the capsule around the implant, and the diagnosis of implant rupture may be

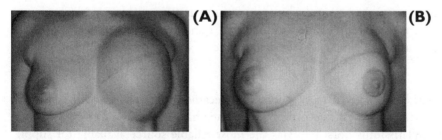

FIGURE 7.1 **(A) Left fully expanded tissue expander; (B) following exchange of expander for permanent implant with reconstructed nipple/areola.**

delayed. Patients with silicone gel ruptures often describe a change in the shape or the feel of the breast after rupture. In cases where physical examination is not conclusive, diagnostic imaging may be helpful. Currently, MRI is the best modality to detect rupture or leakage of silicone gel-filled implants. Surgical removal of the implant and replacement, if desired, is the indicated treatment.

AUTOLOGOUS RECONSTRUCTION

The breast mound can also be reconstructed using a patient's own skin, fat, and muscle, either as a pedicle flap (with its own attached vascular supply), or as a free flap requiring microvascular surgery. Possible flaps include, by donor site, (1) the latissimus dorsi flap (back muscle), (2) the transverse rectus abdominis myocutaneous, or TRAM, flap (abdominal muscle), and (3) the gluteal flap (buttock muscle).

Autologous reconstruction has several advantages. The skin and fat from the donor sites are similar in consistency to a natural breast; therefore, a reconstructed breast simulates a real breast better than an implant, moving naturally with the patient. Since autologous tissue is part of the patient's own body, it does not lead to a foreign-body reaction or capsular contracture. The tissues have excellent vascularity, which can lead to improved wound healing. Nerves can grow into this tissue, leading to improved tactile sensation in the skin. The results tend to improve over time as surgical scars fade and tissue firmness subsides. If the patient gains weight (10 to 15 lbs), the reconstructed breast may also enlarge, leading to fewer problems with asymmetry. The procedure is ideal for patients who have received previous radiation to the breast or in those who are scheduled to receive postmastectomy radiation, because the transposed tissue tolerates the radiation very well.

The complexity of autologous reconstruction procedures is a disadvantage, as it means longer time in the operating room and a longer period of recuperation for the patient. It is therefore absolutely necessary that the surgeon performing these procedures have appropriate training and experience, and that the patient be in relatively good health. Patients who have medical conditions that interfere with microcirculation or that compromise oxygen delivery are not good candidates. These include patients with cardiac disease, such as atherosclerosis and congestive heart failure, and pulmonary disease, such as emphysema. Other poor candidates include those with a diagnosis of uncontrolled insulin-dependent diabetes mellitus, connective-tissue diseases, or morbid obesity, or those who are heavy smokers. Autologous reconstruction also results in additional scars and permanent changes at the donor sites. Blood transfusion, although rare, may be needed during or after the surgery. Patients are asked to donate their own blood, usually two to four weeks prior to surgery.

Latissimus Dorsi Flap. The latissimus dorsi flap became the standard method of breast reconstruction in the 1970s. At that time, most women had deformities from radical mastectomy, and the latissimus dorsi flap was the most reliable source available for supplementing missing skin and replacing the missing pectoralis major muscle. The latissimus dorsi is a flat triangular muscle on the back that arises from the lower thoracic vertebrae, the lumbar and sacral spinal processes, and the iliac crest. It converges into a flat tendon that inserts into the lesser tubercle of the humerus. The thoracodorsal artery provides the dominant vascular supply to the flap.

The latissimus dorsi flap procedure involves rotating the latissimus muscle with an ellipse of skin from the patient's back to the mastectomy site. Because this flap is usually not bulky enough to provide an adequate breast mound, an implant with or without a tissue expander is often also required (Figure 7.2).

In a 2002 study, a procedure called the extended latissimus dorsi flap was evaluated (Chang *et al.*, 2002). In this procedure additional tissue was rotated from the back to add volume to the mastectomy site, thus eliminating the need for a breast implant. Results were good to excellent in patients with small to medium-sized breasts and in obese patients. The main drawback is morbidity at the donor site, which includes prolonged drainage and wound necrosis. Additional studies are needed for further evaluation.

While the latissimus dorsi flap is one of the less frequently performed procedures in autologous reconstruction, in an appropriate candidate it can have excellent results.

Candidates The latissimus dorsi flap is best suited to patients who have inadequate skin at the mastectomy site or whose skin has been severely damaged from previous radiation. This procedure is also offered if patients have failed other methods of reconstruction or are not eligible for other flap procedures (because of insufficient tissue in the abdomen or buttock areas, or because of previous abdominal scars). In a patient with a large contralateral breast who does not want a reduction, insertion of an implant followed by coverage with a latissimus dorsi flap could help to achieve greater symmetry.

Patients who can achieve reasonable results with implant reconstruction alone are not offered this procedure, because it requires the use of both an implant and a flap. Patients who do not want an additional scar on their back are also not good candidates. Professional athletes who use their arms and back muscles during their activities (e.g., tennis, golf) are usually not offered this procedure, because it may alter their performance. In most patients, however, the loss of the latissimus dorsi muscle function is well compensated for by other muscles (teres major and minor) and is virtually not missed.

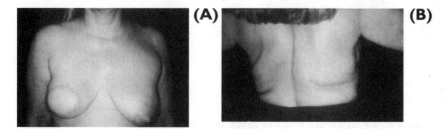

(A) **(B)**

FIGURE 7.2 (A) Right latissimus dorsi flap with implant; **(B)** posterior donor-site scar.

Complications The most common complication is a prolonged seroma (collection of serous fluid) at the donor site. Leaving the surgical drains in place at the donor site for two to three weeks can minimize this complication. Although uncommon, dehiscence of the donor-site incision line can occur when a large amount of skin is removed, causing excess tension. This will heal secondarily but may need scar revision at a later date. Other complications related to the implant, such as capsular contracture, infection, leak, or rupture, can also occur.

Transverse Rectus Abdominis Myocutaneous (TRAM) Flap/Pedicle TRAM Flap. The transverse rectus abdominis myocutaneous flap, simply known as the TRAM flap, is the most widely used autologous tissue procedure today and was first described in 1982 by Hartrampf and colleagues. A TRAM flap creates the breast mound by translocating abdominal skin, fat, and muscle to the mastectomy site (Figure 7.3). In a pedicled TRAM, the rectus muscle is separated in the lower abdomen and is tunneled under the skin of the upper abdomen to the mastectomy site. The superior epigastric artery is the principal blood supply of the rectus muscle, which in turn provides the blood supply to the skin and fat that will form the new breast mound. Either one or both rectus muscles may be used, depending on the amount of tissue required (to reconstruct larger breasts and/or in bilateral breast reconstruction). This is referred to as the unipedicle or double pedicle TRAM flap. The defect in the abdominal wall resulting from moving the rectus muscle upward is often closed with nonabsorbable mesh. In order to close the abdominal donor-site incision, it is necessary to superiorly relocate the umbilicus. This results in a circular scar around the periphery of the umbilicus.

The TRAM flap has many advantages. The procedure provides a large amount of skin and fat and is ideal for reconstruction of a large, ptotic breast. Aesthetic results are usually excellent, and the use of an implant is not necessary. The reconstructed breast is soft and can be contoured to resemble the contralateral breast closely. The long donor-site scar on

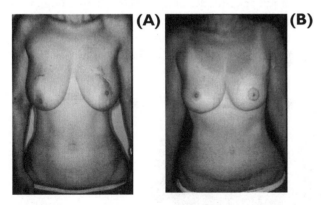

(A) **(B)**

FIGURE 7.3 **(A)** Following bilateral breast biopsies prior to left mastectomy; **(B)** following left **TRAM** flap reconstruction with nipple/areola complex and right reduction mammoplasty. Abdominal donor-site incision also visible.

the abdomen can be kept very low in the suprapubic area. There is often some improvement in abdominal contour (flatter abdomen), although the result is not the same as in abdominoplasty (i.e., tummy tuck). Patients must be informed that the primary goal of this procedure is to reconstruct the breast and not to tighten the abdomen.

Disadvantages include the extensive nature of the procedure and the lengthy recovery period required (often six to eight weeks). Patients will have additional scars at the donor site on the abdomen and around their umbilicus. They will also have numbness on the abdominal skin that may last for six to eight months.

Candidates Candidates for TRAM flap reconstruction must have sufficient tissue at the donor site in the lower abdomen and must be in relatively good health. They must also be motivated to undergo the relatively long recovery period required with this procedure.

TRAM flap reconstruction produces anatomical changes, regardless of whether one muscle or two are used, and therefore cannot be repeated at a later date. As this is the case, special consideration must be given to a patient's risk of developing a contralateral breast cancer. For example, a patient with a BRCA germline mutation who is at greatly increased risk for developing a contralateral breast cancer in the future would be a poor candidate for a unilateral TRAM flap; however, other flap procedures, such as gluteal free flap or latissimus dorsi flap with implant, remain as options. Patients with previous abdominal surgeries or scars that have resulted in anatomical changes in the mid- and upper-abdomen and its blood supply (e.g., abdominoplasty, midline or paramedian scars) may not be candidates for this procedure. However, most patients with low abdominal scars (e.g., cesarean section) may still be candidates.

Complications Complications can include partial flap loss caused by fat necrosis, delayed healing, or necrosis of the umbilicus. Abdominal weakness causing bulge or hernia, although rare, can also be seen. Potential complications due to the extended time in the operating room can include pulmonary emboli, deep-vein thrombosis, and pneumonia.

Free TRAM Flap. The alternative approach to the pedicle TRAM flap is the free TRAM flap. In this procedure, a portion of the rectus muscle, fat, and skin (TRAM flap) is completely detached from the abdominal donor site and its native blood supply (superior and inferior epigastric arteries). This block of tissue is then transplanted to the mastectomy site, and the blood vessels of the flap are reconnected to the vessels at the recipient site (thoracodorsal artery and vein or internal mammary artery and vein) using microvascular surgery. Microvascular surgery involves using a microscope to reconnect the vessels.

Free TRAM flaps are technically more challenging but have specific advantages in addition to the advantages mentioned for the pedicle TRAM flap. In contrast to the pedicle TRAM flap procedure, where the entire muscle is used, the free TRAM flap procedure requires only a small portion of the rectus muscle. This allows the strength of the abdominal wall to be maintained. Vascularization of the free TRAM flap is superior to the pedicle TRAM flap, because the inferior epigastric artery and vein are the dominant blood supply.

This results in less fat necrosis and the ability to transfer more tissue safely. Fat necrosis presents itself as a hard lump and can be easily confused with recurrent disease. Because this flap is freed from the body, it can be easily shaped and positioned to achieve better aesthetic results than are achieved with the pedicle TRAM flap.

Free TRAM flap reconstruction is a complicated microsurgical procedure. Because this procedure is performed using a microscope, it can increase the operating room time significantly. However, in facilities with appropriate equipment and highly trained and experienced plastic surgeons and operating room staff, the average operation time is not substantially different from that of the pedicle TRAM flap procedure.

Candidates   Candidates for the free TRAM flap procedure are similar to those for the pedicle TRAM flap. However, in some cases, patients with high risk factors (obesity, smoking, diabetes, cardiovascular disease, COPD) are also able to undergo this procedure with acceptable complication rates (Serletti & Moran, 2000). This is possible because of the more robust blood supply and more limited donor-site defect in the free TRAM.

Complications   Complications of a free TRAM flap are similar to those of the pedicle TRAM flap but can also include leaks at the sites of anastomosed vessels (bleeding) and/or thrombosis. Failure to correct these complications will result in total flap necrosis/loss (dead flap). If these complications are recognized and reported early, the loss of the flap can be prevented by emergently operating on the patient.

The Deep Inferior Epigastric Perforators (DIEP) Flap.   The DIEP flap breast reconstruction technique, although rare, is a microvascular technique in which the rectus muscle is spared completely and only abdominal skin and fat with its perforators (vessels perfusing the flap) are used (Nahabedian *et al.,* 2002). In this procedure, complications such as abdominal weakness, bulge, or hernia are thought to occur less frequently than with the conventional pedicle or free TRAM flap. However, because of the decreased blood supply to the flap (because no muscle is taken) and added complexity of the surgical procedure, this flap may be associated with an increased risk of total or partial flap loss and fat necrosis. There are no long-term studies concerning this procedure.

Gluteal Free Flap.   In gluteal free flap breast reconstruction, part of the gluteal muscle (superior or inferior portion) with its overlying skin and fat is removed and transplanted at the mastectomy site to reconstruct the new breast mound (Figure 7.4). This can only be done using the microvascular technique described in the section on free TRAM flap reconstruction. The blood supply to this flap is from the superior or inferior gluteal artery. The gluteal flap procedure is technically more demanding than the TRAM flap procedure in terms of the dissection, vascular anastomosis, and the need for repositioning the patient during the surgery (Boustred & Nahai, 1998). Because of the added complexity, this procedure is usually used for unilateral breast reconstruction. If bilateral gluteal reconstruction is needed, the second breast is reconstructed at a later date.

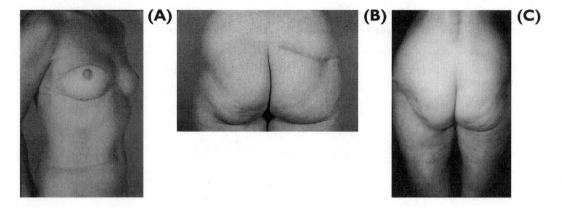

FIGURE 7.4 (A) Right gluteal flap reconstruction; **(B)** superior gluteal flap donor site; **(C)** inferior gluteal flap donor site.

Candidates   Patients who are unable to have TRAM flap or tissue expander/implant reconstruction may be good candidates for this procedure. Patients who prefer to have a donor-site scar on the buttock rather than the back or abdomen may also be considered. Because of the complexity of this procedure, patients must be highly motivated to undergo the long recovery.

Complications   The complications are similar to those mentioned in free TRAM flap reconstruction. Specific complications of gluteal flaps can include increased thrombosis of the vessels and flap loss. Dehiscence of the donor-site incision line is a rare complication and can occur in cases when an excessive amount of skin is taken from the donor site.

Table 7.1 provides a comparison of the different surgical procedures.

TREATMENT OF THE CONTRALATERAL BREAST

Breast reconstruction rarely produces a result that is completely symmetrical to the unaffected contralateral breast. If this is unacceptable to the patient, a number of surgical options are available to correct the asymmetry. In large-breasted women, reduction mammoplasty can be done to decrease the breast size. Women with ptosis who only need a lift of the normal breast without a reduction in volume can benefit from mastopexy (breast lift). Those who are very small-breasted can opt for breast augmentation with the placement of an implant, which is usually placed submuscularly (i.e., underneath the pectoralis muscle). Placement of an implant can make the mammographic follow-up of that breast more difficult. Mammographic techniques, therefore, must be modified to ensure visibility of all areas of the breast. Surgery on the contralateral breast can be performed at any time. These symmetry procedures are most commonly done at the time of the exchange of a tissue expander for a permanent implant or at the time of nipple/areolar reconstruction.

Table 7.1 Comparison of Reconstruction Procedures

Surgical procedure	Anesthesia	OR time	Days in hospital	Shape and consistency	Scars
Insertion of tissue expander	General	1 hr	2–3 with mastectomy, ambulatory if delayed	No natural ptosis, firm (temporary stretching device only)	Through mastectomy scar (no new scar)
Exchange of tissue expander for permanent implant*	General	1 hr	0	Softer than expander; shape and ptosis closer to that of natural breast	Through mastectomy scar (no new scar)
Latissimus dorsi flap	General	3–4 hrs	2–4	Natural shape, soft	Donor-site scar on back
Pedicle TRAM flap	General	4–5 hrs	4–5	Natural shape, soft	Donor-site scar on abdomen
Free TRAM flap	General	5–6 hrs	5–7	Natural shape, soft	Donor-site scar on abdomen
Gluteal free flap	General	6–8 hrs	7–10	Natural shape, soft	Donor-site scar on gluteus (buttock)
Nipple/areolar reconstruction using a skin graft*	Local with IV sedation	1.5 hrs	0	Reconstructed nipple will have tactile but not erectile sensation	Donor-site scar at inner-upper thigh fold (groin fold)
Nipple/areolar reconstruction using micropigmentation (tattooing)*	Local anesthesia in doctor's office	Procedure time: 20 min (approx.)	n/a	Gives illusion of the nipple areolar	n/a

*These procedures are done following initial breast reconstruction.

NIPPLE/AREOLAR RECONSTRUCTION

Creation of the nipple/areolar complex is an important component of breast reconstruction. It enhances the final cosmetic result by changing the appearance of the breast mound to create a more realistic and natural-looking breast. This procedure is ideally performed when the reconstructed breast mound has attained its final shape and the patient and plastic surgeon are satisfied with the results. This is because once created, the new nipple/areola cannot be relocated easily.

Nipple/areolar sharing (borrowing from the opposite breast) allows for a perfect match but is rarely done today, because it can result in change in sensation and depigmentation of the donor nipple. There may also be depigmentation in the grafted nipple.

The most common method of creating the nipple is with the use of local flaps (skin and fat from the center of the new breast mound), which are rotated around each other to create a projecting nipple. The initial color of the reconstructed nipple is the same color as the breast mound. Micropigmentation (tattooing) can be done at a later date to achieve a more natural color. The areola is created using a skin graft. The most common donor site used is from the inner upper thigh. This skin is darker than the breast skin and when grafted, it simulates the color of the areola. The only disadvantage is that it creates an additional scar in the groin. For patients who do not wish to have the skin graft procedure, the areola can be created using micropigmentation.

PSYCHOLOGICAL EFFECTS OF BREAST RECONSTRUCTION

While the need to undergo any surgical procedure can elicit great emotional distress in the individual, the need to undergo a mastectomy for the treatment of breast cancer can be especially difficult. Patients must not only contend with the fear and uncertainty of a cancer diagnosis, but also with the loss of a part of the anatomy that often defines their femininity. It would seem obvious that the reconstruction of a breast mound, particularly at the time of mastectomy, would have profound psychological benefits for the patient. However, there have been conflicting results in the literature.

In a retrospective study of 577 patients, satisfaction with cosmetic results and psychosocial morbidity (anxiety, depression, body image, sexuality, and self-esteem) were compared in women who had breast conservation, mastectomy alone, and mastectomy with reconstruction (Al-Ghazal *et al.,* 2000). Significant statistical differences existed between the three groups, with breast conservation being the most favorable, followed by mastectomy with reconstruction. The greatest morbidity existed in the mastectomy alone group. Rowland *et al.* (2000) interviewed 1957 patients who underwent breast conservation (57%), mastectomy alone (26%), and mastectomy with reconstruction (17%), 1 to 5 years after diagnosis. No differences were seen between groups in terms of emotional and social functioning, or in the women's ability to perform in their normal roles. Surprisingly, women who had mastectomy with reconstruction were the most likely to feel that breast cancer had a negative impact on their sex lives. The authors felt that other factors besides the type of surgery may play a role in determining subsequent quality of life, such as age, exposure to adjuvant therapies, and other health problems.

Nissen *et al.* (2001), in a prospective study, found that women who underwent mastectomy with reconstruction ($N = 40$) had significantly greater mood disturbance and significantly poorer well-being after surgery than women who had mastectomy alone ($N = 55$). These differences persisted 18 months later. In a follow-up qualitative study, Nissen *et al.* (2002)

interviewed 17 women, who had undergone mastectomy with immediate reconstruction between 1.4 and 5 years previously, in a focus group setting to try to explore reasons for the unexpected results of the previous study. Focus group participants felt that possible reasons included timing of the interview (patients may have been overwhelmed at the time), unrealistic patient expectations about the cosmetic outcome, and patient difficulty processing preoperative information.

Al-Ghazal *et al.* (2000), in a retrospective study, examined the benefits of immediate versus delayed reconstruction. They found that patients who underwent immediate reconstruction recalled less distress and had better psychosocial well-being than those who underwent delayed reconstruction. Harcourt and Rumsey (2001) did a thorough review of the existing literature related to psychological aspects of breast reconstruction. They concluded that much of the existing research in this area has methodological flaws, in particular because of the reliance upon retrospective designs and the inappropriate use of randomized controlled trials. They felt that it would be premature to come to any firm conclusions about the psychological benefits of breast reconstruction until more methodologically rigorous studies are carried out.

Since there is great variation in study results, it becomes difficult to make any broad generalizations about the psychological effects of breast reconstruction. For many women it is a positive experience, but for some it is disappointing. Because breast reconstruction is elective surgery, it is vital that the health care professional perform a thorough assessment of the patient during the preoperative consultation to evaluate her motivations, desires, and expectations. Women who anticipate that breast reconstruction will solve preexisting psychological problems, such as long-standing intimacy issues, or those who have unrealistic expectations will likely be disappointed. Some women will forever mourn the loss of their natural breast and will never accept or be happy with their reconstructed breast. By having a frank discussion with the patient and helping her set realistic goals, the health care professional can assist the patient in choosing an option that makes sense for her.

THE ROLE OF NURSING

Nurses have a vital role in their patients' lives by providing quality care, education, and support throughout their hospital stays and in their home settings. During the initial consultation, the nurse should assess the patient for any specific educational, physical, or psychosocial needs that she may have. Specific referrals should be made at this time to avoid any anticipated problems (e.g., social work, smoking cessation program, psychiatry). The nurse should help the patient set realistic goals by providing her with accurate information about what she can expect after surgery. If the patient chooses not to undergo breast reconstruction, then the nurse should support her in that decision. For the patient who opts to have breast reconstruction, she must be informed that while breast reconstruction may approximate the look of the natural breast, it will never precisely duplicate it. General preoperative teaching guidelines are described in Table 7.2. Specific procedure-related teaching points are described in Table 7.3. All information given orally should be supplemented

Table 7.2 General Preoperative Teaching

Topics to cover preoperatively	Teaching points
Things to expect after surgery	Patients undergoing a flap procedure will have an incision and surgical drain(s) at the reconstructed breast site and at the donor site.
	Postoperative swelling is normal and may last for a couple of weeks.
	There may be temporary skin-color changes at the reconstructed site (bruising, pinkish skin). These changes improve with time.
	Patients undergoing a flap procedure will experience temporary tightness at the reconstructed site and at the donor site.
	Any patients having a flap procedure will have a Foley catheter for 2–3 days postoperatively.
	Patients having TRAM or gluteal flap procedure are asked to donate 1–2 units of packed red blood cells in case it is needed during or after surgery.
	Patients are taught breathing and leg exercises to prevent pneumonia and DVT, respectively.
Change in sensation in the reconstructed breast	Patients may experience temporary changes in sensation such as sensitivity to touch, numbness, and tingling (caused by nerve damage during mastectomy).
	Some degree of numbness and change of sensation may be permanent.
Pain management	Pain medication may include PCA pumps, IM, or PO narcotics depending on level of pain (e.g., morphine, Percocet, Darvocet).
Range-of-motion exercises	Exercises generally begin the day after surgery with appropriate modifications for individual procedures.
Home-care needs	Patients having TRAM flap or gluteal flap will need help at home for at least 1 week following discharge.
Time away from work	Approximately 4–6 weeks after implant reconstruction; 6–8 weeks after latissimus dorsi flap; 6–12 weeks after TRAM flap and gluteal flap.

Table 7.3 Procedure-specific Teaching Points

Procedure	Teaching points*
Tissue expander/implant reconstruction	Provide patients with clothing hints to maximize symmetry and improve their appearance during expansion process.
	Instruct patients not to have MRI with tissue expander since port is metal.
	Metal in the port may set off the alarm at security checkpoints in airport.
	Instruct patients to permanently avoid exercises that will develop the pectoralis muscle, which can result in distortion of the reconstructed breast.
	Instruct patients to pad their seat belt when traveling long distances in a car if the seat belt falls directly over the implant.
Latissimus dorsi flap reconstruction	Donor-site incision line causes a great deal of tension in the back.
	Patients will have difficulty extending arm above head for 2–3 weeks. They should not prematurely force the movement.
	Avoid extreme stretching exercises (advanced yoga) for 6–8 weeks to prevent dehiscence of donor-site incision line.
TRAM flap reconstruction	Abdominal donor-site incision causes a great deal of tension in abdominal area.
	To prevent abdominal spasm or dehiscence of incision line, instruct patients to sleep with head elevated 45° and knees bent or on their side in the fetal position during first postoperative week.
	In free TRAM flap, range of motion exercises are delayed 7–10 days to prevent tension on anastomosed vessels.
Gluteal free-flap reconstruction	Patients must avoid lying on their back or on their donor side for 4 weeks because of presence of drains and incision line location.
	Patients must avoid physical activities/movements that could cause tension on posterior thigh until complete healing at donor-site incision.
Nipple/areolar reconstruction	Avoid direct friction on skin-grafted nipple/areola for 2 weeks (i.e., no seat belt on affected side).
	For first 2 weeks, pad seat belt strap if it falls directly on reconstructed site.
	Avoid lower extremity exercises for 3–4 weeks to prevent dehiscence of skin-graft donor site in upper inner thigh.

*Time frames mentioned above may vary depending on physician/nurse experience and preference/condition of patient.

with written booklets. Providing photographs for the patients to view may also help her better envision the actual cosmetic result.

During the initial postoperative period, the nurse must monitor the patient closely to ensure adequate wound healing and pain control. Because of the potential complication of total flap loss in the free flap procedures, it is essential that the flap condition be assessed frequently during the first few days. If a change is noted in the condition of the flap, the patient may need to be brought emergently back to the operating room. Table 7.4 outlines the important components in the assessment of the flap.

Prior to their discharge, patients are taught to look for and report signs and symptoms of infection. Drain and wound care are reviewed. If needed, a referral will be initiated to have a visiting nurse monitor them at home. Patients are asked to demonstrate range of motion exercises to ensure proper form. They should continue the exercises at home, but they should avoid doing high-impact aerobics, jogging, and lifting weights above 5–10 pounds for 6–8 weeks. Patients are instructed to avoid baths and public pools until all incision lines and drain sites have healed completely. Brisk walking, use of stationary bikes and stepping machines, and stretching exercises may begin as soon as the patient feels comfortable doing so. The risk of infection associated with exposure to sun must also be brought to the patient's attention. Because of numbness at the mastectomy site that is common after surgery, patients are generally unable to feel the burning sensation that is caused by sun exposure. Patients are instructed to apply sunscreen (SPF 15 or higher) to the surgical sites whenever they are at risk for sun exposure.

Once the patient is at home, the nurse should be available for any questions, problems, or concerns that she may have. A thorough reassessment can be done during the postoperative visit to evaluate how well the patient is healing, both physically and emotionally. The nurse should provide emotional support throughout the entire process. Patients are at risk for developing emotional problems at any time; these may include poor

Table 7.4 Assessment of Flap Condition After Microvascular Surgery (Free TRAM Flap or Gluteal Free Flap)

Assessment categories	What to look for
Color	Pink: good color Pallor: decreased arterial blood flow Mottling: venous congestion
Circulation with Doppler study	Decreased or absent blood flow indicates blockage of anastomosed vessels
Capillary refill	Press on flap to check refill* Normal refill 3 seconds Arterial problem if > 5 seconds Venous problem if < 2 seconds
Temperature	Flap temperature should not be < 30°C

*Frequency of flap checks: every hour for first 2 days; every 2 hours for days 3 and 4; every 4 hours for days 5 and 6.

adjustment related to their altered body image, inability to function as they did before surgery, and depression related to their cancer diagnosis. Patients should be given the names of available support groups and specific specialists as indicated.

SUMMARY

Today, breast reconstruction is widely accepted as an important component in the rehabilitation process following mastectomy. The majority of women who require or choose to undergo a mastectomy are suitable candidates for some form of breast reconstruction. A variety of options exist, including the use of a breast implant in the form of silicone gel or saline, or reconstruction using the patient's own tissue. The most commonly performed autologous tissue procedures include the latissimus dorsi flap, the pedicle TRAM flap, and the free TRAM flap. Less commonly performed procedures include the gluteal free flap and the DIEP flap. These reconstructive procedures may be done immediately at the time of mastectomy or at a later date. Not every procedure is appropriate for every patient, and careful patient selection is important to ensure a positive outcome.

Finally, breast reconstruction is elective surgery, and the decision to undergo a reconstruction procedure is therefore highly personal. A well-informed patient will have the knowledge and ability to make a decision that feels right for her. Health care professionals provide guidance and information—on reconstructive options, the related risks and benefits, and the advantages and disadvantages of each procedure—that is critical to helping patients set realistic goals. Nurses play an important role by providing their patients with the physical, educational, and emotional care necessary for a return to optimal health.

REFERENCES

Alderman, A.K., Wilkins, E.G., Kim, H., & Lowery, J.C. (2002). Complications in postmastectomy breast reconstruction: two-year results of the Michigan Breast Reconstruction Outcome Study. *Plastic and Reconstructive Surgery, 109,* 2265–2274.

Al-Ghazal, S.K., Fallowfield, L., & Blamey, R.W. (2000). Comparison of psychological aspects and patient satisfaction following breast conserving surgery, simple mastectomy, and breast reconstruction. *European Journal of Cancer, 36,* 1938–1943.

Al-Ghazal, S.K., Sully, L., Fallowfield, L., & Blamey, R.W. (2000). The psychological impact of immediate rather than delayed reconstruction. *European Journal of Surgery, 26,* 17–19.

Allweis, T.M., Boisvert, M.E., Otero, S.E., Perry, D.J., Dubin, N.H., & Priebat, D.A. (2002). Immediate reconstruction after mastectomy for breast cancer does not prolong the time to starting adjuvant chemotherapy. *The American Journal of Surgery, 183,* 218–221.

Bacilious, N., Cordeiro, P.G., Disa, J.J., & Hidalgo, D.A. (2002). Breast reconstruction using tissue expanders and implants in Hodgkin's patients with prior mantle radiation. *Plastic and Reconstructive Surgery, 109,* 102–107.

Boustred, A.M. & Nahai, F. (1998). Inferior gluteal free-flap breast reconstruction. *Clinics in Plastic Surgery, 25,* 275–282.

Carlson, G.W., Losken, A., Moore, B., Thornton, J., Elliott, M., Bolitho, G., & Denson, D.D. (2001). Results of immediate breast reconstruction after skin-sparing mastectomy. *Annals of Plastic Surgery, 46,* 222–228.

Chang, D.W., Youssef, A., Cha, S., & Reece, G.P. (2002). Autologous breast reconstruction with the extended latissimus dorsi flap. *Plastic and Reconstructive Surgery, 110,* 751–759.

Clough, K.B., O'Donoghue, J.M., Fitoussi, A.D., Nos, C., & Falcou, M. (2001). Prospective evaluation of late cosmetic results following breast reconstruction: 1. Implant reconstruction. *Plastic and Reconstructive Surgery, 107,* 1702–1709.

Fisher, B., Redmond, C., Poisson, R., Margolese, R., Wolmark, N., Wickerham, L., Fisher, E., Deutsch, M., Caplan, R., Pilch, Y., Glass, A., Shibata, H., Lerner, H., Terz, J., & Sidorovich, L. (1989). Eight-year results of a randomized clinical trial comparing total mastectomy and lumpectomy with or without irradiation in the treatment of breast cancer. *New England Journal of Medicine, 320,* 822–828.

Foster, R.D., Esserman, L.J., Anthony, J.P., Hwang, E.S., & Do, H. (2002). Skin-sparing mastectomy and immediate breast reconstruction: a prospective cohort study for the treatment of advanced stages of breast carcinoma. *Annals of Surgical Oncology, 9,* 462–466.

Hakelius, L., & Ohlsen, L. (1997). Tendency to capsular contracture around smooth and textured gel-filled silicone mammary implants: a five-year follow-up. *Plastic and Reconstructive Surgery, 100,* 1566–1569.

Harcourt, D., & Rumsey, N. (2001). Psychological aspects of breast reconstruction: a review of the literature. *Journal of Advanced Nursing, 35,* 477–487.

Hartrampf, C.R., Scheflan, M., & Black, P.W. (1982). Breast reconstruction with a transverse abdominal island flap. *Plastic and Reconstructive Surgery, 69,* 216–224.

Janowsky, E.C., Kupper, L.L., & Hulka, B.S. (2000). Meta-analyses of the relation between silicone breast implants and the risk of connective tissue diseases. *New England Journal of Medicine, 342,* 781–790.

Krueger, E.A., Wilkins, E.G., Strawderman, M., Cederna, P., Goldfarb, S., Vicini, F.A., & Pierce, L.J. (2001). Complications and patient satisfaction following expander/implant breast reconstruction with and without radiotherapy. *International Journal of Radiation Oncology, Biology, and Physics, 49,* 713–721.

Nahabedian, M.Y., Momen, B., Galdino, G., & Manson, P.N. (2002). Breast reconstruction with the free TRAM or DIEP flap: patient selection, choice of flap, and outcome. *Plastic and Reconstructive Surgery, 110,* 466–475.

Newman, L.A., Kuerer, H.M., Hunt, K.K., Ames, F.C., Ross, M.I., Theriault, R., Fry, N., Kroll, S.S.,

Robb, G.L., & Singletary, S.E. (1999). Feasibility of immediate breast reconstruction for locally advanced breast cancer. *Annals of Surgical Oncology, 6,* 671–675.

Nissen, M.J., Swenson, K.K., & Kind, E.A. (2002). Quality of life after postmastectomy breast reconstruction. *Oncology Nursing Forum, 29,* 547–553.

Nissen, M.J., Swenson, K.K., Ritz, L.J., Farrell, J.B., Sladek, M.L., & Lally, R.M. (2001). Quality of life after breast carcinoma surgery. *Cancer, 91,* 1238–1246.

Noone, R.B., Frazier, T.G., Noone, G.C., Blanchet, N.P., Murphy, J.B., & Rose, D. (1994). Recurrence of breast carcinoma following immediate reconstruction: a 13-year review. *Plastic and Reconstructive Surgery, 93,* 96–106.

Pollock, H. (1993). Breast capsular contracture: a retrospective study of textured versus smooth silicone implants. *Plastic and Reconstructive Surgery, 91,* 404–407.

Renneker, R., & Cutler, M. (1952). Psychological problems of adjustment to cancer of the breast. *Journal of the American Medical Association, 148,* 833–838.

Rowland, J.H., Desmond, K.A., Meyerowitz, B.E., Belin, T.R., Wyatt, G.E., & Ganz, P.A. (2000). Role of breast reconstructive surgery in physical and emotional outcomes among breast cancer survivors. *Journal of the National Cancer Institute, 92,* 1422–1429.

Rubio, I.T., Mirza, N., Sahin, A.A., Whitman, G., Kroll, S.S., Ames, F.C., & Singletary, S.E. (2000). Role of specimen radiography in patients treated with skin-sparing mastectomy for ductal carcinoma in situ of the breast. *Annals of Surgical Oncology, 7,* 544–548.

Serletti, J.M., & Moran, S.L. (2000). Microvascular reconstruction of the breast. *Seminars in Surgical Oncology, 19,* 264–271.

Vandeweyer, E., & Deraemaecker, R. (2000). Radiation therapy after immediate breast reconstruction with implants. *Plastic and Reconstructive Surgery, 106,* 56–58.

Yule, G.J., Concannon, M.J., Croll, G.H., & Puckett, C.L. (1996). Is there liability with chemotherapy following immediate breast reconstruction? *Plastic and Reconstructive Surgery, 97,* 969–973.

Chapter 8

RADIATION THERAPY

JANA PERUN, MSN, ARNP

INTRODUCTION

While the incidence of breast cancer has increased over the years, mortality has decreased. This change is explained by better cure rates associated with early detection and improved treatment modalities, including radiation therapy. The use of radiation therapy in the treatment of breast cancer has shifted. Initially, radiation was used to treat chest wall recurrences and advanced inoperable cases. Today, radiation is used to treat the intact breast after lumpectomy and many postmastectomy patients at high risk for local chest wall or regional lymph node recurrence. The critical end point of a radiation therapy program's ability to eradicate breast cancer can be judged using rates of response and recurrence through long-term follow-up. Researchers over time have successfully documented that 5000 cGy delivered over 25 fractions with a local boost (1250 cGy) to the primary site of disease is adequate for the eradication of breast cancer in a high percentage of cases.

The practice of radiation oncology has seen remarkable technological advances in both the biomedical and computing and information technology fields. For example, treatment machines have evolved and are now tooled with embedded computer chips and processors, which enables the radiation oncologist to plan even the most complex therapy accurately. Intensity-modified radiation therapy (IMRT) is another revolution in how radiation therapy is delivered. IMRT is able to define the target tissue accurately while excluding nontarget tissues from the treatment field. Targeted internal radiation (i.e., brachytherapy) using the MammoSite® device is currently providing women with a new option for radiation therapy following breast-conserving surgery. This form of therapy restricts the radiation only to the tissues that are likely to harbor residual cancer cells and decreases the treatment course from six weeks to five days. The most recent addition to the field of radiation oncology involves the multileaf collimators, which provide a level of control that was not possible with previously available resources.

The purpose of this chapter is to discuss the use of radiation therapy in the treatment of breast cancer. The associated side effects of treatment, support for patients and their families, and the nurse's role are highlighted.

BACKGROUND

The following discussion provides the reader with background information about the historical development in radiation oncology. In 1895 William Roentgen discovered a new form of radiation that could penetrate various materials. He chose to call it X-ray radiation to distinguish it from other forms of radiation. With remarkable speed, tools were developed and X-ray radiation became a single discovery that changed the course of human existence.

The therapeutic value of ionizing radiation was noted as early as 1896. The first practitioners to demonstrate the ability of X rays to shrink or even eliminate cancerous growths were limited by rudimentary equipment and techniques in treatment and scheduling. The early X-ray machines delivered a maximal dose at the skin surface rather than penetrating to tumors deep within tissue. Massive single doses of radiation produced significant adverse effects on tissue. Practitioners learned that fractionation (i.e., divided radiation dose) of treatment produced greater recovery of normal tissue while allowing for tumor cell death. Supervoltage equipment (cobalt-60 and linear accelerators) did not become available until the 1960s. Physicians used radiation therapy for the treatment of breast cancer within its first decade of use. In 1906, Francis Henry Williams, a physician at Boston City Hospital, Harvard Medical School, published an article in the *Boston Medical Journal* regarding the use of X-ray radiation in the primary treatment of some early cases of breast cancer.

Today, radiation used for the treatment of cancer is called ionizing radiation because it has the ability to dislodge electrons and form ions as it passes through tissues. Ions are atoms that have acquired an electric charge through the gain or loss of an electron. The use of ionizing radiation is based on the premise that radiation interacts with atoms and molecules of tumor cells to produce specific harmful biologic effects. The effect of radiation therapy at the cellular level may be either direct or indirect. The direct effect occurs when any key molecule (DNA/RNA) in the cell is damaged. This is the most effective and lethal injury produced by ionizing radiation. An indirect effect results when ionization occurs in the intracellular water surrounding the molecular structures inside the cell. This form of radiation results in the formation of free radicals that trigger chemical reactions that are toxic to the cell.

RADIATION THERAPY FOR PRIMARY BREAST CANCER

Women with early stage I and II breast cancer who have undergone breast-conserving surgery (BCS) (i.e., excision of the tumor with clear resection of margins) are treated with radiation therapy. After 20 years of follow-up, National Surgical Adjuvant Breast and

Bowel Project (NSABP) studies have shown that for patients with stage I and II breast cancer, BCS followed by breast irradiation is as effective as total mastectomy for the treatment of invasive breast cancer (Fisher *et al.,* 2002). Data continue to indicate that radiation therapy as an adjunct to breast-conserving surgery shows a decrease in distant metastasis and in breast cancer deaths. These results ultimately translate into a substantial survival benefit, as long as the treatment technique avoids long-term pulmonary and cardiac side effects. Women with small breast cancers with carefully cleared surgical margins have a 5% to 6% risk of local recurrence without breast irradiation. Thus, women in the early stages of breast cancer who undergo lumpectomy (BCS) will require some form of breast irradiation. A variety of radiation techniques are now available, providing women with more treatment options and a better chance of survival.

SELECTION OF RADIATION TREATMENT

Stage I or II breast cancer requires a multimodality treatment approach, consisting of surgical resection, radiation therapy, and medical oncology consultation. Choice of local treatment is usually made based on discussions with the patient, her preferences, and surgical and radiation therapy resources. The final decision belongs to the patient and is often influenced by her values and fears. For example, a woman may choose mastectomy based on her concerns about radiation therapy side effects or the inconvenience of the daily treatment schedule. The primary responsibility of the practitioner is to describe the advantages and disadvantages of each treatment strategy.

BCS plus radiation therapy (BCS + RT) involves the total gross removal of the tumor (e.g., lumpectomy or quadrantectomy) and an axillary node dissection, followed by a planned course of radiation therapy, usually over a 6-week period of time (Morrow *et al.,* 2002). Radiation therapy is administered to the entire breast for a total of 4600–5000 cGy in daily fractions of 180–200 cGy. Additionally, the patient will receive a boost to the area of the primary site of disease/biopsy (1000–2000 cGy) by electron beam. Breast irradiation generally starts within 12 weeks of definitive surgery.

Advantages of receiving BCS + RT include breast conservation, decreased deformity of surrounding tissues, and preserved psychological and sexual functioning. Disadvantages of BCS + RT include the inconvenience of daily treatment at the hospital or outpatient treatment center for five to six weeks and skin side effects.

The primary goal of BCS is to completely excise the breast mass with a margin of normal breast tissue in a way that will produce minimal deformity. The surgical technique used during excision determines the degree of postoperative cosmetic effect. Optimal cosmetic results are achieved with the placement of a curvilinear skin incision over the tumor, avoidance of skin retraction (i.e., tunneling), preservation of the fat layer overlying the breast tissue, meticulous hemostasis, and avoidance of drains (Cox & Winchester, 1992). Often metallic clips are placed at the tumor site to assist the radiation oncologist in planning treatment.

SURGICAL MARGINS

Disease recurrence after BCS + RT is lower in the presence of negative surgical margins at the time of resection. Park *et al.* (2000) demonstrated that after eight years, patients with BCS + RT with focally positive margins at the time of resection had a 14% risk of local recurrence (LR), compared to patients with extensively positive margins at the time of resection, who had a 27% risk of LR. Thus, reexcision with positive tumor margins and unknown histologic margins at the time of initial resection is necessary.

Histology. All histologic types of invasive breast cancer may be treated with BCS + RT. Retrospective studies have shown that large tumors (T2 lesions), positive axillary nodes, tumors with extensive intraductal component, palpable tumors, and lobular histology have often required reexcision (Wong & Harris, 2001). Patients with such tumor characteristics may benefit from a more generous initial excision in order to avoid reexcision. Patients who experience persistent positive-tissue margins after surgery are not ideal candidates for BCS + RT and often require a mastectomy.

Age Factors. In the past, age was a determining factor in the selection of BCS + RT. For example, certain prognostic features in younger women increase their risk for local recurrence. However, radiation can be given based on appropriate patient selection and optimal surgical resection. In addition, recent data show that treatment with BCS + RT in women age 65 years or older results in recurrence and survival rates similar to those seen in younger women (Deutsch, 2002).

Other Factors. Other factors are considered when selecting a patient for BCS + RT. For example, contraindications on mammographic evaluation include large tumor size in relation to the breast, two separate malignant lesions in the same breast, and extensive malignant microcalcifications. Such characteristics would require extensive resections and thus compromise the goal of a favorable cosmetic outcome.

Women with larger breasts are not excluded from BCS + RT; however, they require extra care in both surgical and radiation techniques to achieve and maintain a good cosmetic outcome. Patients who are in the first and second trimesters of pregnancy and those who have received previous radiation therapy to the same breast (i.e., radiation therapy for Hodgkin's disease and non-Hodgkin's lymphoma) are not candidates for BCS + RT. Finally, a relative contraindication to BCS + RT includes a history of collagen vascular disease, such as scleroderma or active lupus erythematosus. Omission of radiation therapy after breast conservation surgery is appropriate only for patients with intercurrent diseases and for those who develop metastases while receiving preoperative chemotherapy.

Despite the wide availability of radiation therapy centers across the United States and the current treatment guidelines favoring BCS + RT, fewer than 50% of women with stage I and II breast cancer are treated with BCS + RT. Polednak (2002) found that the number of patients with early-stage breast cancer treated with BCS + RT was 64%. The BCS + RT rate was lower for unmarried women, women age 65–79 years, patients first seen at a hospital without a radiation facility, and patients living in higher poverty areas.

Women may have micrometastases at the time of initial diagnosis. In the presence of micrometastases, adjuvant therapy is given with the intent of curing the patient of residual disease. The combination of chemotherapy and endocrine therapy yields additional benefit when compared with either modality alone. Although there are no current guidelines in the sequencing of chemotherapy with radiation therapy, one strategy is to delay radiation therapy until adjuvant chemotherapy is complete. At times, however, this is not optimal because of the increased risk of local recurrence. (See Chapter 9 for further discussion on the use of adjuvant chemotherapy for breast cancer.)

Follow-up. After BCS + RT, the patient generally receives a physical examination every three to six months for the first three years and then on a biannual basis. The physical examination focuses on evaluation of the primary tumor site and incision, where most recurrences are located. Additionally, assessment of the regional lymph nodes (i.e., cervical, supraclavicular, and axillary) is essential, along with the usual assessment of lungs, heart, muscular/skeletal system and GI/GU. Mammograms are recommended every six months for the first two years and annually thereafter.

POSTMASTECTOMY RADIATION THERAPY

The role of adjuvant postmastectomy radiation therapy (PMRT) has undergone several changes. Historically, PMRT was commonly used based on two rationales: reduction in the risk of local–regional recurrence, and potential for improved survival. Although data demonstrate the effectiveness of PMRT in reducing local recurrence, the potential survival benefit remains controversial.

High Risk for Recurrence. Women at high risk for local–regional recurrence are those who have mastectomy with four or more positive lymph nodes or with an advanced primary tumor. These high-risk women may benefit from PMRT. Data demonstrate a reduction of local–regional recurrence with PMRT from as much as 40% with surgery alone to 10% with surgery and radiation (Metz, *et al.*, 1999).

Several studies have evaluated PMRT in addition to adjuvant chemotherapy, with the largest study from the Danish Breast Cancer Cooperative Group (DBCG). In the DBCG trial 82c, 1375 postmenopausal women having mastectomy for stage II or III breast cancer were randomly assigned to tamoxifen alone or to tamoxifen for 1 year plus local–regional RT. The 10-year rate of local–regional recurrence was reduced from 35% to 8% with RT, and overall survival was improved from 36% to 45% with RT (DeVita, 2001).

It is thought that even with the increased use of anthracycline-based chemotherapy, endocrine therapy, and high-dose chemotherapy, 20–30% of patients at high risk (i.e., those with four or more positive nodes, primary tumor size of 5 cm or greater, and/or involvement of the pectoral fascia) will develop local–regional recurrence. It appears that adjuvant systemic therapy has limited impact on the incidence of local–regional recurrence.

PMRT demonstrates a decrease in the incidence of local–regional recurrence to less than or equal to 10% in this high-risk group. Modifications to PMRT technique now minimize long-term cardiac mortality (Fowble, 1997).

The National Institutes of Health Consensus Statement on Adjuvant Therapy for Breast Cancer (2000) indicates that women with high risk of local–regional tumor recurrence after mastectomy benefit from postoperative radiation therapy. This high-risk group includes women with four or more positive lymph nodes or an advanced primary cancer that meets one or more of the following criteria:

- Original tumor is larger than 5 cm
- Surgical margins of resection are positive for disease
- Tumors are ulcerated or fixed to the skin or chest wall
- Tumor is multicentric

Currently the role of PMRT for women at modest risk of recurrence (one to three positive lymph nodes) is uncertain and needs to be tested in a randomized controlled trial (NIH, 2000). Some experts believe that theoretically, women in this "gray zone" could benefit the most from PMRT because of a low burden of disease. Others believe that although a survival benefit may be achieved, the risk of noncancer deaths secondary to pulmonary or cardiac disorders precludes PMRT. However, favorable evidence shows a dramatic reduction of noncancer deaths, because of the continual improvement of radiation therapy equipment and techniques.

A review of randomized trials suggests an improvement in overall patient survival; however, most patients in these studies had three or fewer positive axillary lymph nodes (Marks & Prosnitz, 1997). More recently, randomized trials, including two studies with a 10- to 15-year follow-up, have demonstrated that PMRT leads to overall survival (Kuske, 1999). This benefit was seen in patients with one to three positive axillary nodes as well as in those with four or more positive nodes. Now, with results showing improved survival after PMRT in both premenopausal and perimenopausal women, with the greatest benefit to women with one to three positive nodes, practice patterns are beginning to shift toward consideration of treatment in women with less tumor involvement (Kuske, 1999).

Treatment Techniques. PMRT is generally given within the first six weeks after mastectomy. Although PMRT may be used in conjunction with chemotherapy, it is not given concurrently with anthracycline-containing regimens in order to avoid cardiac toxicity.

PMRT consists of several fields, including the chest wall and regional lymphatics (i.e., axilla, internal mammary, supraclavicular). The chest wall is treated to a total dose of 5000 cGy over five weeks. Often bolus material is placed over the chest wall to increase the dose of radiation at the skin surface, a common site of recurrence and seeding. Tangential fields are set up when photons are used to treat the chest wall in order to spare underlying structures such as the heart and lungs. In an effort to reduce exposure to the heart and lungs, the internal mammary lymph nodes are usually treated with electrons. Because of the depth of the internal mammary nodes, electron energies of 9–12 MeV are recommended.

Multiple techniques are used to treat the supraclavicular and axillary areas. Often, the radiation beam is angled to reduce the effects to the trachea, esophagus and spinal cord. The usual prescribed dose of therapy to the anterior supraclavicular axillary field is 5000 cGy over 5 weeks (Dow *et al.*, 1997).

STEPS IN THE RADIATION TREATMENT PROCESS

CONSULTATION

Although the plan of treatment traditionally refers to all aspects of the patient's therapy (surgery, chemotherapy, radiation therapy), in radiation therapy it more commonly encompasses the process of selecting the tumor dose prescription, daily dose, fractionation schedule, and arrangement of the radiation beams to achieve the desired radiation dose distribution to the target volume. Before radiation therapy begins, the patient will undergo an initial consultation with the radiation oncologist. Ideally, consultation occurs after diagnosis and before any local or systemic therapy is initiated.

During consultation, the patient will undergo a physical assessment and discussion of the role of radiation therapy in the treatment of her disease. The radiation oncologist will review diagnostic studies and pathology results with the patient and discuss their relationship to the treatment plan. Discussion should include:

- Radiation therapy as a treatment option
- Simulation (what to expect)
- The treatment team
- Treatment schedule
- Daily treatments (what to expect)
- Boost treatment
- Side effects and self-management skills
- Follow-up appointments and procedures
- Question and answer session

It is not uncommon for patients to be frightened and anxious during the initial consultation. It is also not uncommon for women to experience and express frustration at this time. Often women will resent the intrusion in their life. Although it is not always possible, after the initial consultation is completed, it is helpful for the patient to tour the radiation treatment facility, meet the treatment team, and voice any questions or concerns. It is also helpful when family members or significant others can be present to clarify questions and reinforce information from all discussions.

PATIENT TEACHING BEFORE TREATMENT PLANNING

Individual patients should be assessed for their perception of the impact of the diagnosis of breast cancer on their lives. Many cancer care centers have a licensed clinical social worker who can intervene in the planning and early treatment phase to assist the patient in developing and maintaining adequate coping skills. Many institutions use a critical pathway to map the care of the patient during a given timeframe. Institutional pathways may vary, but most will include categories such as patient assessment, patient education, and documentation.

The treatment planning experience may appear frightening, impersonal, and uncomfortable. Pretreatment anxiety, measured by a standardized tool such as the State-Trait Anxiety Scale, is often a predictor of psychological distress during radiation therapy (Smith *et al.*, 2001). By understanding the simulation process, the oncology nurse will be able to accurately explain the process and thereby alleviate many fears that the patient may have. The following are important aspects to consider:

1. Convey a sense of confidence and skill as well as a willingness to answer questions either before or after treatment planning.
2. Convey that the focus is on careful and detailed measurement. It is essential to maintain privacy at all times, which conveys an element of respect and concern for the patient.
3. Inform the patient when the daily radiation treatments will begin. Commonly, within two to four days after treatment planning is complete, 'the patient will receive an appointment date and time to begin the daily treatments.

TREATMENT PLANNING

The area of the body in which the patient will receive treatment is called the treatment field. Before treatment can begin, a planning session, also called a simulation, is scheduled. During this session the radiation oncologist will map out the anatomic areas for radiation treatment. The equipment used in this process is called a simulator. A series of X rays are done on the simulator to delineate the breast and draining lymph node areas.

The ultimate goal of the simulation is to maximize the dose of radiation to the treatment field and minimize the dose to normal surrounding tissues, such as the heart and lungs. Patients are often asked to lie down into a custom-shaped mold that touches just their back and sides. The molds are known as immobilization devices and are made of Styrofoam casts to help ensure consistent patient positioning for daily radiation treatments.

The treatment center may also use a breast board that places the head, arm, and hand in a fixed position. It is important for the patient to understand that padding is not used on the planning or treatment table because it would make the position/treatment field less precise. If a traditional simulator is used during the planning session, the angles and dimensions of the treatment field (i.e., parameters) will be determined. If a CAT scan simulator is used, the parameters will be determined on the planning computer after the planning session is over. Commonly, an X ray will be taken when all planning is completed.

Treatment planning takes approximately one hour. The fields for treatment to the breast or chest wall will be determined clinically. Medially, the target volume is extended to the midline. This is dependent on the shape of the patient and the amount of underlying lung in the radiation field. Laterally, the field will be carried to the midaxillary line.

Inferiorly, the field will fall below the inframammary fold in the intact breast. If the chest wall is to be treated, the inferior field will fall below the contralateral inframammary. Superiorly, the field extends to the base of the clavicular head. Once the angles are established, the radiation therapist will mark the corners of the treatment fields with a permanent small tattoo or nonwashable marker. This marking is a guide to help the radiation therapist consistently target the radiation beam for each treatment. The tattoo is no larger than a small freckle. If the marks are made with a pen, they will eventually fade and will require reapplication (touch-up) during the treatment process.

DAILY RADIATION THERAPY TREATMENT

The most common type of radiation therapy used for women with breast cancer is called external beam radiation (teletherapy). This form of radiation delivers high-energy photons from a linear accelerator (outside of the body) to the specific area (treatment field). The breast is treated with a pair of tangential fields that enter and exit through previously determined medial and lateral borders. The deep edges of the field are coplanar, which allows all divergence to be directed into the air and not deep into the patient's lung. The radiation therapy is given to the entire breast (4500–5000 cGy) in daily fractions of 180–200 cGy.

A third anterior field may be added if the upper axillary and supraclavicular areas are treated. In nearly all treatment techniques, the axilla and supraclavicular fossa are treated with an anterior photon field. The field will be angled laterally so that the cervical spine is eliminated. When the entire axilla needs to be treated, the field will be extended laterally to include a part of the humeral head. Supraclavicular nodes are dosed to a depth of 3 cm, whereas the average midaxillary depth is 7 cm. For this reason a posterior axillary boost is commonly added (Harris *et al.*, 2000).

Chest Wall. The chest wall can also be treated with tangential fields. The field borders are the same, as are the concerns regarding exposure to the underlying heart and lung. Because the overlying skin is a site of recurrence, bolus material must be used to help ensure that the skin receives the full radiation dose. The chest wall can be treated using an electron beam, just as with the intact breast. Such treatment can take several different forms and depends on the radiation oncologist (Harris *et al.*, 2000).

Internal Mammary Nodes. A technique that is useful in treating internal mammary nodes is the medial tangent with supplementation for the missing dose with angled electron fields. This treatment technique can produce satisfactory dose distribution in the majority of patients. Two methods of treating internal mammary nodes have been abandoned: full tangent fields and en face internal mammary photon field matched to shallow tangents. These photon fields deliver a substantial amount of radiation to the heart, which can produce significant cardiac side effects (Harris *et al.*, 2000).

Electron Beam Boost. An electron beam boost is given to the area of the primary site of disease/biopsy (1000–2000 cGy). The electron beam penetrates tissue to a specific depth, allowing treatment of the tumor bed and sparing underlying lungs and ribs from radiation. The goal of the boost is to increase local control to the primary tumor site without decreasing cosmetic outcome. The majority of patients will receive the boost externally. The boost is typically delivered during the final week of radiation treatment. The dose for the boost is based on the pathologic margins of the primary tumor, the reexcisional biopsy, and whether there is presence of tumor in the reexcision specimen. The volume of the electron boost is determined by the clinical features of the size of the primary tumor, pathologic evaluation of the surgical margins, and the need for reexcision. The target volume for the boost is the entire surgical bed. Often the determination of the depth from the skin surface to the surgical marking clips is accomplished by using a CT scanner. Very often patients will receive this dose from the same linear accelerator that was used for their primary therapy and will often lie in the same position. The boost typically brings the total dose to the primary tumor site to 60 Gy (i.e., 6000 cGy) or higher.

Boost Using Radiation Implant. Radiation implants are less commonly used today for boost treatment. This form of radiation is also called brachytherapy, because a radioactive source is implanted internally for a short period of time and then removed. The procedure involves the placement of small catheters under the skin in the excision area where the original tumor was located. Radioactive Iridium 192 (seeds) is placed into the catheters and will emit radiation to the nearby tissue. The "dwell time" for the radiation implant is calculated by a radiation dosimetrist. Typically, the implant is placed for about 24 to 48 hours. Since there are radiation safety concerns, the patient must remain in the hospital during the radiation implant procedure. Radiation precautions, including the time allowed in the implant room and the distance from the radiation source, will apply to staff and visitors. Once the boost is completed, the implant catheters are removed and the patient may be discharged.

Today there is a new method of delivering brachytherapy that involves high-dose radiation. This procedure is done on an outpatient basis. The patient will still require the placement of small catheters to the original site of the tumor bed. In this case the high-dose radiation equipment will deliver the radioactive material inside the catheter for the specified period. This procedure typically takes just a few minutes per day for the number of prescribed days. Once the final boost is completed, the catheters are removed. This form of boost is used as an alternative when boost treatment cannot be accomplished using electrons.

PATIENT AND FAMILY EDUCATION

Primarily, education of patients receiving radiation therapy is aimed to prepare the patient to appropriately cope with the treatment experience and to successfully manage side effects. Women with breast cancer receiving RT have high information needs (Harrison *et al.,* 1999). This finding does not necessarily correlate with patient preference for information. The nurse must assess the patient's desire for information prior to each educational experience.

It is essential to include the patient and family in the care process and encourage both the patient and her loved ones to approach the radiation team as questions or concerns arise. Early in the education experience, telephone numbers for the radiation department and specific personnel should be provided. Many institutions use clinical pathways to coordinate patient care and ensure consistency of education and care provided to all patients.

Because the patient receives treatment daily, the nurse has an opportunity for ongoing assessment and intervention as needs arise. This assessment allows the nurse to connect the patient with appropriate resources, including counseling, nutrition, and financial support services, throughout the treatment experience.

To adequately prepare the patient for the radiation therapy experience, it is helpful to walk the patient through a treatment and to reinforce key points about radiation therapy, including:

1. Radiation is a local treatment that is intended to kill cancer cells that may exist after surgery.
2. Daily treatments are painless (although the radiation will cause pain and discomfort over time).
3. Daily treatments do not make one radioactive.
4. Patients will be able to maintain a normal routine because the treatments last about one half hour. Set-up time is much longer than the treatment time. The actual treatment time is usually less than five minutes.
5. For most breast cancers, radiation therapy significantly decreases the chance of recurrence.

Patients frequently ask, "Why is radiation therapy necessary?" They have been instructed that the surgeon "got it all," which makes it difficult for them to comprehend the need for additional therapy. It is important to explain the concept of microscopic disease in terms that the patient can understand. Once the patient understands that cancer cells too small to be felt or seen can remain after surgery and grow or metastasize, they are more willing to accept the need for additional therapy. Once this is understood, the patient will better accept the total number of treatments needed.

Most patients are not interested in how the radiation therapy works, but they are interested in knowing whether the radiation therapy is working. Because of this concern, radiation port films are a source of confusion to patients. Port films (X ray of the treatment field) are taken weekly throughout radiation and highlight the treatment field for the radiation oncologist. This is a quality control procedure to ensure that the chosen field is receiving the radiation treatment as planned during the simulation. Patients often ask, "What did my X rays show?" A careful explanation of port films and the need for long-term follow-up to monitor progress is indicated.

SIDE EFFECTS OF RADIATION THERAPY

Women undergoing radiation therapy after breast-conserving surgery are expected to tolerate the treatment with minimal side effects. This is due in part to the latest equipment and technologic innovations. Side effects are limited because the breast lies outside of the body. Health care professionals are aware of the need for ongoing assessment and early interventions to continue to limit the severe effects from radiation.

Side effects are a result of cellular damage. The damage is a consequence of the effect of radiation on DNA synthesis and cell division. Ideally, cancer cells die as a result of radiation and are unable to recover, while noncancer cells will recover. Radiation side effects are classified as either acute or late. Acute side effects occur during the treatment and up to six months following the completion of therapy. Side effects that occur after six months are considered late.

Oncology nurses are responsible for clarifying information about the role of radiation therapy, dispelling common misconceptions, and identifying fears about radiation as a treatment modality. It is important to emphasize that radiation therapy is a local treatment and that the patient will not become radioactive. This is a common fear, along with the fear of being burned from the radiation. It is important to emphasize that most patients will experience erythema but will not experience severe side effects unless the patient requires a maximal dose to the skin surface. Patients undergoing radiation therapy will need verbal and written instructions on how to manage their side effects.

The most common side effects resulting from radiation therapy to the breast include skin reactions; intermittent aches and pains in the treated breast, chest wall, or axilla; breast edema; and fatigue. These reactions are normal and will resolve when treatment is completed. Table 8.1 summarizes the acute side effects of radiation therapy to the breast and the nursing management of these side effects.

Skin Reactions. Skin reactions are the primary side effects that occur during therapy. Skin and hair follicle cell lines demonstrate changes more rapidly because of their higher mitotic activity. Early effects are thought to be related to functional cell loss. The effects will generally resolve within two weeks after the completion of treatment. Late effects are caused by injury to the stromal vasculature and endothelial cells and are often considered permanent. (See Chapter 17 for a discussion of late effects of RT.)

Because of today's megavoltage equipment with skin-sparing capabilities, the degree of skin reactions are less severe now than in the past. Typically, the patient will experience mild to moderate erythema that occurs about two weeks after the start of radiation treatment and persists for approximately two weeks after the last treatment. Occasionally, a patient will demonstrate mild erythema after the first radiation treatment. The degree of skin reactions varies from patient to patient and is multifactorial. Fair-skinned individuals appear to be at higher risk for skin reactions. Individuals with darker skin coloring are more prone toward increased skin pigmentation. This type of temporary skin reaction is also considered to be dose-dependent and appears as a series of dark dots in the treatment field. If the supraclavicular region and axillary nodes are in the treatment field, skin reactions may occur in the upper back (i.e., beam exit site). Increased skin reactions also occur along bony prominences such as the clavicle.

TABLE 8.1 Potential Acute Side Effects of Radiation Therapy to Breast/Chest Wall

Side effect	Average onset	Usual duration	Appearance/presentation	Intervention
Radiation dermatitis	Approximately 2 weeks after start of treatment.	Resolution usually within 10 days to 2 weeks after end of treatment for the intact breast. Resolution for chest wall erythema may take as long as 1 month after treatment is completed.	*Grade 0:* no symptoms.* *Grade 1:* (Common) Faint erythema or dry desquamation. *Grade 2:* (Common) Moderate to brisk erythema or patchy moist desquamation frequently confined to skin folds or creases; moderate edema. *Grade 3:* (Rare) Confluent moist desquamation not confined to skin folds; pitting edema. *Grade 4:* (Rare) Skin necrosis or ulceration of full thickness dermis; may include bleeding not induced by minor trauma or abrasion.	Weekly follow-up visits with the nurse and physician for continued assessment and early intervention. *Patient Education:* Instruct patient early to avoid sun exposure to the area receiving radiation therapy. Do not use heating lamps, ice packs, or hot-water bottles. Use only tap water and gentle soaps for cleansing. Do not use harsh soaps. Do not attempt to redraw the markings if they wash off. Do not use adhesive tape in the area receiving radiation therapy. Do not shave or wear deodorant under the arm that is receiving radiation therapy. Avoid tight bras or underwire bras. Wear a sports bra when wearing a bra, if possible. Use only unscented hydrophilic creams (such as Aquaphor, Biafine Unscented), 99–100% pure aloe vera gel (no added perfumes, colors), or Radiacare gel or gel pads.

TABLE 8.1 (continued)

Side effect	Average onset	Usual duration	Appearance/presentation	Intervention
Hyperpigmentation	Approximately 2 weeks after start of treatment. Maybe more pronounced in darker pigmented women.	Resolves slowly after end of treatment. Mild hyperpigmentation may last for months.	Presents as mild to deep tanning of the skin. May be associated with mild discomfort.	As above.
Itching/folliculitis (irritation of hair follicles)	Approximately 10 days to 2 weeks after start of treatment.	Variable—may start to resolve at end of treatment course to entire breast (before start of boost treatment); usually much improved by end of treatment course.	Itchy skin appears slightly red and dry. Folliculitis appears as small red dots, often in sternal, infraclavicular, and supraclavicular area. Occasionally found on back below clavicle 20 exit dose. *Grade 0:* no symptoms.* *Grade 1:* (Common) Mild or localized and relieved immediately by local measures. *Grade 2:* (Common) Intense or widespread and relieved immediately with systemic measures (diphenhydramine). *Grade 3:* (Rare) Intense or widespread and poorly controlled despite treatment.	Use oatmeal colloidal-based soaps. Make paste and apply to affected area, let dry for 3–5 minutes, and rinse off with cool water. Oatmeal colloidal-based bath products may be added to bath. Use 99–100% pure aloe vera gel (no added dyes or perfumes) or unscented hydrophilic creams such as those listed above for erythema. Diphenhydramine (25 mg) may be taken at night for severe itching. For severe cases, IV medication may be required.

TABLE 8.1 (continued)

Side effect	Average onset	Usual duration	Appearance/presentation	Intervention
Fatigue	Highly variable—approximately 2–3 weeks after start of treatment. May be an increased effect with previous or concurrent chemotherapy.	May last up to 2–3 weeks after end of radiation treatments. Average is 10 days to 2 weeks. May be prolonged if receiving chemotherapy.	Increased tiredness in late afternoon or early evening. Most women are able to continue their usual routines.	Earlier bedtime, late afternoon or early evening rest period. Good nutrition—avoid dieting during course of treatment. Conserve energy by having family and friends help as needed. Moderate exercise such as walking has been found to help energy levels.
Dry desquamation (dry peeling)	Approximately 3 weeks after starting radiation.	Usually resolves within 2 weeks of finishing radiation treatments.	Dry flaking or peeling of skin frequently associated with erythema or hyperpigmentation of skin.	As above.
Moist desquamation (moist peeling)	4–5 weeks after start of radiation therapy. Increased occurrence in PMRT.	Usually completely healed within 2–3 weeks after end of radiation treatments.	Moist peeling of the skin with associated erythema. Area may ooze or weep. May be associated with mild to moderate discomfort, depending on severity of reaction. Increased reaction is possible if patient is receiving concurrent chemotherapy. Often occurs in areas with increased shearing friction, such as inframammary fold and axilla.	Gentle rinsing with drying antibacterial solutions, such as chlorhexidine gluconate or ¼–½ strength H2O2. Pat dry with soft clean towel 2–3 times a day. (*Always dilute the H2O2 because full strength will interfere with tissue granulation.*) Above can be followed by application of unscented hydrophilic cream such as Aquaphor, followed by nonadherent dressing such as Aquaphor gauze, covered with a soft ABD pad and held in place by a bra or large-size body netting. Moist soaks can be used, such as aluminum acetate solutions (Bluboro and Domeboro) for 20 minutes 3 times a day. Moisture vapor permeable dressing, such as Op-site, may be used although they can be difficult to adhere in skin folds.

TABLE 8.1 (continued)

Side effect	Average onset	Usual duration	Appearance/presentation	Intervention
				Avoid use of tape on irritated skin. Can use gentle lukewarm shower spray to help debride skin.
				Allow area to be open to air whenever possible.
				If pain is moderate or severe, use of NSAIDs or mild narcotic may be indicated.
				Patient usually requires a break in treatment to promote healing.
Intermittent aches and pains in breast	May occur approximately 1 week after start of radiation.	Can persist for months after radiation finishes, although usually with decreased frequency.	Patients often describe pain as intermittent sharp twinge in the breast.	Reassure patient that this is a normal occurrence and may be alleviated with use of NSAIDs.
Breast edema	As above.	Can persist for months after radiation.	Slight to moderate swelling of treated breast. Breast may feel full or heavy.	As above. Wearing a supportive bra may improve comfort.
Hair loss in treatment portal (fine hair of breast, nipple, and possibly small amount of axillary hair)	Usually starts 3–4 weeks at doses of 30–35 cGy.	Variable. May take 1–6 months for hair to grow back.	Typically not very noticeable or bothersome to patients except when associated with folliculitis or itching.	Follow interventions for itching/folliculitis.

*NCI Common Toxicity Criteria (1999)

Source: Dow, K.H. (1998) *Contemporary Issues in Breast Cancer.* Sudbury, Mass.: Jones & Bartlett. *www.jbpub.com.* Reprinted with permission.

The radiation type and energy may intensify skin reaction. During the boost, the electron beam delivers higher doses to the skin. In patients who receive PMRT, an enhanced skin reaction is intended and expected when bolus material is placed on the skin. Concurrent chemotherapy is a significant promoting factor in skin reactions. Such patients can experience moist desquamation and require careful assessment of the skin shearing areas, including the inframammary fold and axilla. These areas demonstrate increased warmth and moisture and decreased aeration, and often exhibit increased skin reactions.

Additional skin reactions include folliculitis with pruritis, hair loss, and dry/moist desquamations. Folliculitis is often the result of a disruption in the skin's integrity. Areas of higher risk include the skin folds and general breast area. The task of evaluating folliculitis is formidable when the patient is receiving concurrent chemotherapy. In this case it is not safe to assume that the eruption is radiation induced. Collaboration with the medical oncology team is essential to promote diagnosis and proper treatment. Once the practitioner is comfortable with the diagnosis of radiation-induced folliculitis, a mild emollient or lotion will help decrease the pruritis. Oatmeal-based soap applied to the skin may help relieve itchiness. Patients often request approval to use an over-the-counter steroid cream to decrease pruritis. Steroid ointments may decrease itching, but they also increase thinning of the skin and consequently the possibility of increased injury. For this reason, steroid creams should be avoided.

Hair loss in the treated area is considered temporary and for most women is not a concern. On the other hand, dry desquamation (dry peeling) is a common reaction that produces uncomfortable side effects and often becomes a focus of concern for most women. Dry desquamation is predominantly seen on the chest wall and in areas where there is a bony prominence such as the clavicle. It is essential to educate the patient about the use of mild emollients to help soothe the irritated area.

Moist desquamation (moist peeling) most often occurs with concurrent chemotherapy. In fact, it rarely occurs without concurrent chemotherapy and may require a treatment break if the moist reaction is severe. A number of treatments can be instituted for moist desquamation, including the topical application of gentian violet or the application of a moist dressing (hydrocolloid), such as gel pads, to promote wound healing. The effects of such treatments have been studied in relation to radiation-induced moist desquamation. Studies have not demonstrated a significant difference in rate and effectiveness of wound healing (Mak *et al.,* 2000).

Several skin care guidelines are available on managing moist desquamation. It is important for practitioners caring for patients with this side effect to consider the available treatment options as well as adequate pain management. Patients with moist desquamation often require additional efforts to promote pain management, which may involve the use of a mild narcotic. Additionally, patients may require a radiation treatment break if the moist reaction is severe.

The majority of skin-care regimens for patients receiving breast irradiation are not research-based. Recommendations depend on what has worked most effectively in clinical practice and on institutional policies. (See Table 8.2 for guidelines on skin care during and after RT.)

TABLE 8.2 General Skin-Care Guidelines for Radiation Treatment to the Breast/Chest Wall

General skin-care guidelines are provided to patients at the beginning of the course of radiation and are as follows:

1. Keep breast or chest wall clean and dry.
2. Cleanse the treated area with gentle soap (e.g., Ivory, Basis, Pears, Neutrogena, or unscented Dove).
3. Avoid the use of creams, lotions, perfumes, or deodorant in the treatment area unless directed by a radiation oncologist, nurse, or radiation therapist.
4. Avoid extremes of temperature, such as heating pads, hot-water bottles, and ice packs, in the treatment area. Avoid whirlpools and saunas. Avoid swimming pools unless directed by the radiation oncologist, nurse, or radiation therapist.
5. Avoid excess friction or rubbing.
6. Do not use tight clothing or underwire bras; use a sports bra during RT.
7. Use an electric razor to shave under the treated arm during early treatment days. Avoid shaving the treated underarm when there is erythema present.
8. Protect the skin in the treatment field from exposure to direct sunlight by either covering the skin or using a sunblock with SPF of 15 or higher.

Aftercare

General aftercare instructions include the following:

1. Occasional aches and pains in the treated breast/chest wall may continue for weeks or months after finishing RT. Use an NSAID such as ibuprofen.
2. Skin changes will gradually improve over one to two weeks following completion of treatment. The treated skin may look tanned.
3. The breast tissue may feel thicker and firmer after RT. Continue self-breast examinations monthly in order to remain familiar with the feel of the breast tissue.
4. The skin may feel dry after radiation therapy. Use a skin moisturizer for at least two weeks after the end of radiation treatment.
5. If previously irradiated skin is exposed to direct sunlight, cover or protect with SPF 15 or higher sunblock.
6. Call the oncology team with any concerns or questions.
7. If you develop any areas of redness, heat, or swelling in the treated breast, hand, or arm, call your health care provider.

(The following information should be included if patients have had an axillary dissection and/or XRT to the axilla.)

8. Wear gloves when gardening or using harsh chemicals such as bleach.
9. For a long period of time, avoid using the affected arm/hand to carry heavy packages (more than five pounds).
10. If you get a cut or burn on the affected arm/hand, gently cleanse the area and apply antibacterial cream.
11. Use the untreated arm for blood drawing, blood pressures, and vaccinations and/or injections.

Arm and Breast Edema. Arm and breast edema may occur. Lymphedema is seen most often in women who have had a radical mastectomy and an extensive lymph node dissection. It is also seen in women who have had a combination of axillary dissection and radiation to the axilla. The etiology is not well understood, but the edema is believed to be related to obliteration of lymphatics in the axilla by surgery and RT. (See Chapter 15 for a more detailed discussion about lymphedema.)

Breast edema often affects the patient's perception of cosmetic outcome. Axillary node dissection is a significant factor in the incidence of breast edema. Breast edema is more prominent in the first year after treatment and can take up to three years or longer to dissipate. During the course of radiation therapy, patients often complain of a feeling of increasing fullness, swelling, and stiffness in the whole breast. Breast edema combined with skin irritation can produce discomfort. Treatment consists of nonsteroidal anti-inflammatory medications (NSAIDs) and the use of a comfortable cotton sports bra to provide additional support.

After the completion of radiation, edema will slowly subside, and the breast often becomes firmer and rounder and may have a more "youthful" appearance. Such changes are due to the edema and possible scar tissue. Some women complain of a feeling of numbness during their course of therapy. Once the treatments have been completed these symptoms will subside over several weeks.

Women who receive PMRT also complain of a feeling of stiffness and tightness in the chest wall. Over the long term, women feel muscle stiffness in the pectoralis major muscle. This stiffness is caused by scar tissue that results from the radiation treatment. This side effect is usually minor and improves with over-the-counter analgesics.

Intermittent Twinges and Shooting Pains. Patients often report complaints of intermittent twinges and shooting pains in the breast, chest wall, and axilla during their course of treatment and follow-up examinations. It is important to reassure the patient that this is a common but not worrisome side effect. Such pains may be experienced for months to years and can be alleviated with the use of over-the-counter analgesics.

Fatigue. Fatigue is estimated to occur in 72% to 99% of all patients with cancer. For the patient receiving radiation therapy for breast cancer, fatigue can adversely affect her quality of life, both during and after therapy. It usually begins in the second or third week of treatment and typically increases throughout the duration of radiation treatment. The etiologic factors of fatigue relating to radiation therapy are not well known. Fatigue is considered to be multifactorial. It is a result of a variety of physiologic, psychologic, and situational factors. Specific factors that can influence the degree of fatigue in patients receiving radiation therapy include:

- recovering from recent surgery
- previously received chemotherapy or concurrent chemotherapy
- heavier tumor burden

- medications that may cause drowsiness (anti-emetics, pain medication)
- changes in diet and lifestyle from the disruption of the daily treatment schedule
- emotional toll of the months since diagnosis
- effects from the radiation on the body
- sleeplessness and anxiety over the disease and the treatment

Fatigue varies in intensity and duration and is greatly associated with activities that increase the expenditure of energy. For example, many women work a full-time job and maintain a household prior to their diagnosis of cancer and the beginning of their radiation treatments. Fatigue is increased when they have to incorporate the daily radiation treatment into their family and work responsibilities (O'Rourke & Robinson, 1996). Radiation-induced fatigue ranges from none at all to moderate. Patients must be assured that their fatigue will resolve once the treatment ends. Many women fear that the fatigue is a symptom of disease progression. Practitioners are encouraged to develop educational materials and programs aimed at helping women manage and cope with fatigue. It is important to provide them with written and verbal education about how to cope with fatigue during and after their course of therapy. (See Chapter 14 for further discussion of cancer-related fatigue and related interventions.)

EMOTIONAL RESPONSE DURING RADIATION THERAPY

Patients may experience many emotional reactions during the course of radiation therapy. Emotional reactions may not necessarily be related directly to radiation but to the experience of having breast cancer, uncertainty over the future, and the demanding schedule of daily treatments for five to six weeks. Patients often fear the side effects of radiation therapy and its overall effectiveness in preventing the return of their cancer.

D'haese *et al.* (2000) studied the effect of nursing consultation on anxiety, side effects, and self-care of patients receiving radiation therapy. The researchers concluded that nurses can have a positive impact on patient anxiety when education is provided before simulation. Braden *et al.* (1998) assessed self-help interventions through a self-help intervention project (SHIP) for women receiving breast cancer treatment. Women in this study were randomized to one of three intervention groups (self-help course, uncertainty management, or self-help course plus uncertainty management) or to a control group. The authors concluded that a large percentage of women with low resourcefulness who received no SHIP interventions experienced a decrease in self-care, self-help, confidence in cancer knowledge, and psychological adjustment over the time that they received adjuvant therapy.

During the course of treatment, some women may establish supportive relationships with other patients, often forming informal support groups in the waiting areas of the treatment facility. It is important to acknowledge the various emotional responses to the diagnosis of cancer as well as radiation therapy and to provide increased emotional support during this difficult time period. The nurse has a crucial role in assessing patient concerns, providing written and verbal patient education, and coordinating emotional care during and after treatment. Each patient should be given a list of department telephone numbers, including the number for the nurses' station where the patient can call and speak directly to a nurse with questions or concerns.

There may be an age-related difference in the emotional response to treatment. Studies have suggested that young women with breast cancer may be at a greater risk of emotional distress and may experience changes in quality of life and psychosocial adjustment as compared to their older counterparts (Dow & Lafferty, 2000).

Quality of life and psychosocial adjustment may decline during radiation treatment. Thus, it is important for the radiation oncology nurses to assess each patient's psychosocial status before treatment and regularly during treatment. The nurse is encouraged to suggest support groups, discussion groups, and available community resources, and to refer the patient for individual counseling whenever possible.

LATE EFFECTS OF TREATMENT

Fortunately, with advanced surgical and radiotherapeutic techniques, late side effects to radiation therapy are minimal. Late reactions to radiation therapy can include rib fractures, lymphedema, heart and lung effects (including fibrosis and pneumonitis), soft tissue fibrosis, and brachial plexopathy.

Rib Fracture.   Over the years, radiation to the ribcage can make the ribs slightly more likely to fracture. This occurs in fewer than 1% of women and usually happens only after a trauma, injury, or violent movement such as forceful coughing. Fortunately, a rib that fractures usually heals without the need for medical intervention.

Heart and Lung Effects.   In years past, women who received radiation therapy experienced a higher than expected level of cardiac complications. Today, major technological advances have resulted in fewer heart complications. The equipment used today can spare normal tissue from the effects of radiation.

Unfortunately, even with the state-of-the-art equipment, in some women a small part of the lung lies within the treatment field. Scar tissue can form in this small part of the lung in a small percentage of patients. Symptoms are uncommon but can include a dry cough and some shortness of breath. One percent of patients will experience pneumonitis that occurs usually 6 to 18 months after the completion of therapy. The symptoms include a low-grade fever, cough, and shortness of breath. The risk of pneumonitis is increased when the treatment field includes the supraclavicular region and axillary nodes and with concurrent chemotherapy.

Soft Tissue Fibrosis.   With skin-sparing techniques and moderate dose radiotherapy, soft tissue fibrosis is rarely seen. When present, the skin may feel hard with telangiectasia present. Telangiectasias are spiderlike, purple-red vessels in the treatment field that are a result of dilation of the capillaries and increased pressure of blood flowing through superficial vessels. Fibrotic changes in the skin reduce the skin's ability to respond to trauma or such elements as exposure to direct sunlight. Practitioners are encouraged to educate patients on protecting the irradiated skin from sun exposure with sunscreen products.

Brachial Plexopathy. Brachial plexus syndromes can be transient or progressive and irreversible. Signs and symptoms include mild discomfort in the shoulder and arm as well as paresthesias and weakness in the arm and hand. Even though brachial plexopathy is rare, it can occur as a result of radiation to the axilla and supraclavicular regions. Influencing factors include total dose and fractionation schedule. The practitioner must keep in mind that it is important to differentiate brachial plexopathy from disease progression. Once disease progression/tumor involvement is ruled out, treatment is aimed at relieving arm and hand discomfort.

REFERENCES

Asrari, F., & Gage, I. (1999). Radiation therapy in management of breast cancer. *Current Opinion in Oncology, 11*(6), 463–467.

Bartelink, H., Horiot, J., Poortmans, P., Struikmans, H., Van den Bogaert, W., Barillot, I., Fourquet, A., Borger, J., Jager, J., Hoogenraad, W., Collette, L., & Pierart, M. (2001). Recurrence rates after treatment of breast cancer with standard radiotherapy with or without additional radiation. *New England Journal of Medicine, 345*(19), 1378–1387.

Braden, C., Mishel, M., & Longman, A. (1998). Self-help interventions project. Women receiving breast cancer treatment. *Cancer Practice, 6*(2), 87–98.

Bucholz, T., Tucker, S., Masullo, L., Kuerer, H., Erwin, J., Salas, J., Frye, D., Stron, E., McNeese, M., Perkins, G., Katz, A., Singletary, S., Hung, K., Buzdar, A., & Hortobagi, G. (2002). Predictors of local–regional recurrence after neoadjuvant chemotherapy and mastectomy without radiation. *Journal of Clinical Oncology, 20*(1), 17–23.

Cheng, S., Jian, J., Chan, K., Tsai, S., Liu, M., & Chen, C. (1998). The benefit and risk of postmastectomy radiation therapy in patients with high-risk breast cancer. *American Journal of Clinical Oncology, 21*(1), 12–17.

Chow, E. (2002). Radiation treatment for breast cancer: recent advances. *Canadian Family Physician, 48,* 1065–1069.

Cope, D. (2002a). Elderly patients have same survival after breast-conserving treatment. *Oncology Nursing Forum, 28*(3), 456.

Cope, D. (2002b). New devices will reduce breast cancer radiotherapy time. *Clinical Journal of Oncology Nursing, 6*(4), 191–192.

Cox, J., & Winchester, D. (1992). Standards for breast conservation treatment. *CA—A Cancer Journal for Clinicians, 42,* 134–162.

Deutsch, M. (2002). Radiotherapy after lumpectomy for breast cancer in very old women. *American Journal of Clinical Oncology, 25*(1):48–49.

D'haese, S., Vinh-Hung, V., Bijdekerke, P., Spinnoy, M., De Beukeleer, M., Lochie, N., De Roover, P., & Storme, G. (2000). The effect of timing of the provision of information on anxiety and satisfaction of cancer patients receiving radiotherapy. *Journal of Cancer Education, 15*(4), 223–227.

Dow, K.H. (1998). *Contemporary issues in breast cancer.* Sudbury, Mass.: Jones & Bartlett.

Dow, K., & Lafferty, P. (2000). Quality of life, survivorship, and psychosocial adjustment of young women with breast cancer after breast-conserving surgery and radiation therapy. *Oncology Nursing Forum, 27*(10), 1555–1564.

Fisher, B., Anderson, S., Bryant, J., Margolese, R.G., Deutsch, M., Fisher, E.R., Jeong, J.H., & Wolmark, N. (2002). Twenty-year follow-up of a randomized trial comparing total mastectomy, lumpectomy, and lumpectomy plus irradiation for the treatment of invasive breast cancer. *New England Journal of Medicine, 347*(16), 1233–1241.

Fowble, B. (1997). Postmastectomy radiation: then and now. *Oncology, 11*(2), 213–234.

Graydon, J., Galloway, S., Palmer-Wickham, S., Harrison, D., Rich-van der Bij, L., West, P., Burlein-Hall, S., & Evans-Boyden, B. (1997). Information needs of women during early treatment for breast cancer. *Journal of Advanced Nursing, 26*(1), 59–64.

Harrison, D., Galloway, S., Graydon, J., Palmer-Wickham, S., & Rich-van der Bij, L. (1999). Information needs and preference for information of women with breast cancer over a first course of radiation therapy. *Patient Education and Counseling, 38*(3), 217–225.

Hiraoka, M., Mitsumori, M., & Shibuya, K. (2002). Adjuvant radiation therapy following mastectomy for breast cancer. *Breast Cancer, 9*(3), 190–195.

Kurtz, J.M. (1992). Radiation therapy and breast preservation: past achievements, current results, and future prospects. *Seminars in Surgical Oncology, 8*(3), 147–152.

Kuske, R. (1999). Adjuvant irradiation after mastectomy in women with one to three positive axillary nodes: then no; now yes. *Seminars in Radiation Oncology, 9*(3), 254–258.

Lichter, A., & Pierce, L. (2000). Techniques of radiation therapy. In J. Harris, M. Lippman, M. Morrow, & C. Osborne (Eds.), *Diseases of the breast, 2nd ed.,* pp. 589–598. Philadelphia: Lippincott Williams & Wilkins.

Mak, S., Molassiotis, A., Wan, W., Lee, I., & Chan, E. (2000). The effects of hydrocolloid dressing and gentian violet on radiation-induced moist desquamation wound healing. *Cancer Nursing, 23*(3), 220–229.

Marks, L., Hardenbergh, P., & Prosnitz, L. (1999). Mounting evidence for postmastectomy locoregional radiation therapy. *Oncology, 13*(8), 1123–1135.

Marks, L. & Prosnitz, L. (1997). "One to three" or "four or more"? Selecting patients for postmastectomy radiation therapy. *Cancer, 79*(4), 668–670.

Mazanec, S. (1997). Breast cancer. In K.H. Dow, J. Bucholtz, R, Iwamoto, V. Fieler, & L Hilderley. *Nursing Care in Radiation Oncology, 2nd ed.,* pp. 101–135. Philadelphia: W.B. Saunders.

Metz, J., Schultz, D., Fox, K., Glick, J., & Solin, L. (1999). Long-term outcome after postmastectomy radiation therapy for breast cancer patients at high risk for local–regional recurrence. *Cancer Journal from Scientific American, 5*(2), 77–83.

Morrow, M. (1999). Postmastectomy radiation therapy: a surgical perspective. *Seminars in Radiation Oncology, 9*(3), 269–274.

Morrow, M., Strom, E.A., Bassett, L.W., Dershaw, D.D., Fowble, B., Giuliano, A., Harris, J.R., O'Malley, F., Schnitt, S.J., Singletary, S.E., Winchester, D.P. (2002). Standard for breast conservation therapy in the management of invasive breast carcinoma. *CA—A Cancer Journal for Clinicians, 52*(5); 277–300.

National Institutes of Health. (2000). NIH Consensus Development Conference Statement on Adjuvant Therapy for Breast Cancer. Retrieved November 3, 2000, from: *http://consensus.nih.gov.*

Olsen, D., Raub, W., Bradley, C., Johnson, M., Macias, J., Love, V., & Markoe, A. (2001). The effect of aloe vera gel/mild soap versus mild soap alone in preventing reactions in patients undergoing radiation therapy. *Oncology Nursing Forum, 28*(3), 543–547.

O'Rourke, N., & Robinson, L. (1996). Breast cancer and the role of radiation therapy. In K.H. Dow (Ed.), *Contemporary issues in breast cancer*, pp. 43–58. Sudbury, Mass.: Jones & Bartlett.

Park, C.C., Mitsumori, M., Nixon, A., Recht, A., Connolly, J., Gelman, R., Silver, B., Hetelekidis, S., Abner, A., Harris, J.R., Schnitt, S.J. (2000). Outcome at 8 years after breast-conserving surgery and radiation therapy for invasive breast cancer: influence of margin status and systemic therapy on local recurrence. *Journal of Clinical Oncology, 18*(8): 1668–1675.

Polednak, A. (2002). Trends in, and predictors of, breast-conserving surgery and radiotherapy for breast cancer in connecticut, 1988–1997. *International Journal of Radiation Oncology, 53*(1), 157–163.

Roy, I., Fortin, A., & Larochelle, M. (2001). The impact of skin washing with water and soap during breast irradiation: a randomized study. *Radiotherapy and Oncology, 58*(3), 333–339.

Smith, M., Casey, L., Johnson, D., Gwede, C., & Riggin, O.Z. (2001). Music as a therapeutic intervention for anxiety in patients receiving radiation therapy. *Oncology Nursing Forum, 28*(5), 855–862.

Strohl, R. (1998). The nursing role in radiation oncology: symptom management of acute and chronic reactions. *Oncology Nursing Forum, 15*(4), 429–434.

Timothy, S., Teng, S., Stoiler, A., Bolton, J., & Fuhrman, G. (2002). Postmastectomy radiation in patients with four or more positive nodes. *American Surgeon, 68*(6), 539–544.

Vallia, K., Pintile, M., Chong, N., Holowaty, E., Douglas, P., Kirkbride, P., & Wielgoze, A. (2002). Assessment of coronary heart disease morbidity and mortality after radiation therapy for early breast cancer. *Journal of Clinical Oncology, 20*(4), 1036–1042.

Wengstrom, Y., Haggmark, C., Strander, H., & Forsberg, C. (1999). Effects of a nursing intervention on subjective distress, side effects, and quality of life of breast cancer patients receiving curative radiation therapy—a randomized study. *Acta Oncologica, 38*(6), 763–770.

Winer, E., Morrow, M., Osborne, C., & Harris, J. (2001). Cancer of the breast. In V. DeVita, S. Hellman, & S. Rosenberg (Eds.), *Cancer: principles and practice of oncology, 6th ed.,* pp. 1633–1717, Philadelphia: Lippincott Williams & Wilkins.

Wong, J.S., Harris, J.R. (2001). Importance of local tumour control in breast cancer. *Lancet Oncology, 2*(1), 11–17.

Chapter 9

ADJUVANT THERAPY

PATRICIA I. GEDDIE, RN, MS, AOCN

INTRODUCTION

Adjuvant chemotherapy is defined as the administration of cytotoxic chemotherapy or the use of ablative or additive endocrine therapy after primary surgery of breast cancer to kill or inhibit clinically occult micrometastases (Osborne & Ravdin, 2000). Over the last 25 to 30 years, there have been major changes in the use of adjuvant therapy for early-stage breast cancer. In the 1970s, only women with positive nodes received adjuvant therapy until a series of published trials indicated that women with node-negative disease can benefit from adjuvant therapy (Mansour *et al.*, 1989). In the 1980s, doxorubicin-based chemotherapy trials showed an improved survival advantage. In the 1990s, high-dose chemotherapy with autologous bone marrow transplantation, neoadjuvant chemotherapy, and taxanes became available.

Today, the vast array of treatment options available and the factors that determine appropriate treatment can be confusing and overwhelming to the patient. In addition, the public can easily access a variety of information sources, but they may not be adequately prepared to interpret the implications, risks, and benefits. An important role of the oncology nurse and the oncology team is to assist the patient in making an informed decision. The oncology nurse often serves as the patient's advocate and, in doing so, must have a comprehensive understanding of and access to information about available treatment options, treatment goals, and clinical trials available.

The purpose of this chapter is to describe the current adjuvant therapy and targeted therapy regimens, discuss the sequencing of chemotherapy, and describe support for decision-making.

NIH CONSENSUS DEVELOPMENT CONFERENCE STATEMENT ON ADJUVANT THERAPY

Given the many adjuvant therapies, the National Institutes of Health (NIH) convened a Consensus Development Conference on Breast Cancer to evaluate the scientific data

(NIH, 2000). The Statement on Adjuvant Therapy was prepared by a panel representing a variety of fields, including medicine, surgery, epidemiology, public health, statistics, clinical trials, and other oncology fields, to give health care providers, patients, and the general public a current consensus on the use of adjuvant therapy for breast cancer (NIH, 2000). Table 9.1 provides a summary of findings related to adjuvant therapy.

PROGNOSTIC AND PREDICTIVE FACTORS USED TO SELECT ADJUVANT THERAPY

Prognostic and predictive factors are used to determine whether patients are candidates for adjuvant therapy. The most commonly used prognostic factors are TNM staging and hormone receptor status. Prognostic indicators help determine the risk of recurrence. Predictive factors help to select the most effective therapy for reducing that risk (Pritchard, 2002). Any factor has the potential to be both prognostic and predictive, and a factor's importance depends on both the clinical end point and the method of treatment comparison (NIH, 2000).

The College of American Pathologists ranked prognostic factors according to categories:

- *Category I* factors have demonstrated prognostic importance and usefulness in clinical management. These factors include information about TMN staging, histologic grading, histologic type, mitotic figure counts, and hormone receptor status. (See Chapter 5 for more discussion on Category I factors.)
- *Category II* factors have been extensively studied but remain to be statistically validated. These factors include HER-2/neu, proliferation markers, lymphatic and vascular invasion, and p53.
- *Category III* factors are less well studied and include DNA ploidy, microvessel density, EGFR, TGF-alpha, bcl-2, pS2, and cathepsin D (Fitzgibbons *et al.,* 2000).

Table 9.1 Summary of NIH Consensus Development Conference Statement on Adjuvant Therapy for Breast Cancer

- Chemotherapy shows an improvement in both relapse-free survival and overall survival in premenopausal and postmenopausal women (in ages up to 70 years) regardless of node status.
- Adjuvant polychemotherapy is indicated for breast cancers larger than 1 cm in diameter regardless of nodal, menopausal, or hormonal status.
- A small but statistically significant improvement in survival is reported in women who received anthracycline-containing regimens.
- Survival outcomes are not improved in dose-dense chemotherapy regimens (e.g., high-dose chemotherapy with peripheral stem cell support) compared with standard polychemotherapy. Dose-dense chemotherapy regimens should be offered within the setting of a randomized clinical trial.
- Taxanes, such as paclitaxel and docetaxel, are being investigated in the adjuvant treatment of women with node-positive, localized disease. The use of taxanes for treatment in women with node-negative disease should be restricted to randomized clinical trials.

Prognostic and predictive factors can also be divided into three areas: patient characteristics, disease characteristics, and biomarkers. The accepted prognostic and predictive factors are those that have been evaluated in well-designed clinical studies. These factors include age, tumor size, axillary node status, histologic tumor type, standardized pathologic grade, and hormonal receptor status (NIH, 2000). The following is a general discussion about prognostic and predictive factors used to help in decision-making about treatment.

PATIENT CHARACTERISTICS

Age. About 77% of all cancers are diagnosed at age 55 years and older. The risk of developing breast cancer increases with age, peaking at 75 years (ACS, 2002). Age alone is not predictive of response and overall outcome in otherwise healthy older patients. Comorbidities commonly found in older patients, such as cardiovascular disease and renal insufficiency, contribute to the severity of toxicity and decreased tolerability of treatment. The evidence to date suggests that the benefits and toxic effects of chemotherapy in otherwise healthy older patients are comparable to those in younger patients (Early Breast Cancer Trialists' Collaborative Group, 1998; Extermann *et al.,* 2000). The pathologic changes associated with chronic disease and disability are the main determinants of outcome, rather than the physiologic changes associated with aging (Balducci, 2001). Most large clinical trials have set an upper age limit for eligibility, often 65 or 70 years, because of risk for cardiomyopathy and less tolerance for side effects (Hutchins *et al.,* 1999). The NIH Consensus Development Conference Statement suggests that women with node-positive and node-negative disease up to the age of 70 years should be offered chemotherapy.

Race. Race is considered a prognostic factor only. Caucasian women have a higher incidence (115.5/100,000) than African American (101.5/100,000), Asian/Pacific Islander (78.1/100,000), American Indian/Alaskan Native (50.5/100,000), or Hispanic (68.5) women.

African American women have a higher mortality rate (31.0/100,000) than Caucasian (24.3/100,000), Hispanic (14.8/100,000), American Indian/Alaskan Native (12.4/100,000), or Asian/Pacific Islander (11.0/100,000) women (ACS, 2002). African American women who develop breast cancer are generally younger and have larger tumors at diagnosis, and a smaller percentage have hormone receptors in their tumor tissue. These factors contribute to a poorer prognosis.

In cases of similar clinical presentation, however, adjuvant treatment confers similar benefits to African American and Caucasian women (English *et al.,* 2002). Research on the benefits and risks of adjuvant therapy in Hispanic, Asian, and Native American women is continuing (Boyer-Chammard *et al.,* 1999).

DISEASE CHARACTERISTICS

Size of Tumor. Patients with tumor sizes of 2 cm or smaller generally have a better prognosis than those with tumors 3–5 cm or larger. Recurrence rates are greatly increased in tumor sizes 3 cm or more. As tumor size increases, survival decreases regardless of lymph node status (Carter *et al.*, 1989).

Histologic Tumor Type. Infiltrating ductal carcinoma is the most common histologic type, accounting for 75% of breast cancer diagnoses. Axillary lymph nodes are often involved, which carries a poorer prognosis. Other potential metastatic sites include bone, lung, liver, and brain. Infiltrating lobular carcinoma also carries a poor prognosis and occurs approximately 5–10% of the time. Axillary lymph nodes are a common site of metastasis. Tubular (2%), medullary (5–7%), and mucinous (3%) histologies are less common and carry a more favorable prognosis with less common lymph node involvement.

Axillary Nodal Status and Pathologic Grade. Women with node-positive disease are more likely to experience recurrence than women with node-negative disease. Lymph node status serves as an indicator of the tumor's ability to spread (Carter *et al.*, 1989). With both large and small tumors, the rate of recurrence increases with the number of lymph nodes involved, especially with 10 or more positive lymph nodes. Well-differentiated (grade I) tumors tend to have a better prognosis because they generally have lower mitotic counts and low S-phase fraction.

BIOMARKERS

Hormone Receptor Status. Normal breast cells have hormone receptors that respond to estrogen and progesterone stimulus. Well-differentiated breast tumor cells will retain the estrogen and progesterone receptors and demonstrate a better response to hormone manipulation therapy. Women who are postmenopausal generally have positive estrogen receptors, but premenopausal women generally have negative estrogen receptors.

Mitotic Rate. The S-phase fraction is a measurement of the proliferative activity of a tumor. Estrogen receptor-negative tumors tend to have a high S-phase fraction, which indicates a more aggressive metastatic potential. Ploidy analysis is a measurement of the DNA content of tumor cells. Normal cell DNA is diploid, having two sets of chromosomes. Tumors that have an abnormal amount of DNA are aneuploid.

ADJUVANT CHEMOTHERAPY REGIMENS

POLYCHEMOTHERAPY

Cyclophosphamide, methotrexate, and 5-fluorouracil (CMF) was the first polychemotherapy regimen with a demonstrated track record in the adjuvant setting. This combination showed an improvement in both disease-free and overall survival in early breast cancer and was superior to single agent therapy.

Anthracyclines, such as doxorubicin, were also used increasingly in the adjuvant setting. However, the risk of cardiotoxicities is of concern, particularly for the older patient.

Threshold doses and therapeutic effects for doxorubicin are 60 mg/m² and cyclophosphamide at 600 mg/m². In patients without significant preexisting cardiac disease, standard cumulative doses of anthracyclines show no evidence of excessive cardiac toxicity. For patients who have a low risk of recurrence (i.e., node-negative with positive hormone receptors) or a high risk of cardiotoxicity, or previously received anthracyclines for another cancer, CMF is generally recommended (Lohrisch *et al.*, 2001). For patients with a higher risk of recurrence, more dose-intensive anthracycline-based chemotherapy, such as CAF and CEF, has been shown to be superior to CMF in terms of relapse-free survival. Table 9.2 outlines the different adjuvant chemotherapy regimens for both node-negative and node-positive breast cancer.

Treatment regimens with CMF ranged initially from 8 to 24 months. Further studies demonstrated that 4 to 6 courses of therapy provided optimal benefit. Additional therapy did not provide additional benefit and increased the potential for toxicity. Four cycles of doxorubicin and cyclophosphamide (AC) or epirubicin and cyclophosphamide (EC) are found to be equivalent to CMF. (Fisher *et al.*, 1990).

There is currently no convincing evidence to demonstrate that more dose-dense or dose-intensive treatment regimens (high-dose chemotherapy with peripheral stem cell support) result in improved outcomes compared to standard dose levels of polychemotherapy. Stem cell-supported treatment strategies are not recommended outside of a randomized clinical trial.

TAXANES IN THE ADJUVANT SETTING

The taxanes initially showed effectiveness equal to or greater than standard drugs in the treatment of advanced breast cancer. In 1991 and 1996, published studies demonstrated the effectiveness of paclitaxel in the treatment of metastatic breast cancer (Holmes *et al.*, 1991;

Table 9.2 Adjuvant Chemotherapy Regimens

Node-negative disease

- Cyclophosphamide, methotrexate, and 5-fluorouracil (CMF)
- Fluorouracil, doxorubicin, and cyclophosphamide (FAC/CAF)
- Doxorubicin and cyclophosphamide (AC)

Node-positive disease

- Fluorouracil, doxorubicin, and cyclophosphamide (FAC/CAF)
- Cyclophosphamide, epirubicin, and fluorouracil (CEF)
- Doxorubicin and cyclophosphamide (AC)
- AC followed by paclitaxel
- Doxorubicin followed by CMF
- CMF
- Epirubicin and cyclophosphamide (EC)

Nabholtz *et al.*, 1996). The taxanes have demonstrated high activity in metastatic breast cancer and non-cross-resistance with anthracyclines (Henderson *et al.*, 1998). Their use in the adjuvant setting is undergoing continued study (Nabholtz & Riva, 2001; Norton, 2001).

The Cancer and Leukemia Group B (CALGB-9344) randomized study of node-positive patients comparing AC alone to AC followed by paclitaxel showed that the sequential use of AC plus paclitaxel resulted in more than 20% improvement of recurrence-free and overall survival (FDA, 1999). The early results of this study led to FDA approval of paclitaxil in the adjuvant setting. The use of AC with or without sequential paclitaxel is now standard therapy in node-positive disease. There has been no evidence to support adding taxanes to AC in node-negative disease.

Further study in CALBG-9741 compares the benefit of AC for three weeks followed by paclitaxel with the same drugs at higher doses over a two-week period with colony-stimulating factor support. The question is whether the longer duration of treatment versus the addition of paclitaxel is the reason for the significant improvement (Henderson *et al.*, 1998). Further studies need to be conducted to determine benefit of duration of treatment versus the use of new agents. Also, long-term follow-up data for the CALGB-9741 trial is yet to be confirmed.

CHEMOTHERAPEUTIC AGENTS AND SIDE EFFECT PROFILE

The following is a discussion of the common chemotherapy agents used in the adjuvant setting. They include cyclophosphamide, methotrexate, 5-fluorouracil, doxorubicin, epirubicin, paclitaxel, and docetaxel.

Cyclophosphamide is an alkylating agent that causes cross-linking of DNA strands, thus preventing DNA synthesis and cell division. Dosages range from 600 mg/m^2 IV every 21 days or 100 mg/m^2 PO on day 1 through 14 of a 28-day cycle. Common toxicities include nausea and vomiting, alopecia, urotoxicity (including potential for hemorrhagic cystitis) and myelosuppression.

Methotrexate is an antimetabolite (folic acid antagonist) that blocks the enzyme dihydrofolate reductase (DHFR), which inhibits conversion of folic acid to tetrahydrofolic acid, resulting in depletion of critical reduced folates. It also inhibits the precursors of DNA, RNA, and cellular proteins. Dosage ranges are 40 mg/m^2 IV on day 1 and 8 of a 28-day cycle or 40 mg/m^2 IV every 21 days. Side effects include stomatitis (mild to severe), diarrhea, and nausea and vomiting.

5-fluorouracil is a pyrimidine antimetabolite that inhibits the formation of thymidine synthetase (enzyme) needed for DNA synthesis. Dosage ranges from 500 mg/m^2 IV every 21 days or 600 mg/m^2 IV on days 1 and 8 of a 28-day cycle. Side effects include neutropenia and thrombocytopenia; photosensitivity; darkening of skin, veins, and nails; alopecia; and nausea and vomiting (moderate).

Doxorubicin is an anthracycline that binds directly to the DNA base pairs and inhibits DNA and RNA synthesis. Dosage ranges are 60–75 mg/m^2 IV every 21 days or

30 mg/m^2 IV on day 1 and 8 of a 28-day cycle. Doxorubicin has a maximum cumulative lifetime dose of 550 mg/m^2 or less than 400 mg/m^2 if patients have received prior cardiotoxic drug regimens or chest irradiation. Careful observation and monitoring of IV administration (especially peripheral) is recommended because of the vesicant effects if doxorubicin becomes infiltrated. Side effects include cardiotoxicity, nausea and vomiting, myelosuppression, alopecia, and stomatitis.

Epirubicin (EPI) is a doxorubicin analogue that inhibits topoisomerase II by forming a cleavable complex with topoisomerase II and DNA. Dosage ranges are 100–120 mg/m^2 IV every 21 days or 70–90 mg/m^2 IV every 21 days in heavily pretreated patients. An alternative schedule is 12–25 mg/m^2 IV on a weekly basis to decrease the risk of cardiotoxicity. EPI has a higher lifetime cumulative dosage than doxorubicin: 900–1000 mg/m^2. Careful observation and monitoring of IV administration (especially peripheral) is recommended because of the vesicant effects if infiltrated. Toxicities include dose-limiting myelosuppression, nausea and vomiting (common), stomatitis, alopecia, cardiotoxicity, and diarrhea.

Paclitaxel is a taxane, an antimicrotubule agent that enhances the formation and stabilization of microtubules, thereby inhibiting mitotic spindle apparatus and preventing mitosis and cell division. Dosage ranges are 175 mg/m^2 as a 3-hour infusion every 21 days or 80-100 mg/m^2 as a 1-hour infusion every week for 3 weeks with a 1-week rest. Patients receive premedication with dexamethasone 20 mg PO or IV 12 hours and 6 hours prior to IV administration, and diphenhydramine 50 mg IV and cimetadine 300 mg IV 30 minutes prior to IV administration to prevent or reduce the potential for hypersensitivity reaction.

Hypersensitivity reactions can occur within seconds to minutes of the start of paclitaxel infusion and usually occur within the first 10 minutes. Vital signs monitoring is recommended every 15 minutes for the first hour of infusion followed by every 30 minutes in the second hour of infusion. Paclitaxel is formulated in Cremophor EL™ that will cause polyvinylchloride (PVC) from the IV tubing and bag to leach into the infusion fluid. Thus, this agent is administered in either glass or polyolefin containers using a 0.22 micron filter and polyethylene-lined IV administration sets.

Toxicities include dose-limiting neutropenia, mucositis, and neurotoxicity. Frequent side effects are myalgias, arthralgias, and alopecia (including total body). Less common side effects are thrombocytopenia, anemia, nausea, vomiting, diarrhea, and hypersensitivity reaction.

Docetaxel is a semisynthetic taxane that acts by inhibiting mitotic spindle apparatus by enhanced formation and stabilization of microtubules. Dosage ranges from 60 to 100 mg/m^2 as a 1-hour infusion every 21 days. Docetaxel is associated with potential for severe hypersensitivity reaction, including flushing, hypotension, and dyspnea. Patients are premedicated with dexamethasone 8 mg PO twice a day for 3 days starting the day before docetaxel treatment. This agent is administered only in glass or polypropylene bottles or in polypropylene or polyolefin plastic bags for infusion with polyethylene-lined IV administration sets. Toxicities include dose-limiting myelosuppression and hypersensitivity (less common).

SEQUENCING OF ADJUVANT CHEMOTHERAPY

The optimal sequencing of adjuvant chemotherapy with surgery and radiation therapy is the subject of ongoing investigation. However, there are various benefits and drawbacks with the different sequencing, discussed in the following section.

NEOADJUVANT CHEMOTHERAPY

Neoadjuvant chemotherapy refers to chemotherapy administered prior to primary therapy such as surgery. There are several potential advantages and disadvantages of neoadjuvant chemotherapy. Neoadjuvant chemotherapy may be used as a measurement of the response as determined by tumor size pre-and postchemotherapy, for early detection of resistance and sensitivity, and to shrink large tumors prior to surgery. The largest benefit to neoadjuvant chemotherapy may be in patients who present with inoperable, locally advanced breast cancer. These patients may have good tumor response and reduction from neoadjuvant chemotherapy, allowing for less extensive surgery.

One disadvantage of preoperative chemotherapy is the potential for an inadequate biopsy sample size through such techniques as a fine-needle aspiration or core biopsy, which would have otherwise been obtained at complete surgical removal. DNA flow cytometry, receptor status, and other markers and prognostic factors are more difficult to analyze with smaller specimens. An accurate estimate of axillary node status may not be determined prior to administration of preoperative chemotherapy. Although tumors may respond and may be downstaged preoperatively, this has not resulted in improved disease-free and overall survival. Residual disease at tumor margins and local recurrence are potential problems. Moreover, longer follow-up is necessary to assess control of the disease.

PERIOPERATIVE CHEMOTHERAPY

Perioperative adjuvant therapy refers to chemotherapy administered at the time of or just after surgery. Advantages are primarily theory-based and have not significantly been proven in clinical studies (Ludwig Breast Cancer Study Group, 1988). Tumor cells that may be dislodged at the time of surgery may benefit from perioperative chemotherapy. Because chemotherapy is more effective when the cells are in the process of synthesis and proliferation, surgical removal of the primary tumor causes micrometastasis to be more vulnerable to the effects of chemotherapy. Also, the potential for spontaneous drug resistance can be offset by exposing tumor cells to chemotherapy immediately after surgery. One limitation of perioperative chemotherapy is a modest improvement in disease-free survival but not in overall survival (Clahsen *et al.,* 1997).

FUTURE DIRECTIONS

Fewer than 3% of adult patients are participating in clinical trials in the United States. Increased efforts for patient and physician participation are ongoing. Further studies of several areas require exploration: the role of taxanes and high-dose chemotherapy, variations in current dose and schedules, clinical and biologic predictive factors, elderly patients (older than 70 years of age), biological agents, and the role of bisphosphonates as well as newer chemotherapeutic agents.

The taxane paclitaxel has shown promising results in early studies. Long-term follow-up is needed to determine the duration of the results as well as the potential for cardiac toxicities when combined with anthracyclines (Perez, 2001). Another taxane, docetaxel, is being investigated for its role in adjuvant regimens in combination with cyclophosphamide or following standard doxorubicin and cyclophosphamide (AC) therapy.

High-dose chemotherapy study results have not been promising, although future trials are aimed at new agents, combination, and repetitive cycles of therapy. Other chemotherapy trials are evaluating the role of administering individual chemotherapy agents at full dose in a sequential fashion in comparison with combination therapy.

Bisphosphonates such as pamidronate and, more recently, zolendronate inhibit bone reabsorption and release of growth factors, thereby reducing bone metastasis (Mundy & Yoneda, 1998). Further studies are investigating the utilization of well-designed studies to predict the value of treatment with standardized protocols. These studies will require sufficient statistical power to point out clinically important differences.

The lysosomal enzyme cathepsin D, which is synthesized in normal tissues, is also being evaluated. Its activity may be overexpressed and secreted in certain node-negative breast cancers and appears to have a direct role in invasion and metastasis. The use of this predictive factor is not yet a part of clinical practice (Rochefort *et al.*, 1990; Isola *et al.*, 1993).

The inclusion of elderly patients above the age of 70 years is an area of research that is underdeveloped and requires further study.

TARGETED THERAPY

Antineoplastic chemotherapy affects cells particularly in the stages of DNA synthesis and division. Unfortunately, both normal cells and cancer cells undergo the process of DNA synthesis and division, and anticancer chemotherapy does not differentiate between the two. Damage to normal cells from chemotherapeutic agents results in unwanted and sometimes fatal and dose-limiting side effects such as myelosuppression. To have therapies that will selectively target malignant cells offers the advantage for more aggressive treatment without potentially limiting side effects and toxicities.

HER-2 is a gene that encodes the growth factor receptor (Slamon *et al.*, 1989). HER-2 is amplified and overexpressed in 25–30% of patients with breast cancer. HER-2 overexpression is associated with poorer survival. Trastuzumab is a humanized version of the murine monoclonal antibody 4D5 that was approved for the treatment of advanced breast cancer that overexpresses the HER-2/neu oncogene (Nabholtz & Slamon, 2001).

Its mechanism of action inhibits signal transduction from growth factors that stimulate cell proliferation. Ongoing studies will help determine whether HER-2 overexpression should influence the choice of adjuvant cytotoxic therapy.

SUPPORT FOR DECISION-MAKING

The risk of recurrence after local therapy weighed against the benefit versus toxicity from adjuvant therapy requires a collaborative decision-making process involving the health care provider and the patient (Loprinzi & Thome, 2001). Today's health care consumer is more discriminating and is actively seeking information about treatment options. Support for decision-making is important not only at the initial time of planning but throughout the treatment process, rehabilitation, and survivorship. Patients must rely on their health care providers to be their guide, interpreter, and advocate regarding the decisions about adjuvant chemotherapy. Clarifying concerns, expectations, and goals is essential for assisting patients in making a truly informed decision. Health care providers should help the patient evaluate potential and actual risks and benefits of the therapy and how it may impact quality of life, including short-term or long-term lifestyle alterations. The patient's understanding of side effects, both potential and expected, as well as the support available for prevention and management are critical to the overall outcome of therapy.

Patient education must be available in a variety of venues and individualized according to the patient's needs. Teaching methods include verbal interaction, reading, video and audio tapes, and Web sites. Since the Internet contains many sites that provide both credible and unreliable information, patients benefit from assistance in finding sites that are recognized as reputable and approved. There are a multitude of reliable patient educational sources available through the American Cancer Society, the National Cancer Institute, and the Oncology Nursing Society, as well as pharmaceutical and other product companies. Many of the materials are at minimal or no cost. Decision aids improve patients' knowledge about treatment options, reduce anxiety, and enhance comfort with choices to stimulate a more active role in joint decision-making.

SUMMARY

Adjuvant therapy for breast cancer has undergone many significant changes over the past 25 years. Treatments have led to improved disease-free and overall survival, and adjuvant chemotherapy clearly has reduced mortality. Benefits are seen in women with pre-and postmenopausal breast cancer, and in all patients regardless of nodal and ER status. Dose intensity, dose density, and high-dose therapy have not shown effectiveness to date, but further trials are being conducted. The role of taxanes and bisphosphonates has been further elucidated, with follow-up studies in progress. The potential role of trastuzumab as adjuvant therapy is also being evaluated. The long-term side effects of adjuvant therapy show that the risks may outweigh the benefits in subsets of patients who have small tumors, good prognostic features, or favorable histologic subtypes.

REFERENCES

American Cancer Society. (1999). *Operational Statement on Complementary and Alternative Methods of Cancer Management.* Atlanta, Ga.: Author.

American Cancer Society. (2002). *Cancer Facts and Figures.* Atlanta, Ga.: Author.

Balducci, L. (2001). The geriatric cancer patient: equal benefit from equal treatment. *Cancer Control: Journal of the Moffitt Cancer Center, 8*(2), 2–24.

Boyer-Chammard, A., Taylor, T.H., & Anton-Culver, H. (1999). Survival differences in breast cancer among racial/ethnic groups: a population-based study. *Cancer Detection & Prevention, 23*(6), 463–473.

Carter, C.L., Allen, C., & Henson, D.E. (1989). Relation of tumor size, lymph node status, and survival in 24,740 breast cancer cases. *Cancer, 63*(1), 181–187.

Clahsen, P.C., van de Velde, C.J., Goldhirsch, A., Rossbach, J., Sertoli, M.R., Bijnens, L., & Sylvester, R.J. (1997). Overview of randomized perioperative polychemotherapy trials in women in early-stage breast cancer. *Journal of Clinical Oncology, 15,* 2526–2535.

Early Breast Cancer Trialists' Collaborative Group. (1992). Systemic treatment of early breast cancer by hormonal, systemic or immune therapy: 133 randomized trials involving 31,000 recurrences and 24,000 deaths among 75,000 women. *Lancet, 339,* 71–85.

Early Breast Cancer Trialists' Collaborative Group. (1995). Effects of radiotherapy and surgery in early breast cancer: an overview of the randomized trials. *New England Journal of Medicine, 333,* 1444–1455.

Early Breast Cancer Trialists' Collaborative Group. (1998). Polychemotherapy for early breast cancer: an overview of the randomized trials. *Lancet, 352,* 930–942.

Early Breast Cancer Trialists' Collaborative Group. (2000, September 21–23). *Analysis overview results.* Presented at the Fifth Meeting of the Early Breast Cancer Trialists' Collaborative Group, Oxford, United Kingdom.

English, W.P., Cleveland, K.E., & Barber, W.H. (2002). There is no difference in survival between African-American and white women with breast cancer. *American Surgeon, 68*(6), 594–597.

Extermann, M., Balducci, L., & Lyman, G.H. (2000). What threshold for adjuvant therapy in older breast cancer patients? *Journal of Clinical Oncology, 18*(18), 1709–1717.

Fisher, B., Brown, A.M., Dimitrov, N.V., Poisson, R., Redmond, C., Margolese, R.G., Bowman, D., Wolmark, N., Wickerham, D.L., Kardinal, C.G., *et al.* (1990). Two months of doxorubicin-cyclophosphamide with and without interval reinduction therapy compared with six months of cyclophosphamide, methotrexate, and fluorouracil and positive-node breast cancer patients with tamoxifen-nonresponsive tumors: results from the National Surgical Adjuvant Breast and Bowel Project B-15. *Journal of Clinical Oncology, 8,* 1483–1496.

Fitzgibbons, P.L., Page, D.L., Weaver, D., Thor, A.D., Allred, D.C., Clark, G.M., Ruby, S.G., O'Malley, F., Simpson, J.F., Connolly, J.L., Hayes, D.F., Edge, S.B., Lichter, A., & Schnitt, S.J. (2000). Prognostic factors in breast cancer. College of American Pathologists Consensus Statement 1999. *Archives of Pathology & Laboratory Medicine, 124*(7), 966–978.

Food and Drug Administration. (1999). *CALGB-9344.* Presented at a Food and Drug Administration hearing in September 1999.

Henderson, I.C., Berry, D., Demtri, C., et al. (1998). Improved disease-free survival (DFS) and overall survival (OS) from the addition of sequential paclitaxel (T), but not from the escalation of doxorubicin (A) dose level in the adjuvant chemotherapy of patients (PTS) with node-positive primary breast cancer (BC). *Proceedings of the American Society of Clinical Oncology, 17,* 101a.

Holmes, F.A., Walters, R.S., Theriault, R.L., Forman, A.D., Newton, L.K., Raber, M.N., Buzdar, A.U., Frye, D.K., & Hortobagyi, G.N. (1991). Phase II trial of TAXOL, an active drug in the treatment of metastatic breast cancer. *Journal of the National Cancer Institute, 83*(24), 1797–1805.

Hutchins, L.F., Unger, J.M., Crowley, J.J., Coltman, C.A. Jr., & Albain, K.S. (1999). Underrepresentation of patients 65 years of age or older in cancer-treatment trials. *New England Journal of Medicine, 341*(27), 2061–2067.

Isola, J., Weitz, S., Visakorpi, T., Holli, K., Shea, R., Khabbaz, N., & Kallioniemi, O.P. (1993). Cathepsin D expression detected by immunohistochemistry has independent prognostic value in axillary node-negative breast cancer. *Journal of Clinical Oncology, 11,* 36–43.

Lohrisch, C., Di Leo, A., & Piccart, M.J. (2001). Optimal adjuvant cytotoxic therapy for breast cancer. In *American Society of Clinical Oncology 2001 Educational Book,* pp. 61–70. Philadelphia: Lippincott Williams & Wilkins.

Loprinzi, C.L., & Thome, S.D. (2001). Understanding the utility of adjuvant systemic therapy for primary breast cancer. *Journal of Clinical Oncology, 19*(4), 972–979.

Ludwig Breast Cancer Study Group. (1988). Combination adjuvant chemotherapy for node-positive breast cancer: inadequacy of a single perioperative cycle. *New England Journal of Medicine, 319,* 677–683.

Mansour, E.G., Gray, R., Shatila, A.H., Osborne, C.K., Tormey, D.C., Gilchrist, K.W., Cooper, M.R., & Falkson, G. (1989). Efficacy of adjuvant chemotherapy in high-risk node-negative breast cancer intergroup study. *New England Journal of Medicine, 320*(8), 485–490.

Mundy, G.R., & Yoneda, T. (1998). Bisphosphonates as anticancer drugs. *New England Journal of Medicine, 339,* 398–400.

Nabholtz, J.M., Gelmon, K., Bontenbal, M., Spielmann, M., Catimel, G., Conte, P., Klaassen, U., Namer, M., Bonneterre, J., Fumoleau, P., Winograd, B. (1996). Multicenter, randomized comparative study of two doses of paclitaxel in patients with metastatic breast cancer. *Journal of Clinical Oncology. 14*(6): 1858–1867.

Nabholtz, J.M., & Riva, A. (2001). Taxane/anthracycline combinations: setting a new standard in breast cancer. *The Oncologist, 6*(3), 5–12.

Nabholtz, J., & Slamon, D. (2001). New adjuvant strategies for breast cancer. Meeting the challenge of integrating chemotherapy and trastuzumab (Herceptin). *Seminars in Oncology, 118*(3), 1–12.

National Institutes of Health. (2000, November). *NIH Consensus Development Conference Statement on Adjuvant Therapy for Breast Cancer.* Retrieved November 1, 2000, from *http://consensus.nih.gov/cons/114/114_intro.htm.*

Norton, L. (2001). Theoretical concepts and the emerging role of taxanes in adjuvant therapy. *The Oncologist, 6*(3), 30–35.

Nunes, R.A., & Harris, L.N. (2002). The HER2 extracellular domain as a prognostic and predictive factor in breast cancer (review). *Clinical Breast Cancer, 3*(2), 125–135.

Osborne, C.K., & Ravdin, P.M. (2000). Adjuvant systemic therapy of primary breast cancer. In J.R. Harris, M. Lippman, M. Morrow, & C.K. Osborne (Eds.), *Disease of the breast, 2nd ed.,* pp. 599–632. Philadelphia: Lippincott Williams & Wilkins.

Perez, E. (2001). Doxorubicin and paclitaxel in the treatment of advanced breast cancer: efficacy and cardiac considerations. *Cancer Investigation, 19,* 155–164.

Pritchard, K.I. (2002). Controversies in adjuvant systemic therapy: predictive markers in the selection of optimal systemic therapy. In *American Society of Clinical Oncology 2002 Educational Book.* Available at *www.asco.org.*

Rochefort, H., Capony, F., & Garcia, M. (1990). Cathepsin D in breast cancer: from molecular and cellular biology to clinical application. *Cancer Cells, 2,* 383–388.

Slamon, D., Godolphin, W., Jones, L.A., *et al.* (1989). Studies of the HER-2/neu proto-oncogene in human breast and ovarian cancer. *Science, 244,* 707–712.

Slamon, D., & Pegram, M. (2001). Rationale for trastuzumab (Herceptin) in adjuvant breast cancer trials. *Seminars in Oncology, 28*(3), 13–19.

Sparano, J.A. (2001). Cardiac toxicity of trastuzumab (Herceptin): implications for the design of adjuvant trials. *Seminars in Oncology, 28* (1 Suppl 3); 20–27.

Chapter 10

HORMONAL THERAPY

M. JOYCE DIENGER, DNSc, RN

INTRODUCTION

Invasive breast cancer is considered a heterogeneous disease with a strong tendency for systematic involvement. A diagnosis of early-stage disease usually carries a favorable prognosis for long-term survival. However, some micrometastases can remain at distant sites following local therapy. Data indicate that approximately 20% to 30% of women with node-negative disease will develop distant metastases within 10 years when treated by surgery alone (Hellman & Harris, 2000). Since many breast tumors are dependent upon estrogen for growth, hormonal stimulation of residual micrometastases can result in a recurrence or development of metastatic disease (Osborne & Ravdin, 2000).

The use of hormonal therapy in women with hormone receptor-positive tumors following primary treatment of surgery with or without combination chemotherapy and, when indicated, radiation therapy has been found to prevent recurrences and improve survival (Early Breast Cancer Trialists' Collaborative Group [EBCTCG], 1998). Adjuvant hormonal therapy has also been found to reduce the occurrence of disease in the contralateral breast (Fisher, 1999). The goal of hormonal therapy is to prevent breast cancer cells from receiving estrogen stimulation (Osborne & Ravdin, 2000). At this time, tamoxifen, a selective estrogen response modifier (SERM), is the most commonly prescribed oral preparation used as adjuvant hormonal therapy in premenopausal and postmenopausal women with primary breast cancer. Recently, anastrozole, a third-generation aromatase inhibitor, was approved for adjuvant therapy for early breast cancer for postmenopausal women (AstraZeneca, 2002a). This chapter outlines the mechanism of action, efficacy, and use of these hormonal agents in the adjuvant setting.

RATIONALE FOR HORMONE THERAPY

The dependence of many breast tumors on estrogen for growth and the benefits of estrogen deprivation were first recognized by Beatson in 1896 when he documented the regression of metastatic breast tumors following bilateral oophorectomy (Beatson, 1896). However, the nuclear protein estrogen receptor (ER) and its role in the proliferation of breast cancer tissue were not identified until the 1960s (Osborne, 1998). Later, researchers observed the presence of the progesterone receptor (PR), a nuclear protein regulated by the ER. The binding of estrogen, specifically estradiol, to the ER sites on the nuclear cell membrane of breast tumor tissue stimulates gene transcription of several proteins, resulting in cellular proliferation. Therefore, the use of hormonal therapy in breast cancer is centered on the administration of drugs that compete with estrogen for binding at ER sites or reducing the amount of available circulating estrogen. Although the presence of the ER is required for estrogen-stimulated growth, it does not act in isolation. It is now known that the ER is but one component in a complex of proteins that determine the effects of estrogen on a particular tissue or on a particular gene (Osborne, 1998).

The determination of ER and PR status of breast tumor tissue is useful as a prognostic as well as predictive indicator (Osborne, 1998). Generally, an ER+ status carries a more favorable prognosis. ER+ breast tumors tend to be well differentiated with a lower rate of cell proliferation, but ER− tumors tend to have poor tumor differentiation with a higher cellular proliferation rate. More importantly, a positive ER/PR status indicates the likelihood of a favorable response to hormonal therapy.

Approximately 80% of breast tumors in postmenopausal women are ER+, but only 50% to 69% of the tumors in premenopausal women indicate ER expression (Osborne, 1998). Roughly 30% of ER+ tumors are PR−, but fewer than 5% of ER− tumors are PR+. Women whose tumors are ER+/PR+ have the greatest likelihood of responding to hormonal therapy. As many as 33% of postmenopausal women whose tumors are either ER+ or PR+ will also exhibit a favorable response to hormonal therapy. A small percentage of patients whose tumors are ER−/PR− will exhibit some response to hormonal therapy; however, the response is often no more significant than what would have been achieved with other therapy (EBCTCG, 1998; Fisher, Anderson *et al.,* 2001).

TAMOXIFEN AS ADJUVANT THERAPY

Tamoxifen was the first drug released in a class of drugs now known as SERMs (Osborne & Ravdin, 2000). The SERMs exhibit dual estrogen antagonistic and estrogen agonistic effects. Although first introduced in the clinical setting in the early 1970s for the treatment of postmenopausal women with advanced breast cancer, tamoxifen was later approved for use as adjuvant therapy in premenopausal and postmenopausal women with ER+ tumors. Because of tamoxifen's high level of effectiveness and relatively low toxicity profile, it remains the hormonal therapy of choice in the adjuvant setting.

MECHANISMS OF ACTION

The mechanisms of action of tamoxifen are complex. Tamoxifen exhibits estrogen antagonistic effects on breast tumor tissue by competing with estradiol for binding to the ER sites located on nuclear cell membranes (Lindley, 1999). The blocking of the ER sites prevents the stimulation of estrogen-regulated genes that promote cellular proliferation and tumor growth. Tamoxifen also has the capability of interfering with tumor growth by decreasing the production of insulin-derived growth factors while increasing the production of tumor-suppressive growth factors (Vogel, 1996). These later mechanisms of action could explain why some women with ER– tumors exhibit a positive response to tamoxifen therapy.

Tamoxifen exhibits estrogen agonistic effects on other estrogen target cells. Of particular benefit are tamoxifen's positive effects on blood lipid profiles and bone mineral density in postmenopausal women (Osborne & Ravdin, 2000). Tamoxifen has been found to reduce serum concentrations of total cholesterol and low-density lipoproteins while increasing the level of high-density lipoproteins. In some studies, this resulted in a decreased risk for coronary artery disease (Rutqvist & Mattsson, 1993), although others found no reduction in cardiovascular events (Fisher *et al.*, 1998). Tamoxifen has also been shown to maintain, and in some cases increase, bone mineral density (Kristensen *et al.*, 1994; Love *et al.*, 1992). Additionally, a significant reduction in bone fractures was found among postmenopausal women following five years of tamoxifen therapy for the prevention of breast cancer (Fisher *et al.*, 1998).

Tamoxifen also exerts an estrogen agonistic effect on the endometrium (Lindley, 1999). This estrogenic stimulatory effect has resulted in findings of a twofold increase in endometrial cancer in women taking tamoxifen for five years when compared to women receiving placebo (Fisher *et al.*, 1994). Although the increased risk for endometrial cancer is cause for concern, the benefits of tamoxifen are considered to outweigh the risks for women with breast cancer taking the drug (NIH, 2000). Arguments favoring the use of tamoxifen include the fact that the increased risk for endometrial cancer is similar to that found in postmenopausal women taking estrogen replacement therapy and that the type of endometrial cancer most frequently induced by tamoxifen is usually low grade, found early, and easily treated with surgery or other means (Lindley, 1999).

EFFICACY IN THE ADJUVANT SETTING

The Early Breast Cancer Trialists' Collaborative Group has been following women around the world participating in randomized clinical trials comparing adjuvant tamoxifen with a control group for several years. The most recent publication of their meta-analysis included the results of 37,000 women in 55 trials. Analysis of these results demonstrated a definite benefit of adjuvant hormonal therapy with tamoxifen among the 30,000 women studied with ER+ or ER status unknown tumors after about 10 years of follow-up (EBCTCG, 1998). Table 10.1 illustrates the percent of reduction in first recurrence and mortality risk among women in various age groups following five years of therapy. As noted, there is a highly significant reduction in risk of first recurrence and mortality among women of all ages receiving tamoxifen as compared to women in the control group. Additionally, the proportional risk reductions were found to be similar among women with lymph node-positive as well as lymph node-negative disease. The trend for greater recurrence reductions in older women versus younger women was also significant, although the trend for greater decrease in mortality among older women versus younger women was not significant. The lack of significance in mortality trend is thought to be due to the likelihood that many of the deaths that occurred in women who were over age 70 years when randomized were from causes other than breast cancer.

Findings from this meta-analysis also indicate a 46% reduction (SD 9; 2p < 0.00001) in the incidence rate of contralateral breast cancer among women treated with tamoxifen for five years (EBCTCG, 1998). Additionally, this result was independent of age, therefore indicating that five years of tamoxifen therapy can reduce the annual incidence rate of contralateral breast cancer by about half.

Unfortunately, little benefit was observed among the nearly 8000 women in the EBCTCG analysis (1998) with ER– tumors. The reduction in recurrence and mortality risk with five years of tamoxifen therapy in this group was 6% (SD 8; NS) and –3% (SD 11; NS), respectively. However, among 602 women whose tumors were ER– but PR+, the reduction in recurrence risk was 23% (SD 12; 2p = 0.05), and the reduction in mortality risk was 9% (SD 14; NS). Because the number of women in the ER–/PR+ subgroup is small, caution is advised in assuming any real benefit of tamoxifen to these women.

Another large clinical trial of tamoxifen was conducted by the National Surgical Adjuvant Breast and Bowel Project (NSABP). The NSABP B-14 study, a randomized, double-blind

Table 10.1 Tamoxifen Effects on Risk Reduction Based on Age Following Five Years of Therapy

	Recurrence reduction	Mortality reduction
Age < 50 years	45% (SD 8)	32% (SD 10)
Age 50–59 years	37% (SD 6)	11% (SD 8)
Age 60–69 years	54% (SD 5)	33% (SD 6)
Age 70+ years	54% (SD 13)	34% (SD 13)
All patients	47% (SD 3)*	26% (SD 4)*
Trend between effects at different ages	$\chi^2_1 = 4.3$, 2p = 0.04	$\chi^2_1 = 1.5$, 2p > 0.1, NS

SD = Standard deviation; NS = Nonsignificant

* Significance 2p < 0.00001 as compared to women in control group.

Note: Results of women with ER+, lymph node-negative or positive disease.

From: Early Breast Cancer Trialists' Collaborative Group. (1998). Tamoxifen for early breast cancer: an overview of the randomized trials. *Lancet, 351* (9114), 1451–1467.

placebo-controlled trial that started in 1982, recruited over 2800 premenopausal and post-menopausal women with ER+, node-negative breast cancer (Fisher, 1999). Women in the study group were given 20 mg of tamoxifen daily for 5 years. After 10 years of follow-up, a significant recurrence free survival (69% versus 57%, $p < 0.0001$) and overall survival (80% versus 76%, $p = 0.02$) was found among the women in the treatment group versus placebo group. Similar to the findings of the EBCTCG meta-analysis, tamoxifen therapy was also associated with a 37% reduction ($p = 0.007$) in the incidence of contralateral breast cancer.

DOSAGE AND DURATION OF THERAPY

The most frequently prescribed dose of tamoxifen seems to be 20 mg administered once daily, because it has a long biologic half-life (Lindley, 1999). It is recommended that adjuvant hormone therapy begin soon after surgery and the confirmation of ER+ status. Since tamoxifen and chemotherapy may both be used as adjuvant therapy, an exception to this recommendation may be with postmenopausal women who have node-positive disease and have chosen to also receive chemotherapy. In such situations, tamoxifen therapy may be delayed until the course of chemotherapy has been completed. The results of one phase III clinical trial found an estimated disease-free survival (DFS) advantage of 18% in women who received sequential chemohormonal therapy when compared to concurrent therapy (Albain *et al.*, 2002).

The optimal duration of tamoxifen therapy in the adjuvant setting has been the subject of much discussion. Both the EBCTCG meta-analysis (1998) and a review of results from the NSAPB B-14 study (Fisher, Dignam *et al.*, 2001) addressed this issue. As noted in Table 10.2, there is a highly significant trend for greater reductions in recurrence and mortality rates among women with ER+, lymph node-positive or negative disease receiving tamoxifen for 1 versus 2 versus 5 years of therapy with 10 years of follow-up (EBCTCG, 1998). Additionally, the benefits of tamoxifen persist beyond the completion of therapy, and an update from the NSABP B-14 trial (Fisher, Dignam *et al.*, 2001) found that women with ER+, lymph node-negative disease who remained disease free and discontinued tamoxifen after 5 years actually experienced slightly improved overall survival (94% versus 91%) and recurrence-free survival (94% versus 92%) when compared to women who continued taking the drug for an additional 7 years (Fisher, Dignam *et al.*, 2001). Although the optimal duration of tamoxifen

Table 10.2 Effects of Tamoxifen at Any Age Based on Length of Therapy

	Recurrence reduction	Mortality reduction
1 year	21% (SD 3)	12% (SD 3)
2 years	29% (SD 2)	17% (SD 3)
5 years	47% (SD 3)	26% (SD 4)
Trend	$\chi^2_1 = 52.0$, 2p < 0.00001	$\chi^2_1 = 8.8$, 2p = 0.003

SD = Standard deviation

From: Early Breast Cancer Trialists' Collaborative Group. (1998). Tamoxifen for early breast cancer: an overview of the randomized trials. *Lancet, 351*(9114), 1451–1467.

therapy continues to be studied, the current recommendation is that adjuvant treatment with tamoxifen should be limited to 5 years outside the clinical trial setting (Bryant *et al.,* 2001).

SIDE EFFECTS AND ADVERSE EVENTS

Tamoxifen is generally well tolerated. However, some of the side effects experienced from estrogen withdrawal may be bothersome. In the NSABP B-14 trial, the incidence of hot flashes, vaginal discharge, and vaginal bleeding was reported significantly more frequently among women receiving tamoxifen versus placebo (AstraZeneca, 2002b). Other symptoms, such as fluid retention, nausea, and skin changes, were reported at similar frequency with tamoxifen and placebo. Central nervous symptoms such as depression, irritability, headache, insomnia, lethargy, and dizziness have occasionally been observed (Lindley, 1999). In premenopausal women, circulating estrogen levels can become increased because of an interference with the normal hormonal negative feedback mechanism within the pituitary (Knobf, 1996). Thus, menstrual irregularities are experienced by most premenopausal women, with 20% to 30% reporting amenorrhea.

Some laboratory values may also become altered during tamoxifen therapy. Specifically, an increase in SGOT, bilirubin, and creatinine and a decrease in platelet counts were reported during the NSABP B-14 study (AstraZeneca, 2002b). The elevation of liver enzymes has caused some concern, because tamoxifen has been found to be a potent hepatocarcinogen in female rats (Hard *et al.,* 1993). However, only three cases of liver cancer have been associated with tamoxifen use, and all of these were among women taking 40 mg per day in a trial outside the United States (AstraZeneca, 2002b). To date, an increase in the risk for liver damage, hepatoma, or colon cancer has not been observed (Fisher, 1999).

Ocular effects, such as corneal changes, optic neuritis, retinopathy, and macular edema, have been reported with tamoxifen doses greater than 180 mg per day (Lindley, 1999). However, reports of ocular toxicity (retinopathy or keratopathy) with doses of 20 mg per day have been inconsistent. During the NSABP tamoxifen prevention trial, women with preexisting cataracts who were taking tamoxifen did have a slightly increased risk of posterior subcapsular opacities and required cataract surgery (Osborne & Ravdin, 2000). Nevertheless, no vision-threatening ocular toxicities were reported. Monitoring for ocular changes with routine ophthalmic examination is recommended for women with breast cancer receiving tamoxifen therapy (Osborne & Ravdin, 2000).

Reports of an increased incidence of thromboembolic events and endometrial cancer related to long-term tamoxifen therapy (five years) have probably caused the most concern. Deep vein thrombosis, pulmonary embolism, or superficial phlebitis was experienced by 1.7% of the women taking tamoxifen versus 0.4% of women taking placebo in the NSABP B-14 trial (AstraZeneca, 2002b). Endometrial events, including hyperplasia, polyps, and 25 cases of endometrial cancer, have been reported among women in the NSABP B-14 trial (Fisher *et al.,* 1994). Two cases of endometrial cancer were in the placebo group, but 23 cases were in the tamoxifen group. Four women receiving tamoxifen died of uterine cancer. The annual hazard rate for endometrial cancer through all follow-up was 0.2/1000 in the placebo group and 1.6/1000 in the tamoxifen group, which represents a relative risk for endometrial cancer of 2.2 among women receiving tamoxifen when compared with population-based rates. Most of the endometrial cancer found among women in NSABP B-14 was stage I and of good to moderate histologic grade. However, recent reports involving women taking tamoxifen for the prevention of breast cancer indicate a slightly increased risk for developing a more aggressive uterine sarcoma (AstraZeneca, 2002b). Although health care providers are encouraged to discuss the potential risks versus benefits of tamoxifen with women considering use in the prophylactic setting, experts continue to agree that the benefits of tamoxifen therapy among women with breast cancer outweigh the risks (Fisher *et al.*, 1994). All women receiving tamoxifen need to be urged to seek yearly gynecologic exams and immediately report any abnormal vaginal bleeding, menstrual irregularities, changes in vaginal discharge, pelvic pain or pressure, shortness of breath, or leg pain or swelling to their physician (AstraZeneca, 2002b).

ANASTROZOLE AS ADJUVANT THERAPY

Despite tamoxifen's demonstrated ability to reduce recurrence rates in the adjuvant setting, approximately 50% of treated women do not respond (EBCTCG, 1998). There is also evidence that in some cases, breast cancer cells become resistant to tamoxifen and exhibit tamoxifen-stimulated growth (Osborne *et al.*, 1991). These observations, together with the adverse effects of increased incidence of thromboembolic events and endometrial cancer associated with long-term tamoxifen therapy, prompted investigators to search for other agents to use in the adjuvant hormone therapy setting.

The aromatase inhibitors were introduced into the management of metastatic breast cancer more than 20 years ago. Even though the first agent introduced, aminoglutethimide, exhibited a response rate similar to tamoxifen, the associated side effects limited its use (Cocconi, 1994). In the mid-1990s, third-generation aromatase inhibitors became available as second-line treatment of metastatic breast cancer following tamoxifen failure (Geisler *et al.*, 1996). Anastrozole became available in 1995, and based upon findings of effectiveness equal to or superior to tamoxifen in the treatment of metastatic breast cancer, a large randomized clinical trial was initiated evaluating anastrozole against tamoxifen in the adjuvant setting (Bonneterre *et al.*, 2000; Nabholtz *et al.*, 2000). As a result, anastrozole was recently approved as a first-line adjuvant hormonal therapy agent for postmenopausal women with early-stage ER+ breast cancer (AstraZeneca, 2002a).

MECHANISM OF ACTION AND ADMINISTRATION

Anastrozole is a selective nonsteroidal third-generation aromatase inhibitor. In postmenopausal women, most of the circulating estrogens are derived from the conversion of the adrenal androgens androstenedione and testosterone to estrone and estradiol (Gross & Strasser, 2001). The aromatase enzyme is responsible for the conversion process. Anastrozole blocks the aromatase enzyme, thus inhibiting estrogen synthesis and the availability of estrogen for binding at the ER sites. The aromatization reaction occurs mainly in adipose tissue, muscle, and the liver. However, the aromatization of estrogen has also been observed in breast adipose tissue and breast cancer cells. The administration of a third-generation aromatase inhibitor almost completely inhibits the peripheral synthesis of estrogen through the aromatization process. However, in premenopausal women, blocking peripheral synthesis of estrogen does not significantly decrease circulating estrogen levels.

Anastrozole has a very low toxicity profile. It exhibits no estrogen agonistic effects; thus, the incidence of thromboembolic events and endometrial carcinoma experienced with tamoxifen should be reduced (Takanishi, 2001). The 1-mg daily dose is well absorbed by the oral route and has an elimination half-life of about 50 hours.

EFFICACY IN THE ADJUVANT SETTING

The arimidex, tamoxifen alone or in combination (ATAC) trial, a large, double-blind, placebo-controlled, randomized trial involving 381 centers in 21 different countries began recruiting women in July of 1996 (The ATAC Trialists' Group, 2002). The trial was designed to assess the efficacy and safety of anastrozole as compared to tamoxifen and to determine if the combination of anastrozole and tamoxifen was superior to tamoxifen alone as adjuvant therapy in postmenopausal women. The primary end point was DFS defined as time to earliest occurrence of local or distant recurrence, new primary breast cancer, or death from any cause. Secondary end points were time to a recurrence and incidence of new contralateral primary breast tumors. Incidence of distant recurrence and overall survival were also secondary end points, but at this time there is insufficient data on these events for analysis.

Eligible patients were postmenopausal women with ER+ or unknown operable invasive breast cancer who had completed primary surgery and chemotherapy, when indicated (The ATAC Trialists' Group, 2002). Trial therapy could be initiated while the patient was receiving radiation therapy. Patients who met eligibility criteria were randomized to receive active anastrozole 1 mg plus tamoxifen placebo, active tamoxifen 20 mg plus anastrozole placebo, or anastrozole 1 mg and tamoxifen 20 mg daily for 5 years. By the time the trial closed in March of 2000, a total of 9366 women with a mean age of 64 years were enrolled. Patients in each arm were balanced as to tumor size, degree of lymph node involvement, tumor grade, primary treatment received, and demographic characteristics.

Table 10.3 lists the data regarding first events with a median follow-up of 33 months. Of these, 850 (79%) were recurrences or new contralateral tumors and 229 (21%) were deaths without recurrence (The ATAC Trialists' Group, 2002). The noticeably smaller number of primary contralateral breast cancers among women in the anastrozole group as compared to the tamoxifen group is very encouraging.

As noted in Table 10.4, there was no difference in the annual recurrence rates between women receiving tamoxifen or anastrozole alone in the first year of follow-up, but a difference favoring the anastrozole alone arm is seen in the second and third years of follow-up (The ATAC Trialists' Group, 2002). Overall, the DFS estimates at three years for those receiving

Table 10.3 The ATAC Trial: Distribution of Events

	Anastrozole (N = 3125)	Tamoxifen (N = 3116)	Combination (N = 3125)	Total (N = 9366)
First events				
Local recurrence	67	83	81	231
Distant recurrence*	158	182	204	544
Contralateral breast cancer	14	33	28	75
Invasive	9	30	23	62
DCIS	5	3	5	13
Deaths before recurrence	78	81	70	229
Total	317 (10.1%)	379 (12.2%)	383 (12.3%)	1079 (11.5%)

* Including five deaths (two on anastrozole, one on tamoxifen, and two on the combination), which were attributed to breast cancer without prior information about recurrence.

From: The ATAC Trialists' Group. (2002). Anastrozole alone or in combination with tamoxifen versus tamoxifen alone for adjuvant treatment of postmenopausal women with early breast cancer: first results of the ATAC randomized trial. *Lancet, 359,* 2133. Adapted with permission.

anastrozole, tamoxifen, or the combination of anastrozole and tamoxifen were 89.4%, 87.4%, and 87.2%, respectively. The DFS was significantly longer for women on anastrozole alone compared to those receiving tamoxifen, alone (hazard ratio 0.83, $p = 0.013$) or the combination (hazard ratio 0.81, $p = 0.006$). Interestingly, the DFS was not significantly different for those receiving the combination versus tamoxifen alone (hazard ratio 1.02, $p = 0.8$).

The hormone status of some women's tumors that were classified as hormone-receptor unknown at the beginning of the trial was later found to be receptor-negative (The ATAC Trialists' Group, 2002). Therefore, data related to treatment effect were analyzed separately based upon known hormone receptor status. Among those with ER+ tumors, the percentage of women who were disease free at three years follow-up was significantly larger among those in the anastrozole versus tamoxifen group and the anastrozole versus combination group than in the tamoxifen versus combination group. The time to recurrence was also

Table 10.4 The ATAC Trial: Annual Recurrence Rates

	Annual recurrence			Hazard ratio (95% CI)		
	Anastrozole (N = 3125)	Tamoxifen (N = 3116)	Combination (N = 3125)	A/T	C/T	A/C
Year						
1	77 (2.49%)*	71 (2.3%)	87 (2.82%)	1.08	1.23	0.88
2	78 (2.61%)	127 (4.28%)	123 (4.11%)	0.61	0.96	0.63
3	64 (2.94%)	77 (3.72%)	80 (3.71%)	0.77	1.00	0.77

A = anastrozole; T = tamoxifen; C = combination

*Percentages are events per woman-year at risk.

From: The ATAC Trialists' Group. (2002). Anastrozole alone or in combination with tamoxifen versus tamoxifen alone for adjuvant treatment of postmenopausal women with early breast cancer: first results of the ATAC randomized trial. *Lancet, 359,* 2134. Adapted with permission.

significantly longer in the anastrozole group than in the tamoxifen group. Conversely, the recurrence rate was more than three times higher among women with ER– tumors than among women with known positive status. Additionally, no difference in time to recurrence was observed in women with ER– tumors receiving anastrozole alone versus tamoxifen alone.

Based upon results of this first analysis data, the researchers concluded that anastrozole demonstrated better efficacy than tamoxifen, that combination treatment was equivalent to tamoxifen alone but slightly worse than anastrozole alone, and that anastrozole was no more effective than tamoxifen in women with ER- disease (The ATAC Trialists' Group, 2002). It was also noted that in the tamoxifen alone group, the event rate was very similar to that observed in the most recent EBCTCG meta-analysis when adjusted for nodal status. Therefore, the benefits observed in this trial with anastrozole can be attributed to a superior activity of the drug when compared with tamoxifen. However, longer follow-up of the women in this trial is needed to determine if the effects of anastrozole are sustained.

SIDE EFFECTS AND ADVERSE EVENTS

The most frequently reported side effects of anastrozole when used to treat women with metastatic breast cancer are hot flashes, fatigue, nausea, vomiting, headache, peripheral edema, constipation, bone pain, and back pain (Bonneterre *et al.,* 2000; Gross & Strasser, 2001). The occurrences of predefined side effects exhibited during the ATAC trial are listed in Table 10.5.

Table 10.5 ATAC Trial: Comparison of Adverse Effects—Percent of Incidence

	Anastrozole	Tamoxifen	Combination	p (A vs. T)
Hot flashes	34.3%	39.7%	40.1%	< 0.0001
Musculoskeletal sx	27.8%	21.2%	22.1%	< 0.0001*
Fatigue/tiredness	15.6%	15.1%	14.0%	0.5
Mood disturbances	15.5%	15.2%	15.6%	0.7
Nausea/vomiting	10.5%	10.2%	11.7%	0.7
Fractures	5.9%	3.7%	4.6%	< 0.0001*
Vaginal bleeding	4.5%	8.2%	7.7%	< 0.0001
Vaginal discharge	2.8%	11.4%	11.5%	< 0.0001
Cataracts	3.5%	3.7%	3.4%	0.06
Thromboembolic	2.1%	3.5%	4.0%	0.0006
DVT/PE	1.0%	1.7%	2.0%	0.02
CVA	1.0%	2.1%	1.6%	0.0006
Endometrial ca	.1%	.5%	.3%	0.02

A = anastrozole; T = tamoxifen

*Significance in favor of tamoxifen

From: The ATAC Trialists' Group. (2002). Anastrozole alone or in combination with tamoxifen versus tamoxifen alone for adjuvant treatment of postmenopausal women with early breast cancer: first results of the ATAC randomized trial. *Lancet, 359,* 2136. Adapted with permission.

As noted, the incidence of hot flashes, vaginal discharge, vaginal bleeding, ischemic cerebral vascular events, venous thromboembolic events, and endometrial cancer was significantly less in the anastrozole group (The ATAC Trialists' Group, 2002). By contrast, musculoskeletal disorders and fractures were significantly more frequent with anastrozole than with tamoxifen. The differences in these side effect profiles are most likely related to anastrozole's lack of any estrogen agonistic activity and ability to profoundly inhibit the synthesis of estrogen in peripheral tissues. The decrease in thromboembolic and endometrial cancer events is very positive and confirms findings from trials with metastatic breast cancer. However, the increased incidence in the number of fractures does cause concern, and the benefit of concurrent administration of a bisphosphonate preparation in women taking anastrozole is being considered.

CONCLUSION

The efficacy of tamoxifen in reducing the incidence of recurrent and contralateral disease and prolonging survival in premenopausal and postmenopausal women with early-stage ER+ breast cancer was presented in this chapter. Issues regarding the toxicities associated with tamoxifen have raised questions regarding the risks and benefits of treatment. Additionally, the question as to the optimal duration of tamoxifen treatment remains. Many health care professionals face these concerns daily. To help clarify these issues and provide some direction regarding the use of adjuvant therapy for breast cancer, the National Institutes of Health Consensus Development Conference on Adjuvant Therapy for Breast Cancer was held in November 2000. A summary of statements from the conference panel regarding adjuvant hormonal therapy are listed in Table 10.6. The conference panel also provided some direction for new research related to adjuvant hormonal therapy. Suggestions from the panel include further investigations into: (1) the risks and benefits of continuing tamoxifen beyond five years; (2) the value of combined hormonal therapy; and (3) the risks and benefits of new SERMs and aromatase inhibitors and inactivators (NIH, 2000).

Table 10.6 NIH Consensus Development Conference Statement on Adjuvant Hormonal Therapy

- Adjuvant hormonal therapy should be recommended for patients whose breast tumors express hormone receptor protein, regardless of age, menopausal status, involvement of axillary lymph nodes, or tumor size.
- Hormonal therapy should not be recommended to women whose breast cancers do not express hormone receptor protein.
- If tamoxifen is the drug used, therapy should be 20 mg per day for 5 years.
- The risk of recurrence may be further reduced in premenopausal women by combining tamoxifen with combination chemotherapy.
- Even though tamoxifen use has been associated with a slight increased risk of endometrial cancer and thromboembolic events, the benefits of treatment outweigh the risks for most women.
- For some premenopausal women, ovarian ablation is a viable alternative to adjuvant hormonal therapy.

From: National Institutes of Health. (2000). Adjuvant therapy for breast cancer. *NIH Consensus Statement 2000*, 17(4), 8–9.

Since the development of the NIH Consensus Panel's recommendations, preliminary data from the ATAC trial indicating the improved efficacy of anastrozole over tamoxifen in reducing the risk of recurrence and development of a second primary cancer have been released. Many believe these results of the ATAC trial to be very promising. Nonetheless, the American Society of Clinical Oncology continues to endorse a 5-year course of tamoxifen as standard adjuvant hormonal therapy for women with ER+ breast cancer (Ravdin, 2002). The opinion is that while preliminary data from the ATAC trial does indicate superior results with anastrozole, there is insufficient data on long-term side effects to warrant a change in standard therapy. Additionally, with only an average of 33 months of follow-up, the question of whether the improved response will last for 5 or more years is unanswered. There are several substudies from the ATAC trial in progress that will provide additional vital information.

Scientists in the ATAC Trialists' Group emphasize that the favorable findings of anastrozole over tamoxifen in this trial are only applicable to postmenopausal women with newly diagnosed early-stage ER+ disease (The ATAC Trialists' Group, 2002). Additionally, the effects of anastrozole following tamoxifen in the adjuvant setting have not been investigated. The search for effective hormonal therapy in women with ER− breast tumors also continues.

Today, results of medical research are widely publicized in the media, causing patients concern and increasing the difficulty of making a treatment decision. Health care professionals are encouraged to discuss the available data with patients and acknowledge that treatment approaches may change over time.

REFERENCES

Albain, K.S., Green, S.J., Ravdin, P.M., Cobau, C.D., Levine, E.G., Ingle, J.N., et al. (2002). Adjuvant chemohormonal therapy for primary breast cancer should be sequential instead of concurrent: initial results from intergroup trial 0100 (SWOG-8814). Poster presented at ASCO Annual Meeting, Abstract 143. Abstract retrieved September 10, 2002, from *http://www.asco.org/asco/meetings_education/2002posters/abstract143/poster.htm*.

AstraZeneca Pharmaceuticals (2002a). *Arimidex® (anastrozole tablets) Professional Information Brochure 9/02.* Wilmington, Del.: Author.

AstraZeneca Pharmaceuticals. (2002b). *Nolvadex® (tamoxifen citrate) Professional Information Brochure 5/02.* Wilmington, Del.: Author.

Beatson, G.T. (1896). On the treatment of inoperable cases of carcinoma of the mamma: suggestions for a new method of treatment, with illustrative cases. *Lancet, 2,* 104–107.

Bonneterre, J., Thurlimann, B., Robertson, J.F., Krzakowski, M., Mauriac, L., Koralewski, P.,
Vergote, I., Webster, A., Steinberg, M., & von Euler, M. (2000). Anastrozole versus tamoxifen as first-line therapy for advanced breast cancer in 668 postmenopausal women: results of the tamoxifen or Arimidex randomized group efficacy and tolerability study. *Journal of Clinical Oncology, 18,* 3748–3757.

Bryant, J., Fisher, B., & Dignam, J. (2001). Duration of adjuvant tamoxifen therapy. *Journal of the National Cancer Institute Monographs, 30,* 56–61.

Cocconi, G. (1994). First-generation aromatase inhibitors caminoglutethimide and testololactone. *Breast Cancer Research and Treatment, 30,* 57–80.

Early Breast Cancer Trialists' Collaborative Group. (1998). Tamoxifen for early breast cancer: an overview of the randomized trials. *Lancet, 351*(9114), 1451–1467.

Fisher, B. (1999). Highlights from recent National Surgical Adjuvant Breast and Bowel Project studies in the treatment and prevention of breast cancer. *CA— A Cancer Journal for Clinicians, 49,* 159–177.

Fisher, B., Anderson, S., Tan-Chiu, E., Wolmark, N., Wickerham, D.L., Fisher, E.R., Dimitrov, N.V., Atkins, J.N., Abramson, N., Merajver, S., Romond, E.H., Kardinal, C.G., Shibata, H.R., Margolese, R.G., & Farrar, W.B. (2001). Tamoxifen and chemotherapy for axillary node-negative, estrogen receptor-negative breast cancer: findings from National Surgical Adjuvant Breast and Bowel Project B-23. *Journal of Clinical Oncology, 19*(4), 931–942.

Fisher, B., Costantino, J.P., Redmond, C.K., Fisher, E.R., Wickerham, D.L., & Cronin, W.M. (1994). Endometrial cancer in tamoxifen-treated breast cancer patients: findings from the National Surgical Adjuvant Breast and Bowel Project (NSABP) B-14. *Journal of the National Cancer Institute, 86,* 527–537.

Fisher, B., Costantino, J.P., & Wickerham, D.L. (1998). Tamoxifen for prevention of breast cancer: report of the National Surgical Adjuvant Breast and Bowel Project P-1 Study. *Journal of the National Cancer Institute, 90,* 1371–1388.

Fisher, B., Dignam, J., Bryant, J., & Wolmark, N. (2001). Five versus more than five years of tamoxifen for lymph node-negative breast cancer: updated findings from the National Surgical Adjuvant Breast and Bowel Project B-14 randomized trial. *Journal of the National Cancer Institute, 93,* 684–690.

Geisler, J., King, N., Dowsett, M., Ottestad, L., Lundgren, S., Walton, P., Kormeset, P.O., & Lonning, P.E. (1996). Influence of anastrozole (Arimidex), a selective, non-steroidal aromatase inhibitor, on in vivo aromatization and plasma oestrogen levels in postmenopausal women with breast cancer. *British Journal of Cancer, 74,* 1286–1291.

Gross, P.E., & Strasser, K. (2001). Aromatase inhibitors in the treatment and prevention of breast cancer. *Journal of Clinical Oncology, 19,* 881–894.

Hard, G.D., Iatropoulos, M.J., Jordan, K., Radi, L., Kaltenberg, O.P., Imondi, A.R., et al. (1993). Major difference in the hepatocarcinogenicity and DNA adduct forming ability between toremifene and tamoxifen in female rats. *Cancer Research, 53,* 4534–4541.

Hellman, S., & Harris, J.R. (2000). Natural history of breast cancer. In J.R. Harris, M.E. Lippman, M.M. Morrow, & C.K. Osborne (Eds.), *Diseases of the breast, 2nd ed.,* pp. 407–423. Philadelphia: Lippincott Williams & Wilkins.

Knobf, M.T. (1996). Menopausal symptoms associated with breast cancer treatment. In K.H. Dow (Ed.), *Contemporary issues in breast cancer,* pp. 85–97. Sudbury, Mass.: Jones & Bartlett.

Kristensen, B., Ejlertsen, B., Dalgaard, P., Larsen, L., Holmegaard, S.N., Transbol, I., & Mouridsen, H.T. (1994). Tamoxifen and bone metabolism in postmenopausal low-risk breast cancer patients: a randomized study. *Journal of Clinical Oncology, 12,* 992–997.

Lindley, C.M. (1999). Breast cancer. In J.T. DiPiro, R.L. Talbert, G.C. Yee, G.R. Matzke, B.G. Wells, & L.M. Posey (Eds.), *Pharmacotherapy: a physiologic approach, 3rd ed.,* pp. 2013–2042. Norwalk, Conn.: Appleton & Lange.

Love, R.R., Maxess, R.B., Barden, H.S., Epstein, S., Newcomb, P.A., Jordan, V.C., et al. (1992). Effects of tamoxifen on bone mineral density in postmenopausal women with breast cancer. *New England Journal of Medicine, 326,* 852–856.

Nabholtz, J.M., Buzdar, A., Pollak, M., Harwin, W., Burton, G., Mangalik, A., Steinberg, M., Webster, A., & von Euler, M. (2000). Anastrozole is superior to tamoxifen as first-line therapy for advanced breast cancer in postmenopausal women: results of a North American multicenter randomized trial. *Journal of Clinical Oncology, 18,* 3758–3767.

National Institutes of Health. (2000, November 1–3). Adjuvant therapy for breast cancer. *NIH Consensus Statement 2000, 17*(4), 1–35.

Osborne, C.K. (1998). Steroid hormone receptors in breast cancer management. *Breast Cancer Research and Treatment, 51,* 227–238.

Osborne, C.K., Coronado, E., Allred, D.C., Wiebe, V., & DeGregorio, M. (1991). Acquired tamoxifen resistance: correlation with reduced breast tumor levels of tamoxifen and isomerization of trans-4-hydroxytamoxifen. *Journal of the National Cancer Institute, 83,* 1477–1482.

Osborne, C.K., & Ravdin, P.M. (2000). Adjuvant systemic therapy of primary breast cancer. In J.R. Harris, M.E. Lippman, M.M. Morrow, & C.K. Osborne (Eds.), *Diseases of the breast, 2nd ed.,* pp. 599–632. Philadelphia: Lippincott Williams & Wilkins.

Ravdin, P. (2002). Aromatase inhibitors for the endocrine adjuvant treatment of breast cancer. *Lancet, 359,* 2126–2127.

Rutqvist, L.E., & Mattsson, A. (1993). Cardiac and thromboembolic morbidity among postmenopausal women with early-stage breast cancer in a randomized trial of adjuvant tamoxifen. *Journal of the National Cancer Institute, 85,* 1398–1406.

Takanishi, G.C. (2001). A new class of hormonal modulators for the treatment of breast cancer: the aromatase inhibitors. *Women's Health in Primary Care, 4*(368), 371–372.

The ATAC Trialists' Group. (2002). Anastrozole alone or in combination with tamoxifen versus tamoxifen alone for adjuvant treatment of postmenopausal women with early breast cancer: first results of the ATAC randomised trial. *Lancet, 359,* 2131–2139.

Vogel, C.L. (1996). Hormonal approaches to breast cancer treatment and prevention: an overview. *Seminars in Oncology, 23*(4, Suppl 9), 2–9.

Section III

TREATMENT OF RECURRENT AND METASTATIC BREAST CANCER

Chapter 11

TARGETED THERAPY AND TREATMENT OF RECURRENT AND METASTATIC BREAST CANCER

KAREN HASSEY DOW, PHD, RN, FAAN

INTRODUCTION

Despite improvements in treatment of early stage disease, some women will experience recurrence of breast cancer. Annually, about 46,000 women die of metastatic breast cancer. The focus is no longer cure but rather palliation of symptoms, maintenance of quality of life, and even prolonging survival. Advanced breast cancer takes on many faces. For example, women with early stage I or II disease may develop recurrence months to years later. Although the highest risk of recurrence is within two years, recurrence can develop up to 25 years or more later. About 40% of women with node-negative disease and 60% of women with node-positive disease develop recurrence. Other women present with locally advanced stage III breast cancer and may develop disease progression. About 10% of women have newly diagnosed metastatic breast cancer at initial presentation. Advanced breast cancer can be controlled but not cured.

Approximately 50% will live more than 2 years and 10% will live more than 10 years after recurrence. Although the focus has changed from cure to control, there are several new treatments available today, including targeted therapy, chemotherapeutic agents, and hormonal therapies, that have both improved quality of life for women and prolonged their survival. (See Chapter 12 for a discussion of the hormonal treatments available for advanced and metastatic disease.)

The purpose of this chapter is to review the natural history and presentation of recurrent and metastatic disease, discuss the treatment options available, and present nursing management considerations.

NATURAL HISTORY OF RECURRENT AND METASTATIC DISEASE

Breast cancer can spread locally, regionally, and systemically to nearly all organs. The most common routes of spread of metastasis are through the lymphatics and bloodstream. The most frequent sites of recurrence are bone, soft tissue (i.e., skin at scar site and lymph nodes), lung, brain, pleura, and liver. Skin and lymph node involvement will generally precede major visceral organ involvement. Visceral metastasis is associated with a shorter disease-free interval and decreased survival. Bone metastasis is generally considered indolent with a longer disease-free survival. Table 11.1 contains the major sites of breast cancer metastasis/recurrence and the related signs and symptoms.

The risk factors for recurrence include the number of involved axillary nodes with four or more positive nodes, large tumor size at presentation, and negative estrogen and progesterone receptors. Women who overexpress HER-2/neu are also at higher risk of recurrence. Tumors with aneuploid DNA content and a high percentage of cells in the S-phase of the cell cycle contribute to increased risk of recurrence.

Symptoms of advanced disease include nodules on the chest wall after mastectomy, localized back pain that increases in intensity at night, shortness of breath, jaundice, altered mental state, and seizures. Workup generally includes a complete history and physical examination. Blood studies include complete blood count (CBC), platelets, liver function tests (LFTs), chest X ray, bone scan, and CT or MRI of symptomatic areas. Biopsy may be performed to document first recurrence, to distinguish new nodes from benign disease or new primary breast cancer, or differentiate from metastatic disease or from a primary site other than the breast.

SELECTION FOR TREATMENT

Treatment selection is influenced by a combination of patient and disease factors. Patient factors include age, treatment preference and choice, physical status, presence of comorbid disease, and family, social, and insurance considerations. Disease factors include prognostic indicators, extent of recurrent or metastatic disease, menopausal status, estrogen receptor status, prior chemotherapy, prior hormonal therapy, time to relapse, and the extent of recurrence (local vs. systemic).

SYSTEMIC THERAPY

Chemotherapy, targeted therapy, and hormonal therapy are indicated for advanced and metastatic disease. Chemotherapy is indicated in the following conditions: multiple metastatic sites and/or nonskeletal metastasis, aggressive visceral metastasis, and ER/PR tumors that are refractory to hormonal treatment. Side effects are more difficult when chemotherapy is used rather than hormonal therapy. There is no evidence that patients will respond to chemotherapy sooner than with endocrine therapy. Doxorubicin-containing

Table 11.1 Summary of Physical Sequelae Secondary to Major Sites of Breast Cancer Metastasis/Recurrence

Metastatic Site	Incidence	Signs & Symptoms	Associated Clinical Problems	Standard Symptom Management
Skeletal	• 2/3 of patients diagnosed with breast cancer; vertebrae most common site • Marrow involved in about half of patients with bone metastasis on x-ray or scan	• Localized pain of gradually increasing intensity; tendency to worsen at night and with positional change; percussion tenderness at involved sites • Anemia secondary to neoplastic marrow involvement	• *Pathologic fracture* secondary (2°) to involvement of bone cortex • *Hypercalcemia* 2° to skeletal metastasis or endocrine therapy	• Fractures treated with surgical stabilization followed by radiation therapy (RT). Large lesions in weight-bearing bones occasionally treated prophylactically with RT • Hydration; administration of diuretics with K supplementation; administration of agents that directly reduce Ca^{++} levels (mithramycin, calcitonin, prostaglandin inhibitors or etidronate); mobilization
Spinal Cord		• Progressive back pain (localized and radicular) • Muscular weakness (usually lower extremities) • Paresthesias in one or more extremities • Bowel/bladder sphincter dysfunction	• *Paralysis* 2° to epidural spinal cord compression induced by tumor encroachment or vertebral fracture	• RT, to vertebral locations identified as metastatic sites on MRI or myelogram, plus corticosteroids • Decompression laminectomy or anterior decompression if deterioration progresses during RT, if recurrence is in previously irradiated area, or if there is evidence of vertebral instability
Brain (including cerebral & leptomeningeal metastases)	• 9%–25% of all patients with breast cancer • 25%–50% of all patients with metastatic breast cancer	• Headache • Unilateral sensory loss • Focal muscular weakness • Hemiparesis • Incoordination (ataxia) • Visual defects • Speech disorders (aphasia) • Impaired cognition (memory loss, ↓ concentration) • Behavioral/mental changes • Loss of sphincter control • Papilledema • Persistent nausea/vomiting	• *Seizure activity* • *Progressive loss of consciousness*	• Whole brain RT and administration of dexamethasone (8–16 mg/day) • *For meningeal involvement,* intrathecal chemotherapy with methotrexate, cytosine arabinoside, or thiotepa via lumbar puncture or Ommaya reservoir q 3–6 days until cerebral spinal fluid clears

Table 11.1 (continued)

Metastatic Site	Incidence	Signs & Symptoms	Associated Clinical Problems	Standard Symptom Management
Pulmonary (including lung nodules, lymphangetic spread, and pleural effusions)	• 59%–69% of all breast cancer patients on autopsy • Lymphangetic spread in 24%–34% of all patients on autopsy; <20% diagnosed ante-mortem • Pleural effusion experienced by 50% of all patients with metastatic breast cancer	• Depends on sites and extent of pulmonary metastasis; patients may be asymptomatic or experience any combination of the following symptoms; • Chest pain (pleuritic if inflammatory process present) • Dyspnea on exertion; shortness of breath; tachypnea • Nonproductive cough (unless pneumonia is present, then productive) • With pleural effusion, adventitious breath sounds, dullness to percussion, and restricted chest wall expansion on affected site	• *Symptomatic pleural effusion* 2° lymphatic and venous obstruction by tumor	• Thoracentesis followed by closed thoracostomy tube drainage to minimize or eliminate effusion • Instillation of sclerosing agent (eg, tetracycline) via chest tube to cause fibrosis and obliteration of pleural space
Liver	• 58%–65% of all breast cancer patients on autopsy	• Abdominal dissension • RLQ abdominal pain ± radiation to scapular region • Nausea/vomiting, anorexia, weight loss • Weakness/fatigue • Hepatomegaly • Jaundice • Peripheral edema • Elevated LFTs; alkaline phosphatase, total bilirubin	• *Ascites* 2° to peritoneal tumor seeding or hepatic failure	• Sodium and fluid restriction with diuretic therapy • Administration of albumin • Paracentesis ± instillation select chemotherapeutic agents

From Engelking, C., and Kalinowski, B. (1996). *A comprehensive guide to breast cancer treatment current issues and controversies,* Triclinica Communications.

regimens associated with higher response may last from several months to a year. Both monotherapy and combination therapy are used. Long-term complete remissions are achievable in 10–20% of patients. Clinical response is generally evaluated after two cycles of chemotherapy.

CHEMOTHERAPY IN ADVANCED BREAST CANCER

The optimal approach to chemotherapy treatment in metastatic breast cancer has not yet been determined (Miles *et al.,* 2002). Sequential therapy allows the optimal delivery of single-drug therapy and potentially reduces the risk of toxicity, which may improve quality of life. Sequential therapy may be especially appropriate in frail or elderly patients, who may be unable to tolerate the toxicity of combination therapy, or in patients with slowly growing tumors. Sequential single-agent treatment (monotherapy) has been preferable to combination therapy, because older drug combinations were found to be no more effective and were often more toxic than monotherapy. However, more recent studies show that combination and sequential therapy have use in the treatment of metastatic breast cancer.

Sequential Therapy or Monotherapy

Capecitabine Capecitabine is an orally administered systemic prodrug of 5'-deoxy-5-fluorouridine (5'-DFUR) (accessed at: *http://www.xeloda.com*). The enzyme, thymidine phosphorylase (dThdPase), hydrolyzes 5'-DFUR to the active drug 5-FU. Many tissues throughout the body express thymidine phosphorylase and some cancers overexpress this enzyme in higher concentrations than surrounding normal tissues. Capecitabine monotherapy is indicated for the treatment of patients with metastatic breast cancer resistant to both paclitaxel and an anthracycline-containing chemotherapy regimen, or resistant to paclitaxel and for whom further anthracycline therapy is not indicated (e.g., patients who have received cumulative doses of 400 mg/m^2 of doxorubicin or doxorubicin equivalent).

As monotherapy, capecitabine was evaluated in an open-label single-arm trial conducted in 24 centers in the United States and Canada. A total of 162 patients with stage IV breast cancer were enrolled. Patients received a dose of 1255 mg/m^2 twice daily for 2 weeks followed by a 1 week rest period and given as 3 week cycles. The efficacy and safety of capecitabine monotherapy compares favorably with CMF in chemotherapy-naive patients, and with paclitaxel in patients having anthracycline-based chemotherapy.

Vinorelbine Vinorelbine is a semisynthetic vinca alkaloid derived from vinblastine. Vinorelbine inhibits cell growth by binding to the tubulin of the mitotic microtubules. Like other mitotic inhibitors, vinorelbine also promotes apoptosis in cancer cells. Norris *et al.* (2000) evaluated anthracyclines in combination with vinorelbine. Both agents are associated with myelosuppression. Patients experience higher incidence of neurotoxicity/neuropathy, constipation, and venous reactions when compared to monotherapy (anthracycline) alone.

Gemcitabine Gemcitabine, a cytotoxic nucleoside analogue, is structurally similar to cytarabine but has a wider spectrum of antitumor activity because of its different cellular pharmacology and mechanism of action. Gemcitabine is metabolized intracellularly to two active metabolites, gemcitabine diphosphate (dFdCDP) and gemcitabine triphosphate (dFdCTP). The cytotoxic effects of gemcitabine are exerted through incorporation of dFdCTP into DNA with the assistance of dFdCDP, resulting in inhibition of DNA synthesis and induction of apoptosis. Gemcitabine is cell-cycle phase specific (S- and G_1/S-phases).

Gemcitabine has demonstrable single-agent antitumor activity in metastatic breast cancer. Nearly 20 phase II clinical trials of gemcitabine alone or as part of combination therapy have confirmed its role in this disease (Qu & Perez, 2002). As a single agent, gemcitabine has response rates ranging from 16% to 37% in first-line and/or refractory settings. Gemcitabine has been combined with platinum, taxanes, vinorelbine, and anthracyclines. Qu and Perez (2002) reported response rates in the range of 50% to 80% in small phase II clinical trials. There is a mild toxicity profile with gemcitabine. It is being evaluated in combination with targeted drugs such as trastuzumab, tyrosine kinase inhibitors, and angiogenesis inhibitors.

Combination Therapy. Newer drug combinations, such as paclitaxel/trastuzumab or capecitabine/docetaxel, show survival advantages over single-agent therapy and have manageable safety profiles. Paclitaxel and trastuzumab each have single-agent activity against breast cancer with distinct mechanisms of action and no cross-resistance. This combination has shown a survival advantage of 25% over paclitaxel alone in women with metastatic breast cancer who overexpress HER-2 (Slamon *et al.*, 2001).

Capecitabine has been evaluated in clinical trials in combination with docetaxel (Taxotere®) (accessed at: *http://www.rocheusa.com/products/xeloda*). The combination dose regimen was selected based on the tolerability profile of the 75 mg/m^2 administered in 3 week cycles of docetaxel in combination with 1250 mg/m^2 twice daily for 14 days of capecitabine administered in 3 week cycles. As combination therapy, capecitabine was evaluated in combination with docetaxel in an open-label, multicenter, randomized trial in 75 centers in Europe, North America, South America, Asia, and Australia. A total of 511 patients with metastatic breast cancer resistant to, or recurring during or after, an anthracycline-containing therapy, or relapsing during or recurring within two years of completing an anthracycline-containing adjuvant therapy, were enrolled. Two hundred and fifty-five (255) patients were randomized to receive capecitabine 1250 mg/m^2 twice daily for 14 days followed by one week without treatment and docetaxel 75 mg/m^2 as a 1-hour intravenous infusion administered in 3 week cycles. Capecitabine plus docetaxel significantly reduced the risks of disease progression and death by 35% ($p = 0.0001$) and 23% ($p < 0.05$), respectively, and significantly increased median survival ($p < 0.05$) and objective response rates ($p < 0.01$) (Wagstaff *et al.*, 2003).

Capecitabine in combination with docetaxel has distinct mechanisms of action and single-agent activity. It is thought that the potential mechanisms that underlie the synergy are thymidine phosphorylation (TP) upregulation and Bcl-2 downregulation (O'Shaughnessy *et al.*, 2002). There are no overlapping toxicities with the major toxicity of docetaxel being myelosuppression and capecitabine monotherapy having a low incidence of myelosuppression.

Capecitabine plus paclitaxel (which further upregulates thymidine phosphorylase [TP] in tumor tissue) has demonstrated activity in two Phase II studies in advanced/metastatic breast cancer. Capecitabine plus vinorelbine shows activity in patients with metastatic breast cancer who have previously received chemotherapy. Capecitabine in triple combinations with an anthracycline and a taxane or cyclophosphamide have also shown to be highly active. In the future, capecitabine may be combined with novel biologic agents, such as trastuzumab and bevacizumab, the former combination has already shown encouraging results in a pilot trial.

Side Effects with Combination Chemotherapy.

Physical side effects are similar to those resulting from adjuvant therapy regimens. The most common side effects are bone marrow depression, nausea, vomiting, weight gain or loss, alopecia, fatigue, and sleep disturbance. (See Chapter 13 for a discussion of side effect management.)

There are additional side effect management issues with the use of agents such as capecitabine because it is a self-administered, home-based therapy (Mrozek-Orlowski *et al.*, 1999). The recommended dose is 1250 mg/m^2 twice a day for 2 weeks followed by a 1 week rest period every three weeks. The capecitabine dose is taken daily in two divided doses (about 12 hours apart) within 30 minutes after the end of a meal. The tablets should be taken with water. Compliance with daily oral medication is a concern. Patients must be taught to take the medication as prescribed. They should not "double up" after missed or skipped doses. In addition, if they experience side effects and decreased dose modification is necessary, they must not increase the dose at a later date.

Side effects specific to capecitabine are hand-foot syndrome (i.e., palmar-plantar erythrodysesthesia) and diarrhea (Mrozek-Orlowski *et al.*, 1999). Mild to moderate anemia is a frequent side effect. Other side effects that have been reported include stomatitis, nausea, vomiting, dyspepsia, anorexia, abdominal pain, constipation, fatigue, and transient hyperbilirubinemia. When capecitabine is combined with docetaxel, additional common adverse effects that occur over 20% of the time include leukopenia, alopecia, edema, pyrexia, asthenia, and constipation (Mrozek-Orlowski *et al.*, 1999; *http://www.xeloda.com/web*).

Hand-foot syndrome (HFS) is the dose-limiting toxicity. The cause of HSF is unknown. HFS usually appears during the first cycle of capecitabine but can occur at anytime. Symptoms may occur during treatment or during the seven-day rest period. Once HFS occurs, it tends to persist even if in a mild stage (Mrozek-Orlowski *et al.*, 1999).

In the early mild stage, patients describe HFS as a tingling sensation with mild erythema, painless swelling, tenderness, rash, or dry and itchy skin on the palms of the hands and the soles of the feet. Patients need to be educated to stop the medication and wait until the problem resolves. In addition, patients should be taught to use emollient lotions, creams containing lanolin, Vitamin B6, and cotton gloves, and they should minimizing pressure on the soles of their feet. Dose modification may be necessary when patients resume taking the medication.

Hand-foot syndrome can progress to painful erythema, swelling of the hands and feet, discomfort causing alterations in daily activities, moist desquamation, or blistering, and severe pain. When severe side effects occur, it is recommended that patients stop therapy until toxicity is resolved. Dose modification may also be necessary.

Capecitabine is also associated with diarrhea, which can be severe (accessed at: *http://www.rocheusa.com/products/xeloda/*). Gastrointestinal (GI) symptoms are thought to result from the antiproliferative activity of capecitabine on epithelial cells in the GI mucosa. Patients with severe diarrhea should be carefully monitored. In the clinical safety trial, the median time to first occurrence of grade 2 to 4 diarrhea was 34 days (ranging from 1 to 369 days). The median duration of grade 3 to 4 diarrhea was 5 days. If grade 2, 3, or 4 diarrhea occurs, patients should discontinue the drug until the diarrhea resolves or decreases in intensity to grade 1. After a recurrence of grade 2 diarrhea or occurrence of any grade 3 or 4 diarrhea, capecitabine doses should be decreased. In general, the recommended treatment for diarrhea is loperamide and diet modification.

Drug interactions occur with antacids containing magnesium and aluminum-hydroxides, which affect the absorption of capecitabine. Drug interactions also occur if patients are on warfarin or phenytoin with changes in bleeding levels.

Capecitabine is contraindicated in patients with creatinine clearance less than 30mL/min. Patients having mild to moderate renal impairment must be carefully monitored. There are no recommended dose modifications for patients with mild to moderate hepatic dysfunction. However, should renal or hepatic toxicity occur during therapy, capecitabine is discontinued until the impairment resolves. Subsequent dosing recommendations are based on the severity and frequency of toxicity.

Since certain oral cancer drugs are covered by Medicare, nurses can assist patients in contacting the reimbursement hotline of the company Hoffman-LaRoche Pharmaceuticals (800-443-6676). A benefit of the oral fluorinated pyrimidines is that patients do not need implanted venous access devices and ambulatory pumps (Mrozek-Orlowski *et al.*, 1999).

TARGETED THERAPY

HER-2 is a proto-oncogene that encodes a 185 kDa transmembrance receptor, tyrosine kinase (Slamon *et al.*, 1989). HER-2 is amplified or overexpressed in 25–30% of human breast and ovarian cancers. Tumor cells may have extra copies of the HER-2/neu gene. Extra copies of HER-2/neu are associated with rapid proliferation and growth that metastasizes beyond the original site. Overexpression is related to poor prognosis in women with breast cancer.

Trastuzumab is a humanized version of the murine monoclonal antibody 4D5 that was approved for the treatment of advanced breast cancer that overexpresses the HER-2/neu oncogene (Nabholtz & Slamon, 2001). The mechanism of action targets extracellular domain of HER-2 growth factor receptor and inhibits signal transduction and cell proliferation.

Trastuzumab is approved for use in women with progressive, metastastic breast cancer that overexpresses HER-2, and in women with disease progression after one to two prior chemotherapy regimens. Trastuzumab has demonstrated effectiveness both as a single agent and when used in combination with chemotherapy. The U.S. Food and Drug Administration approved the use of trastuzumab and paclitaxel as first-line treatment of HER-2-overexpressing metastatic breast cancer, based on the results of a randomized phase III clinical trial showing that this combination produced higher response rates and longer survival duration than treatment with chemotherapy alone.

Ongoing trials are underway to evaluate the use of trastuzumab in combination with other forms of chemotherapy, including vinorelbine, docetaxel, anthracyclines, and platinum agents. It is thought that information from these trials will help resolve questions regarding the efficacy of various combinations and dosing schedules (Ligibel & Winer, 2002).

Initial therapy is a loading dose of 4 mg/kg IV over 90 minutes followed weekly with 2 mg/kg IV over 30 minutes. Chills and fever range from mild to moderate and diminishing in severity with subsequent infusions. Other side effects include nausea, vomiting, myelosuppression, and diarrhea.

Cardiac Dysfunction. Patients previously treated with anthracyclines are at higher risk for developing cardiac toxicity. Cardiac toxicity was also an unexpected side effect of trastuzumab treatment in the pivotal trials. The incidence of cardiac dysfunction increased with prior or concurrent doxorubicin exposure. When patients had minimal prior exposure to anthracyclines, the risk of cardiac dysfunction was 1%. When patients had more extensive prior doxorubicin exposure, the risk of cardiac dysfunction was 7% when trastuzumab was used as monotherapy. The incidence increased to 12% when trastuzumab was combined with paclitaxel. When patients received trastuzumab concurrently with doxorubicin, the risk of cardiac dysfunction increased 29% (Sparano, 2001).

The etiology of trastuzumab-associated cardiac dysfunction is unknown. However, concurrent or prior exposure to doxorubicin suggests a common pathophysiologic basis with anthracycline-induced myocardial injury. Several clinical trials are in progress to evaluate the efficacy and safety of trastuzumab in patients with early-stage disease and to develop strategies to minimize or prevent cardiac toxicity (Sparano, 2001). Sequential trastuzumab and anthracycline therapy is being studied rather than combination treatment (Nabholtz & Slamon, 2001).

HER-2 Tests. HER-2 overexpression may be a significant predictor of patient response to taxanes and anthracyclines. HER-2-positive status is the sole criterion for identifying patients with breast cancer for trastuzumab therapy, with demonstrated efficacy in women with metastatic breast cancer. Immunohistochemistry (IHC) and fluorescence in-situ hybridization (FISH), which measure the HER-2 protein and gene, respectively, are currently the most widely used HER-2 tests in the clinical setting. However, results from these assays are influenced by many variables, including choice of antibody or probe, methodology, level of user experience, and laboratory variability.

Although there is no widespread standard testing algorithm, the importance of HER-2 in clinical practice demands accurate and reproducible tests. Polymerase chain reaction (PCR) and chromogenic in-situ hybridization (CISH) are newer ways to assess HER-2 gene amplification. Enzyme-linked immunosorption assay (ELISA), a semiautomated technique that can be used to measure the level of the HER-2 extracellular domain (ECD) in serum, may also be useful. Although these technologies show great promise, they will need to be validated against IHC or FISH before being accepted into routine clinical practice.

LOCAL TREATMENT FOR METASTATIC DISEASE

RADIATION THERAPY

Radiation therapy may be used to palliate symptoms when the disease has spread to the bone, chest wall, axilla, spinal column, and brain. Palliative radiation is effective in reducing the distressing symptoms of metastasis and may be given in an emergency to treat the spinal column and brain.

Bone Metastasis. Patients with bone metastasis usually present with pain and possibly loss of mobility in the involved extremity (O'Rourke & Robinson, 1996). The diagnosis is confirmed by physical exam and bone scan or plain film. If the involved areas cannot be seen from these tests, a CT scan or MRI may be done to locate the lesion. The goals of radiation for bone metastasis are to alleviate the pain and prevent pathologic fracture.

Spinal Cord Compression. Spinal cord compression is one of the most serious complications of metastatic breast cancer. Compression may be caused by tumor growth placing pressure on the spinal cord or fracture of the vertebrae weakened by tumor cells. It can present as numbness, weakness, or paralysis of an extremity, with loss of bladder or bowel sphincter control. Patients may also experience moderate to severe pain. This condition requires emergency radiation treatment to prevent further damage to the spinal cord and to decrease pain.

Brain Metastasis. Breast cancer is one of the major cancers that metastasize to the brain, causing many sensory and perceptual changes. Symptoms include headache, dizziness, visual changes, gait changes, mental status changes, seizure activity, and weakness. Brain metastasis is confirmed by CT or MRI. Once confirmed, emergency treatment with radiation therapy is indicated. Steroids are given to help reduce intracranial pressure. Side effects include cranial hair loss, skin erythema, and potential for transient increase in neurological symptoms (O'Rourke & Robinson, 1996).

NURSING MANAGEMENT IN ADVANCED BREAST CANCER

The most important nursing consideration in advanced breast cancer is to help the patient and family plan and assist in the scheduling of treatments, in order to maintain the highest level of functioning with the least amount of disruption. Nurses must have a unique understanding of the dilemmas facing women with advanced disease who have to restart a long course of treatment and endure and manage side effects again. Patients face major changes in responsibilities at home and at work and face the difficulties of a shortened life expectancy. They must manage an uncertain future while coping with and managing advanced and metastatic breast cancer. Table 11.2 summarizes the quality of life issues that face these patients.

Nursing considerations are focused on explaining that treatment options and goals are different for advanced disease. Helping patients and their families interpret survival data is vital. Recurrence is viewed as more distressful than initial diagnosis, and patients may experience more difficulty in making decisions about treatment. Other nursing roles are to teach patients to set priorities, provide emotional support, and strengthen patients' coping abilities. The nurse should also help spouses, significant others, children, and other family members understand issues in advanced breast cancer. Referral to supportive networks, groups, and social workers for supportive and expressive therapy may also be useful.

Table 11.2 Quality of Life Issues with Recurrent and Metastatic Breast Cancer

Physical well-being
- Physical symptoms such as pain, metastatic skin lesions, and side effects of treatment
- Metastatic skin lesion management

Psychological well-being
- Anxiety and depression are generally underdiagnosed and undertreated
- Concerns about physical decline, changes in body image, threats to sexuality and self-esteem, and becoming a burden

Social well-being
- Work, financial, and family concerns
- Change in work patterns or sick leave
- Health insurance and financial considerations
- Family fears over uncertain treatment outcomes and changes in family roles and responsibilities

Spiritual well-being
- Uncertainty
- Concerns about dying and death
- Maintaining and promoting hope

REFERENCES

Biganzoli, L., Martin, M., & Twelves, C. (2002). Moving forward with capecitabine: a glimpse of the future. *Oncologist, 7*(Suppl 6), 29–35.

Carlson, R. (1998). Quality of life issues in the treatment of metastatic breast cancer. *Oncology, 12*(3 Suppl 4), 27–31.

Engelking, C., & Kalinowski, B. (1996). *A comprehensive guide to breast cancer treatment: current issues and controversies.* New York: Triclinica Communications.

Fossati, R., Confalonieri, C., Torri, V., *et al.* (1998). Cytotoxic and hormonal treatment for metastatic breast cancer: a systematic review of published randomized trials involving 31,510 women. *Journal of Clinical Oncology, 16,* 3439–3460.

Hortobagyi, G.N. (2002). Gemcitabine in combination with vinorelbine for treatment of advanced breast cancer. *Clinical Breast Cancer, 3*(Suppl 1), 34–38.

Hudis, C.A. (2002). Single-agent versus combination therapy in advanced breast cancer: potential roles of capecitabine. *Oncology (Huntingt). 16*(10 Suppl 12), 13–16.

Ligibel, J.A., & Winer, E.P. (2002). Trastuzumab/chemotherapy combinations in metastatic breast cancer. *Seminars in Oncology, 29*(3 Suppl 11), 38–43.

McEvilly, J.M., & Dow, K.H. (1998, April). Treating metastatic breast cancer: principles and current practice. *American Journal of Nursing* (Supplement), 26–29.

Miles, D., Von Minckwitz, G., & Seidman, A. (2002). Combination versus sequential single-agent therapy in metastatic breast cancer. *Oncologist, 7*(Suppl 6), 13–19.

Mrozek-Orlowski, M., Frye, D., & Sanborn, H. (1999). Capecitabine: nursing implications of a new oral chemotherapeutic agent. *Oncology Nursing Forum, 26*(4), 753–762.

Nabholtz, J., & Slamon, D. (2001). New adjuvant strategies for breast cancer. Meeting the challenge of integrating chemotherapy and trastuzumab (Herceptin). *Seminars in Oncology, 118*(3), 1–12.

Norris B., Pritchard K.I., James K., Myles J., Bennett K., Marlin S., Skillings J., Findlay B., Vandenberg T., Goss P., Latreille J., Rudinskas L., Lofters W., Trudeau M., Osoba D., Rodgers A.(2000). Phase III comparative study of vinorelbine combined with doxorubicin versus doxorubicin alone in disseminated metastatic/recurrent breast cancer: National Cancer Institute of Canada Clinical Trials Group Study MA8. *Journal of Clinical Oncology, 18*(12), 2385–2394.

O'Rourke, N., & Robinson, L. (1996). Breast cancer and the role of radiation therapy. In K.H. Dow (Ed.), *Contemporary issues in breast cancer,* pp. 43–58. Sudbury, Mass.: Jones & Bartlett.

O'Shaughnessy, J., Miles, D., Vukelja, S., *et al.* (2002). Superior survival with capecitabine plus docetaxel combination therapy in anthracycline-pretreated patients with advanced breast cancer: Phase III trial results. *Journal of Clinical Oncology, 20,* 2812–2823.

Qu, G., & Perez, E.A. (2002). Gemcitabine and targeted therapy in metastatic breast cancer. *Seminars in Oncology, 29*(3 Suppl 11), 44–52.

Slamon, D., Godolphin, W., Jones, L.A., *et al.* (1989). Studies of the HER-2/neu proto-oncogene in human breast and ovarian cancer. *Science, 244,* 707–712.

Slamon, D.J., Leyland-Jones, B., Shak, S., *et al.* (2001). Use of chemotherapy plus a monoclonal antibody against HER2 for metastatic breast cancer that overexpresses HER2. *New England Journal of Medicine, 344,* 783–792.

Wagstaff, A.J., Ibbotson, T., & Goa, K.L. (2003). Capecitabine: a review of its pharmacology and therapeutic efficacy in the management of advanced breast cancer. *Drugs, 63*(2), 217–236.

12

HORMONAL THERAPY IN ADVANCED AND METASTATIC DISEASE

M. JOYCE DIENGER, DNSc, RN

INTRODUCTION

Many advances have been made in the treatment of breast cancer during the last several decades. Nonetheless, no woman with a history of invasive breast cancer is ever completely free of the threat of recurrence. As many as 20% to 30% of women diagnosed with node-negative disease and treated with standard therapy will experience return of their disease (Ellis *et al.,* 2000). Each year, 28% of women diagnosed with breast cancer have regional involvement, and 6% have metastatic disease at the time of diagnosis (American Cancer Society, 2002).

Metastatic breast cancer is not curable (Ellis *et al.,* 2000). Therefore, the goal of systemic therapy in metastatic breast cancer is palliation or a prolonged survival and improved quality of life. Because hormonal therapy is less toxic than chemotherapy, it is often the treatment of choice, especially in women with estrogen receptor-positive (ER+) tumors. The purpose of hormonal therapy is to inhibit estrogen-stimulated tumor growth through the administration of agents that either compete for binding at ER sites or reduce the amount of circulating estrogen (Osborne, 1998). The common approach to treatment of metastatic ER+ breast cancer consists of sequential hormonal therapies, reserving chemotherapy until the disease becomes refractory to all hormonal options (Osborne, 1999). An exception might be a woman with serum HER-2/neu-positive tumors even if they are ER+. Data indicate that these patients are less likely to exhibit a favorable response to hormonal therapy and that in those who do respond, the duration of response and median survival is shorter than in those without tumor HER-2/neu protein expression (Lipton *et al.,* 2002).

Approximately 30% of women with metastatic breast cancer will have a favorable response to hormonal therapy (Muss, 1999). The response to hormonal therapy is slow, often requiring three to four months of follow-up before a response is observed. The average duration of response with any one of the various agents is six months to one year. However, in some patients the disease can be controlled, neither progressing nor regressing for longer periods of time. The response rate is somewhat higher with combination chemotherapy (40% to 70%), but the toxicities associated with chemotherapy often result in a reduced quality of life. Additionally, the average duration of response with chemotherapy for metastatic disease is about nine months, and a sustained response is seldom achieved.

SELECTION OF HORMONAL THERAPY

The selection of patients for hormonal therapy over chemotherapy as treatment for metastatic breast cancer needs to be individualized. Treatment priorities should be reviewed with each patient and the risks and benefits of each modality weighed carefully. Once the diagnosis of metastatic disease has been established, it is suggested that the clinician discuss with the patient prognostic factors and treatment goals then choose a treatment modality that offers the highest efficacy with the least toxicity (Ellis *et al.*, 2000).

Generally, patients most likely to respond favorably to a course of hormonal therapy for metastatic disease are postmenopausal, have an ER+ and/or progesterone receptor-positive (PR+) tumor, experienced a five-year or longer disease-free interval, have metastatic disease limited to bone and soft tissue, and have disease that is not progressing rapidly (Ellis *et al.*, 2000). Patients who exhibited a previous positive response to hormonal therapy and subsequently experienced disease progression will usually respond again when given another hormonal agent in a different class. This implies that resistance to a particular hormonal agent does not necessarily indicate loss of estrogen dependence of the breast tumor and resistance to all hormonal therapy. It is important, however, to confirm the ER status of the metastases as well as the primary tumor, because around 20% of ER+ primary tumors have ER– metastases (Elledge & Fuqua, 2000). In metastatic disease, the ER status of the metastatic site may be more predictive of treatment response than the ER status of the primary tumor (Kuukasjarvi *et al.*, 1996). (See Chapter 10 for a more complete discussion of the significance of ER/PR tumor status in hormonal therapy.)

TYPES OF HORMONAL AGENTS

Table 12.1 outlines the hormonal agents commonly used today in the treatment of metastatic breast cancer. Tamoxifen was introduced as a treatment for metastatic breast cancer in the early 1970s and, due to high response rates and tolerability, quickly became first-line therapy for the treatment of metastatic disease in premenopausal and postmenopausal women (Ellis *et al.*, 2000). Tamoxifen, a selective estrogen response modifier (SERM), remains the most commonly used hormonal agent in the treatment of breast cancer and the agent to which all other hormonal agents for breast cancer are compared.

Table 12.1 Hormonal Agents Used in the Treatment of Metastatic Breast Cancer

Class/agent	Administration	Major adverse reactions
Selective estrogen receptor modulators		
Tamoxifen (Novaldex®)	20 mg PO/daily	Hot flashes, vaginal discharge, bleeding
Toremifene (Fareston®)	60 mg PO/daily	Irregular menses, nausea, increased risk for endometrial cancer, thromboembolic events
Progestins		
Megestrol acetate (Megace®)	40 mg PO/qid	Weight gain, fluid retention, hypertension, vaginal bleeding, nausea, thromboembolic events
Aromatase inhibitors		
Anastrozole (Arimidex®)	1 mg p PO/daily	Hot flashes, headache,
Letrozole (Femara®)	2.5 mg PO/daily	nausea/vomiting, fatigue,
Exemestane (Aromasin®)	25 mg PO/daily	bone pain
Pure antiestrogen/estrogen downregulation		
Fulvestrant (Faslodex®)	250 mg IM/monthly	GI disturbances, hot flashes, pharyngitis, headache, back pain, arthralgia, UTI, thromboembolic events

PO = by mouth; qid = four times a day; IM = intramuscular

Note: Administration of prescribed drug is continued until disease progression becomes evident.

Data from Ellis *et al.*, 2000; Howell *et al.*, 2002; Lindley, 1999; and Osborne *et al.*, 2002.

Unfortunately, not all tumors respond to tamoxifen, and many women experience a progression of disease following a course of tamoxifen adjuvant therapy. Megestrol was frequently, then, given as second-line therapy. However, hormonal agents in another class, aromatase inhibitors, have proven more efficacious than megestrol and are now approved as first- and second-line therapy in postmenopausal women with ER+ metastatic breast cancer. Recently, fulvestrant, a pure antiestrogen, was approved as treatment for postmenopausal women whose disease progressed following a course of hormonal therapy. Consequently, megestrol is now considered by many to be third- or fourth-line therapy (Dow, 2002). A discussion of each of these agents and their use in the treatment of metastatic breast cancer follows.

SELECTIVE ESTROGEN RECEPTOR MODULATORS

The SERMs are a classification of agents known for their ability to exert both estrogen antagonistic and agonistic effects on various target tissues (Lindley, 1999). Tamoxifen and toremifene are the two nonsteroidal agents belonging to this class that have approval for treatment of premenopausal and postmenopausal women with ER+ metastatic breast cancer. They exhibit estrogen antagonistic effects by blocking estradiol from binding to the ER sites on the nuclear membrane of breast tumor cells. Thus, the stimulus for continued tumor proliferation is removed, resulting in tumor regression. Beneficial estrogen agonistic effects are exhibited by the maintenance of bone mineral density and improved blood lipid profiles. Unfortunately, estrogen agonistic effects are also exhibited on endometrial tissue and blood coagulation processes. Therefore, the adverse effects of the increased risk for endometrial cancer and thromboembolic events (Table 12.1) cause the most concern, although to a lesser degree in the treatment of metastatic disease versus use in the adjuvant setting (Lindley, 1999). (See Chapter 10 for a complete discussion of the benefits and risks of tamoxifen therapy.)

TAMOXIFEN

Tamoxifen remains the initial standard hormonal therapy for postmenopausal women with advanced disease who have not previously received tamoxifen as adjuvant therapy (Ellis *et al.*, 2000). It is also a first-line alternative to oophorectomy or therapy with a luteinizing hormone-releasing hormone (LHRH) agonist in premenopausal women. Overall, tamoxifen achieves tumor regression in 16% to 56% of women, with a mean duration of response between 12 and 18 months in women with metastatic disease (Osborne *et al.*, 2000). Another 20% of patients will experience stable disease lasting for at least six months. Women with ER+/PR+ or unknown metastatic disease have a greater likelihood of response than those with ER– and/or PR– disease (Osborne, 1998). In one prospective study, premenopausal women with ER+ tumors achieved an overall 24% response rate to tamoxifen therapy, but postmenopausal women with ER+ tumors experienced an 86% response rate (Ravdin *et al.*, 1992). Women in the study with ER+/PR– tumors achieved a clinically significant benefit from tamoxifen therapy, but to a lesser degree than women with ER+/PR+ tumors.

In addition to the adverse reactions noted in Table 12.1, women with metastatic disease may also experience an increase in the number and size of metastatic skin nodules and bone pain two days to three weeks after beginning therapy (Ellis *et al.*, 2000). This is often called tumor flare, as the skin nodules often develop erythema. In approximately 5% of patients, the symptoms are accompanied by hypercalcemia. These symptoms are thought to be related to the drug's estrogen agonistic properties and usually subside. Supportive therapy with analgesics and/or prednisone for one to two weeks is helpful in reducing the erythema (Wilson, 1993). If symptoms persist, therapy may be stopped for a few weeks and then reintroduced slowly with increasing doses until the desired dose is achieved. Twice weekly monitoring of serum calcium levels and astute observation for signs and symptoms of hypercalcemia are suggested for the first several weeks, as the hypercalcemia, when present, can be life threatening and may warrant discontinuing tamoxifen.

TOREMIFENE

Toremifene is an alternative to tamoxifen and exhibits similar tissue-specific estrogen antagonistic and agonistic effects (Minton, 1999). Results of phase III clinical trials indicate that treatment of metastatic breast cancer with toremifene results in response rates comparable to tamoxifen. Results of preclinical studies indicated that toremifene may possibly exert less of an effect on the DNA in the endometrium and thus carries a lower risk for endometrial cancer than tamoxifen. Unfortunately, a 12-month study of post-menopausal women with breast cancer receiving tamoxifen or toremifene demonstrated similar estrogenic endometrial effects with both drugs. However, toremifene is known to have a 14% rise in serum high-density lipids (HDLs), but tamoxifen is known to have a 5% decrease in HDLs. The significance of this finding remains unclear, and toremifene is now being compared with tamoxifen in adjuvant clinical trials.

As previously mentioned, women with metastatic breast cancer almost always develop resistance to treatment with SERMs for reasons not entirely understood (Osborne *et al.*, 2000). Changes in the ER and growth factor signaling are thought to be contributing factors. Additionally, tamoxifen's intrinsic agonistic activity can result in disease progression resulting from actual drug-stimulated tumor growth. Thus, a regression of tumor growth has been observed following withdrawal of tamoxifen in women whose disease progressed while on therapy. The SERMs are typically cross-resistant. Therefore, if treatment with tamoxifen has failed, it is unlikely that treatment with toremifene will be effective. However, treatment with another hormonal agent may be effective in further controlling the disease.

PROGESTINS

Until a few years ago, treatment with a progestin, such as megestrol acetate, was the frequent choice for second-line hormonal therapy in metastatic breast cancer (Lindley, 1999). However, with the development of new agents, such as the aromatase inhibitors and pure antiestrogens, the progestins are used more today as third- or fourth-line therapy (Dow, 2002). The mechanism of action of megestrol in tumor regression is not completely understood. Suggested modes of action include inhibition of aromatase activity, an increase in rate of estrogen catabolism, and/or blockage of PR sites (Ellis *et al.*, 2000). Megestrol has an efficacy comparable to tamoxifen, exhibiting response rates between 20% and 40% in clinical trials (Wasaff, 1997). As many as 50% of women will experience weight gain while taking megestrol. Often, weight gain is accompanied by fluid retention leading to hypertension. The added weight can affect body image in some women, although it can be a benefit for those who are experiencing cancer-induced weight loss.

AROMATASE INHIBITORS

In postmenopausal women, most of the circulating estrogens are derived from the conversion of the adrenal androgen androstenedione and testosterone to estrone and estradiol by the aromatase enzyme in peripheral tissues (Gross & Strasser, 2001). Aromatase inhibitors decrease the level of circulating estrogen by blocking the action of the aromatase enzyme in adipose tissue as well as in cells of muscles, the liver, breast tissue, and the breast tumor itself. Therapy with aromatase inhibitors is contraindicated in premenopausal women, as blocking the aromatization process in premenopausal women results in polycystic ovaries and androgen excess (Ellis *et al.*, 2000).

The aromatase inhibitors were first approved as second-line hormonal therapy for use in women whose disease progressed following treatment with tamoxifen. Aminoglutethimide, a nonselective agent, was the first aromatase inhibitor used in the United States. As a nonselective inhibitor, it affects the synthesis of the other adrenal hormones, such as aldosterone and cortisol, as well as androstenedione and testosterone. Consequently, treatment with aminoglutethimide resulted in adrenal insufficiency syndrome, necessitating the concurrent administration of glucocorticoids (Cocconi, 1994). Due to the development of the selective third-generation aromatase inhibitors, aminoglutethimide is rarely, if ever, used today.

The third-generation aromatase inhibitors available today include the nonsteroidal agents anastrozole and letrozole and the steroidal agent exemestane (Lindley, 1999). Anastrozole and letrozole have similar chemical structures and bind reversibly to the aromatase enzyme. Exemestane binds irreversibly to aromatase, inactivating and destroying the enzyme. Thus, exemestane is sometimes called a "suicide" aromatase inhibitor. The third-generation agents selectively inhibit the aromatase enzyme and, therefore, are well tolerated without the toxicities experienced with aminoglutethimide. They are very effective in lowering circulating estrogen levels. A daily 1-mg dose of anastrozole provides more than a 95% inhibition of whole-body aromatase activity in postmenopausal women with advanced breast cancer (Geisler *et al.*, 1996). Both anastrozole and letrozole are now approved as first-line hormonal therapy in postmenopausal women with ER+ or unknown metastatic breast cancer, while exemestane remains as an agent for second-line therapy.

In clinical trials of second-line therapy with patients who progressed while on tamoxifen therapy, anastrozole, letrozole, and exemestane demonstrated antitumor activity equal to or superior to megestrol. Patients in these studies taking one of the aromatase inhibitors were able to experience an average clinical benefit of 38.2% versus 35.6% with megestrol and objective responses (complete remission [CR] + partial remission [PR]) of 12.6% versus 12.2%, 23.6% versus 16.4%, and 15.0% versus 12.4%, respectively (Buzdar *et al.*, 1998; Dombernowsky *et al.*, 1998; Kaufmann *et al.*, 2000). Additionally, in a quality of life assessment in one study comparing anastrozole and megestrol, women taking anastrozole had better physical and psychologic scores than women taking megestrol (Buzdar *et al.*, 1997).

Anastrozole has also exhibited equal or superior efficacy compared to tamoxifen in studies of first-line hormonal therapy for postmenopausal women with advanced breast cancer. Two randomized double-blind multicenter clinical trials (one with 668 women and the other with 353 women) compared anastrozole 1 mg/day to tamoxifen 20 mg/day (Bonneterre *et al.*, 2000; Nabholtz *et al.*, 2000). Women in both trials had locally advanced or metastatic ER+ and/or PR+ or estrogen receptor unknown tumors. Some women had received prior adjuvant therapy with tamoxifen. In the trial conducted by Bonneterre *et al.* (2000), women in the anastrozole and tamoxifen groups experienced fairly equal median time to progression (TTP) (8.2 months versus 8.3 months) and overall response (OR) (32.9% versus 32.6%). A clinical benefit (defined as CR + PR + stabilization of disease ≥ 24 weeks) was achieved by 56.2% and 55.5% of the women, respectively.

In the trial conducted by Nabholtz *et al.* (2000), women taking anastrozole experienced a significantly longer TTP than the women taking tamoxifen (11.1 months versus

5.6 months, p = .005). The percentage of women experiencing a clinical benefit was also significantly larger among the women taking anastrozole than among the women taking tamoxifen (59% versus 46%, p = .0098). Both drugs were well tolerated in each trial. In both trials, there were fewer incidences of thromboembolic events and vaginal bleeding among the women taking anastrozole.

Comparable findings have been reported in studies using letrozole and exemestane. In a large clinical trial comparing letrozole to tamoxifen as first-line therapy, 907 post-menopausal women with advanced breast cancer were randomized to receive either letrozole 2.5 mg/day or tamoxifen 20 mg/day (Mouridsen *et al.*, 2001). Results indicated that letrozole was significantly superior to tamoxifen regarding TTP (median 41 weeks versus 26 weeks) and significantly reduced the risk of progression by 30% (hazard ratio 0.70, p = .0001). Likewise, time to treatment failure was longer with letrozole than with tamoxifen (median 40 weeks versus 25 weeks), as was the overall response rate (30% versus 20%, p = .0006) and rate of clinical benefit (49% versus 38%, p = .001). In a smaller randomized phase II clinical trial comparing exemestane 25 mg/day and tamoxifen 20 mg/day, median TTP was 31 months versus 32 months, although an objective response (CR + PR) was experienced by 42% versus 16% of the women in the exemestane and tamoxifen groups, respectively (Paridaens *et al.*, 2000).

FULVESTRANT, PURE ANTIESTROGEN

Even though treatment with an aromatase inhibitor significantly reduces the level of circulating estrogens, breast tumors can adapt to low estrogen concentrations, and disease can progress following only a brief period of remission (Osborne, 1999). Thus, a more effective hormonal agent might be one that causes total loss of the ER from the cell. A pure steroidal antiestrogen, namely fulvestrant, is such an agent. Fulvestrant is the purest ER antagonist available today. It has an affinity for binding to the ER near that of 17α-estradiol but exhibits no estrogenic activity. Fulvestrant has the unique ability to bind to the ER of the nuclear cell membrane, blocking most, if not all, of the estrogen-regulated gene transcription activity, as well as causing loss of the ER protein from the cell, known as ER downregulation (Robertson, 2002). Cultured cells and breast tumors from *in vivo* experimental model systems revealed markedly decreased ER levels following exposure to fulvestrant (Osborne, 1999).

In animal studies, the administration of fulvestrant resulted in greater tumor regression and a longer duration of remission compared to tamoxifen (Osborne *et al.*, 1995). Additionally, tumors previously resistant to tamoxifen responded to fulvestrant, suggesting different mechanisms of resistance between SERMs and a pure estrogen antagonist. Since fulvestrant has no estrogenic effect, there is no endometrial tissue stimulation and no increased risk for endometrial cancer (Robertson, 2002). Fulvestrant does not cross the blood-brain barrier, which should decrease the incidence of hot flashes.

Favorable responses to fulvestrant were achieved in an early phase II trial with 19 postmenopausal women with advanced breast cancer resistant to tamoxifen (Howell *et al.*,

1995). In all, 13 or 69% of the women experienced some clinical benefit. Seven women experienced a partial response and six women experienced stable disease for a median duration of 18 months with minimal side effects.

Two similarly designed phase III trials, one in Europe and one in North America, compared the safety and efficacy of fulvestrant as a 250-mg monthly intramuscular injection with anastrozole 1 mg per day given orally in postmenopausal women with advanced breast cancer (Howell *et al.*, 2002; Osborne *et al.*, 2002). A total average of 56.4% of the women had experienced disease progression with previous hormonal therapy. Data illustrating the efficacy end points is listed in Table 12.2. The mean follow-up time was 14.6 months for the European study and 17.0 months for the North American study. Overall, fulvestrant demonstrated efficacy similar to anastrozole in terms of TTP, OR, and clinical benefit in both studies.

In the North American study, the difference in median duration of response was notable at 19.0 months for fulvestrant and 10.8 months for anastrozole. Both fulvestrant and anastrozole were well tolerated by the women in both trials. The common adverse reactions are listed in Table 12.1. The incidence of study withdrawal due to drug-related adverse events was 0.9% for fulvestrant and 1.2% for anastrozole. Results of these studies indicate that fulvestrant is at least as effective as anastrozole and provides an additional treatment option for postmenopausal women with metastatic breast cancer that progressed on other hormonal therapy.

Fulvestrant cannot be absorbed orally; therefore, it is administered monthly as a 250-mg intramuscular injection (AstraZeneca, 2002). It is to be administered into the dorsogluteal muscle either as a single 5-ml injection or in a divided dose of two 2.5-ml injections. Fulvestrant is packaged as one syringe containing 5 ml (250 mg) or two syringes containing 2.5 ml (125 mg) each with a 21-gauge Safety Glide™ needle. It must be stored in a refrigerator 2°–8°C (36°–46°F) and brought to room temperature prior to administration. The injection(s) should be given slowly. The Z-track intramuscular injection technique can be

Table 12.2 Comparison of Efficacy Results of European and North American Trials with Fulvestrant and Anastrozole

| | European study | | North American study | |
	Fulvestrant $N = 222$	Anastrozole $N = 229$	Fulvestrant $N = 206$	Anastrozole $N = 194$
Clinical end points				
TTP (months)	5.5	5.1	5.4	3.4
OR	20.7%	15.7%	17.5%	17.5%
CB rate	44.6%	45.0%	42.2%	36.1%
DOR (months)	15.0	14.5	19.0	10.8

TTP = time to progression; OR = objective response; CB = clinical benefit (complete response + partial response + stable disease ≥ 24 weeks); DOR = duration of response

Data from Howell *et al.*, 2002; Osborne *et al.*, 2002.

used to prevent leakage of the drug into the subcutaneous tissue as the needle is withdrawn (Lynn, 2002). Injection site reactions with mild transient pain and inflammation were seen in 7% of patients (1% of treatments) who received a single 5-ml injection (Howell *et al.*, 2002) and in 27% of patients (4.6% of treatments) given the two 2.5-ml injections (Osborne *et al.*, 2002).

NURSING MANAGEMENT

Metastatic breast cancer is usually very distressing. However, the availability of several hormonal agents in the clinical setting now allows more treatment choices. Nurses have a greater role than ever before in helping women to understand and cope with their advanced disease and hormonal therapy. Women receiving fulvestrant will see the oncology nurse monthly for injections. This timing offers excellent opportunities to enhance the nurse's role as liaison between patients and the treatment team. Additionally, the nurse can help the patient and family to cope with treatment by explaining the purpose and action of the hormonal therapy, why previous hormonal therapy may have failed and the need for a change in therapy, the goal of the therapy (i.e., palliation, not cure), and the usual adverse effects of the drug and how to manage them (Lynn, 2002). Table 12.3 offers

Table 12.3 Advice to Patients on Coping with Adverse Reactions Caused by Hormonal Therapy

Adverse reaction experienced	Advice
Hot flashes	• Wear absorbent cotton clothing • Wear layers of clothes that can be easily removed if overheated • Avoid caffeine, spicy foods, and alcohol
Weight gain	• Exercise 20 to 30 minutes daily (also improves symptoms of fatigue) • Eat foods low in fat, such as fruits and vegetables
Nausea	• When preparing foods, present them in an appealing way, such as using colorful vegetables
Vaginitis	• Wear cotton underwear • Use vaginal lubricants
Thromboembolism	• Report immediately any symptoms of shortness of breath and/or swelling, tenderness in lower extremities
Urinary tract infections	• Drink at least 6 to 8 glasses of fluid (including water and cranberry juice) daily
Decreased sex drive (due to lack of estrogen/vaginal lubrication)	• Use vaginal lubrication prior to intercourse
Joint disorders	• Take OTC NSAIDs or acetaminophen
Pain at needle injection site (with fulvestrant)	• Use a topical anesthetic cream • Use warm/cold compresses on injection site

OTC = over-the-counter; NSAIDs = nonsteroidal anti-inflammatory drugs

From: Lynn, J. (2002). The oncology nurse's role in educating patients on endocrine therapy for metastatic breast cancer—focus on fulvestrant. *Cancer Nursing*, 25(2S), 16S. Adapted with permission.

some advice to give to patients for coping with the common adverse reactions experienced with hormonal therapy. It is suggested that women keep a written summary of symptoms they are experiencing (related to hormonal therapy or advancing disease) and share it with the nurse during routine visits to the clinic or office. The nurse can determine which symptoms are causing the patient appreciable concern, share these with the health care team, and provide advice on symptom management techniques.

SUMMARY

Several hormonal agents have demonstrated effectiveness in prolonging survival while maintaining the quality of life in women with metastatic breast cancer. The availability of the aromatase inhibitors as first-line hormonal therapy offers additional options for women with concerns regarding the increased risk for endometrial cancer and thromboembolic events associated with the SERMs. Figure 12.1 provides a proposed sequence of hormonal therapies for postmenopausal women with ER+ advanced breast cancer. Only tamoxifen and LHRH are approved for use in premenopausal women. However, the idea of giving premenopausal women with advanced disease a combination of LHRH analogues and aromatase inhibitors is being considered (Ellis *et al.*, 2000). Additionally, studies seeking information as to the efficacy and optimal dose of fulvestrant for use with premenopausal women and fulvestrant versus tamoxifen as first-line therapy are underway (Dow, 2002).

FIGURE 12.1 Options for Sequencing of Hormonal Therapy in Metastatic Breast Cancer.

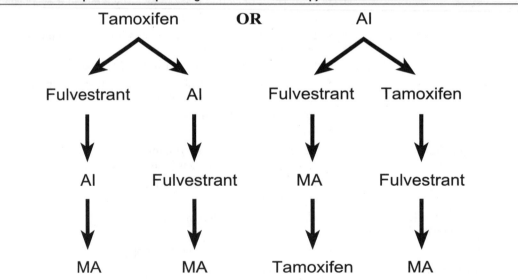

AI= Aromatase inhibitor; MA= Megestrol acetate

From: Dow, K.H. (2002). Existing and emerging endocrine therapies for breast cancer. *Cancer Nursing, 25*(2S), 10S. Reprinted with permission.

REFERENCES

American Cancer Society. (2002). *Breast cancer facts and figures, 2001–2002*. Atlanta, Ga.: Author.

AstraZeneca Pharmaceuticals. (2002). *Faslodex® fulvestrant injection. Prescribing information, 7/02*. Wilmington, Del.: Author.

Bonneterre, J., Thurlimann, B., Robertson, J.F., Krzakowski, M., Mauriac, L., Koralewski, P., Vergote, I., Webster, A., Steinberg, M., & von Euler, M. (2000). Anastrozole versus tamoxifen as first-line therapy for advanced breast cancer in 668 postmenopausal women: results of the tamoxifen or Arimidex randomized group efficacy and tolerability study. *Journal of Clinical Oncology, 18*, 3748–3757.

Buzdar, A.U., Jonat, W., Howell, A., Jones, S.E., Blomqvist, C.P., Vogel, C.L., Eiermann, W., Wolter, J.M., Steinberg, M., Webster, A., & Lee, D. (1998). Anastrozole versus megestrol acetate in the treatment of postmenopausal women with advanced breast carcinoma: results of a survival update based on a combined analysis of data from two mature phase III trials. *Cancer, 83*, 1142–1152.

Buzdar, A.U., Jones, S.E., Vogel, C.L., Wolter, J., Plourde, P., & Webster, A. (1997). A phase III trial comparing anastrozole (1 and 10 milligrams), a potent and selective aromatase inhibitor, with megestrol acetate in postmenopausal women with advanced breast carcinoma. *Cancer, 79*, 730–739.

Cocconi, G. (1994). First-generation aromatase inhibitors caminoglutethimide and testololactone. *Breast Cancer Research and Treatment, 30*, 57–80.

Dombernowsky, P., Smith, I., Falkson, G., Leonard, R., Panasci, L., Bellmunt, J., Bezwoda, W., Gardin, G., Gudgeon, A., Morgan, M., Fornasiero, A., Hoffmann, W., Michel, J., Hatschek, T., Tjabbes, T., Chaudri, H.A., Hornberger, U., & Trunet, P.F. (1998). Letrozole, a new oral aromatase inhibitor for advanced breast cancer: double-blind randomized trial showing a dose effect and improved efficacy and tolerability compared with megestrol acetate. *Journal of Clinical Oncology, 16*, 453–461.

Dow, K.H. (2002). Existing and emerging endocrine therapies for breast cancer. *Cancer Nursing, 25*(2S), 6S–11S.

Elledge, R.M., & Fuqua, S.A. (2000). Estrogen and progesterone receptors. In J.R. Harris, M.E. Lippman, M.M. Morrow, & C.K. Osborne (Eds.), *Diseases of the breast, 2nd ed.*, pp. 471–488. Philadelphia: Lippincott Williams & Wilkins.

Ellis, M.J., Hayes, D.F., & Lippman, M.E. (2000). Treatment of metastatic breast cancer. In J.R. Harris, M.E. Lippman, M.M. Morrow, & C.K. Osborne (Eds.), *Diseases of the breast, 2nd ed.*, pp. 749–797. Philadelphia: Lippincott Williams & Wilkins.

Geisler, J., King, N., Dowsett, M., Ottestad, L., Lundgren, L., Walton, P., Kormeset, P.O., & Lonning, P.E. (1996). Influence of anastrozole (Arimidex), a selective, non-steroidal aromatase inhibitor, on *in vivo* aromatization and plasma oestrogen levels in postmenopausal women with breast cancer. *British Journal of Cancer, 74*, 1286–1291.

Gross, P.E., & Strasser, K. (2001). Aromatase inhibitors in the treatment and prevention of breast cancer. *Journal of Clinical Oncology, 19*, 881–894.

Howell, A., DeFriend, D., Robertson, J., Blamey, R., & Walton, P. (1995). Response to a specific antiestrogen (ICI 182780) in tamoxifen-resistant breast cancer. *Lancet, 345*(8941), 29–30.

Howell, A., Robertson, J.F., Quaresma Albano, J., Aschermannova, A., Mauriac, L., Kleeberg, I., Vergote, I., Erikstein, B., Webster, A., & Morris, C. (2002). Fulvestrant, formerly ICI 182,780, is as effective as anastrozole in postmenopausal women with advanced breast cancer progressing after prior endocrine treatment. *Journal of Clinical Oncology, 20*, 3396–3403.

Kaufmann, M., Bajetta, E., Dirix, L.Y., Fein, L.E., Jones, S.E., Zilembo, N., Dugardyn, J.L., Nasurdi, C., Mennel, R.G., Cervek, J., Fowst, C., Polli, A., di Salle, E., Arkhipov, A., Piscitelli, G., Miller, L.L., & Massimini, G. (2000). Exemestane is superior to megestrol acetate after tamoxifen failure in postmenopausal women with advanced breast cancer: results of a phase III randomized double-blind trial. *Journal of Clinical Oncology, 18*, 1399–1411.

Kuukasjarvi, T., Kononen, J., Helin, H., Holli, K., & Isola, J. (1996). Loss of estrogen receptor in recurrent breast cancer is associated with poor response to endocrine therapy. *Journal of Clinical Oncology, 14*, 2584–2589.

Lindley, C.M. (1999). Breast cancer. In J.T. DiPiro, R.L. Talbert, G.C. Yee, G.R. Matzke, B.G. Wells, & L.M. Posey (Eds.), *Pharmacotherapy: a physiologic approach, 3rd ed.*, pp. 2013–2042. Norwalk, Conn.: Appleton & Lange.

Lipton, A., Ali, S.M., Leitzel, K., Demers, L., Chinchilli, V., Engle, L., Harvey, H.A., Brady, C., Nalin, C.M., Dugan, M., Carney, W., & Allard, J. (2002). Elevated serum HER-2/neu level predicts decreased response to hormone therapy in metastatic breast cancer. *Journal of Clinical Oncology, 20,* 1467–1472.

Lynn, J. (2002). The oncology nurse's role in educating patients on endocrine therapy for metastatic breast cancer—focus on fulvestrant. *Cancer Nursing, 25*(2S), 13S–17S.

Minton, S.E. (1999). New hormonal therapies for breast cancer. *Cancer Control, 6*(3), 247–255. Retrieved September 18, 2002, from *http://www.moffitt.usf.edu/pubs/cc/index.htm.*

Mouridsen, H., Gershanovich, M., Sun, Y., Perez-Carrion, R., Boni, C., Monnier, A., Apffelstaedt, J., Smith, R., Sleeboom, H.P., Janicke, F., Pluzanska, A., Dank, M., Becquart, D., Bapsy, P.P., Salminen, E., Snyder, R., Lassus, M., Verbeek, J.A., Staffler, B., Chaudri-Ross, H.A., & Dugan, M. (2001). Superior efficacy of letrozole versus tamoxifen as first-line therapy for postmenopausal women with advanced breast cancer: results of a phase III study of the International Letrozole Breast Cancer Group. *Journal of Clinical Oncology, 19,* 2596–2606.

Muss, H.B. (1999). New hormones for advanced breast cancer. *Cancer Control, 6*(5, Supp). Retrieved September 18, 2002, from *http://www.moffitt.usf.edu/pubs/ccj/v6s2/article.htm.*

Nabholtz, J.M., Buzdar, A., Pollak, M., Harwin, W., Burton, G., Mangalik, A., Steinberg, M., Webster, A., & von Euler, M. (2000). Anastrozole is superior to tamoxifen as first-line therapy for advanced breast cancer in postmenopausal women: results of a North American multicenter randomized trial. *Journal of Clinical Oncology, 18,* 3758–3767.

Osborne, C.K., Coronado-Heisohn, E.B., Hilsenbeck, S.G., McCue, B.L., Wakeling, A.E., McClelland, R.A., Manning, D.L., Nicholson, R.I. (1995). Comparison of the effects of a pure steroidal antiestrogen with those of tamoxifen in a model of human breast cancer. *Journal of the National Cancer Institute, 87*(10); 746–50.

Osborne, C.K. (1998). Steroid hormone receptors in breast cancer management. *Breast Cancer Research and Treatment, 51,* 227–238.

Osborne, C.K. (1999). Aromatase inhibitors in relation to other forms of endocrine therapy for breast cancer. *Endocrine-Related Cancer, 6,* 271–276.

Osborne, C.K., Pippen, J., Jones, S.E., Parker, L.M., Ellis, M., Come, S., Gertler, S.Z., May, J.T., Burton, G., Dimery, I., Webster, A., Morris, C., Elledge, R., Buzdar, A. (2002). Double-blind, randomized trial comparing the efficacy and tolerability of fulvestrant versus anastrozole in postmenopausal women with advanced breast cancer progressing on prior endocrine therapy: results of a North American trial. *Journal of Clinical Oncology, 20,* 3386–3395.

Osborne, C.K., Zhao, H., & Fuqua, S.A.W. (2000). Selective estrogen receptor modulators: structure, function, and clinical use. *Journal of Clinical Oncology, 18,* 3172–3186.

Paridaens, R., Dirix, L., Beex, L., Nooij, M., Cufer, T., Lorhisch, L., *et al.* (2000, May). Exemestane (Aromasin) is active and well tolerated as first-line hormonal therapy (HT) of metastatic breast cancer (MBC) patients (Pts): results of a randomized phase II trial. In *Program and Abstracts of the 36th Annual American Society of Clinical Oncology*, New Orleans, La. Abstract 316.

Ravdin, P.M., Green, S., Dorr, T.M., McGuire, W.L., Fabian, C., Pugh, R.P., Carter, R.D., Rivkin, S.E., Borst, J.R., Belt, R.J., *et al.* (1992). Prognostic significance of progesterone receptor levels in estrogen receptor-positive patients with metastatic breast cancer treated with tamoxifen: results of a prospective Southwest Oncology Group study. *Journal of Clinical Oncology, 10,* 1284–1291.

Robertson, J. (2002). Estrogen receptor downregulators: new antihormonal therapy for advanced breast cancer. *Clinical Therapeutics, 24*(Suppl. A), A17–A30.

Wasaff, B. (1997). Current status of hormonal treatments for metastatic breast cancer in postmenopausal women. *Oncology Nursing Forum, 24,* 1515–1520.

Wilson, B.A. (1993). Tamoxifen for breast cancer therapy: nursing implications. *Medsurg Nursing, 2*(6), 494–495.

Section IV

SYMPTOM MANAGEMENT

13

ACUTE SIDE EFFECT MANAGEMENT

PATRICIA I. GEDDIE, RN, MS, AOCN

INTRODUCTION

The majority of women with early breast cancer are able to tolerate adjuvant chemotherapy very well. The maintenance of working and daily life routines continues in spite of the lifestyle changes that are often required during the four to six months of treatment. Oncology nurses play a major role in coordination of direct and indirect patient care. Interventions include patient and family education as well as the emotional and psychological support that patients often need. Facilitation and involvement in support groups, in both the private and community settings, is an example of support offered to patients and their families for short-term and/or long-term needs.

Side effect and symptom management often is initiated by the nurse through telephone triage, outpatient clinics, and inpatient settings. Side effects commonly observed are neutropenia (grade 3 and 4), alopecia, nausea and vomiting, thromboembolism, weight gain, mucositis and stomatitis, fatigue, and arthralgia and myalgia. The Common Toxicity Criteria Rating from the National Cancer Institute grade side effects and toxicities on a scale of one to four (NCI, 1999). These criteria are provided in Table 13.1.

The purpose of this chapter is to discuss the common acute and expected side effects of adjuvant chemotherapy with emphasis on the nursing role in management of these side effects.

NEUTROPENIA

Chemotherapy-induced neutropenia is a major dose-limiting toxicity. Chemotherapy dose delays and reductions may compromise treatment effectiveness. Neutropenia is defined as the reduction in the number of circulating neutrophils to less than 1000/µL. Grade 3 and 4 neutropenia on the NCI scale (absolute neutrophil count [ANC] < 1000)

Table 13.1 Common Toxicity Criteria of the National Cancer Institute

Toxicity	Grade 0	Grade 1	Grade 2	Grade 3	Grade 4
Neutropenia	Normal	ANC > 1.5	ANC < 1.0	ANC < 0.5	ANC < 1.0
Alopecia	Normal	Mild	Pronounced	—	—
Nausea	None	Able to eat acceptable amount	Significant decrease in intake but able to eat	No significant intake	> 10 episodes in 24 hours
Vomiting	None	1 in 24 hours	2–5 in 24 hours	6–10 in 24 hours	> 10 in 24 hours, requiring parental support
Stomatitis	None	Painless ulcers, redness, mild soreness	Painful redness, edema, ulcers, able to eat	Painful redness, edema, ulcers, unable to eat	Requires parental or enteral support
Arthralgia/ myalgia	None	Mild, able to function	Moderate, interfering with function but not ADLs	Severe, interfering with ADLs	Disabling

ANC = Absolute neutrophil count; ADL = Activity of daily living

is common, leading to an increased risk of life-threatening infections, hospitalizations, and IV antibiotic use. Several factors contribute to the risk of neutropenia and its associated complications, such as age, prior therapy (both chemotherapy and radiation therapy), bone metastases, classification of chemotherapy drugs, and duration of therapy (Wujcik, 1999).

The ANC is calculated by the following formula: percent neutrophils (segmented and banded) × white blood cell (WBC) count = ANC. Anthracyclines such as doxorubicin, antimetabolites such as cyclophosphamide and methotrexate, and the taxanes place the patient at risk when these are combined in polychemotherapy regimens (Skeel, 1999). Short-term neutropenia lasts less than a week and long-term neutropenia exceeds 1–2 weeks. Nadir, or lowest WBC count, is predictable at approximately 10–14 days after treatments, with recovery observed at 3–4 weeks after treatment.

Signs and symptoms observed include fever of 100° F (38° C) to 100.4° F in a 24-hour period or a temperature spike of 101.3° F (38.5° C), pain and tenderness, change in elimination of urine and stool, lethargy, myalgia, and malaise. Observed signs of infection are generally absent in moderate to severe neutropenia because of the lack of circulating neutrophils. Early assessment, identification, and patient education regarding signs and symptoms of infection are crucial to the effective management and treatment. Good hand washing and meticulous personal hygiene is essential in promoting prevention and reducing neutropenia-related infections. Treatment includes antibiotic, antiviral, or antifungal therapy, depending on the source of the infection as detected in blood and other body fluid cultures (Hughes *et al.*, 1997).

In the 1990s, colony-stimulating factors dramatically changed the impact and complications of neutropenia management, both in intensity and duration. Filgrastim and sargramostim were the first two colony-stimulating factors used in the treatment and management of neutropenia. The serum half-life of filgrastim (approximately 3 hours) and subsequent neutrophil response necessitate daily injections given 24 hours after therapy, in daily doses (including weekends) of 5 μg/kg/day over 10–14 days for filgrastim (Amgen, 2001) and 250 μg/m²/day over 10–14 days for sargramostin (Immunex, 2000). Patients are required to make daily visits to the physician's office or outpatient center to receive injections because of reimbursement issues.

Those patients who are home-bound could benefit from home health nurses administering the injections in the home care setting. Daily office visits for injections can be quite challenging for patients who are also experiencing anemia, fatigue, and other side effect-related complications.

In 2001, a long-acting form of filgrastim, pegfilgrastim, was approved for chemotherapy-induced neutropenia (Amgen, 2000). Polyethylene glycol (PEG) is a nontoxic, water-soluble polymer that has been used extensively to modify proteins in order to extend their half-life and ultimately improve their pharmacologic profile over that of unmodified proteins. PEG is a technology used with other drugs, including anti-fungals such as amphotericin and liposomal doxorubicin.

The molecule is of sufficient size to minimize renal clearance, making it possible for the serum levels to remain elevated during the nadir and decline as the neutrophils recover. Pegfilgrastim increases its plasma half-life, making possible sustained plasma drug concentrations and injections given once, provided that the chemotherapy administrations are at least 14 days apart. Side effects from pegfilgrastim are similar to those from filgrastim, and both are equally well tolerated. Once-a-cycle dosing requires fewer office visits by patients and adds to their overall quality of life (Amgen, 2000).

NAUSEA AND VOMITING

Nausea and vomiting are two of the most common and dreaded side effects of chemotherapy. Chemotherapy agents can be rated on their level of emetic potential: mildly emetogenic (i.e., vinblastine, vincristine), moderately emetogenic (i.e., cyclophosphamide, 5-fluorouracil), or highly emetogenic (i.e., cisplatin, carmustine) (Wilkes *et al.,* 2000; Hesketh, 1999).

Other characteristics that contribute to the risks associated with nausea and vomiting include female gender, very young or very old age, history of motion sickness, hyperemesis gravidarum, previous exposure to chemotherapy, alcohol use, and cigarette smoking (Wickham, 1999).

The nausea and vomiting experience is also divided into three categories: anticipatory (a conditioned response), acute (within 24 hours) and delayed (after 24 hours). Anticipatory nausea and vomiting occurs in 25% to 67% of patients and can be potentially prevented with adequate control prior to therapy (Wickham, 1999). Dopamine antagonists such as prochlorperazine, metaclopramide, and triethylperazine offer control of nausea and vomiting but are often associated with side effects such as sedation, confusion, hypotension, drowsiness, and the potential for extrapyramidal reactions. Benzodiazepines such as lorazepam are CNS depressants that can cause sedation, amnesia, and confusion. The amnesic effect is effective for anticipatory nausea, but lorazepam should be used with caution for patients with hepatic or renal compromise. The exact mechanism of corticosteroids is unknown and may cause gastric irritation, complicate diabetes mellitus, and induce insomnia, anxiety, and hypertension.

Acute nausea and vomiting has been largely reduced with the use of serotonin antagonists (5HT-3). Serotonin antagonists were approved for the management of the acute phase of chemotherapy-induced nausea and vomiting in the early 1990s and have dramatically changed and added to the pharmacologic management options. Dexamethasone has been shown to increase efficacy of antiemetic agents, especially when combined with ondansetron, granisetron, and dolasetron. Side effects are greatly reduced and are moderate in nature: headache, hypotension, constipation, and sedation. Often, an adjustment in the rate of administration can alleviate these side effects.

Although acute nausea and vomiting are under greater control and management, the issue of delayed nausea and vomiting remains a challenge. Metoclopramide, prochlorperazine, and dexamethasone have historically proven effective in the pharmacologic management of delayed nausea and vomiting.

A new class of antiemetics, the neurokinin-1 (NK-1) receptor antagonists (RAs), is being studied. Studies have shown that they improve control in the acute phase when used in conjunction with standard antiemetic regimens. They also show promising results for control in the delayed phase of nausea and vomiting when used alone or with dexamethasone (Rittenberg, 2002). Phase III studies are ongoing.

ANTIEMETIC BEHAVIORAL INTERVENTIONS

Alternatives to pharmacologic interventions are behavioral interventions that the patient can be taught to perform independently. A trained therapist is usually required to assist the patient with techniques such as guided imagery, hypnosis, and biofeedback. Used more frequently are relaxation techniques (controlled breathing and progressive muscle relaxation) that can be taught by a nurse or other licensed health care professional. Distraction aids such as readily available audiotapes, television, and music in the treatment areas are helpful to minimize symptoms and are useful adjuncts with antiemetics. These techniques and interventions also give the patient a sense of control and help relieve anxiety that can often exacerbate symptoms (King, 1997). There are no clinical guidelines of criteria for patient selection and appropriate interventions to select and combine (Redd, 1994).

Another nonpharmacologic intervention is based on the principles of acupuncture. Acupressure is a form of touch therapy where specific points on the body are stimulated with finger pressure to relieve a variety of symptoms. In the treatment of nausea and vomiting, there is a point on the dominant arm called the Neiguan point or P6 (McMillan *et al.,* 1991). The P6 point is located on the inner wrist about three finger widths above the crease of the wrist and falling between the tendons of the palmaris longus and fexor carpi radialis. Elastic wrist bands with a bead or stud placed over the P6 are commercially available. These wrist bands can be placed on one or both wrists.

Nausea and vomiting may be avoided by changing to a bland diet or to foods that do not have offensive odor or spicy taste, or by consuming cold or room-temperature foods, clear liquids, carbonated beverages, and soda crackers. Patients should avoid high-fat foods, which can delay gastric emptying. The use of ginger as a tea or in capsules, which are available in health food stores, has been found to impact nausea and vomiting in the postoperative arena (Phillips *et al.,* 1993).

STOMATITIS/MUCOSITIS

Stomatitis and mucositis are general terms referring to inflammation and ulceration of the oral mucosa. It can often be predicted and proactively treated to reduce the severity and duration. Cells in the oral mucosa are vulnerable because they live approximately 5 days with a rapid turnover rate of every 7–14 days. Without anticipatory and effective prevention measures and treatment, stomatitis and mucositis can and often do lead to other complications such as pain, difficulty swallowing, anorexia, weight loss, dehydration, and infections.

Fluorouracil, doxorubicin, and methotrexate are chemotherapy agents associated with a high risk for the development of stomatitis and mucositis (Skeel, 1999). Other high-risk factors include poor oral hygiene, cavities, and alcohol consumption (Beck, 1999). Stomatitis often occurs within two to five days and lasts up to 14 days. Patients may benefit from a pretreatment dental exam to assess any preexisting compromise that can be effectively treated.

Early preventive measures such as saline or sodium bicarbonate rinses can effectively remove debris without causing harm to granulating tissue, as hydrogen peroxide does. Lubricating agents and topical anesthetics offer soothing relief to this distressing symptom. In 1992, Beck documented an oral assessment rating scale to measure changes in oral mucosa with the goal of maintaining a pink, smooth, moist, and intact oral mucosa, including lips, teeth, tongue, and saliva. Patients wearing dentures should be instructed to remove dentures daily and inspect the oral cavity for signs of breakdown and injury. Dramatic weight loss can cause dentures to lose their original fit, and patients may require a dental assessment and refitting of dentures.

Patient education should also include foods and products that may contribute to irritation and injury to the oral mucosa, such as citrus or acid-containing foods, spicy foods, rough textures, extreme temperatures of hot and cold, alcohol, caffeine, and tobacco (Beck, 1999). Early signs and symptoms include sensitivity to temperatures and citrus, redness, dryness, and roughness. The prevention of local and systemic infections avoids the potential complication of systemic sepsis. Vitamin E applied topically has shown effectiveness in patients experiencing stomatitis. Some advocate the use of cryotherapy, or ice, to constrict capillary vessels and reduce swelling and pain (Rocke *et al.,* 1993). The management and reduction of neutropenia severity and duration utilizing colony-stimulating factors has been effective in reducing the risk for stomatitis and mucositis. Nystatin rinses, Mycelex™ troches, and oral fluconazole are effective treatments for local fungal infections commonly manifested as candida albicans. Acyclovir is the preferred treatment for the viral infection herpes simplex. Broad-spectrum antibiotics are required to treat bacterial infections such as Pseudomonas and Streptococcus.

ALOPECIA

Hair cell follicles are in a continuous cycle of regrowth and proliferation, especially at the scalp. With repeated chemotherapy doses and duration, other body hair in the pubic, facial, and axillary areas are also affected. Alopecia, or hair loss, is usually temporary and begins around two to three weeks after treatment with continued loss over three to four weeks (Reeves, 1999). Regrowth will occur about three months after completion of therapy, but not without initial changes in color, texture, and pattern. Hair will return to its pretreatment condition within approximately one year after treatment is completed.

The amount of hair loss, from thinning to complete loss, is usually determined by the quantity of hair prior to treatment and the type of chemotherapy. Total hair loss can be expected with doxorubicin, high potential with cyclophosphamide and paclitaxel, moderate potential with methotrexate and 5-fluorouracil, and thinning with cyclophosphamide, methotrexate, and 5-fluorouracil (CMF) polychemotherapy (Williams *et al.,* 1999).

Patients are counseled about when to expect hair loss and advised to proactively seek covering for their scalp in the form of scarves, hats, and wigs. Often patients are advised to cut long hair in order to minimize the amount of perceived hair loss. The American Cancer Society's program Look Good… Feel Better assists patients experiencing alopecia and skin changes. Licensed and experienced cosmetologists and beauticians participate in this program to offer professional advice and support regarding skin care, make-up techniques, and wig styling. Some insurance providers will cover the costs of a wig if a prescription for a "scalp prosthesis" is ordered with the medical indications for alopecia from cancer chemotherapy treatment. Methods and techniques to preserve hair, such as scalp hypothermia and tourniquets, are controversial at best and are generally ineffective, potentially allowing for hidden metastases to the scalp.

WEIGHT GAIN

Weight gain incidence varies from 50% to 90%, with a weight gain greater than 10% (up to 22 pounds) and duration up to two years after treatment. Several factors may contribute to this phenomenon, including fatigue, depression, hormonal changes, and metabolic imbalances. Premenopausal and perimenopausal women experience more weight gain than those in the postmenopausal stage of life. A decrease in circulating estrogen accounts for the weight gain seen in menopause.

Women who receive alkylating agents, such as cyclophosphamide, experience ovarian toxicity, resulting in a premature medically induced state of menopause (Goodman, 1999). This could account for the seemingly increased weight gain among premenopausal women versus women who were postmenopausal and had already experienced weight gain prior to treatment (McInnes, 2001). Studies have compared variables of activity, resting metabolic rate, and oral intake in weight-gaining and non-weight-gaining women with no significant differences. Compensatory eating related to depression has been postulated as a potential cause. Regular exercise and a reduced-fat diet can counteract weight gain and can ultimately increase function and provide a perceived higher quality of life. Patient education about the risks, preventive strategies, and interventions are key strategies for avoiding or reducing this side effect.

CANCER-RELATED FATIGUE AND SLEEP DISTURBANCE

See Chapter 14 for further discussion about cancer-related fatigue and sleep disturbance.

ARTHRALGIA/MYALGIA

Arthralgia is joint pain; myalgia is diffuse muscle pain. Myalgias and arthralgias occur in 96% of patients receiving paclitaxel in doses of 175 mg/m^2 and increase during the time of granulocyte–colony-stimulating factor administration (Martin, 1999). Symptoms are dose related. Paclitaxel at doses less than 170 mg/m^2 causes mild discomfort but at doses greater than 200 mg/m^2 is associated with more severe discomfort and pain (McGuire *et al.*, 1989). Effects occur 48 to 72 hours after infusion and can persist for up to 7 days. Effects occur primarily in large joints but can involve the whole body. Pharmacologic interventions such as nonsteroidal analgesics or narcotics are usually required (Natale, 1996). Nonpharmacologic interventions include warm baths, relaxation techniques, and massage therapy (Martin, 1999).

THROMBOEMBOLIC EVENTS

Thromboembolic disease has long been recognized as a complication of cancer (Levine *et al.*, 1988). The etiology is multifactoral and includes release of procoagulants by tumor cells as well as comorbidities and predisposing factors in anticancer drugs. This has been most often reported when chemotherapy is combined with endocrine therapy (Rutqvist & Mattsson, 1993). However, another study has shown that thromboembolic events have occurred more often and been more severe in the tamoxifen plus chemotherapy treatment versus tamoxifen alone (Pritchard *et al.*, 1996). Most patients have only reported superficial phlebitis and did not require hospitalization.

The rate of thrombosis in women with stage II breast cancer receiving adjuvant chemotherapy is approximately 5% (Levine, 1997). This rate is increased in metastatic breast cancer. Since postmenopausal women with breast cancer are more likely to receive endocrine therapy, their risk for thromboembolism is greater and potentially lethal. Low-dose warfarin given prophylactically and concurrently with chemotherapy has shown a significantly reduced rate of thromboembolism. Central venous catheters may increase the risk of catheter-related clots (Falanga *et al.*, 1998).

SUMMARY

In summary, acute side effects from breast cancer can be effectively managed by the oncology nurse through anticipatory teaching and patient education. The available pharmacologic and nonpharmacologic interventions help patients with breast cancer to maintain their quality of life while on treatment.

REFERENCES

Amgen. (2000). *Pegfilgrastim* (Neulasta™). *Prescribing information*. Thousand Oaks, Calif.: Author.

Amgen. (2001). *Filgrastim* (Neupogen®). *Prescribing information*. Thousand Oaks, Calif.: Author.

Beck, S.L. (1992). Prevention and management of oral complications in the clinical practice. In *Current Issues in Cancer Nursing Practice Updates*, pp. 27–38. Philadelphia: Lippincott.

Beck, S. (1999). Mucositis. In C.H. Yarbro, M.H. Frogge, & M. Goodman (Eds.), *Cancer symptom management, 2nd ed.*, pp. 307–321. Sudbury, Mass.: Jones & Bartlett.

Falanga, A. Levine, M.N., Consonni, R. Gritti, G., Delaini, F., Oldani, E., Julian, J.A., and Barbui, T. (1998). The effect of very-low-dose warfarin on markers of hypercoagulation in metastatic breast cancer: results from a randomized trial. *Thrombosis & Haemostasis, 79*(1), 23–27.

Goodman, M. (1999). Menopausal symptoms. In C.H. Yarbro, M.H. Frogge, & M. Goodman (Eds.), *Cancer symptom management, 2nd ed.*, pp. 307–321. Sudbury, Mass.: Jones & Bartlett.

Hesketh, P. (1999). Defining the emetogenicity of cancer chemotherapy regimens: relevance to clinical practice. *Oncologist, 4,* 191–196.

Hughes, W.T., Armstrong, D., Bodey, G.P., Brown, A.E., Edwards, J.E., Feld, R., Pizzo, P., Rolston, K.V., Shenep, J.L., & Young, L.S., (1997). Guidelines for the use of antimicrobial agents in neutropenic patients with unexplained fever. *Clinical Infectious Diseases, 25,* 551–573.

Immunex. (2000). *Sargramostim* (Leukine ®). *Prescribing information*. Seattle, Wash.: Author.

King, C.R. (1997). Nonpharmacologic management of chemotherapy-induced nausea and vomiting. *Oncology Nursing Forum, 24,* 41–48.

Levine, M.N. (1997). Prevention of thrombotic disorders in cancer patients undergoing chemotherapy. *Thrombosis & Haemostasis, 78,* 133–136.

Levine, M.N., Gent, M., Hirsh, J., Arnold, A., Goodyear, M.D., Hryniuk, W., & DePauw, S. (1988). The thrombogenic effect of anticancer drug therapy in women with stage II breast cancer. *New England Journal of Medicine, 318*(7), 404–407.

Martin, V. (1999). Arthralgias and myalgias. In C.H. Yarbro, M.H. Frogge, & M. Goodman (Eds.), *Cancer symptom management, 2nd ed.*, pp. 35–42. Sudbury, Mass.: Jones & Bartlett.

McInnes, J.A., & Knobf, M.T. (2001). Weight gain and quality of life in women treated with adjuvant chemotherapy for early-stage breast cancer. *Oncology Nursing Forum, 28*(4), 675–683.

McGuire, W.P., Rowinsky, E.K., Rosenshein, N.B., Grumbine, F.C., Ettinger, D.S., Armstrong, D.K., & Donehower, R.C. (1989). Taxol: a unique antineoplastic agent with significant activity in advanced ovarian epithelial neoplasms. *Annals of Internal Medicine, 111,* 273–279.

McMillan, C., Dundee, J.W., & Abram, W.P. (1991). Enhancement of the antiemetic action of ondansetron by transcutaneous electrical stimulation of the P6 antiemetic point, in patients having highly emetic cytotoxic drugs. *British Journal of Cancer, 64,* 971–972.

Natale, R.B. (1996). Preliminary results of phase I/II clinical trial of paclitaxel and carboplatin in non-small cell lung cancer. *Seminars in Oncology, 23*(16), 51–54.

National Cancer Institute. (1999). Common Toxicity Criteria. National Institutes of Health, Department of Health and Human Services, Version 2.0. Retrieved November 13, 2000, from *http://ctep.info.nih.gov/CTC3/ctc.htm.*

Phillips, S., Ruggier, R., & Hutchinson, S.E. (1993). *Zingiber officinale* (ginger)—an antiemetic for day case surgery. *Anaesthesia, 48*(8), 715–717.

Pritchard, K.I., Paterson, A.H., Paul, N.A., Zee, B., Fine, S., & Pater, J. (1996). Increased thromboembolic complications with concurrent tamoxifen and chemotherapy in a randomized trial of adjuvant therapy for women with breast cancer. *Journal of Clinical Oncology, 14,* 2731–2737.

Redd, W.H. (1994). Behavioral intervention for cancer treatment side effects. *Acta Oncologica, 33,* 113–116.

Reeves, D. (1999). Alopecia. In C.H. Yarbro, M.H. Frogge, & M. Goodman (Eds.), *Cancer symptom management, 2nd ed.,* pp. 307–321. Sudbury, Mass.: Jones & Bartlett.

Rittenberg, C.N. (2002). A new class of antiemetic agents. *Clinical Journal of Oncology Nursing, 6*(2), 103–104.

Rocke, L.K., Loprinzi, C.L., Lee, J.K., et al. (1993). A randomized clinical trial of two different durations of oral cryotherapy for prevention of 5-fluorouracil-related stomatitis. *Cancer, 72,* 2234–2238.

Rutqvist, L.E., & Mattsson, A. (1993). Cardiac and thromboembolic morbidity among post-menopausal women with early-stage breast cancer in a randomized trial of adjuvant tamoxifen. *Journal of the National Cancer Institute, 85,* 1398–1406.

Skeel, R. (1999). *Handbook of cancer chemotherapy* (5th ed.). Philadelphia: Lippincott Williams & Wilkins.

Wickham, R. (1999). Nausea and vomiting. In C.H. Yarbro, M.H. Frogge, & M. Goodman (Eds.), *Cancer symptom management, 2nd ed.,* pp. 307–321. Sudbury, Mass.: Jones & Bartlett.

Wilkes, G., Ingwersen, K., & Barton-Burke, M. (2000). Nausea and vomiting. In *Oncology nursing drug handbook,* pp. 418–447. Sudbury, Mass.: Jones & Bartlett.

Williams, J., Wood, C.L., & Cunningham-Warburton, P. (1999). A narrative study of chemotherapy-induced alopecia. *Oncology Nursing Forum, 26,* 1463–1468.

Wujcik, D. (1999). Infection. In C.H. Yarbro, M.H. Frogge, & M. Goodman (Eds.), *Cancer symptom management, 2nd ed.,* pp. 307–321. Sudbury, Mass.: Jones & Bartlett.

Chapter 14

FATIGUE, SLEEP DISTURBANCE, AND PAIN

GLORIA VELEZ-BARONE, ARNP, MSN, AOCN

INTRODUCTION

Despite the trends in decreased mortality rates, breast cancer incidence rates continue to increase (ACS, 2002b). More women will be living with the diagnosis and sequelae of breast cancer treatment. Distressing and common side effects, such as fatigue, insomnia, and pain, require assessment and interventions to improve the quality of life for breast cancer survivors.

This chapter will discuss the incidence, etiology, and treatment of fatigue, insomnia, and pain. A review of the literature indicates that previous research focused on these symptoms individually and with unidimensional approaches (Piper *et al.*, 1998; Winningham *et al.*, 1994). More recent research studies are expanding and advancing symptom management. The concepts of multidimensional assessment (Stein *et al.*, 1998) and symptom clusters, which may have a synergistic adverse effect on future morbidity (Dodd *et al.*, 2001), may have an impact on how nurses assess and implement interventions.

FATIGUE

INCIDENCE

Fatigue is the most common and distressing symptom of cancer and cancer therapy (Clark & Lacasse, 1998; Winningham *et al.*, 1994). In patients with breast cancer, fatigue may be attributed to surgical interventions, radiation therapy, or adjuvant chemotherapy. The exact mechanisms are not clear; however, observations have been made on the duration and patterns of fatigue. In a comparison of patients receiving chemotherapy and radiation therapy, Irvine *et al.* (1994) found that patients receiving radiation therapy had a significant increase in fatigue over a 5- or 6-week course, and patients receiving chemotherapy experienced fatigue

14 days after treatment, when compared with individuals who were not receiving therapy. The researchers found that the prevalence of fatigue in patients receiving therapy was 61%.

Broeckel *et al.* (1998) compared a control group of 59 women to a group of 61 women who had undergone adjuvant chemotherapy. The findings of the study indicate that breast cancer patients experience a heightened fatigue after completion of adjuvant therapy. Severe fatigue was significantly related to poor sleep quality, menopausal symptoms, and poor coping strategies. Bower *et al.* (2000) studied 2000 women diagnosed with early breast cancer who had completed local or systemic adjuvant therapy. They found that energy levels were lower 1 year after treatment but improved after 2 years and remained stable for years 3, 4, and 5. Postsurgical fatigue is self-limiting and usually resolves with time. However, it is difficult to assess the true impact of surgery on fatigue because of additional treatments the patient may receive prior to healing (Nail & Jones, 1995).

ETIOLOGY

Fatigue is a common side effect of cancer treatment; despite the numerous studies on fatigue, the pathophysiology remains unknown (Nail & Jones, 1995; Winningham *et al.,* 1994; Ream & Richardson, 1999). Mechanisms that may be responsible for fatigue include biochemical factors (such as electrolyte imbalance), altered sleep and rest, psychosocial factors (e.g., distress, decreased coping skills), environmental factors (such as pain) and possible altered nutritional status (decreased albumin and protein) (Winningham *et al.,* 1994; Nail & Jones, 1995; Brophy & Sharp, 1991). A study by Beach *et al.* (2001) found that weight loss and nutritional changes did not correlate with fatigue in lung cancer patients; however, the authors suggested that the study be duplicated in other patient populations using a different fatigue instrument. More clinical studies are required to clarify the etiology of cancer-related fatigue.

FATIGUE ASSESSMENT

Fatigue, like pain, is a subjective phenomenon that is multidimensional. Unidimensional scales provide limited information about the patient's experience (Stein *et al.,* 1998). Several scales have been developed that can be used in clinical practice for the assessment of fatigue. The Multidimensional Fatigue Symptom Inventory (MFSI) (Stein *et al.,* 1998) has clinical as well as research applicability. The MFSI can be administered frequently, so that a clinician can obtain data prior to beginning therapy (as a baseline), throughout therapy (to follow progression of fatigue), and after implementation of interventions (to assess effectiveness).

The Schwartz Cancer Fatigue Scale (Schwartz, 1998) may provide information about the multidimensional aspect of cancer-related fatigue as well as a valid and reliable description of the patient's experience.

The revised Piper Fatigue Scale (PFS) (Piper *et al.,* 1998) was evaluated using a test group of 382 women with breast cancer. The scale measures four dimensions of subjective fatigue: severity, affective, sensory, and cognitive/mood. Information from the revised PFS can be used to make appropriate referrals and individualize supportive interventions in fatigue management.

MANAGEMENT

The evaluation and management of fatigue remains an important focus of nursing care. In patients with breast cancer, fatigue may occur when there is an increase in physical and psychosocial demands. Fatigue limits the ability to function (Winningham, 1995), and if not addressed it may have quality of life consequences, such as changes in interpersonal relationships, adverse health care encounters, changes in work performance, issues with self-esteem, and difficulty in processing information (Nail & Jones, 1995).

There are several nursing theories that can be used to provide guidelines in developing a fatigue management plan. Ryden's Conceptual Framework of Energy Expenditure (1977) proposes that fatigue occurs when there is an energy deficit, or the energy required, exceeds the supply. Piper *et al.* (1987) developed the Integrated Fatigue Model, which considers multiple etiologies for fatigue, such as treatment patterns, activity and rest patterns, symptom patterns, and innate host patterns. The Integrated Fatigue Model can be used to develop interventions, but it does not predict relationships. Winningham's Psychobiological–Entropy Model (1995) proposes that fatigue is a result of energy deficits related to illness, treatment, environmental influences, and decreased activity. Winningham's interventions focus on effectively managing symptoms and restoring the balance between rest and activity.

Fatigue management begins with patient education on the various behavioral interventions. Although there are no set guidelines for energy conservation techniques in the cancer patient, the guidelines listed in Table 14.1 have been used in patients with physical illnesses. Patients must also learn to plan activities and energy expenditures, prioritize activities, and incorporate rest periods during the day. Theories on fatigue describe it as an energy imbalance, so a proper amount of rest and sleep is an essential part of the management plan (discussed further in the section on insomnia).

Alternative or integrative therapies such as relaxation therapy, biofeedback, and massage therapy may have a role in fatigue management, but they have yet to be evaluated in clinical studies to document their effectiveness.

Exercise as an intervention for fatigue has been evaluated in clinical trials and has shown evidence of effectiveness (Mock *et al.*, 1997, 2001). Schwartz *et al.* (2001) studied the effect of exercise on women undergoing treatment for breast cancer. The women were asked to exercise 15–30 minutes a day 3–4 days a week; the type of exercise was chosen by the participant. This study found that women who participated in an exercise program had significantly reduced fatigue, and as the duration of the exercise increased, the intensity of fatigue decreased. This study, and others that evaluate exercise as an intervention, provide data that increased rest is not the appropriate method to reduce cancer-related fatigue and that a certain amount of moderate exercise is beneficial.

There are a few contraindications to an exercise program for patients with breast cancer. Exercise should be restricted on days of chemotherapy administration, in the presence

Table 14.1 Suggested Strategies for Energy Conservation

Activities of daily living

- Sit down to bathe and dry off. Wear a terry robe instead of drying off.
- Use a shower/bath organizer to decrease leaning and reaching.
- Install grab rails in the bathroom.
- Use extension handles on sponges and brushes.
- Use an elevated toilet seat.
- Organize time to avoid rushing.
- Lay out clothes and toiletries before dressing.
- Minimize leaning over to put on clothes and shoes. Bring your foot to your knee to apply socks and shoes. Fasten bra in front then turn to back.
- Modify the home environment to maximize efficient use of energy. Example: Place chairs to allow rest stops (e.g., along a long hallway).
- Wear comfortable clothes and low-heeled, slip-on shoes. Wear button-front shirts rather than pullovers.

Housekeeping

- Schedule household tasks throughout the week.
- Do housework sitting down when possible. Use long-handled dusters, dust mops, etc. Use a wheeled cart or carpenter's apron to carry supplies.
- Delegate heavy housework, shopping, laundry, and child care when possible.
- Drag or slide objects rather than lifting. Use proper body mechanics. Use your leg muscles, not your back, when working.
- Sit when ironing and take rest periods.
- Stop working *before* becoming tired.

Shopping

- Organize list by aisle.
- Use a grocery cart for support.
- Shop at less busy times.
- Request assistance in getting to the car.
- Purchase clothing that doesn't require ironing.

Meal preparation

- Use convenience foods/easy-to-prepare foods.
- Use small appliances (they take less effort to use).
- Arrange the preparation environment for easy access to frequently used items.
- Prepare meals sitting down.
- Soak dishes instead of scrubbing and let dishes air-dry.
- Prepare double portions and freeze half.

Child care

- Plan activities to allow for sitting down (e.g., drawing pictures, playing games, reading, computer games).
- Teach children to climb up on the lap or into the highchair instead of being lifted.
- Make a game of the household chores so that children will want to help.
- Delegate child care when possible.

Workplace

- Plan workload to take advantage of peak energy times. Alternate physically demanding tasks with sedentary tasks.
- Arrange work environment for easy access to commonly used equipment and supplies.

Leisure

- Do activities with a companion.
- Select activities that match energy level.
- Balance activity and rest (don't get overtired).

Based on information from Donovan, E. (1995, October 25). Energy conservation. In *Fatigue Initiative through Research and Education (FIRE®)* course. Educational program sponsored by the Oncology Nursing Society and Ortho Biotech Inc., Phoenix, Arizona. Printed with permission from the Oncology Nursing Society.

of a fever, or if there is metastatic bone involvement of greater than 25% of the cortex. High-impact aerobics are contraindicated during chemotherapy and recurrent disease; walking is appropriate and effective in this patient population. Lab values also need to be evaluated prior to exercise. If the WBC is less than 3000 mm^3, the absolute neutrophil count is less than 2500 mm^3, Hgb is less than 10 g/dl, and platelets are less then 25,000 mm^3, exercise should be restricted and resumed when lab values rise above these criteria. Exercise is a useful intervention in the management of cancer-related fatigue; however, patients must be educated and followed throughout the process.

SUMMARY

Management plans for fatigue should be individualized. They should contain strategies for energy balance incorporating energy conservation techniques (See Table 14.2) and an exercise plan, attention-restoring activities, and patient education information (Winningham *et al.,* 1994; Berger & Farr, 1999; Sarna & Conde, 2001; Clark & Lacasse, 1998; Schwartz *et al.,* 2001). Nursing interventions can help in decreasing the severity of this symptom, as well as promote quality of life.

INSOMNIA

INCIDENCE

Insomnia affects 50% of the adult population, and at some point 90% of the adult population has had difficulty with sleep patterns (Lippmann *et al.,* 2001). The following groups have higher reported rates of insomnia: women, especially those in minority groups; people who are unemployed or separated; members of lower socioeconomic groups; and those with medical or psychiatric disorders (Holbrook *et al.,* 2000).

Insomnia is a prevalent yet poorly studied phenomenon in the cancer patient population (Savard & Morin, 2001). Owen *et al.* (2000) compared the subjective sleep quality

Table 14. 2 Resources

National Comprehensive Cancer Network
50 Huntington Pike, Suite 200
Rockledge, PA 19046
Phone: 215-728-4788 / 1-888-909-NCCN
Fax: 215-728-3877
www.nccn.org

Oncology Nursing Society
125 Enterprise Drive
Pittsburgh, PA 15275-1214
Phone: 1-866-257-4ONS (toll-free)
Fax: 1-877-369-5497 (toll-free)
www.ons.org

of a group of patients receiving cancer treatment to that of healthy individuals. The authors found that the cancer patients had poor subjective sleep quality when compared to the healthy subjects. The cancer patients also had difficulty falling asleep, shorter and less efficient nocturnal sleep, and an increased use of sleeping medications.

ETIOLOGY

Insomnia is the patient's inability to obtain an adequate amount of quality sleep, manifesting itself as nonrefreshing or nonrestorative rest. Insomnia may present itself as difficulty falling asleep, an inability to stay asleep (with frequent awakening during the night), or early morning awakening with the inability to return to sleep.

Insomnia can be acute, occurring for days to weeks at a time. One type of insomnia known as transient insomnia is related to emotional distress during a personal crisis or to the use of stimulants (such as caffeine) or other pharmaceutical drugs. Chronic insomnia lasts for several weeks and is associated with medical illnesses or psychiatric disorders such as anxiety or depression. Females experience insomnia twice as often as men. Advancing age and a personal or family history of insomnia are also predisposing factors (Morin, 1993).

MANAGEMENT

Management of insomnia is essential because chronic sleep deprivation may lead to difficulties in concentration, irritability, depression, fatigue, and mood disturbances. Physical consequences of insomnia include headache, diarrhea, GI discomfort, palpations, and nonspecific pain (Savard & Morin, 2001). There are two categories for the management of insomnia—nonpharmacologic or behavioral and pharmacologic interventions.

Nonpharmacologic interventions fall into three categories: stimulus control, temporal control, and sleep restriction (Holbrook *et al.*, 2000; Kupfer & Reynolds, 1997). In stimulus control the bedroom should only be used for sleep and intimacy activities. Watching TV, reading, and work should be performed in other designated areas. If the patient retires to bed and does not fall asleep within 20 minutes, the patient should leave the bedroom until she becomes drowsy. The goal is to associate the bedroom with sleep and not insomnia (Holbrook *et al.*, 2000). In temporal control the patient arises at the same time each day, regardless of the hour they fell asleep, and there is a restriction on daytime napping. Sleep restriction minimizes the amount of time spent in bed; the time is gradually increased as long as 85% of the time spent in bed is used for sleep (Kupfer & Reynolds, 1997).

The concept of sleep hygiene, although not well researched, can be helpful. Assessment through using a sleep journal may be useful in identifying habits that lead to poor sleep quality and insomnia. The journal should contain information regarding sleep patterns (sleep onset, duration of sleep, naps, etc.) and the use of sleep aids, as well as activities and environmental factors that may influence rest. The patient should also avoid stimulants (such as caffeine, chocolate, and nicotine), alcohol, heavy meals, and exercise just prior to sleep. Patient education is important because in an effort to promote rest and relaxation, patients may inappropriately use alcohol, smoking, and warm drinks.

Other sleep hygiene interventions, such as a warm bath or shower and the use of muscle relaxation techniques, cognitive control techniques, and priority symptom management (pain, nausea, vomiting), may be beneficial in inducing a state of relaxation and drowsiness.

Pharmacologic interventions for insomnia include benzodiazepine, nonbarbiturates, nonbenzodiazepine, antidepressants, and antihistamines. The principles that govern pharmacological intervention include using the lowest effective dose for the shortest duration (less than two weeks) and discontinuation of the medication gradually with monitoring for rebound effects. Because of the potential for adverse effects of hypnotic drugs and their limited use, these drugs should be used as an adjunct to the nonpharmacologic approach to insomnia.

SUMMARY

Insomnia is a complex phenomenon that may have various etiologies. The nurse may have an invaluable role in the assessment and management of transient and chronic insomnia through implementation of behavioral and nonpharmacological interventions. Insomnia has not been well studied in the cancer patient population; as more research studies are conducted, better treatment modalities may arise.

PAIN

During the last several years there has been an increased focus on pain and its assessment and management. Through research, knowledge in this area has become highly specialized. Studies specifically on the topic of breast cancer pain syndromes are beginning to emerge and will assist clinicians with this phenomenon.

PREVALENCE AND ETIOLOGY

Pain associated with breast cancer may result from direct tumor involvement or from treatment. Pain from direct tumor involvement may manifest itself in connection with bone metastases, neural metastases, peripheral neuropathy resulting from tumor infiltration, or visceral metastasis. The most common cause of pain in breast cancer patients is metastatic bone disease (MacDonald *et al.,* 1998). Pain related to treatment may occur from chemotherapy, radiation therapy, or surgery.

Chemotherapy may produce severe and painful mucositis, and, depending on the chemotherapy agents used, specific adverse events such as neuropathy, cystitis, or extravasation may occur.

Radiation therapy may lead to chronic pain syndromes such as plexopathies and radiation myelopathy (Portenoy, 1997). A study by Norman (2002) evaluated 33 women for clinical presentation and natural history of radiation-induced brachial plexopathy. The author found that symptoms begin from 6 months to 20 years after radiation therapy. Seventeen patients required long-term opioid therapy for pain management; symptoms were progressive and pain was common and chronic in nature.

Between 10% and 30% of breast cancer patients will suffer with postsurgical pain. The incidence increases with axillary node dissection or total mastectomy (MacDonald *et al.,* 1998). From 10% to 64% of women experience phantom pain after mastectomies; 80% of the sensations have some degree of pain, and the incidence is higher if there was breast pain prior to the mastectomy (McCaffery, 1999). Baron *et al.* (2000) evaluated 132 patients for the prevalence, severity, and level of distress of postsurgical breast sensations. Certain sensations such as numbness and tenderness were prevalent. Severe and distressing sensations such as burning, cramping, and pain interfered with activities of daily life (ADLs). Postsurgical alterations in sensation result from injury to nerves in the operation field. The sensory nerve is often damaged to gain access to the axillary nodes (Baron, 1998). Postsurgical pain may also be attributed to complications of surgery, such as infection, seroma, or bleeding, which may increase the risk for developing chronic pain syndromes (Baron, 1998).

ASSESSMENT

The cornerstone for any pain management plan begins with assessment. Pain in breast cancer is due to various etiologies; it may be acute and nociceptive in nature (e.g., mucocitis), chronic and nociceptive (e.g., bone metastasis), or chronic and neuropathic (e.g., neuropathies). A patient may experience any one of these, individually or in combination. An assessment will assist in identifying the cause of the pain and will guide the treatment plan.

The first step is to identify the location of the area(s) of discomfort. Next is to obtain the pain intensity. Pain is subjective and there are tools, such as the pain intensity scale, that can be used to measure pain perception. The key is that all clinicians use the same tool. Alleviating and aggravating factors, along with the patient's acceptable level of pain (pain goal), should be documented. The patient should then be asked to qualify the pain (burning, tingling, sharp, constant, achy, etc.). This will assist in determining if the pain is nociceptive or neuropathic in nature. Temporal features should be evaluated next (onset, duration, course, and pattern). Finally, an assessment of the effect of pain on quality of life should be obtained—whether the pain is interfering with sleep, ADLs, physical activity, appetite, and/or mood.

Assessment should also include diagnostics as appropriate (bone scans, CT scans, PET scans) to monitor for disease progression or metastatic disease.

MANAGEMENT

Effective management of pain is an interdisciplinary process that should incorporate pharmacologic and nonpharmacologic interventions. The National Comprehensive Cancer Network is a consortium of 18 nationally recognized cancer centers that publish consensus guidelines on cancer diagnosis and symptom management. The pain treatment guidelines have "decision trees" that are based on patient assessment and pain intensity. The guidelines provide an evidence-based systematic approach to providing adequate relief.

The classification of medications used will depend on the pain that is being experienced. Nociceptive pain responds well to nonsteroidal anti-inflammatory agents and to opioids, while neuropathic pain is best managed by adjuvant drugs such as antidepressants and anticonvulsants (McCaffery, 1999, MacDonald, *et al.*, 1998). Substance P inhibitors are being evaluated for their ability to reduce hyperalgesia. Capsaicin, a substance P inhibitor, has been evaluated for use in postmastectomy pain (Dini *et al.*, 1993). Lecuona Navea *et al.* (1999) applied 0.025% topical capsaicin three times a day for one month, and every patient had a statistically significant decrease in pain. Although the results of this study are encouraging due to small sample size ($N = 33$), more clinical trials are required to substantiate the therapy's effectiveness.

Nonpharmacological interventions may be physical or psychosocial modalities, and some may easily be implemented by the nursing staff. Physical modalities include cutaneous stimulation (thermal, cryotherapy), massage, pressure, vibration, exercise, immobilization, and the use of counterstimulation (TENS). The use of immobilization should be limited, because excessive use may lead to atrophy and muscle weakness. Cryotherapy should be used with caution in patients who have vascular disease.

Psychosocial interventions include relaxation techniques, distraction, psychotherapy, structural support, and patient education. These interventions may assist in diminishing the emotional component of pain, increasing the sense of control, and improving patients' ability to cope with pain (McCaffery, 1999), but care must be taken not to assume the pain is "all in the patient's head" if these modalities are effective in decreasing the perception of pain. It is also important to remember that nonpharmacological therapies are not intended to replace pharmacological interventions; they are to be used in addition to appropriate medical management. Nonpharmacological interventions are a long-standing component of oncology nursing care (Hogan, 1997), and nurses have an integral role in the coordination of pharmacological and nonpharmacological interventions.

Patients also use complementary or alternative methods to manage pain. Some therapies such as tai chi, yoga, meditation, prayer, music therapy, aroma therapy, art therapy, therapeutic touch, and acupuncture may increase relaxation and enhance well-being (ACS, 2002a); other therapies, such as herbal remedies, need to be monitored closely for potential interactions with existing medicines. The National Cancer Institute is funding clinical trials to prove the effectiveness of complementary therapies; however, most have not undergone controlled scientific evaluations. Nevertheless, health care professionals need to discuss these therapies with their patients and encourage participation in clinical trials, so that in the future these alternative methods may be part of evidence-based practice.

SUMMARY

Breast cancer remains the number one cancer diagnosis for women. More women are surviving this disease but are living with long-term sequelae. Adequate control of fatigue, sleep disorders, and pain will enhance the quality of life for this patient population. Much of the research on these distressing symptoms has been conducted in the general oncology population. More clinical trials are required to focus on the specific needs and issues for the breast cancer patient population.

REFERENCES

American Cancer Society. (1996). *Exercises after breast surgery.* Atlanta, Ga.: Author.

American Cancer Society. (2002a). *ACS guide to complementary and alternative cancer methods.* Atlanta, Ga.: Author.

American Cancer Society. (2002b). *Cancer facts and figures.* Atlanta, Ga.: Author.

Baron, R. (1998). Sensory alterations after breast cancer surgery. *Oncology Nursing Forum, 2,* 17–23.

Baron, R.H., Kelvin, J.F., Bookbinder, M., Cramer, R., Borgen, P.I., & Jhaler, H.T. (2000). Patients' sensation after breast cancer surgery: a pilot study. *Cancer Practice, 8,* 215–222.

Beach, P., Siebeneck, B., Fenn Buderer, N., & Ferner, T. (2001). Relationship between fatigue and nutritional status of patients receiving radiation therapy to treat lung cancer. *Oncology Nursing Forum, 28,* 1027–1031.

Berger, A.M. (1998). Patterns of fatigue and activity rest during adjuvant breast cancer chemotherapy. *Oncology Nursing Forum, 25,* 51–62.

Berger, A.M., & Farr, L. (1999). The influence of daytime inactivity and nighttime restlessness on cancer-related fatigue. *Oncology Nursing Forum, 26,* 1663–1671.

Bower, J.E., Ganz, P.A., Desmond, K.A., Rowland, J.H., Meyerewitz, B.E., & Belin, T.R. (2000). Fatigue in breast cancer survivors: occurrence, correlates, and impact on quality of life. *Journal of Clinical Oncology, 18,* 743–755.

Broeckel, J.A., Jacobsen, P.B., Horton, J., Balducci, L., & Lymen, G.H. (1998). Characteristics and correlates of fatigue after adjuvant chemotherapy for breast cancer. *Journal of Clinical Oncology, 16,* 1689–1696.

Brophy, L., & Sharp, E. (1991). Physical symptoms of combination biotherapy: a quality of life issue. *Oncology Nursing Forum, 18* (Suppl 1), 25–30.

Clark, P.M., & Lacasse, C. (1998). Cancer-related fatigue: clinical practice issues. *Clinical Journal of Oncology Nursing, 2,* 45–53.

Dini, D., Bertelli, G., Gozza, A., & Forno, G.G. (1993). Treatment of the post-mastectomy pain syndrome with topical capsaicin. *Pain, 54,* 223–226.

Dodd, M.J., Miaskowski, C., & Paul, S.M. (2001). Symptom clusters and their effect on the functional status of patients with cancer. *Oncology Nursing Forum, 28,* 465–470.

Hogan, C.M. (1997). Cancer nursing: the art of symptom management. *Oncology Nursing Forum, 24,* 1335–1341.

Holbrook, A.M., Crowther, R., Lotter, A., Chang, C., & King, D. (2000). The diagnosis and management of insomnia in clinical practice: a practical evidence-based approach. *Canadian Medical Association Journal, 162,* 216–221.

Irvine, D., Vincent, L., Graydon, J.E., Bubela, N., & Thompson, L. (1994). The prevalence and correlates of fatigue in patients receiving treatment with chemotherapy and radiotherapy. A comparison with the fatigue experienced by healthy individuals. *Cancer Nursing, 17,* 367–378.

Jacox, A., Carr, D.B., Payne, R., *et al.* (1994). Management of cancer pain: clinical practice guideline. *AHCPR, 94, 0592.* Rockville, Md.: Agency for Health Care Policy and Research, Public Health Service, U.S. Department of Health and Human Services.

Kupfer, D.J., & Reynolds, C.F. (1997). Management of insomnia. *New England Journal of Medicine, 336,* 341–346.

Lecuona Navea, M., Higelmo Benavides, M.A., & Ayala Ortueta, C. (1999). Capsaicina tópica en el síndrome del dolor postmastectomía. *Rehabilitatión, 33* (5), 321–326.

Lippmann, S., Mazour, I., & Shahab, H. (2001). Insomnia: therapeutic approach. *Southern Medical Journal, 94,* 866–873.

MacDonald, R.N., Hugi, M.R., *et al.* (1998). The management of chronic pain in patients with breast cancer. *Canadian Medical Association Journal, 158,* 71–82.

McCaffery, M. (1999). Selected pain problems. In M. McCaffery, & C. Pasero (Eds.), *Pain: clinical manual, 2nd ed..* St. Louis: Mosby.

Miaskowski, C., & Lee, K. (1999). Pain, fatigue, and sleep disturbances in oncology outpatients receiving radiation therapy for bone metastasis: a pilot study. *Journal of Pain and Symptom Management, 17,* 320–332.

Mock, V., Dow, K.H., Meares, C.J., Grimm, P.M., Dienemann, J.A., Haisfield-Wolfe, M.E., Quitasol, W., Mitchell, S., Chakravarthy, A., & Gage, I. (1997). Effects of exercise on fatigue, physical functioning, and emotional distress during radiotherapy treatment for breast cancer. *Oncology Nursing Forum, 24,* 991–1000.

Mock, V., Pickett, M., Ropka, M.E., Lin, E.M., Stewart, K.J., Rhodes, V.A., McDaniel, R., Grimm, P.M., Krumm, S., & McCorkele, R. (2001). Fatigue and quality of life outcomes of exercise during cancer treatment. *Cancer Practice, 9,* 119–128.

Morin, C.M. (1993). *Insomnia: psychological assessment and management.* New York: The Guilford Press.

Nail, L., & Jones, L.S. (1995). Fatigue as a side effect to cancer treatment: impact on quality of life. *Quality of Life, 4,* 8–13.

National Comprehensive Cancer Network. (2001). *Cancer pain treatment guidelines,* (Version 1). National Comprehensive Cancer Network: Author.

Norman, A.M. (2002). Radiation-induced brachial plexopathy in women treated for carcinoma of the breast. *Clincal Rehabilatation, 16,* 160–166.

Owen, D.C., Parker, K.P., & McGuire, D.B. (2000). Comparison of subjective sleep quality in patients with cancer and healthy subjects. *Oncology Nursing Forum, 26,* 1649–1651.

Piper, B.F., Dibble, S.I., Dodd, M.J., Weiss, M.C., Slaughter, R.E., & Paul, S.M. (1998). The revised Piper Fatigue Scale: psychometric evaluations in women with breast cancer. *Oncology Nursing Forum, 25,* 677–684.

Piper, B., Lindsey, A., & Dodd, M. (1987). Fatigue mechanisms in cancer patients: developing a nursing theory. *Oncology Nursing Forum, 14*(6), 17–23.

Portenoy, R. (1997). The physical examination in cancer pain assessment. *Seminars in Oncology Nursing, 13,* 25–29.

Portenoy, R., & Intri, L.M. (1999). Cancer-related fatigue: guidelines for evaluation and management. *The Oncologist, 4,* 1–10.

Ream, E., & Richardson, A. (1999). From theory to practice: designing interventions to reduce fatigue in patients with cancer. *Oncology Nursing Forum, 26,* 1295–1303.

Ryden, M. (1977). Energy: a crucial consideration in the nursing process. *Nursing Forum, 16*(1), 71–82.

Sarna, L., & Conde, F. (2001). Physical activity and fatigue during radiation therapy: a pilot study using actigraph monitors. *Oncology Nursing Forum, 28,* 1043–1046.

Savard, J., & Morin, C.M. (2001). Insomnia in the context of cancer: a review of a neglected problem. *Journal of Clinical Oncology, 19,* 895–908.

Schwartz, A.L. (1998). The Schwartz Cancer Fatigue Scale: testing reliability and validity. *Oncology Nursing Forum, 25,* 711–717.

Schwartz, A., Mori, M., & Jao, R. (2001). Exercise reduces chemotherapy fatigue in breast cancer patients. *Physician & Sports Medicine, 29,* 5–6.

Stein, K.D., Martin, S.C., Hann, D.H., & Jacobsen, P.B. (1998). A multidimensional measurement of fatigue for use with cancer patients. *Cancer Practice, 6,* 143–151.

Winningham, M. (1995). Fatigue: the missing link to quality of life. *Quality of Life: A Nursing Challenge, 4,* 2–7.

Winningham, M., Nail, L., Burke, M., Brophy, L., Cimprich, B., Jones, L.S., Pickard-Holley, S., Rhodes, V., St. Pierre, B., Beck, S., Glass, E., Mock, V., Mooney, K., & Piper, B. (1994). Fatigue and the cancer experience: the state of the knowledge. *Oncology Nursing Forum, 21,* 23–36.

Chapter 15

LYMPHEDEMA

JANE ARMER, PHD, RN

SCOPE OF THE PROBLEM OF LYMPHEDEMA

In the Western world, breast cancer and its treatment are the leading causes of lymphedema. In the United States, some 180,000 women develop breast cancer annually (ACS, 2002). The literature suggests that as many as 20 to 40 of every 100 women treated for breast cancer will experience lymphedema in their lifetimes. More than 2 million women living with breast cancer in the United States, accounting for nearly 25% of all cancer survivors, are at risk for development of lymphedema throughout their lifetimes.

Lymphedema occurs as both an acute and chronic condition in which significant persistent swelling associated with an abnormal accumulation of protein-rich fluid is experienced in the affected area (Casley-Smith, 1992; Mortimer, 1998). For breast cancer patients, the affected area is generally the arm on the same side as the affected breast. Lymphedema may also affect the trunk, specifically the breast, axilla, and scapular area. Both surgical and radiation fields and nearby distal areas may be affected, as well as areas impacted by reconstruction or infection.

The impact of unmanaged and unresolved lymphedema on quality of life among women surviving breast cancer is extensive, encompassing interpersonal and family relationships, functional abilities, occupational roles, self-image, and, perhaps most importantly, self-esteem (Casley-Smith, 1992; Mirolo *et al.*, 1995; Passik & McDonald, 1998; Petrek & Heelan, 1998; Tobin *et al.*, 1993). In addition, significant health-related complications of unmanaged lymphedema include cellulitis, lymphadenitis, open wounds, and potentially life-threatening septicemia and angiosarcoma (Humble, 1995; Mortimer, 1998; Petrek & Heelan, 1998).

PATHOPHYSIOLOGY AND CLASSIFICATION OF LYMPHEDEMA

Lymphedema is a condition characterized by an abnormal collection of excessive tissue proteins, edema, chronic inflammation, and fibrosis (Brennan, 1992). It occurs when there is an imbalance between the amount of arteriovenous fluid diffusing into interstitial tissue to nourish cells and the ability of the lymphatic system to carry away the fluid containing the larger protein molecules, which cannot move back into the venous system. Lymphedema is the result of a functional overload of the lymphatic system in which interstitial lymph volume exceeds lymph transport capabilities. The protein-rich fluid left behind causes increased interstitial pressure (leading to swelling); provides a rich breeding ground for bacteria (leading to localized and, if not treated aggressively, sometimes regional and systemic infections); and, left unmoved, leads to fibrosis, which may in turn further impede lymphatic drainage.

Lymphedema is categorized as either primary or secondary. Primary lymphedema is caused by congenital absence or abnormalities of lymphatic tissue and is relatively infrequent. Secondary lymphedema is generally caused by obstruction or interruption of the lymphatic system, usually involving the lymph nodes, as a result of infection, trauma, malignancy, or scar tissue (Brennan, 1992). Lymphedema associated with breast cancer is classified as secondary lymphedema. It is caused by removal of lymph nodes and mechanical obstruction of lymphatic channels after breast cancer surgery and/or radiation therapy and/or infection. Secondary lymphedema may be characterized by its chronicity and duration.

Acute lymphedema lasts days, weeks, or possibly several months and has a pitting quality (Brennan, 1992; NCI, 2002). Excess fluid is accommodated by a large expandable subcutaneous tissue space. Noticeable fluctuations in arm size are typical, with the largest increase noted at night. Acute lymphedema may take one of four forms:

- Transient and mild lymphedema may occur within a few days of surgery; the affected area may be warm and erythematous, but generally not painful; it often responds within one week of onset to limb elevation and gentle muscle pumping (making a fist and releasing).
- A second form of acute lymphedema may occur six to eight weeks postoperatively, possibly as acute lymphangitis, phlebitis, or radiation response; the affected area is tender, warm or hot, and erythematous; it often responds to elevation and anti-inflammatory medication, although more involved treatment may be needed.
- The erysipeloid form of acute lymphedema occurs after an insect bite or minor injury or burn; often superimposed on a chronic edematous limb, the affected area is erythematous, very tender, and hot; it requires limb elevation and antibiotics (no compression pumps or wrapping recommended).
- The fourth and most common form of acute lymphedema is usually insidious and not necessarily associated with erythema; with variable onset, aching and skin discomfort are often apparent 18–24 months after cancer treatment, although it may appear a few months to many years later; treatment is discussed later in this chapter.

Transient lymphedema typically lasts less than six months and is associated with pitting edema and absence of brawny skin changes (Brennan, 1992). Chronic lymphedema lasts longer than six months. Change occurs over time as fluid becomes embedded in subcutaneous connective tissues, restricting joint movement and gradually causing edema to be nonpitting. Affected skin becomes hard, thick, and brawny in appearance.

Lymphedema can be further categorized as mild, moderate, or severe. Three stages are identified:

- Grade I, in which pitting occurs upon application of pressure and edema reverses with limb elevation;
- Grade II, in which edema becomes larger and harder and no longer pits under pressure; and
- Grade III, in which swelling worsens and skin changes occur—the skin may become very thick and develop huge folds associated with elephantiasis (Casley-Smith, 1992).

Clinicians may find the following staging criteria particularly helpful:

- 1+: Edema that is barely detectable;
- 2+: A slight indentation is visible when the skin is depressed;
- 3+: A deeper fingerprint returns to normal in 5 to 30 seconds;
- 4+: The extremity may be 1.5 to 2 times normal size (NCI, 2002).

National criteria are currently under development with the goal of standardizing diagnostic staging for improvement of patient care and outcomes-based research (Cheville, 2002).

DIAGNOSIS OF LYMPHEDEMA

Lack of uniform definition and absence of standardized measurement methods with acceptable reliability and validity limit the diagnosis of lymphedema (Petrek *et al.*, 2000; Rockson *et al.*, 1998). Circumferential measurement at selected points (every 2–10 cm, or at 1–5 anatomic points) is the most commonly used anthropometric assessment for lymphedema in the clinical setting, even though it suffers from problems with reliability (between measurers and over time, and even within the same measurer) (see Figure 15.1). Water displacement, the "gold standard" of limb volume estimation, is bulky and messy in the clinical setting (see Figure 15.2). Estimation of limb volume by infrared perometry, equipment marketed for custom fitting of compression garments, is now in research trials (Armer, 2002) (see Figure 15.3).

Physical examination with findings of a greater than 2 cm (or 200 ml) difference between affected and contralateral limbs is one diagnostic criterion for establishment of the diagnosis of lymphedema. Optimally, such a finding (2 cm or 200 ml difference) between preoperative baseline measurement of the affected limb and postoperative measurement of the same limb would support the diagnosis of lymphedema, since the bilateral limbs may not be equal in volume.

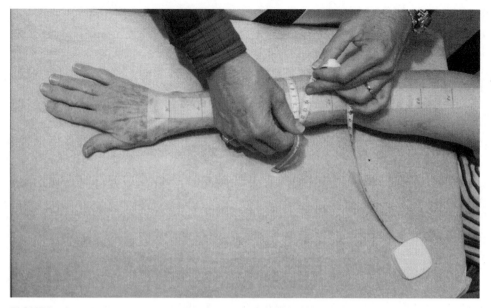

FIGURE 15.1 Sequential circumferential arm measurements.

Photo courtesy of University of Missouri, Sinclair School of Nursing, Lymphedema Research Project.

Symptoms of sensation changes and functional changes must also be assessed, in addition to anthropometric measurements (see Figure 15.4). Location, quality, intensity, duration, and precipitating and alleviating factors related to the swelling must be assessed. Venous thrombosis must be ruled out. Lymphoscintigraphy (imaging of the lymphatic system with dye) can be used to differentiate primary and secondary lymphedema and rule out other etiologies (Rockson *et al.*, 1998).

INCIDENCE, PREVALENCE, AND IMPACT OF LYMPHEDEMA

Perhaps in part because of difficulties in measurement and diagnosis, the reported incidence of lymphedema varies greatly among women treated for breast cancer with surgery and radiation. Reviews of the literature have estimated the incidence of lymphedema from 6% to 30% (Petrek & Heelan, 1998) and from 6% to 62.5% (Passik & McDonald, 1998). Petrek and Heelan noted that the study with the shortest follow-up (12 months) reported the lowest incidence (6%); likewise, one of the studies with the longest follow-up (11 years) reported the highest incidence. Among 1151 women treated with radiation for breast cancer, 23% reported lymphedema at 0 to 2 years after treatment and 45% at 15 or more years after treatment (Mortimer *et al.*, 1996). Among patients treated with surgery alone, prevalence increased from 20% at 0 to 2 years after surgery to 30% at 15 or more years after surgery.

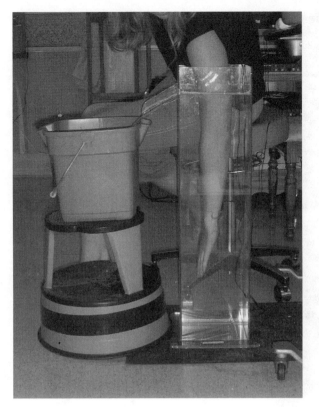

FIGURE 15.2 Water displacement, the "gold standard" for limb volume.

FIGURE 15.3 Assessment of limb volume using perometry.

Photos courtesy of University of Missouri, Sinclair School of Nursing, Lymphedema Research Project.

FIGURE 15.4 Assessment of subjective symptoms of limb change in a breast cancer survivor.
Photo courtesy of University of Missouri, Sinclair School of Nursing, Lymphedema Research Project.

This broad statistical range of findings probably reflects major breakthroughs in breast cancer treatment, including progress in breast conservation and therapeutic combinations leading to increased survivorship (Erickson *et al.,* 2001; Meek, 1998; Tobin *et al.,* 1993); inconsistent criteria for defining lymphedema in the literature; and small samples, retrospective rather than prospective analyses, and the difficulties (particularly reliability) in assessing lymphedema. Lymphedema among breast cancer patients, even using the lowest incidence estimates for the United States alone, affects hundreds of thousands of women and represents a major societal need. Management of the physical and psychosocial aspects of lymphedema is a significant—and largely unrecognized—need in the health care community.

In addition to risk of infection associated with the cellulitis and lymphangitis that often result from the protein-rich stagnant lymph fluid, the swelling associated with post-breast cancer lymphedema often causes discomfort and disability. Some 50% of women with mild lymphedema report heaviness or fullness in the limb. Symptoms experienced most commonly among a group of breast cancer survivors with measurable lymphedema were limb swelling, heaviness, tenderness, and numbness (Armer & Whitman, 2002). Breast cancer survivors with lymphedema, when compared to those without swelling, reported more signs and symptoms.

Hull (1998) noted a wide impact of lymphedema on women's daily lives, including the following: (1) sleeping becomes difficult as women try to position their arms; (2) carrying items, such as heavy pots or groceries, becomes difficult; (3) many forms of exercise, even walking, become difficult; and (4) fit and comfort of clothing become problematic (e.g., blouses need to be larger, long sleeves are worn even in the summer to cover the swelling or pressure garment). Treatment for chronic lymphedema, such as compression bandaging (overnight only for routine long-term maintenance or 23 hours a day during intensive treatment), further impacts activities of daily living and caring for self and family. Thus, the physical impact of lymphedema on a wide range of daily activities is significant. Despite the widespread impact of lymphedema on women's lives, it is underrecognized and undertreated.

WHY LYMPHEDEMA IS UNDERRECOGNIZED AND UNDERTREATED

Reasons for the underrecognition and undertreatment of lymphedema are threefold:

- There is a lack of standard criteria for measuring and diagnosing lymphedema.
- Lymphedema onset may be insidious, developing gradually over several years.
- Lymphedema has not been considered a "life-threatening" complication.

Quantification of lymphedema has been problematic, despite the fact that various methods have been used to measure the swollen arm (Petrek & Heelan, 1998). Among these measurement approaches are circumferences (using a nonstretch flexible tape measure to assess limb girth at certain intervals), water displacement (using a volumeter, the "gold standard" of limb volume estimation), tonometry (a measure of interstitial pressure with limited reliability testing), and perometry (which uses infrared laser technology to estimate volume and graph shape) (Petlund, 1991). The lack of standard measurement protocols and reliability studies contributes to the measurement quandary (see Armer *et al.*, 2002).

Perhaps the most common criterion for diagnosis of lymphedema has been a finding of 2 cm or more difference in arm circumference (or 200 ml difference in limb volume if water displacement is used) between affected and nonaffected limbs (Meek, 1998). These measurement criteria alone are dichotomous: all or none, without specification as to severity. They may also overlook latent stage of disease when early intervention may be most effective in reversing swelling.

Another key measurement issue stems from the common lack of a preoperative limb volume baseline for postoperative comparison. Current diagnoses are generally based on differences between ipsilateral and contralateral limbs, or limbs not known to be equal in size or shape prior to breast cancer treatment.

Another factor inhibiting the recognition of the extent of the problem of lymphedema, in terms of numbers affected and the extent of the impact on lives, is the apparent under-diagnosis by health care providers. As noted earlier, it is conservatively estimated that 20 to 40 of every 100 women treated for breast cancer with contemporary treatment modalities will experience lymphedema in their lifetimes. Indeed, in one prevalence study, researchers found 39% of 103 women returning for follow-up after breast cancer treatment (mean time since diagnosis = 36 months) had greater than or equal to 2 cm difference in circumference between the affected and nonaffected limbs at one or more points (Armer & Whitman, 2002). However, among the 99 corresponding medical records reviewed, only 21 charts (21%), just over half of the 39% with measurable LE, were found to have a medical diagnosis of lymphedema. Further, an additional 40% of the 103 women had differences between limbs at one or more points of greater than or equal to 1 cm but less than 2 cm, a difference that some consider latent or mild lymphedema (Meek, 1998; NCI, 2002).

In addition, although oncology physicians might be aware of the general risk for lymphedema, some early findings indicate that physicians might not always be aware of the existing condition of lymphedema, perhaps because of its insidious nature (Armer & Whitman, in press). For example, in one case, a breast cancer lymphedema patient reported that the referring physician informed her about the lymphedema study and suggested she consider participating, because even though she did not have lymphedema, she was at risk of someday developing lymphedema. In fact, circumferential arm measurements revealed greater than or equal to 2 cm difference between the affected and non-affected arms at two of five measurement sites, sufficient for a diagnosis of lymphedema. Upon questioning, the patient reported several signs and symptoms of lymphedema, including nonreversing swelling of the affected hand and wrist.

This anecdotal example underscores two important points. First, most often patients' limbs are not measured routinely in the clinical setting—radiation oncology, surgical oncology, or medical oncology—during acute treatment or routine follow-up. Thorough assessment requires objective measures of visual inspection, palpation, and volume estimation (by circumferences, water displacement, or perometry) in comparison to the non-affected limb. Assessment also requires patient survey of possible signs and symptoms associated with lymphedema, including self-reported symptoms such as limb heaviness, swelling, change in fit of garments, redness, and tenderness.

Secondly, in both the prevalence study and the case cited in the previous paragraph, a one-time comparison of circumferences of the ipsilateral and contralateral limbs was carried out. Although comparison with the nonaffected limb is critical, for the optimal assessment both limbs would be assessed over time, as changes in daily activities, treatment effects, weight changes, and fluid-balance shifts are but four of the possible factors that potentially affect limb volume. Limb volume changes over time, and comparison to the contralateral limb provides the most complete objective assessment data for lymphedema diagnosis and treatment decisions. Similarly, self-reporting of signs and symptoms over time is revealing of limb changes that may indicate a need for further follow-up in assessment of lymphedema. Optimally, these assessments (limb volume and symptom experience) will begin preoperatively and continue throughout the months and years of post-breast cancer follow-up (see Figure 15.5).

After reviewing the lymphedema literature, Petrek and Heelan (1998) noted that the scanty evaluation of lymphedema may be attributed to several factors, including a history of relative neglect of women's health problems and, perhaps most importantly, the traditional view that quality of life is less important than the eradication of cancer and detection of recurrence. Unfortunately, neglect of lymphedema has not only meant that many women go undiagnosed and fail to receive basic preventive information (see Maunsell *et al.,* 1993), but has also inhibited the development of effective psychosocial interventions. As Passik and McDonald (1998) concluded, "what recommendations to make to women are anything but clear and well studied at this time" (p. 2819). Treatment of lymphedema has been, and continues to be, a major challenge for health care professionals—and for breast cancer survivors (Hull, 1998; Tobin *et al.,* 1993).

RISK FACTORS FOR LYMPHEDEMA

Over the past decade, breast conservation techniques, most often coupled with radiotherapy, have been used widely in an effort to diminish unpleasant, lasting side effects (such as lymphedema) long associated with more radical treatments without sacrificing survivorship (Pressman, 1998). Similar medical optimism regarding reduction in lymphedema has been

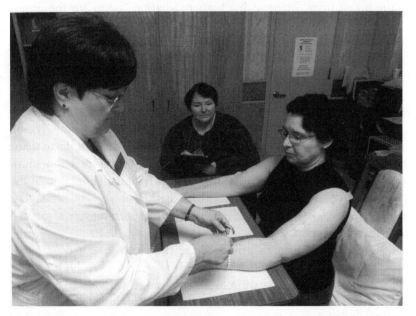

FIGURE 15.5 Assessment of baseline and follow-up circumferential measurements after breast cancer diagnosis and treatment.

Photo courtesy of University of Missouri, Sinclair School of Nursing, Lymphedema Research Project.

associated in recent years with the advent of sentinel lymph node biopsy procedures that spare the breast cancer patient the more invasive and traumatic axillary lymph node dissection. However, preliminary observations indicate that the incidence of lymphedema following breast conservation surgical methods, such as lumpectomy and partial mastectomy combined with radiotherapy, may be equal to or, in fact, greater than the incidence following traditional surgical treatment (mastectomy with or without radiation) (Pressman, 1998; Rockson, 1998).

Axillary lymph node dissection (ALND) of level I, II, and III nodes is believed to be the greatest contributor to development of lymphedema (Brennan, 1992). Level I nodes are located at the tail of the breast. Level II nodes are closest to the breast and drain the breast area. Level III nodes are located between the pectoralis muscle along subscapular vessels and the chest wall. (See Chapter 6 for additional information about axillary lymph node dissection.)

Sentinel lymph node biopsy (SLNB) is being evaluated in two national clinical trials as a diagnostic alternative to ALND in terms of mortality and morbidity. Intuitively, many believe SLNB may be associated with a decreased incidence of lymphedema, but research findings based on long-term follow-up are not yet available. Early evidence suggests that SLNB alone does not eliminate the risk of lymphedema (see Thiadens *et al.*, 2002). Lymphedema risk may be increased when both SLNB and ALND are carried out.

Radiation therapy is also believed to be associated with increased lymphedema risk (Meek, 1998). Conservative breast surgery (lumpectomy) is routinely combined with radiation therapy to the breast (most often with a higher radiation "boost" to the tumor field) as an alternative to mastectomy. This more common treatment of radiation combined with conservative surgical treatment of the breast may not reduce the woman's risk of lymphedema, as compared to mastectomy; long-term follow-up examining lifetime risk is not yet available to fully document lymphedema morbidity related to breast cancer treatment.

Incidence of lymphedema appears to be highest when both ALND and axillary radiation are performed (Meek, 1998). While lymphatic vessels are resistant to radiation, lymph nodes are sensitive and undergo a process of reduced lymphocyte production, fatty tissue replacement, and localized fibrosis following radiation. Studies suggest that radiation-induced fibrosis of the venous vessels may subsequently impede lymphatic function in the limb (see Meek, 1998). Research examining predictors of radiation skin reactions suggests seroma aspiration to be predictive of severe skin reactions, which in turn may be associated with higher occurrence of lymphedema (Porock, 2002; Porock *et al.*, 1998).

Among the multiple factors believed to influence the individual breast cancer survivor's risk for post-breast cancer lymphedema development are extent of ALND; axillary radiation therapy and scatter from breast radiation therapy; postoperative infection; severity of radiation skin reaction (and, indirectly, seroma formation); weight gain during or following treatment; older age at diagnosis; poor nutritional status; and certain comorbid conditions, including obesity and diabetes (Coward, 1999; Humble, 1995; Kalinowski, 2001; Porock, 2002; Porock *et al.*, 1998; Rockson, 1998).

There remain many unanswered questions regarding individual risk for post-breast cancer lymphedema. Of two breast cancer survivors with similar history, stage of disease, and treatment, one may develop lymphedema in the immediate postoperative period and the other may remain free of lymphedema symptoms over her lifetime. Three examples of unexplored research questions regarding individual risk follow.

1. Although lymphedema prevalence and age have not been rigorously examined, it has been assumed that older women, at higher risk for breast cancer, are at higher risk for lymphedema. However, assumptions of higher prevalence for lymphedema among older survivors may be related to the higher number of breast cancer cases over age 65 years (see Armer & Fu, 2002; Armer & Heckathorn, under review).
2. Influence on capillary permeability by common breast cancer therapies has not been studied. Might certain agents that influence fluid retention and capillary wall permeability also impact risk for development of lymphedema?
3. Individual differences in lymphatic anatomy and physiology are not routinely studied preoperatively to inform surgical and radiation treatment decisions. Theoretically, the potential to individualize the treatment approach (e.g., surgical incision, radiation field/shielding) based on the person's underlying lymphatic structure and function might reduce risk of lymphedema formation.

SYMPTOMS COEXISTING WITH POST-BREAST CANCER LYMPHEDEMA

Changes in pain, range of motion, and sensations may be indicators of developing lymphedema or other treatment-related sequelae and must be carefully assessed at each follow-up visit and over time. Notation of location, intensity, and actions that elicit, exacerbate, and relieve the pain, functional impairment, and altered sensations is an important component of a thorough assessment.

In one study, between one third and two thirds of breast cancer survivors with greater than or equal to 2 cm difference between limb circumferences reported experiencing swelling, heaviness, tenderness, and/or numbness (Armer & Whitman, 2002). Numbness, tightness, and heaviness were reported by approximately one fourth (23%) to one half (55%) of all women. Limb tenderness, limb swelling, and aching were reportedly experienced "over the past year" by one third (34%) to two fifths (42%) of all women. Those with greater than or equal to 2 cm difference between limb circumferences reported more symptoms. Some 50% of women with even mild swelling reported sensations of heaviness and fullness in the affected limb.

Differentiation of etiology of posttreatment pain, function, and sensation changes may be difficult. Pain may be related to nerve damage during surgery, known as postmastectomy pain syndrome (PMPS). (See Carpenter *et al.*, 1998; Kwekkeboom, 1996; Stevens *et al.*, 1995; and Wallace *et al.*, 1996, for further reading on postmastectomy pain syndrome.) Stretching of skin and interstitial tissue to accommodate the buildup of lymph fluid may also cause discomfort. Pressure of increased lymph fluid on nerve endings also causes pain.

When the lymph fluid increases, the arm becomes visibly swollen and may feel heavy, with an observable and/or measurable increase in arm size.

Early postoperative range of motion (ROM) changes in the ipsilateral arm and shoulder may result from tissue manipulation and positioning during surgery. Later ROM changes may result from scar tissue and fibrosis related to surgery and/or radiation. Swelling and fibrosis from lymphedema may also cause ROM restrictions in the shoulder, elbow, wrist, and fingers.

Posttreatment sensation changes may be related to the surgical incision or to nerve irritation or injury during ALND. Sensations may be decreased, increased, or altered. Sensations include phantom breast sensations, numbness, hyperesthesias, and "pins and needles" sensations. Dysesthesia, described as a cutting or burning pain, may be reported. Sensation changes may also be related to pressure on nerve endings by increased lymph fluid.

Sensation changes may be the earliest indicator of increasing interstitial pressure changes associated with lymphedema, even before visually observable changes or measurable volume changes. The breast cancer survivor may be the first to notice that a ring or watch or favorite sleeve may no longer fit as before or that a sensation has changed (reduced, increased, altered).

Although it is little acknowledged, those with breast cancer-related lymphedema may experience a level of fatigue that is moderately severe and moderately disruptive to daily living (Armer & Porock, 2002). Fatigue may also be an early cue of health status change (e.g., cellulitis).

In general, symptoms associated with lymphedema are treated with targeted interventions. For example, pain associated with lymphedema may be treated with analgesics, relaxation techniques, adjuvant drugs such as amitriptyline, and/or transcutaneous electrical nerve stimulation (TENS) (NCI, 2002). In general, however, the most successful treatment is reduction of volume in the limb associated with the lymphedema.

INTERVENTIONS FOR LYMPHEDEMA

Early detection and intervention hold the greatest promise of reducing this widespread condition (Petrek et al., 2000; Rockson, 1998). Identification of epidemiological and clinical factors associated with risk and incidence will provide the necessary foundation for preventive intervention. Once lymphedema is established, general supportive care of balanced nutrition with adequate protein, limb volume reduction, and symptom management are required (see Table 15.1). More rigorous research examining type and frequency of treatments and optimal outcomes is needed.

A range of medical approaches with varying levels of success in the management of lymphedema have been reported (Casley-Smith, 1992; Casley-Smith et al., 1998; Hutzschenreuter et al., 1991; Mason, 1993; Rockson et al., 1998). These approaches include limb elevation, diuretics, benzopyrones, compression sleeves, sequential pressure devices, directional-flow gradient-foam devices, exercise, infection control, and maintenance of skin integrity

Table 15.1 Lymphedema Treatment Approaches

Treatment approaches	Effectiveness and comments
Limb elevation	Effective in acute (early) lymphedema when swelling is reversible.
Diuretics	Noneffective for protein-rich lymphedema. May be effective for systemic or vascular non-protein-rich edema; may cause adverse reactions in lymphedema (see Brennan, 1992).
Benzopyrones Coumarin	Unproven effectiveness (no rigorous randomized double-blind clinical trials showing greater effectiveness than placebo); not FDA-approved; discontinued in Australia following liver complications (see Loprinzi *et al.*, 1997, 1999).
Anticoagulants Pantothenic acid Pyridoxine Hyaluronidase	These drugs have no proven therapeutic value in lymphedema management and may cause adverse reactions; no rigorous randomized double-blind clinical trials showing greater effectiveness than placebo (see Brennan, 1992).
Surgical interventions	Not recommended as they are not generally successful in curing lymphedema. Several techniques have been attempted with minimal success and high complication rates of skin necrosis, infection, and sensory difficulties (NCI, 2002; Savage, 1985).
Sequential pressure device Pump	Mixed findings; not currently first line of treatment recommended by consensus of the National Lymphedema Network; further damage to lymphatics possible with inappropriate use/pressure.
Compression sleeve	Effective for maintaining limb volume when properly fitted and periodically replaced (alone not generally effective for reduction).
Exercise	Effective for management and reduction of swelling with carefully individualized graduated exercise plan, with limb appropriately compressed, avoiding extreme repetitions, excessive weights, and extreme temperatures.
Infection control	Essential and highly effective; prevention and early treatment most effective; history of cellulitis, lymphangitis, erysipelas, septicemia denotes higher risk for infection; may require standing prescription for antibiotics.
Nutrition	Well-balanced diet sufficient in protein is essential to enhance healing and avoid hypoalbuminemia, which can exacerbate excess protein movement into the interstitium; goal of achieving optimal weight while well-nourished.
Skin integrity	Essential and highly effective: prevention of skin breaks, skin cleansed with mild soaps and moisturized with pH-neutral lotions.
Comprehensive (Complex, Complete) Decongestive Physiotherapy (Therapy) (CDP, CDT): manual lymph drainage, bandaging and compression garments, exercise, and meticulous skin care (inclusive)	Highly effective; comprehensive program of specialized manual lymph drainage to stimulate lymphatic function locally, regionally, and systemically, regime of bandaging and daytime compression, exercise, and skin care; usually specified period of intensive treatment until maximal limb volume reduction achieved, followed by continuing self-care program, sometimes with occasional "boosts" of intensive treatment; optimal dosing (length of each treatment [60 vs. 90 minutes, scheduled daily vs. 3 times a week, 3 to 4 to 6 weeks]) not yet established by rigorous research.

(Table 15.1). To date, many of these approaches lack rigorous research evaluation. With the exception of antibiotics to manage infections, pharmaceuticals and surgical interventions play no significant role in lymphedema management (Loprinzi *et al.,* 1997, 1999; Mortimer *et al.,* 1996; NCI, 2002); successful treatment to reduce limb volume hinges on manual/mechanical therapies.

Certain approaches currently under more rigorous study, such as complete decongestive physiotherapy (including a program of manual lymph drainage, bandaging, exercise, and meticulous skin care), show the greatest effectiveness in reducing lymphedema.

MANAGEMENT OF LYMPHEDEMA USING COMPLEX DECONGESTIVE PHYSIOTHERAPY

The most widely recommended treatment for lymphedema, complex decongestive physiotherapy (CDP), has four components and two phases. The four components include meticulous skin care; manual lymph drainage; compression bandaging; and exercise. There are two phases of CDP, with the first (intensive) phase lasting four to six weeks to establish lymphedema reduction and the second (maintenance) phase involving preservation of initial reduction. Resources for locating trained and certified therapists specializing in CDP can be located at the National Lymphedema Network Web site (see Table 15.2).

The recommended skin care regime includes liberal use of pH-neutral lotions and oil-based soaps to keep skin moist and supple; careful inspection to find and treat even minute breaks in skin; and avoidance of injury or even minor damage (e.g., bruises, sunburn, insect bites, abrasion) to the affected arm and trunk.

Manual lymphatic drainage (MLD) or manual lymphatic therapy (MLT) is first carried out by a trained and certified MLD therapist and continued by the patient and/or family as instructed by the therapist. The goal of MLD is to stimulate lymphatic flow in truncal regions of the body before treatment of the limb, with the proximal arm massaged before the distal arm. Massage is performed slowly and rhythmically, with minimal pressure and friction.

Compression bandages (or later, daytime garments) are applied immediately after massage to maintain reduction in volume and to enhance effectiveness of the muscle pump in moving lymph fluid from the limb during exercise and activities of daily living. Two-way low-stretch (non-elastic wrap) bandages are applied from the distal to the proximal limb. Compression garments for daytime wear are fitted by trained fitters or certified therapists.

Table 15.2 Selected Internet Resources on Lymphedema Management for Patients and Professionals

Organization	Web site
National Lymphedema Network	*http://www.lymphnet.org/resource.html*
National Cancer Institute	*http://www.nci.nih.gov/cancerinfo/pdq/ supportivecare/lymphedema/patient/*

Exercises are individualized and sequenced to facilitate movement of fluid from the interstitium into the lymphatics and the trunk. Jarring, pounding, or highly repetitive exercises are not generally recommended. Each individual is instructed to monitor for increased swelling as new levels of exercise are initiated. Swimming and water exercise in moderate temperatures are optimal exercises, as the water pressure provides support for the limb during muscle contraction.

SELF-MANAGEMENT

Because lymphedema tends to be a lifelong and chronic condition, appropriate self-management is critical to the prevention of complications and other untoward effects that diminish functional abilities and quality of life related to breast cancer lymphedema survivorship. Although personal and historic characteristics such as age, weight, infection, comorbidities such as diabetes, and axillary dissection are believed to affect a woman's risk for onset of lymphedema, patient compliance has been identified as the most important factor in treating lymphedema (Petrek *et al.*, 2000; Rose *et al.*, 1991). Even so, little is known about factors influencing patient compliance and promoting effective self-management strategies for lymphedema symptoms. For example, many of the most promising lymphedema management techniques are time consuming and very difficult to accomplish by the patient herself, so that the patient may be vulnerable to incomplete compliance without strong support and practical assistance from family or friends.

In one study, the most frequently reported lymphedema symptom management strategy was "no action" (Armer & Whitman, 2002). One breast cancer survivor with moderately severe lymphedema in her dominant limb reported that she was unable to comply with the bandaging regime when her husband traveled or was too tired to assist her. It was evident that the patient experienced difficulties with both social support and problem solving, which negatively influenced her lymphedema symptom management—and ultimately, limb volume and functional health status.

One study involving women with post-breast cancer lymphedema focused on the impact of the under-recognition of lymphedema. In particular, patients' understandings of lymphedema causes and treatments were examined in order to better understand their perceived receipt of accurate medical information and information utilization (Radina *et al.*, under review). Findings indicate that participants were generally aware of the fundamental cause of their lymphedema—breast cancer treatment. They also attributed onset of lymphedema to other incidents such as physical activity and skin damage, consistent with existing empirical evidence. Participants' treatment choices were both consistent and inconsistent with empirical evidence. Choices consistent with empirical knowledge included the use of compression treatment, massage, elevation, pumps, therapists/therapy centers, and positive attitude/faith. Areas of inconsistency in patients' knowledge that are deserving of further investigation were the effectiveness of both exercise and medication in the management of lymphedema (Radina *et al.*, under review). This study highlights the need to not only improve diagnosis and treatment of lymphedema, but to also increase awareness of the condition within the medical community, ultimately improving patient education.

Lymphedema support groups are one tool for effective education, peer support, and problem solving. Unfortunately, support groups and training in practical problem solving are not yet readily available to all patients. Lymphedema support groups are listed by state at the Web site of the National Lymphedema Network (*http://www.lymphnet.org/support.html*). In total, there were 128 lymphedema support groups listed, covering all 50 states, in 2002. Credible web sites and electronic communications have potential to create virtual support groups, "pen pals," and resources wherever Internet access exists (see Figure 15.6).

PSYCHOSOCIAL ISSUES RELATED TO LYMPHEDEMA

THE VIEW FROM WITHIN

Lymphedema is not a trivial problem. Not only are there the physical symptoms and risks noted earlier, but the associated challenges may also lead to posttreatment psychosocial distress. Research suggests that the impact of secondary lymphedema on psychosocial dimensions extends beyond that of the breast cancer itself. For many survivors, the onset and chronic nature of lymphedema represents a daily distressful reminder of the breast cancer and its life-changing impact. Women may experience depression and anxiety relating to functional impairment; body image concerns relating to the appearance of the arm; and increased feelings of social isolation.

Tobin *et al.* (1993) were among the first researchers to examine the psychological morbidity of lymphedema. They observed that breast cancer patients who did not experience arm swelling seemed more successful in assimilating the experience of breast cancer and moving on. However, patients with arm swelling reported more difficulty in several domains of psychosocial adjustment. One patient aptly depicted the difficulty: "The breast is not so bad.

FIGURE 15.6 Lymphedema support group and family members united to raise money for cancer research.

At least it is hidden, but everybody keeps asking about my arm" (Tobin *et al.*, 1993, p. 3252). In addition, Tobin and colleagues observed that some patients reported complete loss of interest in dress and appearance, difficulties in sexual and interpersonal relations, and loss of occupational aspirations, with subsequent loss in self-esteem and depression. One 88-year-old breast cancer survivor who has lived 41 years with posttreatment lymphedema reports that her extended experience living with lymphedema was far more life changing than her treatment for breast cancer itself (Armer, in press). In short, coping with lymphedema is not only stressful, but it potentially results in serious psychosocial problems that directly influence the quality of life of breast cancer survivors.

PSYCHOSOCIAL INTERVENTIONS

As limited as the proven effective physiologic interventions in lymphedema management are, testing of psychosocial interventions has been even more limited. Preliminary research suggests that lack of social support and avoidant coping are related to psychosocial and functional morbidity in lymphedema patients. In one study, women who had poor social support, pain, and/or passive and avoidant coping styles reported the highest levels of disabilities (Passik *et al.*, 1995). Thus, psychosocial factors such as social support and problem-solving style may serve as personal and environmental resources. If available, these resources may allow women to successfully manage lymphedema and its emotional and psychological impact; if lacking, they may exacerbate the functional impact of their condition. These findings suggest that further study is needed of psychosocial factors, especially problem-solving capacity and style and social support, in relationship to the progression of lymphedema (Armer *et al.*, 2002).

FAMILY IMPACT

In a qualitative study examining the impact of lymphedema on women's family roles, the Family Adjustment and Adaptation Response Model was used to interpret data regarding how lymphedema affected the women and their families in terms of task completion and family functioning. Research findings indicate that families who are more flexible in modification for completing daily tasks and who have preexisting resources for coping with stressors have more positive outcomes than those families who are more rigid and cope with stressors poorly (Radina & Armer, 2001). Further work in this area has potential to provide the foundation for family-level interventions in dealing with chronic illness such as lymphedema.

PREVENTION OF LYMPHEDEMA

Prevention is the major goal, because there is currently no cure for lymphedema. Since we understand that lymphedema may occur immediately after surgery or radiation or many years later, preventive education must begin at preoperative teaching and continue through the months and years of follow-up. The focus of prevention is minimizing injury or damage to the involved extremity. Precautions recommended by the National Lymphedema Network (2001) include:

- Do not ignore any swelling.
- Do not allow injection or blood draw in the affected arm.
- Check blood pressure on the unaffected arm.
- Maintain skin and nail care.
- Avoid vigorous exercises using the affected arm.
- Do not lift heavy objects with the affected arm.
- Avoid excessive heat, saunas, sunburns, tans, and hot baths.
- Do not wear constricting garments, jewelry, and sleeves.
- Prevent arm swelling and infection.
- Use sunscreen on the affected arm.
- Wear gloves while doing housework and gardening; wear oven mitts when cooking.
- Wear a compression sleeve during air travel.
- Use an electric razor to remove axillary hair.
- Maintain ideal body weight; avoid smoking and alcohol.

NURSING MANAGEMENT OF LYMPHEDEMA

Nursing strategies for management of post-breast cancer lymphedema include:

- Initiate education on lymphedema prevention at the preoperative visit; review understanding at each follow-up visit.
- Ensure that the patient has written guidelines and educational materials for future reference.
- Review lymphedema pathophysiology and steps to prevention.
- Instruct the patient on establishing routine circumferential measurements of both the affected and the nonaffected limb at easy-to-find landmarks (such as a freckle or nevus) for self-monitoring of limb volume changes.
- Ask patients about lymphedema or "limb swelling" and other signs and symptoms; patients may not volunteer information unless asked directly.
- Monitor patients closely when lymphedema occurs; evaluate and manage symptoms.
- Facilitate referral to a certified manual lymph drainage therapist for assessment, intensive treatment, and teaching on self-management.
- Instruct the patient to report any rash, redness, tenderness, swelling of the affected area (hand, arm, breast, and/or scapular region), and increased temperature immediately.
- Be alert to risk of repeated infections in the patient who has experienced a single infection.
- Do not dismiss even a seemingly minor injury.
- Encourage a well-balanced, protein-sufficient diet; review nutritional status and lab work routinely for hypoalbuminemia (goal of serum albumin above 2.5 g/dL).
- Assess psychosocial concerns as well as physical and functional changes.

- Explore perceived barriers to self-management and compliance and provide resources for problem solving.
- Assist patients in assessing personal short-term and long-term goals and placing self-management actions in the context of these self-concordant goals.
- Suggest that patients wear a medical alert bracelet.

Although optimal treatment benefits are seen with early intervention, with appropriate therapy improvement can be seen even after substantial time of swelling. See also Hull (2000); Fu and Armer (2002); Kalinowski (2001); Erickson *et al.* (2001); and National Cancer Institute (2002) for further reading in the area of nursing management strategies.

SUMMARY

Lymphedema is a major problem affecting a significant number of women treated for breast cancer. In fact, 20% to 40% of the 2 million breast cancer survivors in the United States may be affected by lymphedema during their lifetimes. This chronic condition has long been underdiagnosed and underreported, in part because of difficulties with standard and reliable measurement approaches. When one takes a lifespan perspective, the impact of chronic lymphedema is viewed as being far more life changing than the acute treatment for breast cancer itself. Over the years, both professional and self-care actions in management of lymphedema have been limited and little studied. Comprehensive decongestive physiotherapy is considered the most effective treatment for lymphedema. Intensive CDP must be followed by continuing maintenance care and vigilant self-management. With careful assessment and management, the potential negative impact of chronic lymphedema on functional health and quality of life can be minimized.

REFERENCES

American Cancer Society. (2002). *Cancer Facts & Figures – 2002.* Atlanta, Ga.: Author.

Armer, J.M. (2002). Estimation of breast cancer limb volume by perometry and circumferences: a prospective longitudinal study [Abstract]. *Proceedings of the International National Lymphedema Network Conference, Chicago, Illinois, 5,* 15.

Armer, J.M. (in press). Living with lymphedema: a case study of secondary lymphedema in an elderly breast cancer survivor. *Lymphology.*

Armer, J.M., & Fu, M. (2002, August). Age differences in post-breast cancer lymphedema signs and symptoms [Abstract]. *Proceedings of the International National Lymphedema Network Conference, Chicago, Illinois, 5,* 20.

Armer, J.M., & Heckathorn, P. (under review). Post-breast cancer lymphedema and the older survivor. *Journal of Gerontological Nursing.*

Armer, J.M., Heppner, P.P., & Mallinkrodt, B. (2002). Post-breast cancer treatment lymphedema: the hidden epidemic. *Scope on Phlebology and Lymphology, 9*(1), 334–341.

Armer, J.M., & Porock, D. (2002). Self-management of fatigue among women with lymphedema. *Lymphology, 35* (Suppl), 208–213.

Armer, J.M., & Whitman, M. (2002). The problem of lymphedema following breast cancer treatment: prevalence, symptoms, and self-management. *Lymphology, 35* (Suppl), 153–159.

Brennan, M.J. (1992). Lymphedema following the surgical treatment of breast cancer: a review of pathophysiology and treatment. *Journal of Pain and Symptom Management, 7*(2), 110–116.

Carpenter, J.S., Andrykowski, M.A., Sloan, P., Cunningham, L., Cordova, M.J., Studts, J.L., McGrath, P.C., Sloan, D., & Kenady, D.E. (1998).

Postmastectomy/postlumpectomy pain in breast cancer survivors. *Journal of Clinical Epidemiology, 51*(12), 1285–1292.

Casley-Smith, J.R. (1992). Modern treatment of lymphoedema. *Modern Medicine of Australia, 5,* 70–83.

Casley-Smith, J.R., Boris, M., Weindorf, S., & Lasinski, B. (1998). Treatment for lymphedema of the arm—the Casley-Smith method. *Cancer Supplement, 83*(12), 2843–2863.

Cheville, A. (2002, September). Update on common toxicity criteria system. Paper presented at the 5th International National Lymphedema Network Conference. Chicago, Illinois.

Coward, D. (1999). Lymphedema prevention and management knowledge in women treated for breast cancer. *Oncology Nursing Forum, 26,* 1047–1053.

Erickson, V., Pearson, M., Ganz, P., *et al.* (2001). Arm edema in breast cancer patients. *Journal of the National Cancer Institute, 93,* 96–111.

Fu, M., & Armer, J.M. (2002, August). Self-concordant goals and lymphedema management. Poster presented at the 5th International National Lymphedema Network Conference. Chicago, Illinois.

Hull, M.M. (1998). Functional and psychosocial aspects of lymphedema in women treated for breast cancer. *Innovations in Breast Cancer Care, 3*(4), 97–100, 117–118.

Hull, M. (2000). Lymphedema in women treated for breast cancer. *Seminars in Oncology Nursing, 16*(3), 226–237.

Humble, C.A. (1995). Lymphedema: incidence, pathophysiology, management, and nursing care. *Continuing Education, 22*(10), 1503–1509.

Hutzschenreuter, P.O., Wittlinger, H., Wittlinger, G., & Kurz, I. (1991). Postmastectomy arm lymphoedema: treated by manual lymph drainage and compression bandage therapy. *European Journal of Physical Medicine and Rehabilitation, 1*(6), 166–170.

Kalinowski, B. (2001). Lymphedema. In C.H. Yarbro, M.H. Frogge, & M. Goodman (Eds.), *Cancer symptom management, 2nd ed.,* pp. 457–486. Sudbury, Mass.: Jones & Bartlett.

Kwekkeboom, K. (1996). Postmastectomy pain syndromes. *Cancer Nursing,* 19(1), 37–43.

Loprinzi, C.L., Kugler, J.W., Sloan, J.A., *et al.* (1999). Lack of effect of coumarin in women with lymphedema after treatment for breast cancer. *New England Journal of Medicine, 340*(5), 346–350.

Loprinzi, C.L., Sloan, J., & Kugler, J. (1997). Coumarin-induced hepatotoxicity. *Journal of Clinical Oncology, 15*(9), 3167–3168.

Mason, M. (1993). The treatment of lymphoedema by complex physical therapy. *Australian Physiotherapy, 39*(1), 41–45.

Maunsell, E., Brisson, J., & Deschenes, L. (1993). Arm problems and psychological distress after surgery for breast cancer. *Cancer Journal of Surgery, 36*(4), 315–320.

Meek, A.G. (1998). Breast radiotherapy and lymphedema. *Cancer Supplement, 83*(12), 2788–2797.

Mirolo, B.R., Bunce, I.H., Chapman, M., Olsen, T., Eliadis, P., Hennessy, J.M., Ward, L.C., & Jones, L.C. (1995). Psychosocial benefits of postmastectomy lymphedema therapy. *Cancer Nursing, 18*(3), 197–205.

Mortimer, P.S. (1998). The pathophysiology of lymphedema. *Cancer Supplement, 83*(12), 2798–2802.

Mortimer, P.S., Bates, D.O., Brassington, H.D., *et al.* (1996). The prevalence of arm oedema following treatment for breast cancer. *Quarterly Journal of Medicine, 89,* 377–380.

National Cancer Institute. (2002). *Lymphedema (PDQ®)* (updated September 2002). Retrieved September 19, 2002, from *http://www.nci.nih.gov/cancerinfo/pdq/ supportivecare/lymphedema/patient/.*

National Lymphedema Network. (2001). 18 steps to prevention for arm lymphedema. Retrieved September 19, 2002, from *http://www.lymphnet.org/ prevention.html.*

Passik, S.D., & McDonald, M.V. (1998). Psychosocial aspects of upper extremity lymphedema in women treated for breast carcinoma. *Cancer Supplement, 83*(12), 2817–2820.

Passik, S.D., Newman, M.L., Brennan, M., & Tunkel, R. (1995). Predictors of psychological distress, sexual dysfunction and physical functioning among women with upper extremity lymphedema related to breast cancer. *Psycho-Oncology, 4,* 255–263.

Petlund, C.F. (1991). Volumetry of limbs. In W.L. Olszewski (Ed.), *Lymph stasis: pathophysiology, diagnosis, and treatment,* pp. 309–330. Boca Raton, Fla.: CRC Press.

Petrek, J.A., & Heelan, M.C. (1998). Incidence of breast carcinoma-related lymphedema. *Cancer Supplement, 83*(12), 2776–2781.

Petrek, J.A., Pressman, P.I., & Smith, R.A. (2000). Lymphedema: current issues in research and management.

CA—A Cancer Journal for Clinicians, 50(5), 292–307.

Porock, D. (2002, August). Impact of seroma on the development of radiation skin reactions. Poster presented at the International Society for Nurses in Cancer Care 12th International Conference. London, UK.

Porock, D., Kristjanson, L., Nikoletti, S., Cameron, F., & Pedler, P. (1998). Predicting the severity of radiation skin reactions in women with breast cancer. *Oncology Nursing Forum, 25*(6), 1019–1029.

Pressman, P.I. (1998). Surgical treatment and lymphedema. *Cancer Supplement, 83*(12), 2782–2787.

Radina, M.E., & Armer, J.M. (2001). A qualitative investigation of families coping with chronic illness: lymphedema and the family. *Journal of Family Nursing, 7*(3), 281–299.

Radina, M.E., Armer, J.M., Culbertson, S.D., & Dusold, J.M. (under review). Self-regulation theory and the health information needs of women with post-breast cancer lymphedema. *Nursing Oncology Forum.*

Rockson, S.G. (1998). Precipitating factors in lymphedema: myths and realities. *Cancer Supplement, 83*(12), 2814–2816.

Rockson, S.G., Miller, L.T., & Senie, R. (1998). Workgroup III. Diagnosis and management of lymphedema. *Cancer Supplement, 83*(12), 2882–2885.

Rose, K.E., Taylor, H.M., & Twycross, R.G. (1991). Long-term compliance with treatment in obstructive arm lymphedema in cancer. *Palliative Medicine,* 52–55.

Savage, R.C. (1985). The surgical management of lymphedema. *Surgery, Gynecology, and Obstetrics, 160*(3), 283–290.

Stevens, P.E., Dibble, S.L., & Miaskowski, C. (1995). Prevalence, characteristics, and impact of postmastectomy pain syndrome: an investigation of women's experiences. *Pain, 61,* 61–68.

Thiadens, S.R.J., Armer, J.M., & Porock, D. (2002). NLN preliminary statistical analysis of survey data on lymphedema. *National Lymphedema Network LymphLink, 14*(1), 5, 6, 8, 9.

Tobin, M.B., Lacey, H.J., Meyer, L., & Mortimer, P.S. (1993). The psychological morbidity of breast cancer-related arm swelling. Psychological morbidity of lymphoedema. *Cancer, 72,* 3248–3252.

Wallace, M.S., Wallace, A.M., Lee, J., & Dobke, M.K. (1996). Pain after breast surgery: a survey of 282 women. *Pain, 66,* 195–205.

chapter 16

MENOPAUSAL SYMPTOMS

JANET S. CARPENTER, PHD, RN, AOCN

JULIE L. ELAM, RN, MSN

INTRODUCTION

Assessment and management of menopausal symptoms following breast cancer treatment is an increasingly important issue for several reasons. First, the number of women surviving breast cancer is increasing (ACS, 2001). Current estimates suggest that as many as 2.5 million breast cancer survivors may be living in the United States (Swain *et al.,* 1999a). This increase is attributable to decreased breast cancer mortality, relatively high five-year survival rates for local and regional stage tumors (ACS, 2001) and the aging of the United States population (U.S. Bureau of the Census, 1996). Changing treatment trends indicate that hot flashes and other menopausal symptoms may be a problem not only for breast cancer survivors, but also for those with recurrent or metastatic disease. In addition, menopausal symptoms affect women of all ages—young, middle-aged, and older—because of side effects of breast cancer treatment. Finally, a growing body of evidence suggests that hot flashes and other menopausal symptoms can significantly impact quality of life (Carpenter *et al.,* 1998, 2002; Carpenter & Andrykowski, 1999; Swain *et al.,* 1999a, 1999b, 1999c, 1999d, 1999e, 1999f). Taken together, these factors suggest that a growing number of women with breast cancer will experience hot flashes and other menopausal symptoms. Thus, careful assessment and appropriate management of menopausal symptoms are key to improving quality of life among women diagnosed with breast cancer.

This chapter is divided into several sections. In the first section, definitions of menopause and basic changes in the hormonal milieu occurring during menopause are presented. Several factors that predispose women with breast cancer to menopausal symptoms are then discussed. The chapter then divides into discussion of major target tissues affected during menopause, including vasomotor effects (hot flashes) and effects on the skeletal system, cardiovascular system, and urogenital tract. Each of these target tissues is discussed in terms of the physiologic effects of menopause, pharmacologic and nonpharmacologic management of symptoms or effects on target tissues, and implications for nursing practice.

MENOPAUSE

Over the years, there have been several attempts to unify terms and definitions used to describe the menopausal transition. Consensus statements from two panels, the 1994 World Health Organization (WHO) Scientific Group on Research on the Menopause and the 2001 Stages of Reproductive Aging Workshop (STRAW), are discussed.

WHO TERMINOLOGY

In 1994, the WHO convened a panel of scientists to revisit menopause-related terms and definitions first published by that same organization in 1981 (WHO, 1981, 1994). The following definitions emerged from that panel and are widely used today. Natural menopause was defined as occurring after 12 or more months of amenorrhea not associated with obvious pathologic or physiologic cause. Conversely, induced menopause was defined as the absence of menses following either surgical removal of both ovaries or iatrogenic ablation of ovarian function, such as that caused by chemotherapy or radiation. Perimenopause was defined as the time immediately prior to menopause. The term premenopause was used to describe (1) the entire reproductive period prior to perimenopause or (2) only the 1–2 years immediately prior to perimenopause. Finally, because the median age at menopause is widely recognized to occur around ages 50–51 years, premature menopause was defined as occurring prior to the age of 40 years. Thus, using these terms, a 38-year-old woman who stops menstruating as a result of breast cancer chemotherapy can be classified as experiencing induced and premature menopause.

STRAW TERMINOLOGY

The STRAW panel was convened to revisit commonly used terms and definitions and to create a staging system for female reproductive aging (Soules *et al.,* 2001). The outcome of the panel's discussion and their published recommendations involve a seven-stage system for healthy women who age spontaneously to natural menopause. Three stages are used to describe the premenopausal reproductive period, two stages encompass perimenopause (early and late), and two stages encompass postmenopause (early and late). Menopause is again defined as occurring after 12 months of amenorrhea. The menopausal transition encompasses early and late perimenopause as well as the first 12 months following the final menstrual period. Each of the seven stages is defined in terms of two objective criteria: the menstrual cycle and endocrine function, specifically levels of follicle-stimulating hormone (FSH). The panel noted that not all women will follow a clear progression through the seven stages; some women may skip a stage altogether and others might move backwards and forwards through the stages.

Because this chapter focuses on menopause, the four STRAW stages related to the perimenopause and postmenopause are defined here (Soules *et al.,* 2001; see this source for definitions of the reproductive or premenopausal stages). Early perimenopause is defined in terms of variable menstrual cycles with a change of more than 7 days in normal menstrual cycle length and elevated FSH levels. Late perimenopause is defined as two or more skipped menstrual cycles with an interval of 60 or more days between cycles and elevated FSH levels. Early postmenopause encompasses the first year following the final menstrual period and the subsequent four years. It is defined in terms of the absence of menses and elevated FSH levels. Late postmenopause encompasses the time period after the first five years following the final menstrual period and is again characterized by elevated FSH levels.

The panel recommended not using the stages for the following situations: cigarette smoking, extremes of body weight (BMI < 18 or > 30 kg/m^2), heavy exercise (> 10 h/wk or aerobic exercise), chronic menstrual cycle irregularity, prior hysterectomy, and abnormal uterine or ovarian anatomy (e.g., fibroids or endometrioma) (Soules *et al.,* 2001). In addition, STRAW stages should be applied with caution to women with breast cancer taking tamoxifen, because this drug has been known to decrease FSH levels (Kostoglou-Athanassiou *et al.,* 1995).

CHANGES OCCURRING DURING MENOPAUSE

The transition from regular menstrual cycles to amenorrhea encompasses morphologic changes in the ovaries and resulting changes in the hormonal profile (Utian, 1990; Knobf, 1996). The ovaries become smaller, fibrotic, and devoid of any functional follicles. Estradiol, the dominant source of estrogen for the premenopausal woman, dramatically declines. Estrone becomes the principal source of estrogen for the postmenopausal woman. Estrone is derived from peripheral conversion of androstenedione. Levels of gonadotrophins (e.g., FSH, luteinizing hormone [LH]) rise significantly after menopause because of estrogen loss. The decline in circulating estrogen then affects various target tissues of the body.

Hormone levels in women with breast cancer taking tamoxifen will be altered from this normal menopausal pattern. In a study of 42 postmenopausal women with breast cancer, hormone levels after 6 months of tamoxifen therapy reflected significant ($p < .05$) decreases in FSH, LH and free testosterone, and significant increases in estradiol and sex hormone-binding globulin levels compared to pretamoxifen baseline levels (Kostoglou-Athanassiou *et al.,* 1995). Similarly, in a prospective study of 47 women with breast cancer, estradiol levels were 239% higher after two years of tamoxifen therapy in comparison to pre-tamoxifen baseline levels ($p < .05$) (Lum *et al.,* 1997). Thus, FSH levels with or without estradiol may not be reliable indicators of menopausal status among women with breast cancer taking tamoxifen.

MENOPAUSE AND CANCER

Several factors predispose women with breast cancer to menopausal symptoms. First, as in healthy women, estrogen withdrawal related to the natural aging process may precipitate menopausal symptoms (Kronenberg, 1990; Stanford *et al.*, 1987). However, unlike healthy women, hormone replacement therapy (HRT) for managing hot flashes and other symptoms is controversial at best (Canney & Hatton, 1994; Cobleigh *et al.*, 1994; Smith *et al.*, 1996; Swain *et al.*, 1999b; Wile *et al.*, 1993) and often is contraindicated for women with breast cancer (Brzezinski, 1995; Runowicz, 1996). Although some authors advocate the use of HRT in women with breast cancer (Cobleigh *et al.*, 1994; Smith *et al.*, 1996), data suggest that only 31% of women with breast cancer would be willing to consider HRT if offered (Couzi *et al.*, 1995) and only 5% or less would actually take HRT after diagnosis (Carpenter *et al.*, 2002; Swain *et al.*, 1999d). Women often discontinue HRT at the time of their cancer diagnosis based upon recommendations from health care providers (Brzezinski, 1995; Runowicz, 1996; Ganz, 2001), thus precipitating or exacerbating hot flashes.

Second, women with breast cancer may experience menopausal symptoms in response to estrogen withdrawal related to chemotherapy. Chemotherapy-induced ovarian disruption and subsequent early and artificial menopause may predispose women to menopausal symptoms. In women with breast cancer, chemotherapy-induced menopause may occur in women as young as 36 years old (Carpenter *et al.*, 1998). The effects of chemotherapy on the ovary are dependent on age, dose, and duration of treatment. Younger women and those receiving higher dosages or longer periods of chemotherapy are at greatest risk for ovarian disruption (Reichman & Green, 1994). In a survey of 114 postmenopausal breast cancer survivors, younger women were shown to experience a higher prevalence and severity of hot flashes in comparison to older women (Carpenter *et al.*, 1998).

Third, hot flashes in particular are a known side effect of tamoxifen citrate, a commonly prescribed selective estrogen receptor modulator (Love, 1989; Love *et al.*, 1991; Pasacreta & McCorkle, 1998). In a randomized, double-blind, placebo-controlled study, women with breast cancer using tamoxifen ($N = 70$) were significantly more likely to report hot flashes in comparison to women using placebo ($N = 70$) after 6 months of treatment (67% vs. 45%, $p < .01$) (Love *et al.*, 1991). In addition, the proportion of women reporting severe hot flashes was significantly higher in the tamoxifen treated group after 3, 6, and 12 months of treatment ($p < .05$) (Love *et al.*, 1991). Similarly, among 114 postmenopausal women with breast cancer, tamoxifen users were 2.6 times more likely to experience severe hot flashes than nonusers (Carpenter *et al.*, 1998).

Newer drugs that are increasingly being used in lieu of tamoxifen are also associated with hot flashes (e.g., raloxifene, letrozole, anastrozole). Raloxifene is a selective estrogen receptor modulator like tamoxifen (Johnston, 2001; Gadjos & Jordan, 2002). Letrozole and anastrozole are aromatase inhibitors (e.g., they inhibit estrogen synthesis), which lower plasma estrogen levels and also may cause menopausal symptoms (Mouridsen *et al.*, 2001). These latter agents are used in the treatment of advanced and metastatic breast cancer, but, like tamoxifen, they will most likely move from use in metastatic to primary breast cancer in the near future.

Taken together, these factors suggest that the etiology of menopause in women with breast cancer is unique. Because of this, knowledge that is learned from menopausal experiences of healthy women may not translate to the experiences of women with breast cancer. For example, data on symptom prevalence, severity, and distress in healthy, naturally menopausal women may not generalize to women with breast cancer who (1) are not using HRT, (2) have experienced induced and premature menopause resulting from chemotherapy, and/or (3) are using tamoxifen.

As a second example, data on the temporal pattern of symptoms in healthy women may not generalize to women with breast cancer. For example, in healthy women, hot flashes begin during perimenopause, peak in frequency during the first 6 years postmenopause, and gradually decrease over time (Kronenberg, 1990). However, in women with breast cancer taking tamoxifen, this temporal pattern may be substantially altered. Women who begin 5 years of tamoxifen therapy in their 60s may reexperience hot flashes 10 or more years postmenopause. Therefore, although menopausal symptoms are generally regarded as uncomfortable results of a "normal" life transition in healthy women (Matthews, 1992), factors discussed above (contraindications against HRT, use of chemotherapy, tamoxifen, and other agents) suggest that this may not be true for women with breast cancer. For these women, menopausal symptoms can be considered "abnormal" and requiring intervention.

The remainder of this chapter focuses on target tissues affected by menopause. Specifically, vasomotor symptoms and effects on the skeletal system, cardiovascular system, and urogenital tract are discussed. Whenever possible, research specific to women with breast cancer is presented. When that information is limited or not available, research pertaining to healthy women without cancer is discussed.

VASOMOTOR SYMPTOMS: HOT FLASHES

Hot flashes are the most frequently occurring symptom of menopause. They are a subjective and transient sensation of heat, most commonly felt in the upper body and head. Kronenberg (1994) defined hot flashes as "transient episodes of flushing, sweating, and a sensation of heat, often accompanied by palpitations and a feeling of anxiety, and sometimes followed by chills" (p. 320). Hot flashes in breast cancer survivors have been similarly defined (Finck *et al.*, 1998; Knobf, 2001; Carpenter *et al.*, 2002). When 102 women with breast cancer were asked to describe their hot flashes, descriptions were similar to those found in the literature on healthy women (e.g., sensation of heat, heart irregularities, associated perspiration, etc.) (Finck *et al.*, 1998). In another study directly comparing the responses of 69 breast cancer survivors and 63 healthy women, Carpenter *et al.* (2002) found no differences in the number or types of hot flash descriptors chosen. The most commonly endorsed descriptors were heat (93%), sweating or perspiring (89%), flushed (77%), and clammy (46%). Similarly, in a grounded theory study of 27 women with breast cancer, hot flashes were described as being from mild ("I might be standing there and all of a sudden feel very warm and it would pass") to severe ("I have awful hot flashes... I had a huge one today... [it] was a doozy... it was a construction worker in 95 degree weather") (Knobf, 2001, p. 203).

Hot flashes are also a discrete physiologic event that can be measured using sternal skin conductance monitoring (Freedman, 1989; Carpenter *et al.,* 1999). Increases in sternal skin conductance of greater than or equal to 2 μmho in a 30-second period correspond to self-reported hot flashes in healthy women (Freedman, 1989) and in women with breast cancer (Carpenter *et al.,* 1999). Sternal skin conductance monitoring can be used to obtain objective hot flash frequency counts (i.e., number of hot flashes per day) as well as the precise time of day each hot flash occurred (hour, minute, second).

ETIOLOGY OF HOT FLASHES

The exact etiology of hot flashes remains elusive (Kronenberg, 1990, 1994; Rosenberg & Larsen, 1991; Lomax & Schonbaum, 1993; Freedman *et al.,* 1995; Freedman, 1998; Freedman & Krell, 1999). Most recently, hot flashes have been thought to result from increases in core body temperature occurring within a reduced thermoregulatory null zone (Freedman, 1998; Freedman & Krell, 1999). The thermoregulatory null zone is defined as the threshold between sweating (high end) and shivering (low end). If the thermoregulatory null zone is decreased (Figure 16.1), increases in core body temperature can lead to a ceiling effect of sweating, but decreases in core temperature can lead to a floor effect of shivering. This results in the sensation of a hot flash. It is believed that restoring or increasing the thermoregulatory null zone helps to prevent the ceiling effect of sweating and the floor effect of shivering (Figure 16.2).

Interestingly, central norepinephrine has been thought to play a key role in the reduced thermoregulatory null zone (Freedman, 1998; Freedman & Krell, 1999). Norepinephrine is a catecholamine that is released in response to sympathetic nervous system activation (e.g., in response to stress or activity/exercise) (Guyton & Hall, 2000). Norepinephrine decreases the thermoregulatory null zone in animals and, therefore, may be responsible for decreasing the null zone among women with hot flashes (Freedman & Krell, 1999). As further support for this hypothesis, agents that inhibit norepinephrine, such as clonidine and venlafaxine, can alleviate hot flashes (Nagamani *et al.,* 1987;

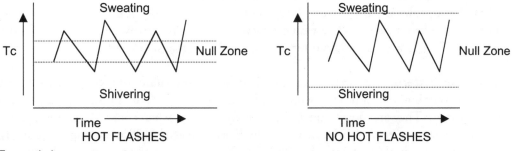

Tc = core body temperature

FIGURE 16.1 and 16.2 Fluctuations in Core Body Temperature and the Thermoregulatory Null Zone.

Goldberg *et al.,* 1994; Loprinzi *et al.,* 1998; Freedman & Dinsay, 2000), whereas agents that stimulate norepinephrine release (e.g., yohimbine) can cause hot flashes (Freedman & Krell, 1999). The exact mechanism(s) accounting for the hypothesized elevation in central norepinephrine is unknown.

It is likely that other unknown disruptions in thermoregulation and neuroendocrine pathways contribute to hot flashes (Rosenberg & Larsen, 1991; Lomax & Schonbaum, 1993; Freedman, 1998; Freedman & Krell, 1999). For example, estrogen withdrawal, rather than absolute estrogen level, has been linked to hot flashes. Estrogen replacement therapy appears to alleviate hot flashes by raising the sweating threshold (Freedman & Blacker, 2002). Whether estrogen raises the sweating threshold independent of changes in norepinephrine is unknown.

HOT FLASH PREVALENCE, SEVERITY, AND DISTRESS

Among women with breast cancer, hot flashes are a prevalent, severe, and distressing symptom. Studies have indicated that 65% of women with breast cancer report hot flashes, with the majority rating the symptom to be severe (Couzi *et al.,* 1995; Carpenter *et al.,* 1998; Harris *et al.,* 2002). As many as 72% of women with breast cancer taking tamoxifen and 78% of women who have received breast cancer chemotherapy report experiencing hot flashes (Carpenter *et al.,* 1998). Significantly more women with breast cancer reported hot flashes: 65% of 69 women with breast cancer versus 16% of 63 age-matched healthy women with intact uteri and ovaries ($p < .001$) (Carpenter *et al.,* 2002). In addition, when asked to rate hot flash severity and distress using a 10-point scale, women with breast cancer reported significantly more severe and more distressing hot flashes ($p < .001$) in comparison to age-matched healthy women.

The severity and distress associated with hot flashes among women with breast cancer may be related to the high daily frequency at which this symptom is experienced. Prior research suggests that 45% to 63% of postmenopausal women with breast cancer experience daily hot flashes (Carpenter *et al.,* 1999, 2002). Using a prospective diary methodology, women with breast cancer reported experiencing approximately three times as many hot flashes per day compared to age-matched women without cancer (Carpenter *et al.,* 2002). In addition, using more precise objective measurements (e.g., sternal skin conductance monitoring), Carpenter and colleagues (2001) counted as many as 31 hot flashes per day in some women with breast cancer. Breast cancer survivors experience an average of 10 hot flashes per day (SD = 7) when monitored for 24 hours using sternal skin conductance methods.

Temporal Pattern. Research on temporal patterns of hot flashes in women with breast cancer is very limited. In healthy women without cancer, hot flashes follow a daily (circadian) pattern. They are most frequent in the early evening, when core body temperature is highest (Freedman *et al.,* 1995). In a study by Freedman *et al.* (1995), among 10 naturally postmenopausal healthy women, hot flashes varied with core body temperature by time of day, reaching a peak frequency at 18:25 hours (6:30 P.M.). However, in women with breast cancer, one study suggests that hot flashes seem to occur throughout the day and night with no clear pattern (Carpenter *et al.*, 2001).

Hot Flash Triggers. Factors that may trigger hot flashes have been studied in survey research. When 437 healthy women without breast cancer were asked to identify factors that triggered their hot flashes, the most commonly cited trigger was stress, which was endorsed by 59% of women (Kronenberg, 1990). Using a similar questionnaire, Carpenter *et al.* (2002) surveyed 69 breast cancer survivors and 63 age-matched healthy women. The only trigger more commonly endorsed by breast cancer survivors in comparison to healthy women was stressful or emotional situations (52% of breast cancer survivors vs. 12% of healthy women; $p < .01$).

In another grounded theory study of menopausal symptoms, women with breast cancer identified work stress and anxiety as hot flash triggers. Published quotes included "When I'm in my classroom [at work], I get them [hot flashes] more often..." and "... sometimes stress or anxiety, even a good anxiety, a happy anxiety brings them on..." (Knobf, 2001, p. 204). Other triggers that were endorsed by the 69 women with breast cancer surveyed in the Carpenter *et al.* study (2002) included "nothing, hot flashes just seem to happen" (59%), external heat sources (stove, sunshine, hot room) (46%), alcoholic beverages (23%), confined spaces (18%), caffeine (14%), and other (not specified) (9%). Thus, women with breast cancer may find some relief from hot flashes if they are able to identify and then avoid such factors that may trigger their hot flashes.

Impact on Quality of Life. Hot flashes in women with breast cancer can interfere with quality of life. The symptom has been associated with fatigue and disruptions in mood, affect, daily activities, and sleep in women with breast cancer. In one survey (Carpenter *et al.*, 2002), hot flash severity and distress in breast cancer survivors were associated with greater mood disturbance on the Profile of Mood States (POMS) (McNair *et al.*, 1981), higher negative affect on the Positive and Negative Affect Scale (PANAS) (Watson *et al.*, 1998), and greater interference with daily activities as measured by the Hot Flash Related Daily Interference Scale (Carpenter, 2001). Compared to breast cancer survivors who did not have hot flashes, or who had only mild hot flashes, those with moderate to severe hot flashes reported significantly greater total mood disturbance, depression, tension, anger, fatigue, and confusion ($p < .01$); significantly more negative affect ($p < .001$); and significantly greater interference with daily activities, including mood, sleep, concentration, and sexuality ($p < .001$) (Carpenter *et al.*, 2002). Other research has also related hot flashes to chronic sleep disturbances in healthy women (Erlik *et al.*, 1981) and to fatigue in women with breast cancer (Broeckel *et al.*, 1998).

PHARMACOLOGIC MANAGEMENT OF HOT FLASHES

Pharmacologically based interventions that have been evaluated as treatments for hot flashes are reviewed in the following section. The majority of these studies are limited by use of self-reported hot flash frequency data using daily diaries. Self-reported data may not be an accurate measure of hot flashes as women have been shown to underestimate the number of hot flashes they experience per day (Carpenter *et al.*, 1999). In addition, self-reported data may be prone to intervention expectancy effects (expectation that the intervention will work) and testing effects (decreasing compliance over time makes it appear that hot flashes improve over time) (Carpenter, 2000).

Venlafaxine hydrochloride. The antidepressant venlafaxine hydrochloride appears safe, effective, and minimally toxic in alleviating hot flashes in women with breast cancer (Loprinzi *et al.*, 1998, 2000; Barton, Levasseur, *et al.*, 2002). Venlafaxine is a phenylethylamine derivative that potently inhibits the reuptake of neuronal serotonin and norepinephrine (selective serotonin and norepinephrine inhibitor [SSNRI]) (Horst & Preskorn, 1998; Beique *et al.*, 1999). The mechanism of action of venlafaxine in alleviating hot flashes most likely occurs through inhibition of norepinephrine. Inhibition of norepinephrine may alleviate hot flashes by restoring the thermoregulatory null zone (Freedman & Krell, 1999). Paradoxically, one case study report describes the return of hot flashes attributed to venlafaxine (75 mg PO qid) in a woman who had experienced complete relief of hot flashes for eight years with estrogen replacement therapy (Grady-Welicky & Hartmann, 2001).

Venlafaxine was first evaluated in a phase II clinical trial involving 23 women with breast cancer and 5 men with prostate cancer (Loprinzi *et al.*, 1998). The dosage of venlafaxine used was 25 mg PO qid (taken as 12.5 mg PO bid). Participants completed prospective daily hot flash diaries throughout a 1-week baseline and 4-week treatment period. Mean hot flash frequency decreased from 6.6 hot flashes per day to 4.3 per day at the end of treatment (no standard deviations or *p* values provided). In addition, 54% of participants reported a decrease in hot flash frequency of at least 50%. Using calculated hot flash scores, the number of severe and very severe hot flashes decreased from a mean of 1.4 per day at baseline to 0.1 per day at the end of treatment (no standard deviations reported; $p < .001$).

Venlafaxine was also evaluated in a dose response study (Loprinzi *et al.*, 2000). Women with breast cancer or those at high risk for developing breast cancer were stratified by age, hot flash frequency, tamoxifen use, and duration of hot flashes ($N = 191$). Groups received 37.5 mg, 75 mg, or 150 mg of oral venlafaxine daily for 4 weeks. Dose response curves indicated that the 75-mg dosage was significantly more effective in decreasing self-reported hot flashes than the 37.5-mg dose and placebo. In a follow-up dose continuation study, data for only 102 of the original 191 who completed the dose response study were available (53%). Attrition was related to lack of information regarding dosing, lack of diary information, and disinterest in continuing the medication (Barton *et al.*, 2002). Side effects of venlafaxine include nausea, nervousness, and constipation.

Other Antidepressants and St. John's Wort. Interestingly, other antidepressants that are not in the same classification as venlafaxine and that do not have a major impact on norepinephrine may also improve hot flashes. The exact mechanism of action of these other antidepressants on hot flashes remains unknown. Because some of these antidepressants have the potential for interaction with other medications, they should be thoroughly researched before being recommended for any individual patient. For example, paroxetine was evaluated in an open-label, non-placebo-controlled trial (Stearns *et al.,* 2000). Women with breast cancer completed a baseline week and then received 10 mg of paroxetine daily for 1 week followed by 20 mg of paroxetine daily for 4 weeks. Significant improvements in self-reported hot flash frequency, severity, mood, anxiety, and quality of life were noted. Similarly, Roth and Scher (1998) reported on 5 men with prostate cancer who noted anecdotal improvement in hot flashes with use of sertraline. In another study, fluoxetine was found to be moderately effective in treating hot flashes in women with a history of breast cancer (Loprinzi *et al.,* 2002). Unfortunately, fluoxetine is known to inhibit cytochrome P450 isoenzymes involved in the metabolism of tamoxifen and other medications (Cheer & Goa, 2001; Crewe *et al.,* 2002). Thus, fluoxetine may raise levels of tamoxifen and other medications and should be used with caution because of high potential for drug–drug interactions.

St. John's wort, an herbal preparation that is believed to have antidepressant properties, has been proposed as a potential hot flash treatment, at least for men with prostate cancer (Moyad, 2002). However, St. John's wort mitigates the effects of several medications and is generally regarded as having high potential for interaction with prescription medications that are metabolized through cytochrome P450 (Mansky & Straus, 2002). Thus, St. John's wort should not be used to treat hot flashes, especially among women taking tamoxifen after breast cancer.

Gabapentin. Two separate case study reports describe improvement in hot flashes after prescription of gabapentin in women taking tamoxifen and men with prostate cancer (Guttuso, 2000; Jeffery *et al.,* 2002). Dosages ranged from 200 mg to 900 mg per day with improvement noted within 1–3 days. Although the mechanism of action of this agent is unclear, controlled clinical trials are needed to carefully evaluate the benefits and side effects associated with this medication when used for treating hot flashes.

Clonidine Hydrochloride. Clonidine hydrochloride appears effective in reducing hot flashes but can be associated with significant side effects. Clonidine is a centrally (medullary) acting antiadrenergic agent effective for reducing hot flashes in healthy women (Nagamani *et al.,* 1987) and in women with breast cancer (Goldberg *et al.,* 1994). A total of 110 women with breast cancer participated in a 9-week randomized, double-blind, crossover trial of transdermal clonidine (equivalent to 0.1 mg PO qid) versus placebo (Goldberg *et al.,* 1994). Women completed daily hot flash diaries throughout the study period. Significant decreases in subjective hot flash frequency, severity, and mean daily hot flash score (mean frequency × mean severity) were seen at the end of the clonidine treatment period ($p < .05$). However, significantly more side effects were seen with clonidine as compared to placebo, including dry mouth, constipation, itching under the patch, and drowsiness ($p < .05$). Marginal differences in dizziness were seen between treatment periods ($p < .10$). When asked which was more effective, only 48% of participants chose clonidine. When asked to indicate preference while taking into account side effects, only 31% preferred clonidine. Thus, clonidine may not be acceptable to women with breast cancer.

Bellergal Retard. Bellergal retard, belladonna alkaloids, and phenobarbital have been used for treating hot flashes. Bellergal retard was studied in an 8-week double-blind study of 66 healthy women, 33 assigned to placebo and 33 assigned to receive bellergal 1 tablet per day (Bergmans *et al.,* 1987). Bellergal retard is composed of ergomatine tartrate and phenobarbital. Although self-reported hot flashes decreased during the study, differences were not significant after 8 weeks of treatment. Thus, in addition to lack of demonstrated efficacy, the potential addictive risk and the availability of safer alternatives limit the usefulness of these agents.

Megestrol Acetate. Similar to clonidine, megestrol acetate, a progestin used in the treatment of late-stage breast cancer, appears effective in decreasing hot flashes in women with breast cancer, but it is also associated with significant side effects (Loprinzi *et al.,* 1994; Quella *et al.,* 1998). A total of 97 women with breast cancer and 66 men with prostate cancer were enrolled in a 9-week crossover trial (Loprinzi *et al.,* 1994). Participants completed a 1-week baseline period and 4 weeks of treatment or placebo before crossing over to an additional 4 weeks on the opposite study arm. Hot flashes were measured using a daily prospective diary methodology. Hot flashes decreased significantly with megestrol acetate (20 mg PO qid) (Loprinzi *et al.,* 1994). Data from the first treatment arm for 80 women with breast cancer indicated that (1) hot flash frequency decreased by 74% over baseline in the megestrol acetate group and by 27% in women treated with placebo ($p < .001$) and (2) the median hot flash score decreased by 83% over baseline with megestrol acetate and by only 27% with placebo (Loprinzi *et al.,* 1994). However, when participants were followed over the long term (3 years after the original study), 69% of the women with breast cancer had discontinued the drug; 75% of the women were still having hot flashes (Quella *et al.,* 1998). In addition, 41% of those who continued taking the drug reported breakthrough hot flashes (Quella *et al.,* 1998). Reported side effects included vaginal bleeding, chills, depression, and numbness and tingling in the hands (Loprinzi *et al.,* 1994; Quella *et al.,* 1998).

Vitamin E. Vitamin E is relatively inexpensive and has been recommended for hot flashes at least since the mid-1940s (Christy, 1945; Finkler, 1949; McLaren, 1949; Miller, 1992; Jubelirer, 1995). However, only one published study was found examining vitamin E's efficacy within the last 20 years (Barton *et al.,* 1998). Women with breast cancer ($N = 104$) completed nine weeks of a randomized, crossover trial of vitamin E versus placebo. Women completed a one-week baseline, four weeks of placebo or treatment involving 800 IU of vitamin E PO qid, and an additional four weeks of treatment or placebo. Hot flashes were assessed subjectively using a daily prospective diary methodology at baseline and during the last week of treatment for each arm. Compared to baseline and placebo treatment periods, no significant differences were seen in mean daily hot flash frequency, severity, or mean daily hot flash score (mean frequency × mean severity). Thus, vitamin E does not appear to be effective for alleviating hot flashes in women with breast cancer (Barton *et al.*, 1998). In addition, women with heart disease, diabetes, or hypertension must consult their physicians before taking vitamin E.

NONPHARMACOLOGIC MANAGEMENT OF HOT FLASHES

The following nonpharmacologic treatments for hot flashes may be beneficial when used alone or in combination with pharmacologic agents.

Relaxation Training. Relaxation training is recommended for alleviating hot flashes in women with breast cancer. Types of relaxation training shown to reduce hot flashes in healthy women include progressive muscle relaxation (Germaine & Freedman, 1984), relaxation combined with temperature control biofeedback training (Stevenson & Delprato, 1983), paced respiration (Freedman & Woodward, 1992), at-home relaxation audiotapes (Irvin *et al.*, 1996), and applied relaxation (Wijma *et al.*, 1997). These strategies appear to decrease subjective hot flash severity (Irvin *et al.*, 1996) and hot flash frequency, as measured using diaries or objective monitoring of sternal skin conductance (Germaine & Freedman, 1984; Freedman & Woodward, 1992).

Phytoestrogens. Increasing phytoestrogen intake, either through soy-based or other botanical products, is another strategy commonly recommended for alleviating hot flashes. Recommendations to increase soy consumption stem from data regarding the low incidence of hot flashes in Asian women, a population known to consume large amounts of soy (Albertazzi *et al.*, 1998; Adlercreutz, 1990; Adlercreutz & Mazur, 1997; Murkies *et al.*, 1995; Soffa, 1996). Herbs recommended for hot flashes (or menopausal symptoms) include dong quai (*Angelica sinensis*), black cohosh, ginseng, gotu kola, licorice root, chaste tree, sage, and wild yam root (Israel & Youngkin, 1997; Soffa, 1996; Waldman, 1998). Recently, soy proteins and other plant estrogens have been described as phyto-SERMs (selective estrogen receptor modulators) rather than phytoestrogens (Messina, 2002).

Studies on the use of soy for the management of hot flashes have produced conflicting results (Albertazzi *et al.*, 1998; Knight *et al.*, 2001; Murkies *et al.*, 1995; Nagata *et al.*, 2001; Quella *et al.*, 2000; Upmalis *et al.*, 2000; Scambia *et al.*, 2000; St Germain *et al.*, 2001; Van Patten *et al.*, 2002). For example, in one randomized study, 40 women received 60 g soy protein and 39 women received 60 g casein protein (placebo) for 10 weeks (Albertazzi *et al.*, 1998). When compared to the 2-week baseline, soy significantly decreased the number, but not the severity, of subjectively recorded hot flashes ($p < .001$). In contrast, another randomized, double-blind study compared the effectiveness of soy flour versus wheat flour in decreasing hot flashes in healthy postmenopausal women (Murkies *et al.*, 1995). Although women who added 45 g of soy flour per day to their diets reported a significant decrease in subjective hot flash frequency and severity during the 12 weeks of the study, no significant differences between soy and wheat flour supplementation were seen: soy flour (highly phytoestrogenic) was no more effective than wheat flour (minimally phytoestrogenic) in reducing hot flashes. Thus, although soy is commonly recommended, the definitive benefits of soy in alleviating hot flashes are unclear (Swain *et al.,* 1999d).

Similarly, the efficacy of herbs in alleviating hot flashes is largely unresearched. In addition, variations in the quality of herbs and unanswered questions about dosing regimens contribute to the questionable safety of these products (Israel & Youngkin, 1997). Although phytoestrogens or phyto-SERMs may be safe alternatives to HRT for healthy women, studies of the long-term effects of phytoestrogens among women with breast cancer are lacking (Swain *et al.,* 1999d). One paper indicated that black cohosh did not exhibit estrogenic activity when studied in vivo and had no effect on breast cancer cell lines in vivo (Tsai *et al.,* 2002). Another published study of black cohosh demonstrating a decrease in hot flashes over time did not contain a control group, so the improvement in hot flashes could not be differentiated from a placebo-like effect (Liske *et al.,* 2002). In general, phytoestrogens (soy or herbs) appear to have limited empirical support for their safety and/or effectiveness in alleviating hot flashes in women with breast cancer.

Other Dietary Changes.   Recommendations to decrease caffeine and alcohol consumption to control hot flashes are commonly made but appear to be untested. In previous studies, alcohol has been endorsed by only a minority of women as a trigger of hot flashes (e.g., 14–23%) (Kronenberg, 1990; Carpenter *et al.,* 2002). Women who identify caffeine and alcohol as hot flash triggers may benefit from reducing or eliminating these products from their diets.

Exercise.   The role of regular physical activity or exercise in the etiology or management of hot flashes is controversial. It is widely understood that core body temperature can increase 1ºC to 4ºC during vigorous physical activity (Brenner *et al.,* 1997; Guyton & Hall, 2000). When this increase in core body temperature exceeds the sweating threshold, sweating is triggered in both men and women during exercise. However, because the sweating threshold is reduced in women with hot flashes (Freedman & Krell, 1999), only minor elevations in core body temperature during activity/exercise may be needed to trigger hot flashes. Such minor elevations in core body temperature may occur during mild intensity or short duration activity/exercise such as that which occurs during everyday activities (e.g., walking from one's car into a building). Thus, women who are prone to hot flashes may be more likely to experience hot flashes during even minimal levels of physical activity/exercise.

In addition, both the intensity and duration of exercise are positively associated with norepinephrine release (for review see Fry and Kraemer, 1997). This norepinephrine release may decrease the thermoregulatory null zone and lead to hot flashes as a short-term, immediate effect. If the immediate effect of activity/exercise is to trigger hot flashes through elevations in core body temperature and/or norepinephrine release, women may reduce the frequency, intensity, and duration of exercise in order to avoid hot flashes. This behavioral adaptation could then have long-term detrimental health effects.

In contrast, although core body temperature increases during activity/exercise, over time exercise lowers the thermoregulatory set point (lower core body temperature) (Brenner *et al.*, 1997). This lowering of core body temperature may have a longer-term effect of reducing hot flashes by preventing core body temperature from reaching the sweating threshold. Thus, women who exercise may have fewer hot flashes overall in comparison to women who do not exercise.

No studies have evaluated the immediate effect of physical activity/exercise on hot flashes (e.g., activity/exercise as a hot flash trigger). However, four descriptive studies have examined the relationship between exercise and hot flashes. All reported similar findings regarding a long-term beneficial effect of activity/exercise on hot flashes. Healthy women without breast cancer who undertook more physical activity reported fewer hot flashes (Hammar *et al.*, 1990; Ivarsson *et al.*, 1998; Stadberg *et al.*, 2000; Gold *et al.*, 2000). In contrast, Sternfeld *et al.* (1999) evaluated the relationship between habitual physical activity prior to the final menstrual period and hot flashes using 82 perimenopausal women experiencing daily symptoms and 89 symptom-free perimenopausal women. Although the sample was small, findings indicated that self-reported activity during the year prior to the final menstrual period was not associated with fewer hot flashes (OR = 1.03).

Acupuncture.   Acupuncture may be an effective method for treating hot flashes in women with breast cancer. One study evaluated the effects of 10 weeks of twice daily acupuncture treatments on men with prostate cancer and hot flashes due to castration therapy (Hammar *et al.*, 1999). Self-reported hot flashes decreased by an average of 70% over the course of the 10-week period. Additional research is needed to clarify the acupuncture points and frequency and duration of treatments needed to provide optimal relief from hot flashes. Studies by nurse researchers regarding this important intervention for women with breast cancer are currently underway.

Multimodal Interventions.   Very few studies have evaluated multimodal or multicomponent interventions for reducing hot flashes. Ganz *et al.* (2000) studied a comprehensive menopausal assessment intervention program for relief of menopausal symptoms, including hot flashes. The intervention included an educational component, nonhormonal medications for hot flashes (e.g., clonidine, bellergal, and megestrol acetate), and slow abdominal breathing. Compared to a usual care group (N = 39), the intervention group (N = 33) evidenced improvement in menopausal symptom bother, including hot flash bother, measured using seven items ($p < .001$). Thus, use of several interventions in combination may be the most effective method for reducing hot flashes in women with breast cancer.

OSTEOPOROSIS

Osteoporosis, a skeletal disorder, is characterized by an increased susceptibility to fracture because of low bone mass (Berger, 2000). It has been reported that four to six million postmenopausal white females in the United States have been diagnosed with osteoporosis, resulting in $13.8 billion in health care expenditures for pathological fractures (Lobo, 1999). Of the cases reported, hip fractures are stated to be the most lethal, with a mortality rate of 10–20% within one year of occurrence (Lobo, 1999).

ETIOLOGY

During menopause, bone loss occurs at a more rapid rate (Twiss *et al.*, 2001). Reduction in bone mass, which leads to osteoporosis, can be attributed to decreased estrogen that occurs during menopause. Normal remodeling of bone consists of resorption and formation phases (Mahon, 1998). These events transpire in temporary bone remodeling units called osteoblasts and osteoclasts. Osteoblasts facilitate bone formation, and osteoclasts are cells that facilitate bone resorption. Osteoblasts are located on the surface of the bone and secrete collagen to form a matrix making a seam or border (Berger, 2000). Physiologically, the osteoclasts make a cavity in the bone, termed the resorption pit, that is then filled by osteoblasts to form new bone. Bone turnover is the rate at which this process occurs (Mahon, 1998). The pathophysiology of osteoporosis occurs with impaired matching of bone-remodeling units. As the osteoclast creates the resorption pit, it is not replenished by osteoblast units. The net result is a decrease in the total bone formation and thus a decrease in bone mass (Mahon, 1998).

Bone mass reflects the balance achieved during peak bone mass present in the fourth decade of life and the amount of bone lost during aging (Brincat & Galea, 1999). Low bone mass with microarchitectural deterioration can cause structural changes in the skeletal structure, causing bones to be fragile and more prone to fracture (Mahon, 1998). These pathologic changes in the bone structure contribute to the increased risk of osteoporotic fractures of the distal forearm, spine, and hip (Berger, 2000). Healthy women are able to take HRT, which can slow the progression of osteoporosis. Without HRT, women can lose up to 30% of bone mass during menopause (Riis, 1995). As postmenopausal women age, this risk of osteoporosis increases at a steady rate. Those who remain estrogen deficient have an even greater chance of developing osteoporosis with pathologic manifestations such as fracture (Mahon, 1998). However, the exact mechanism by which estrogen protects against bone loss remains unclear (Lindsey & Cosman, 1999).

Women with breast cancer are at higher risk for osteoporosis because of estrogen depletion secondary to treatment and lack of HRT. Women who receive chemotherapy experience premature menopause at an earlier age and have lower bone mineral density (BMD) compared with women not receiving chemotherapy (Headley *et al.*, 1998). Breast cancer survivors may lose up to 30% of bone mass within the first year of menopause without estrogen (Twiss *et al.*, 2001).

Table 16.1 lists additional risk factors for osteoporosis in women with breast cancer (Mahon, 1998; Goodman, 1996).

DETECTION

Bone mineral density studies, such as a dual energy X-ray absorptiometry (DEXA) scan, are often used for bone mass evaluation and measurement (Van Kuijk & Genant, 1999). In addition to estrogen depletion, women with noted osteopenia on X ray, primary hyperparathyroidism, and chronic steroid therapy should obtain a DEXA scan to determine if systemic therapy is needed. Other methods of detection include peripheral DEXA, computerized tomography, ultrasound, single X-ray absorptiometry, and radiographic absorptiometry (Mahon, 1998). Once osteopenia has been found, other lifestyle factors must be evaluated in order to determine the cause or contributing factors. In breast cancer survivors, bone mass loss may also be attributed to metastatic lesions and should be carefully evaluated (Mahon, 1998).

PHARMACOLOGIC MANAGEMENT OF OSTEOPOROSIS

The goal of management is to prevent osteoporosis from occurring whenever possible or to limit the amount of bone loss. The following agents are useful in the prevention and/or treatment of osteoporosis.

Calcitonin. Calcitonin is indicated for the treatment (not prevention) of osteoporosis. Calcitonin is a naturally occurring hormone that is involved in calcium regulation and reduces bone loss in the spine. This hormone, secreted by the thyroid gland, inhibits the osteoclastic function through antiresorptive activities (Mahon, 1998). It has been shown to increase BMD by 2–4% in postmenopausal women who experienced vertebral fractures (Mahon, 1998). The drug comes in an intranasal preparation. In research studies calcitonin was reported to increase spinal bone mass in women with established postmenopausal osteoporosis (Mahon, 1998).

Table 16.1 Additional Osteoporosis Risk Factors

- Advancing age

- Family history of osteoporosis

- Ethnicity

  - White and Asian women have higher risk

  - African American and Hispanic women have lower risk

- Small body size and low body weight (less than 127 pounds)

Data from: Mahon, 1998; Goodman, 1996.

Bisphosphonates. Bisphosphonates can reduce bone loss by inhibiting the action of osteoclasts, thus reducing vertebral fractures (Delmas *et al.,* 1997). They are resorption inhibitors and decrease the rate of bone resorption (Christiansen, 1999). Alendronate is the first FDA-approved nonhormonal therapy for osteoporosis (Mahon, 1998). Spinal bone mass has been reported to increase with the use of alendronate, with a decrease in the risk of pathologic fractures (Mahon, 1998). Patient teaching is essential for patients who are prescribed alendronate because of its adverse effects and administration methods. Risedronate is a new bisphosphonate approved for postmenopausal osteoporosis, steroid-induced osteoporosis, and Paget's disease, and it is reported to be an effective treatment (Umland & Boyce, 2001).

Nursing care includes teaching patients and monitoring for adverse reactions (Springhouse Corporation, 2002). Side effects of bisphosphonates include abdominal pain, nausea, dyspepsia, constipation, diarrhea, acid regurgitation, esophageal ulcer, gastritis, and musculoskeletal pain. In addition, antacids may interfere with drug absorption. Taking bisphosponates with aspirin or nonsteroidal anti-inflammatory drugs can increase the likelihood of experiencing adverse gastrointestinal side effects. Because food can decrease absorption, patients should be instructed to take these medications on an empty stomach, at least 30 minutes prior to meals. Contraindications include renal insufficiency, because the drugs are metabolized through the kidneys, and gastrointestinal disorders. Calcium and phosphate levels should be monitored throughout therapy.

Hormones, Tamoxifen, and Raloxifene. Estrogen/hormone replacement therapy is a treatment for osteoporosis but is generally contraindicated in women with breast cancer. However, like estrogen replacement therapy, SERMs may also augment BMD. Raloxifene acts as an estrogen receptor antagonist in endometrial and breast tissue but as an estrogen agonist in the cardiovascular and skeletal systems (Christiansen, 1999). It was reported to slow bone loss and stabilize bone turnover in early postmenopausal healthy women (Christiansen, 1999). The utilization of raloxifene in breast cancer treatment has increased in the past several years because of new research results. Tamoxifen continues to be prescribed for adjuvant therapy as the first-line treatment. The side effect profile of raloxifene has been well documented and is cause for concern for some patients. Side effects can include hot flashes and venous thromboembolism events (Jordan *et al.,* 2001). More extensive, comparative studies are in progress to determine the overall efficacy of raloxifene for use in treating osteoporosis in breast cancer patients. Although the majority of women with primary breast cancer take tamoxifen, women with estrogen receptor-negative tumors or those who stop tamoxifen after five years of therapy continue to be at high risk for osteoporosis.

NONPHARMACOLOGIC MANAGEMENT OF OSTEOPOROSIS

Nonpharmacologic interventions are also appropriate for patient management of osteoporosis. Table 16.2 lists tips for osteoporosis prevention and management. Available resources for further recommendations can be obtained from the National Osteoporosis

Table 16.2 Osteoporosis Prevention

- Exercise 30 minutes a day, 3 times a week.
- Adhere to a weight-bearing, strength, and weight-training program that is frequent and progressive in intensity.
- Improve environment to reduce the risk of falls (wear sturdy, low-heeled shoes; secure rugs in home).
- Follow a high-calcium diet, including dairy products (i.e., milk, yogurt, ice cream, cheese), fruits, vegetables (e.g., broccoli, legumes, kale), and soy products (i.e., tofu, soy milk).
- Take calcium supplements of 1500 mg/day in divided doses of 500 mg, with vitamin D 200 to 400 IU to help absorb calcium.
- Do not take calcium supplements with caffeine, which can affect the absorption of calcium.
- Stop smoking and decrease alcohol intake.

Data from: Slemenda & Johnston, 1999; Mahon, 1998.

Foundation (NOF), a nonprofit, voluntary health organization dedicated to reducing the prevalence of osteoporosis. Access is available at *http://www.nof.org*.

CARDIOVASCULAR EFFECTS

Cardiovascular disease is the leading cause of death in women in the United States. The incidence of coronary heart disease (CHD) is 4 in 1000 women from ages 45 to 54 years (Sotelo & Johnson, 1997). As healthy menopausal women reach 50 years of age, CHD incidence increases more rapidly, as a result of various physiologic changes during this time (Sotelo & Johnson, 1997). There are few studies to evaluate the incidence of cardiovascular disease in breast cancer survivors, specifically in relation to the role of menopause in incidence, prevalence, and severity.

ETIOLOGY

Risk of cardiovascular disease increases with estrogen deficiency, because estrogen has a protective cardiovascular effect. When estrogen is decreased, it causes changes in plasma total cholesterol and lipid profile. Decreased estrogen results in a higher level of low-density lipoprotein (LDL) cholesterol and a lower concentration of high-density lipoprotein (HDL) cholesterol (Vega, 2001). In addition, estrogen decreases hepatic HDL receptor sites, thus decreasing HDL catabolism. The net result is a reduction of cholesterol accumulation in peripheral tissues, elimination through biliary fluid, inhibited accumulation of lipids in coronary arteries, and increased arterial blood flow (Goodman, 1996).

In a review of past epidemiologic studies regarding the cardioprotective mechanism of estrogen, it was found that because the population sampling came from healthy women with no listed comorbidities, the cardioprotective effects may be exaggerated (Schenck-Gustafsson, 1996). The controversy of prescribing estrogen for potential cardioprotective effects has been publicized in the media and is of much concern for the medical community in regards to healthy women. Publicized findings from the Women's Health Initiative (USA) indicated that continuous combined conjugated equine estrogen and medroxyprogesterone acetate was associated with increased CHD, stroke, and pulmonary embolism compared to women taking placebo.

Tamoxifen and other SERMs are commonly prescribed for women at high risk for developing breast cancer as well as for women with estrogen receptor-positive breast cancer. Although tamoxifen and raloxifene have been noted to have beneficial effects on bone density and breast cancer, there are potential cardiovascular-related side effects that should be considered. Data from the National Surgical Adjuvant Breast and Bowel Project Breast Cancer Prevention Trial found an increased risk of thrombotic events among healthy women taking tamoxifen/raloxifene for breast cancer prevention, including stroke, deep vein thrombosis, and pulmonary embolism (Fisher *et al.*, 1998). However, the unique relationship between menopausal changes in cardiac tissue and risks associated with cardiotoxic chemotherapy (e.g., doxorubicin) remains unclear. The potential synergistic effects between chemotherapy and menopause have not been clearly defined in women with or without preexisting cardiac damage.

Tamoxifen was found to have a neutral effect on the endothelial function in postmenopausal breast cancer patients (Ong *et al.*, 2001). Ultrasounds were performed on the subjects ($N = 16$), all of whom were currently receiving tamoxifen therapy. The first group ($N = 10$) contained newly diagnosed patients just starting therapy. The second group consisted of patients taking tamoxifen for 3–5 years ($N = 6$). The technician was blinded to therapeutic status during the procedure. The results showed no significant differences in epithelial function between those just starting on tamoxifen and those taking the drug for 3–5 years. Although the findings are compelling, the study consisted of a small cohort with various confounding variables that affect endothelial function, such as cigarette smoking and high body mass. This suggests a need for further large-scale studies to determine the validity of these findings.

MANAGEMENT OF CARDIOVASCULAR EFFECTS

Management strategies to reduce the risk of cardiovascular disease are based on results from the longitudinal Framingham Heart Study and are listed in Table 16.3 (Castelli, 2000; Goodman, 1996; Gorodeski & Utian, 1994).

Table 16.3 Management Strategies to Reduce Cardiovascular Disease Risk

- Stop smoking.
- Exercise 30 minutes a day, 3 times a week.
- Eat a moderate diet to lower fat intake and control blood lipid levels.
- Take vitamin E, 400 to 800 units per day.
- Take dietary supplements of folate plus vitamins B6 and B12 to reduce homocysteine levels.
- Take aspirin 75 to 325 mg per day.
- Prescribe lipid- and cholesterol-modifying medications for patients with unfavorable profile.
- Maintain a healthy body weight.

Data from: Castelli, 2000; Goodman, 1996; Gorodeski & Utian, 1994.

Exercising and maintaining a healthy body weight may be particularly difficult for women with breast cancer. Exercise may be difficult because of treatment-related fatigue and loss of stamina. Weight gain is a commonly reported side effect of breast cancer chemotherapy. Since the late 1970s, clinicians and researchers have been reporting significant weight gain among breast cancer survivors (Dixon *et al.*, 1978; Knobf *et al.*, 1983; Subramanian *et al.*, 1991; McInnes & Knobf, 2001). In one descriptive correlation study, it was found that premenopausal women who completed adjuvant therapy for breast cancer had a greater tendency for weight gain. The women who experienced significant weight gain tended to maintain this excess weight after completion of therapy. Thus, weight gain associated with cancer chemotherapy may increase the impact of menopausal changes on the cardiovascular system. Women with breast cancer may need particular help in reducing these risk factors.

UROGENITAL TRACT

Noted drops in estrogen levels during menopause or related to chemotherapy's or tamoxifen's effects on the ovaries can cause certain target tissues such as vaginal epithelium, skin, and mucous membranes, to have altered function and changes in structure (Knobf, 1998). Urogenital changes can be painful and negatively impact quality of life. In healthy women, urogenital side effects can be treated with estrogen with improvement (Rymer & Morris, 2000), but, as noted above, this treatment is contraindicated in breast cancer patients. Breast cancer patients are at risk for urogenital changes resulting from chemotherapy, radiation, or surgically induced menopause.

ETIOLOGY

Cellular proliferation and growth of reproductive tissues and sex organs depend on the principal function of estrogens (Guyton & Hall, 2000). The vagina and urethra have active estrogen receptor sites in the epithelium (Griebling & Nygaard, 1997). Estrogen assists in cell productivity (assisting in replacement of the cell lining), increases blood flow to the urethral structure, sensitizes urethral sphincter alpha adrenergic receptors, and stimulates metabolism of connective tissue (Hextall & Cardozo, 2001). Therefore, reduced estrogen support, as well as aging, result in changes in the vagina and lower urinary tract. During menopause, the anatomy of the vagina changes. It becomes narrower and shorter, with decreased elasticity of the epithelium in response to lowered estrogen. This tissue atrophy results in vaginal dryness, dyspareunia, and vaginitis (Gardner, 1999). In addition, vaginitis may be a result of decreased blood flow and increased pH of the vaginal area (Knobf, 1998). Changes in vaginal flora may result in urinary tract infections. In addition, because of the decrease in estrogen, urethral closure pressure, abdominal pressure, and transmission to the proximal urethra all decrease (Hextall & Cardozo, 2001). These changes can result in generalized incontinence issues and/or dysuria. In addition, the sensation of bladder fullness increases, leading to frequency and urgency of urination and nocturia.

PREVALENCE, SEVERITY, AND IMPACT ON QUALITY OF LIFE

Studies focusing on vaginal dryness and urogenital symptoms in women with breast cancer are somewhat limited. Studies on sexual functioning in this patient group do not always assess vaginal dryness, and studies on menopausal symptoms do not always assess urogenital changes. In addition, studies may focus on one menopausal group (premenopause or perimenopause only) or one category of women with breast cancer (survivors only) rather than considering all menopausal groups and women with recurrent or metastatic disease.

Despite these limitations, research indicates that urogenital symptoms do occur and may interfere with quality of life (Carpenter & Andrykowski, 1999; Ganz *et al.,* 2000; Knobf, 2001; Harris *et al.,* 2002). In a qualitative study of 27 young women who received adjuvant therapy for breast cancer, women reported experiencing vaginal dryness but did not discuss this symptom with their health care providers (Knobf, 2001). Harris *et al.* (2002) surveyed 110 women with breast cancer (cases) and 73 healthy women (controls). Only 5% of cases reported experiencing vaginal dryness, an incidence that was not significantly higher than controls. Incontinence was not assessed. In contrast, in a survey of 114 postmenopausal breast cancer survivors, 36% reported experiencing vaginal dryness (Carpenter & Andrykowski, 1999). Of those women reporting the symptom, 27% reported the symptom to be mild, 32% reported moderate dryness, and 42% reported the symptom to be quite a bit to extremely severe (Carpenter & Andrykowski, 1999). Unfortunately, this survey did not inquire about incontinence (stress, urge, or other), nor did it include a comparison group of healthy women. In another study, 71% of 72 postmenopausal breast cancer survivors involved in an intervention study reported vaginal dryness at baseline, and 51% reported stress urinary incontinence (Ganz *et al.,* 2000). Symptom severity was rated using a scale of 0 to 4 points. Mean severities for vaginal and urogenital symptoms were mild (M = 1.07, SD = 1.01 and M = .59, SD = 0.82, respectively). Of the 72 women, 39% reported both vaginal dryness and urinary incontinence, 69% reported vaginal dryness and hot flashes, and 49% reported urinary incontinence and hot flashes. These symptoms were correlated with quality of life on the CARES Global, Psychosocial, and Sexual Summary Scales (*r*'s = 0.29–0.42). Interestingly, vaginal dryness was found to significantly increase over time among 817 respondents involved in a longitudinal study of menopausal symptoms in women with breast cancer (*p* < .05) (Ganz *et al.,* 2002).

In regards to urogenital symptoms, future research needs to focus on all groups of women who have been diagnosed with breast cancer. For example, women with bone metastases often have stable disease and may be living with these symptoms. Research could be expanded to include more culturally and ethnically diverse groups of women, as well.

MANAGEMENT OF VAGINAL DRYNESS

Limited management options are available because of the contraindication of estrogen-containing interventions. Literature from clinical trials continues to be published in this area, as there are limited standard treatment options. One meta-analysis of healthy women reviewed various HRT trials and suggested that estrogen vaginal cream was just as effective as the oral route of administration (Cardozo *et al.,* 1998). For the breast cancer population, it remains controversial whether vaginal creams containing estrogen are appropriate for symptomatic treatment of urogential problems.

Water-soluble lubricants have been the historical intervention when estrogen (systemic or cream) is contraindicated. The use of such lubricants can provide comfort during sexual intercourse (Bachmann *et al.,* 1999). Vaginal lubricants such as K-Y® Jelly, Replens® and Astroglide® are examples of available treatment options for vaginal dryness. These methods do not contain estrogen and provide comfort for dyspareunia. It has been reported that Replens® can improve vaginal elasticity, increase moisture, and normalize vaginal pH to premenopausal levels (Nachtigall, 1994). In comparison studies regarding vaginal lubricants versus placebo, no conclusive findings were able to report one product as being superior for treatment (Barton, Loprinzi, & Gostout, 2002).

Topical estrogen creams and tablets also are used in treatment of vaginal dryness. These preparations are suggested to provide more effective relief of symptoms but can be cumbersome and messy to apply (Barton, Loprinzi, & Gostout, 2002). Two intravaginal preparations exist, Vagifem® and Estring®. Vagifem®, which resembles a tablet, is inserted into the vagina utilizing an applicator. It contains 25 µg of 17 beta-estradiol and is inserted once daily for 2 weeks then decreased to biweekly (Barton, Loprinzi, & Gostout, 2002). The vaginal ring, or Estring®, is a 55-mm round and 9-mm thick device that is inserted into the upper, posterior vaginal vault and contains 2 mg of 17 beta-estradiol (Bachmann, 1998). It remains in the vagina for 3 months and does not need to be removed for sexual intercourse or other hygienic activities unless the patient desires (Bachmann, 1998). The absorption of the estrogen contained in both treatment modalities is reported to be low and remains comparable to nontreatment cohorts (Barton, Loprinzi, & Gostout, 2002). Because the amount of systemic absorption is thought to be minimal, clinicians may favor using such methods for symptomatic relief.

MANAGEMENT OF URINARY SYMPTOMS

There are medical, surgical, and behavioral treatment options for women with urinary incontinence. Pharmacologic interventions for urinary symptoms benefit mainly patients with urge incontinence and stress incontinence (Davis, 2000). Accurate assessment of patient history is vital in prescribing certain options because of side effect profiles of several drug classifications.

Several drug classifications are utilized in therapy. Smooth muscle relaxant drugs such as hyoscyamine and oxybutynin are commonly used for urge incontinence (DeMarco, 1999). They provide an antimuscarinic action, which suppresses muscle contractility and potentially provides local anesthetic relief for pain (DeMarco, 1999). These particular drugs possess side effects similar to anticholinergic drugs and are prescribed with caution because of potential adverse side effects. In current research studies, tolterodine, an antispasmodic drug, possessed the fewest reported side effects but is expensive for patients (Davis, 2000). Other classifications of drugs that can be utilized for urge incontinence include antihistamines (e.g., phenylpropanolamine, chlorpheniramine) and tricyclic antidepressants (e.g., imipramine, amitriptyline) (Davis, 2000). The use of estrogen for urinary incontinence remains questionable.

Although the effects of estrogen replacement may decrease or slow the progression of urinary tract symptoms, limitations in research methods have provided conflicting results.

For stress incontinence, minimal pharmacologic interventions are available; treatment is focused on behavioral and surgical modifications. Alpha-adrenergic agonists such as ephedrine, pseudoephedrine, and phenylpropanolamine stimulate the smooth muscle of the bladder anatomy causing urethral closure (DeMarco, 1999). Surgical interventions for stress incontinence are reported to have more effective results and may potentially be more effective than drug therapy (Barton, Loprinzi, & Gostout, 2002). Modern surgical techniques using laparoscopic methods have improved success and provided long-term relief.

Physiotherapy and behavior interventions are also thought to improve urinary complaints:

- Kegel strengthening exercises enhance the muscle of the pelvic floor, which is specifically utilized for stress incontinence. Exercises should be performed 2 times per day for 6–12 weeks in order to see improvement (Barton, Loprinzi, & Gostout, 2002; DeMarco, 1999).
- Implement a bladder training program. Bladder training includes both behavioral and physical re-training to improve urinary continence. Behavioral training includes emptying the bladder upon waking in the morning, establishing a set schedule for voiding throughout the day, and avoiding liquids 2–3 hours prior to bedtime. Physical re-training, mainly used for stress incontinence, consists of strengthening the pelvic floor muscles by performing Kegel exercises which improve the urethra function and provide more urinary control.
- Encourage women to void at regular intervals to avoid accidents.
- Promote adequate fluid intake (eight glasses of water per day) with decreased caffeine intake.

Lower urinary tract infections (UTIs) are attributed to the relaxation of the pelvic muscles, causing increased postvoid residual urine. This physiologic change can promote bacterial growth, causing frequent and recurrent UTIs (DeMarco, 1999). Antibiotic therapy is suggested for primary uncomplicated episodes of cystitis (DeMarco, 1999). A general 3–5 day course for the first episode may be effective, utilizing sulfa-based drugs for first-line use. A urine culture should be obtained to assess culture and sensitivity and to ensure appropriate antibiotic choice. For recurrent infections, a longer course of 7–14 days should be considered (DeMarco, 1999).

In addition to the behavioral interventions listed earlier, patients should be instructed on general hygiene techniques. Below are recommended practices for prevention of UTI in postmenopausal women.

- Change undergarments daily, utilizing cotton fabrics.
- Avoid hot tubs or highly chlorinated pools.
- Avoid using perfumed toilet paper, wiping front to back after bowel movements.
- Avoid feminine hygiene products that potentially irritate the urethra.

RECOMMENDATIONS FOR PRACTICE

The implications for clinical practice related to menopausal symptom management are substantial. Practice implications related to assessment, patient education, symptom management, monitoring of treatment outcomes, and research are discussed below. Practice guidelines are relevant not only to oncology specialists but also to primary care practitioners because of increasing survival rates and the need for long-term, routine care of these women.

ASSESSMENT

Assessment is the primary step in preventing and managing menopausal symptoms in women with breast cancer. Assessment should focus on a multisystem profile of demographic factors, breast cancer treatment-related factors, and the extent of current physical effects of menopausal symptoms. Demographic factors should include body mass index, age, menopausal status, exercise and dietary habits, and family history of osteoporosis or cardiovascular disease. Breast cancer treatment factors include current stage of disease, extent of systemic therapy, surgical/radiation intervention, and indications for tamoxifen/raloxifene or aromatase inhibitors. Extent of current physical effects can be assessed using standardized assessment methods (e.g., symptom severity ratings, DEXA scans, etc). Although routine standard of care involves assessment of multiple systems, such as cardiovascular and bone health, it is particularly important for clinicians to relate these findings to menopausal status and breast cancer treatment.

Women with hot flashes and urogenital symptoms in particular should undergo a standard symptom assessment. For example, descriptions of frequency, severity, and distress associated with such symptoms should be addressed, and patients should be encouraged to describe the impact these symptoms have on quality of life. Because these symptoms may be difficult or embarrassing for patients to discuss, it is important for clinicians to be comfortable initiating conversation regarding these issues. In addition, because hot flashes in particular have been associated with mood and sleep disturbances, women who present with primary complaints of mood and/or sleep difficulty should also be assessed for hot flashes.

The impact of hot flashes on quality of life can be quickly and easily assessed using the Hot Flash Related Daily Interference Scale (Carpenter, 2001). This scale was modeled on the Wisconsin Brief Pain Inventory (Daut *et al.*, 1983) and the Fatigue Symptom Inventory (Hann *et al.*, 1998). It consists of a series of 10-point numeric rating scales ranging from zero (does not interfere) to 10 (completely interferes). Patients are asked to rate the degree to which hot flashes impact each of 10 quality of life domains, including work, social activities, leisure activities, sleep, mood, concentration, relations with others, sexuality, enjoyment of life, and overall quality of life. This assessment provides a comprehensive segue to the extent and severity of hot flashes and can therefore form the basis for in-clinic symptom assessment. Scores can be totaled to create a baseline index that can be followed over time and related to the effectiveness of therapy.

Other symptom checklists can be quickly designed and easily implemented in clinic. Checklists might consist of a list of menopausal symptoms (hot flashes, vaginal dryness, dyspareunia) with columns for patients to mark "yes" or "no" to indicate if they are experiencing the symptom and another column for patients to rate severity. Such checklists again can form the start of conversations regarding these symptoms, or they can be indexed and followed over time as an indicator of response to symptom management interventions. Although such checklists are commonly used in clinics, they often include only acute treatment-related side effects (e.g., nausea, vomiting) or are general measures of symptoms relevant to all persons with cancer. As such, they may not include menopausal symptoms or other breast cancer-specific side effects. Therefore, existing symptom checklists should be revisited and modified as necessary to include these important menopausal symptoms.

EDUCATION

Historically, patient education has focused on acute side effects of cancer treatment (e.g., nausea, vomiting). Educating women and family members regarding the possibility of menopausal symptoms is equally as important. Women should be taught risk factors for menopausal symptoms and the impact that they may have on quality of life. Personalized risk factor assessment is particularly important to differentiate young women undergoing chemotherapy-induced menopause from older, postmenopausal women taking tamoxifen. Women need to understand how their own personal experiences with menopause may differ from their mothers', sisters', or friends' experiences. Preparing women in advance for the possibility of frequent, severe, or bothersome hot flashes or urogenital side effects may allow them to better cope with these symptoms. In addition, it is important to communicate the expected temporal pattern of side effects. For example, hot flashes may not begin until chemotherapy or tamoxifen is started, and osteoporosis can remain essentially invisible until bone loss is found on a DEXA scan.

Practitioners should be mindful of cultural/ethnic diversity, learning styles, or learning disabilities when educating patients and family members. Assessing appropriate teaching methods during symptom assessment is important for adequate education. Education facilitates open communication with clinicians and therefore can become the cornerstone of quality care. The need for a multidisciplinary team, particularly a dedicated symptom management team that is accessible to patients, may be especially useful in education and management of these long-term symptom issues.

MANAGEMENT

Pharmacologic and nonpharmacologic treatments have been outlined throughout this chapter. Unfortunately, there is no algorithm-type standard of care for implementing these treatments. Instead, it may be necessary to try one treatment after another in order to find the one that is effective and acceptable to patients. Utilizing multiple pharmacologic interventions, such as antidepressants, may mask other problems (e.g., depression) or may lead to tolerance, rendering them ineffective in the long term.

Patients are often most interested in finding a balance between effectiveness and side effects. Treatments with unacceptable or severe side effects, even when completely effective, may not be preferred to no treatment at all. For example, previous research has shown that a significant number of women prefer not to take pharmacologic interventions for hot flashes (Carpenter *et al.*, 1998, 2002). These women should be educated regarding risk/benefit ratios of medications and options for nonpharmacologic management. In addition, patients may be reluctant to use estrogen-containing vaginal preparations to alleviate vaginal dryness and dyspareunia, even though systemic absorption of these products has been shown to be minimal.

Awareness of herbal remedies and other complementary and alternative treatments and their potential side effects is necessary. Because research is continually evolving regarding alternative therapies, it is particularly important for the clinician to stay abreast of the latest treatments. Information regarding effectiveness, the potential for herb–drug interactions, and contraindications for alternative treatments is rapidly expanding. This information should be shared with patients on a routine basis to ensure that any herbal or alternative remedies selected are safe for use.

Perhaps the most effective way to manage menopausal symptoms is to carefully monitor the outcome of therapies. Routine assessment and reevaluation of effectiveness and side effects associated with symptom management modalities is critical for promoting quality of life. When all symptom management strategies have been exhausted and a woman continues to report severe and/or debilitating symptoms, it may be necessary to consider hormone replacement therapy. The risks and benefits of hormone replacement therapy for that individual patient should be carefully discussed.

In summary, several unique factors predispose women with breast cancer to menopausal symptoms. As presented, these symptoms can have profound impact on quality of life. This chapter has focused on an overview of menopause, risk factors for menopausal symptoms, and etiology and management of various menopausal symptoms, including hot flashes, osteoporosis, cardiovascular effects, and urogenital symptoms. Practice implications presented are patient specific and should be evaluated on a patient-by-patient basis.

REFERENCES

Adlercreutz, H. (1990). Western diet and western diseases: some hormonal and biochemical mechanisms and association. *Scandinavian Journal of Clinical Laboratory Investigations, 50*(Suppl), 3–23.

Adlercreutz, H., & Mazur, W. (1997). Phyto-oestrogens and western diseases. *Annals of Medicine, 29,* 95–120.

Albertazzi, P., Pansini, F., Bonaccorsi, G., Zanotti, L., Forini, E., & De Aloysio, D. (1998). The effect of dietary soy supplementation on hot flushes. *Obstetrics & Gynecology, 91,* 6–11.

American Cancer Society. (2001). *Breast cancer facts and figures 2001–2002* (01-50M-No. 8610.01R). Atlanta, Ga.: Author.

Bachmann, G.A. (1998). The clinical platform for the 17 beta-estradiol vaginal releasing ring. *American Journal of Obstetrics and Gynecology, 178,* S257–260.

Bachmann, G.A., Ebert, G.A., & Burd, I.D. (1999). Vulvovaginal complaints. In R.A. Lobo (Ed.), *Treatment of the postmenopausal woman: basic and clinical aspects, 2nd ed.,* pp. 195–201. Philadelphia: Lippincott Williams & Wilkins.

Barton, D., LaVasseur, B., Loprinzi, C., Novotny, P., Wilwerding, M.B., & Sloan, J. (2002). Venlafaxine for the control of hot flashes: results of a longitudinal continuation study. *Oncology Nursing Forum, 29,* 33–40.

Barton, D.L., Loprinzi, C., & Gostout, B. (2002). Current management of menopausal symptoms in cancer patients. *Oncology (Huntington), 16,* 67–72, 74; discussion 75–76, 79–80.

Barton, D.L., Loprinzi, C.L., Quella, S.K., Sloan, J.A., Veeder, M.H., Egner, J.R., Fidler, P., Stella, P.J., Swan, D.K., Vaught, N.L., & Novotny, P. (1998). Prospective evaluation of vitamin E for hot flashes in breast cancer survivors. *Journal of Clinical Oncology, 16,* 495–500.

Beique, J.C., de Montigny, C., Blier, P., & Debonnel, G. (1999). Venlafaxine: discrepancy between in vivo 5-HT and NE reuptake blockade and affinity for reuptake sites. *Synapse, 32,* 198–211.

Berger, B.M. (2000). Osteoporosis. In B.A. Eskin (Ed.), *The menopause: comprehensive management, 4th ed.,* pp. 105–116. New York: Parthenon.

Bergmans, M.G.M., Merkus, J.M.W.M., Corbey, R.S., Schellekens, L.A., & Ubachs, J.M.H. (1987). Effect of Bellergal Retard on climacteric complaints: a double-blind, placebo-controlled study. *Maturitas, 9,* 227–234.

Brenner, I., Shek, P.N., Zamecnik, J., & Shephard, R.J. (1997). Stress hormones and the immunological responses to heat and exercise. *International Journal of Sports Medicine, 19,* 130–143.

Brincat, M.P., & Galea, R. (1999). Collagen. The significance in skin, bone, and carotid arteries. In R.A. Lobo (Ed.), *Treatment of the postmenopausal woman: basic and clinical aspects, 2nd ed.,* pp. 203–212. Philadelphia: Lippincott Williams & Wilkins.

Broeckel, J.A., Jacobsen, P.B., Horton, J., Balducci, L., & Lyman, G.H. (1998). Characteristics and correlates of fatigue after adjuvant chemotherapy for breast cancer. *Journal of Clinical Oncology, 16,* 1689–1696.

Brzezinski, A. (1995). Management of menopause in women with breast cancer. *Israel Journal of Medical Science, 3,* 163–168.

Canney, P.A., & Hatton, M.Q. (1994). The prevalence of menopausal symptoms in patients treated for breast cancer. *Clinical Oncology, 6,* 297–299.

Cardozo, L., Bachmann, G., McClish, D., & Fonda, D. (1998). Meta-analysis of estrogen therapy in the management of urogenital atrophy in postmenopausal women: second report of the Hormones and Urogenital Therapy Committee. *Obstetrics and Gynecology, 92,* 722–727.

Carpenter, J. (2000). Hot flashes and their management in breast cancer. *Seminars in Oncology Nursing, 16,* 214–225.

Carpenter, J.S. (2001). The Hot Flash Related Daily Interference Scale: a tool for assessing the impact of hot flashes on quality of life following treatment for breast cancer. *Journal of Pain and Symptom Management, 22,* 979–989.

Carpenter, J.S., & Andrykowski, M.A. (1999). Menopausal symptoms in breast cancer survivors. *Oncology Nursing Forum, 26,* 1311–1317.

Carpenter, J.S., Andrykowski, M.A., Cordova, M.J., Cunningham, L., Studts, J., McGrath, P., Sloan, D., Kenady, D.E., & Munn, R. (1998). Hot flashes in postmenopausal women treated for breast carcinoma: prevalence, severity, correlates, management, and relation to quality of life. *Cancer, 82,* 1682–1691.

Carpenter, J.S., Andrykowski, M.A., Freedman, R.R., & Munn, R. (1999). Feasibility and psychometrics of an ambulatory hot flash monitoring device. *Menopause, 6,* 209–215.

Carpenter, J.S., Gautam, S., Andrykowski, M., & Freedman, R.R. (2001). Circadian rhythm of objectively recorded hot flashes in postmenopausal breast cancer survivors. *Menopause, 8,* 181–188.

Carpenter, J.S., Johnson, D.H., Wagner, L., & Andrykowski, M.A. (2002). Hot flashes and related outcomes in breast cancer survivors and matched comparison women. *Oncology Nursing Forum, 29,* 476. Published as an online exclusive with full text available at *www.ons.org.*

Castelli, W.P. (2000). Menopause and cardiovascular disease. In B.A. Eskin (Ed.), *The menopause: comprehensive management, 4th ed.,* pp. 1117–1135. New York: Parthenon.

Cheer, S.M., & Goa, K.L. (2001). Fluoxetine: a review of its therapeutic potential in the treatment of depression associated with physical illness. *Drugs, 61,* 81–110.

Christiansen, C. (1999). Treatment of osteoporosis. *Treatment of the postmenopausal woman: basic and* clinical aspects, 2nd ed., pp. 315–328. Philadelphia: Lippincott Williams & Wilkins.

Christy, C.J. (1945). Vitamin E in menopause. *American Journal of Obstetrics & Gynecology, 50,* 84–87.

Cobleigh, M.A., Berris, R.F., Bush, T., Davidson, N.E., Robert, N.J., Sparano, J.A., Tormey, D.C., & Wood, W.C. (1994). Estrogen replacement therapy in breast cancer survivors: a time for change. *Journal of the American Medical Association, 272,* 540–545.

Couzi, R.J., Helzlsouer, K.J., & Fetting, J.H. (1995). Prevalence of menopausal symptoms among women with a history of breast cancer and attitudes toward estrogen replacement therapy. *Journal of Clinical Oncology, 13,* 2737–2744.

Crewe, H.K., Notley, L.M., Wunsch, R.M., Lennard, M.S., & Gillam, E.M. (2002). Metabolism of tamoxifen by recombinant human cytochrome P450 enzymes: formation of the 4-hydroxy, 4'-hydroxy and N-desmethyl metabolites and isomerization of trans-4-hydroxytamoxifen. *Drug Metabolism and Disposition, 30,* 869–874.

Daut, R.L., Cleeland, C.S., & Flanery, R.C. (1983). Development of the Wisconsin Brief Pain Inventory to assess pain in cancer and other diseases. *Pain, 17,* 197–210.

Davis, N.S. (2000). Urological problems. In B.A. Eskin (Ed.), *The menopause: comprehensive management, 4th ed.,* pp. 171–184. New York: Parthenon.

Delmas, P.D., Balena, R., Confravreux, E., Hardouin, C., Hardy, P., & Bremond, A. (1997). Bisphosphonate risedronate prevents bone loss in women with artificial menopause due to chemotherapy of breast cancer: a double-blind, placebo-controlled study. *Journal of Clinical Oncology, 15,* 955–962.

DeMarco, E.F. (1999). Urinary tract disorders in perimenopausal and postmenopausal women. In R.A. Lobo (Ed.), *Treatment of the postmenopausal woman: basic and clinical aspects, 2nd ed.,* pp. 213–230. Philadelphia: Lippincott Williams & Wilkins.

Dixon, J.K., Moritz, D.A., & Baker, F.L. (1978). Breast cancer and weight gain: an unexpected finding. *Oncology Nursing Forum, 5,* 5–7.

Erlik, Y., Tataryn, I.V., Meldrum, D.R., Lomax, P., Bajorek, J.G., & Judd, H.L. (1981). Association of waking episodes with menopausal hot flushes. *Journal of the American Medical Association, 245,* 1741–1744.

Finck, G., Barton, D.L., Loprinzi, C.L., Quella, S.K., & Sloan, J.A. (1998). Definitions of hot flashes in breast cancer survivors. *Journal of Pain and Symptom Management, 16,* 327–333.

Finkler, R.S. (1949). The effect of vitamin E in the menopause. *Journal of Clinical Endocrinology and Metabolism, 9,* 89–94.

Fisher, B., Costantino, J.P., Wickerham, D.L., Redmond, C.K., Kavanah, M., Cronin, W.M., Vogel, V., Robidoux, A., Dimitrov, N., Atkins, J., Daly, M., Wieand, S., Tan-Chiu, E., Ford, L., Wolmark, N., et al. (1998). Tamoxifen for prevention of breast cancer: report of the National Surgical Adjuvant Breast and Bowel Project P-1 study. *Journal of the National Cancer Institute, 90,* 1371–1388.

Freedman, R.R. (1989). Laboratory and ambulatory monitoring of menopausal hot flashes. *Psychophysiology, 26,* 573–579.

Freedman, R.R. (1998). Biochemical, metabolic, and vascular mechanisms in menopausal hot flashes. *Fertility and Sterility, 70,* 332–337.

Freedman, R.R., & Blacker, C.M. (2002). Estrogen raises the sweating threshold in postmenopausal women with hot flashes. *Fertility and Sterility, 77,* 487–490.

Freedman, R.R., & Dinsay, R. (2000). Clonidine raises the sweating threshold in symptomatic but not in asymptomatic postmenopausal women. *Fertility and Sterility, 74,* 20–23.

Freedman, R.R., & Krell, W. (1999). Reduced thermoregulatory null zone in postmenopausal women with hot flashes. *American Journal of Obstetrics and Gynecology, 181,* 66–70.

Freedman, R.R., Norton, D., Woodward, S., & Cornelissen, G. (1995). Core body temperature and circadian rhythm of hot flashes in menopausal women. *Journal of Clinical Endocrinology and Metabolism, 80,* 2354–2358.

Freedman, R.R., & Woodward, S. (1992). Behavioral treatment of menopausal hot flashes: evaluation by ambulatory monitoring. *American Journal of Obstetrics and Gynecology, 167,* 436–439.

Fry, A.C., & Kraemer, W.J. (1997). Resistance exercise overtraining and overreaching: neuroendocrine responses. *Sports Medicine, 23,* 106–129.

Gadjos, C., & Jordan, V.C. (2002). Selective estrogen receptor modulators as a new therapeutic drug group: concept to reality in a decade. *Clinical Breast Cancer, 2,* 272–281.

Ganz, P.A. (2001). Menopause and breast cancer: symptoms, late effects, and their management. *Seminars in Oncology, 28,* 274–283.

Ganz, P.A., Desmond, K.A., Leedham, B., Rowland, J.H., Meyerowitz, B.E., & Belin, T.R. (2002). Quality of life in long-term, disease-free survivors of breast cancer: a follow-up study. *Journal of the National Cancer Institute, 94,* 39–49.

Ganz, P.A., Greendale, G.A., Petersen, L., Zibecchi, L., Kahn, B., & Belin, T.R. (2000). Managing menopausal symptoms in breast cancer survivors: results of a randomized controlled trial. *Journal of the National Cancer Institute, 92,* 1054–1064.

Gardner, L.A. (1999). Hormonal contraceptives and related drugs. In K. Gutierrez (Ed.), *Pharmacotherapeutics: clinical decision-making in nursing,* pp. 1129–1153. Philadelphia: W.B. Saunders.

Germaine, L.M., & Freedman, R.R. (1984). Behavioral treatment of menopausal hot flashes: evaluation by objective methods. *Journal of Consulting and Clinical Psychology, 52,* 1072–1079.

Gold, E.B., Sternfeld, B., Kelsey, J.L., Brown, C., Mouton, C., Reame, N., Salamone, L., & Stellato, R. (2000). The relation of demographic and lifestyle factors to symptoms in a multi racial/ethnic population of women aged 40–55 years of age. *American Journal of Epidemiology, 152,* 463–473.

Goldberg, R.M., Loprinzi, C.L., O'Fallon, J.R., Veeder, M.H., Miser, A.W., Maillard, J.A., Michalak, J.C., Dose, A.M., Rowland, K.M., & Burnham, N.L. (1994). Transdermal clonidine for ameliorating tamoxifen-induced hot flashes. *Journal of Clinical Oncology, 12,* 155–158.

Goodman, M. (1996). Menopausal symptoms. In C.H. Yarbro, M.H. Frogge, & M. Goodman (Eds.), *Cancer symptom management,* pp. 77–99. Sudbury, Mass.: Jones & Bartlett.

Gorodeski, G.I., & Utian, W.H. (1994). Epidemiology of risk factors of cardiovascular disease in postmenopausal women. In R.A. Lobo (Ed.), *Treatment of the postmenopausal woman: basic and clinical aspects,* pp. 199–221. New York: Raven Press.

Grady-Welicky, T.A., & Hartmann, D.M. (2001). Flushing in a menopausal woman taking venlafaxine. *American Journal of Psychiatry, 158,* 1330.

Griebling, T.L., & Nygaard, I.E. (1997). The role of estrogen replacement therapy in the management of urinary incontinence and urinary tract infection in postmenopausal women. *Endocrinology and Metabolism Clinics of North America, 26,* 347–360.

Guttuso, T.J. (2000). Gabapentin's effects on hot flashes and hypothermia. *Neurology, 54,* 2161–2163.

Guyton, A.C., & Hall, J.E. (2000). *Textbook of Medical Physiology, 10th ed.* Philadelphia: W.B. Saunders.

Hammar, M., Berg, G., & Lindgren, R. (1990). Does physical exercise influence the frequency of postmenopausal hot flushes? *Acta Obstetricia Gynecologica Scandinavica, 69,* 409–412.

Hammar, M., Frisk, J., Grimas, O., Hook, M., Spetz, A.C., & Wyon, Y. (1999). Acupuncture treatment of vasomotor symptoms in men with prostatic carcinoma: a pilot study. *Journal of Urology, 161,* 853–856.

Hann, D.M., Jacobsen, P.B., Azzarello, L.M., Martin, S.C., Curran, S.L., Fields, K.K., Greenberg, H., & Lyman, G. (1998). Measurement of fatigue in cancer patients: development and validation of the Fatigue Symptom Inventory. *Quality of Life Research, 7,* 301–310.

Harris, P.F., Remington, P.L., Trentham-Dietz, A., Allen, C.I., & Newcomb, P.A. (2002). Prevalence and treatment of menopausal symptoms among breast cancer survivors. *Journal of Pain and Symptom Management, 23,* 501–509.

Headley, J.A., Theriault, R.L., LeBlanc, A.D., Vassilopoulou-Sellin, R., & Hortobagyi, G.N. (1998). Pilot study of bone mineral density in breast cancer patients treated with adjuvant chemotherapy. *Cancer Investigation, 16,* 6–11.

Hextall, A., & Cardozo, L. (2001). The role of estrogen supplementation in lower urinary tract dysfunction. *International Urogynecology Journal, 12,* 258–261.

Horst, D.W., & Preskorn, S.H. (1998). Mechanisms of action and clinical characteristics of three atypical antidepressants: venlafaxine, nefazodone, buproprion. *Journal of Affective Disorders, 51,* 237–254.

Irvin, J.H., Domar, A.D., Clark, C., Zuttermeister, P.C., & Friedman, R. (1996). The effects of relaxation response training on menopausal symptoms. *Journal of Psychosomatic Obstetrics & Gynecology, 17,* 202–207.

Israel, D., & Youngkin, E.Q. (1997). Herbal therapies for perimenopausal and menopausal complaints. *Pharmacotherapy, 17,* 970–984.

Ivarsson, T., Spetz, A.C., & Hammar, M. (1998). Physical exercise and vasomotor symptoms in postmenopausal women. *Maturitas, 29,* 139–146.

Jeffery, S.M., Pepe, J.J., Popovich, L.M., & Vitagliano, G. (2002). Gabapentin for hot flashes in prostate cancer. *Annals of Pharmacotherapy, 36,* 433–436.

Johnston, S.R. (2001). Endocrine manipulation in advanced breast cancer: recent advances with SERM therapies. *Clinical Breast Cancer Research, 7,* 4367s–4387s.

Jordan, V.C., Gapstur, S., & Morrow, M. (2001). Selective estrogen receptor modulation and the reduction in risk of breast cancer, osteoporosis, and coronary heart disease. *Journal of the National Cancer Institute, 93,* 1449–1457.

Jubelirer, S.J. (1995). The management of menopausal symptoms in women with breast cancer. *The West Virginia Medical Journal, 91,* 54–56.

Knight, D.C., Howes, J.B., Eden, J.A., & Howes, L.G. (2001). Effects on menopausal symptoms and acceptability of isoflavone-containing soy powder dietary supplementation. *Climacteric, 4,* 13–18.

Knobf, M.T. (1996). Menopausal symptoms associated with breast cancer treatment. In K.H. Dow (Ed.), *Contemporary issues in breast cancer,* pp. 85–97. Boston: Jones & Bartlett.

Knobf, M.T. (1998). Natural menopause and ovarian toxicity associated with breast cancer therapy. *Oncology Nursing Forum, 25,* 1519–1530.

Knobf, M.T. (2001). The menopausal symptom experience in young mid-life women with breast cancer. *Cancer Nursing, 24,* 201–210.

Knobf, M.T., Mullen, J.C., Xistris, D., & Moritz, D.A. (1983). Weight gain in women with breast cancer receiving adjuvant chemotherapy. *Oncology Nursing Forum, 10,* 28–33.

Kostoglou-Athanassiou, I., Ntalles, K., Gogas, J., Markopoulos, C., Alevizou-Terzaki, V., Athanassiou, P., Georgiou, E., & Proukakis, C. (1995). Sex hormones in postmenopausal women with breast cancer on tamoxifen. *Hormone Research, 47,* 116–120.

Kronenberg, F. (1990). Hot flashes: epidemiology and physiology. *Annals of the New York Academy of Sciences, 592,* 52–86.

Kronenberg, F. (1994). Hot flashes: phenomenology, quality of life, and search for treatment options. *Experimental Gerontology, 29,* 319–336.

Lindsey, R., & Cosman, F. (1999). Pathophysiology of bone loss. In R.A. Lobo (Ed.), *Treatment of the postmenopausal woman: basic and clinical aspects, 2nd ed.,* pp. 305–314. Philadelphia: Lippincott Williams & Wilkins.

Liske, E., Hänggi, W., Henneicke-von Zepelin, H.H., Boblitz, N., Wüstenberg, P., Rahlfs, V.W., & Stat, C. (2002). Physiological investigation of a unique extract of black cohosh (*Cimicifugae racemosae rhizoma*): A 6-month clinical study demonstrates no systemic estrogenic effect. *Journal of Women's Health and Gender-Based Medicine, 11,* 163–174.

Lobo, R.A. (1999). Clinical aspects of hormonal replacement: routes of administration. In R.A. Lobo (Ed.), *Treatment of the postmenopausal woman: basic and clinical aspects, 2nd ed.,* pp. 125–154. Philadelphia: Lippincott Williams & Wilkins.

Lomax, P., & Schonbaum, E. (1993). Postmenopausal hot flushes and their management. *Pharmacological Therapy, 57,* 347–358.

Loprinzi, C.L., Kugler, J.W., Sloan, J.A., Mailliard, J.A., LaVasseur, B.I., Barton, D.L., Novotny, P.J., Dakhil, S.R., Rodger, K., Rummans, T.A., & Christensen, B.J. (2000). Venlafaxine in management of hot flashes in survivors of breast cancer: a randomised controlled trial. *Lancet, 356,* 2059–2063.

Loprinzi, C.L., Michalak, J.C., Quella, S.K., O'Fallon, J.R., Hatfield, A.K., Nelimark, R.A., Dose, A.M., Fischer, T., Johnson, C., Klatt, N.E., Bate, W.W., Rospond, R.M., & Oesterling, J.E. (1994). Megestrol acetate for the prevention of hot flashes. *New England Journal of Medicine, 33,* 347–352.

Loprinzi, C.L., Pisansky, T.M., Fonseca, R., Sloan, J.A., Zahasky, K.M., Quella, S.K., Novotny, P.J., Rumman, T.A., Dumesic, D.A., & Perez, E.A. (1998). Pilot evaluation of venlafaxine hydrochloride for the therapy of hot flashes in cancer survivors. *Journal of Clinical Oncology, 16,* 2377–2381.

Loprinzi, C.L., Sloan, J.A., Perez, E.A., Quella, S.K., Stella, P.J., Mailliard, J.A., Halyard, M.Y., Puthi, S., Novotny, P.J., & Rummans, T.A. (2002). Phase III evaluation of fluoxetine for treatment of hot flashes. *Journal of Clinical Oncology, 20,* 1578–1583.

Love, R.R. (1989). Tamoxifen therapy in primary breast cancer: biology, efficacy, and side effects. *Journal of Clinical Oncology, 7,* 803–815.

Love, R.R., Cameron, L., Connell, B.L., & Levanthal, H. (1991). Symptoms associated with tamoxifen treatment in postmenopausal women. *Archives of Internal Medicine, 151,* 1842–1847.

Lum, S.S., Woltering, E.A., Fletcher, W.S., & Pommier, R.F. (1997). Changes in serum estrogen levels in women during tamoxifen therapy. *American Journal of Surgery, 173,* 399–402.

Mahon, S.M. (1998). Osteoporosis: a concern for cancer survivors. *Oncology Nursing Forum, 25,* 843–851.

Mansky, P.J., & Straus, S.E. (2002). St. John's wort: implications for cancer patients. *Journal of the National Cancer Institute, 94,* 1187–1188.

Matthews, K.A. (1992). Myths and realities of the menopause. *Psychosomatic Medicine, 54,* 1–9.

McInnes, J.A., & Knobf, M.T. (2001). Weight gain and quality of life in women treated with adjuvant chemotherapy for early-stage breast cancer. *Oncology Nursing Forum, 28,* 675–684.

McLaren, H.C. (1949). Vitamin E in the menopause. *British Medical Journal, 2,* 1378–1381.

McNair, P.M., Lorr, M., & Droppelman, L. (1981). *POMS Manual, 2nd ed.* San Diego: Educational and Testing Service.

Messina, M. (2002, October). Soy intake and breast cancer risk. Abstract presented at the 13th Annual Meeting of the North American Menopause Society, Chicago, Illinois.

Miller, K.L. (1992). Alternatives to estrogen for menopausal symptoms. *Clinical Obstetrics and Gynecology, 35,* 884–893.

Mouridsen, H., Gershanovich, M., Sun, Y., PérezCarrión, R., Boni, C., Monnier, A., Apffelstaedt, J., Smith, R., Sleeboom, H.P., Jänicke, F., Pluzanska, A., Dank, M., Becquart, D., Bapsy, P.P., Salminen, E., Snyder, R., Lassus, M., Verbeek, J.A., Staffler, B., Chaudri-Ross, H.A., & Dugan, M. (2001). Superior efficacy of letrozole (Femara) versus tamoxifen as first-line therapy for postmenopausal women with advanced breast cancer: results of a phase III study of the International Letrozole Breast Cancer Group. *Journal of Clinical Oncology, 19,* 2596–2606.

Moyad, M.A. (2002). Complementary/alternative therapies for reducing hot flashes in prostate cancer patients: reevaluating the existing indirect data from studies of breast cancer and postmenopausal women. *Urology, 59,* 20–33.

Murkies, A.L., Lombard, C., Strauss, B.J.G., Wilcox, G., Burger, H.G., & Morton, M.S. (1995). Dietary flour supplementation decreases post-menopausal hot flushes: effect of soy and wheat. *Maturitas, 21,* 189–195.

Nachtigall, L.E. (1994). Sexual function in the menopause and post-menopause. In R.A. Lobo (Ed.), *Treatment of the postmenopausal woman: basic and clinical aspects,* pp. 301–306. New York: Raven Press.

Nagamani, M., Kelver, M.E., & Smith, E.R. (1987). Treatment of menopausal hot flashes with transdermal administration of clonidine. *American Journal of Obstetrics and Gynecology, 156,* 561–565.

Nagata, C., Takatsuka, N., Kawakami, N., & Shimizu, H. (2001). Soy product intake and hot flashes in Japanese women: results from a community-based prospective study. *American Journal of Epidemiology, 153,* 790–793.

Ong, P.J.L., Linardou, H., Graham, H.A., Savage, P., Hayward, C.S., Coombes, R.C., & Collins, P. (2001). Tamoxifen is not detrimental to endothelial function in postmenopausal women with breast cancer. *American Heart Journal, 142,* E6.

Pasacreta, J.V., & McCorkle, R. (1998). Providing accurate information to women about tamoxifen therapy for breast cancer: current indications, effects and controversies. *Oncology Nursing Forum, 25,* 1577–1583.

Quella, S.K., Loprinzi, C.L., Barton, D.L., Knost, J.A., Sloan, J.A., LaVasseur, B.I., Swan, D., Krupp, K.R., Miller, K.D., & Novotny, P.J. (2000). Evaluation of soy phytoestrogens for the treatment of hot flashes in breast cancer survivors: a North Central Cancer Treatment Group trial. *Journal of Clinical Oncology, 18,* 1068–1074.

Quella, S., Loprinzi, C.L., Sloan, J., Vaught, N., Dekrey, W., Fischer, T., Fink, G., Pierson, N., & Pisansky, T. (1998). Long-term use of megestrol acetate by cancer survivors for the treatment of hot flashes. *Cancer, 82,* 1784–1788.

Reichman, B.S., & Green, K.B. (1994). Breast cancer in young women: effect of chemotherapy on ovarian function, fertility, and birth defects. *Journal of the National Cancer Institute Monographs, 16,* 125–129.

Riis, B.J. (1995). The role of bone loss. *American Journal of Medicine, 98,* 29S–32S.

Rosenberg, J., & Larsen, S.H. (1991). Hypothesis: pathogenesis of postmenopausal hot flush. *Medical Hypotheses, 35,* 349–350.

Roth, A.J., & Scher, H.I. (1998). Sertraline relieves hot flashes secondary to medical castration as treatment of advanced prostate cancer. *Psychooncology, 7,* 129–132.

Runowicz, C.D. (1996). Hormone replacement therapy in cancer survivors: a con opinion. *CA—A Cancer Journal for Clinicians, 46,* 365–373.

Rymer, J., & Morris, E.P. (2000). Extracts from "clinical evidence": menopausal symptoms. *British Medical Journal, 321,* 1516–1519.

Scambia, G., Mango, D., Signorile, P.G., Anselmi-Angeli, R.A., Palena, C., Gallo, D., Bombardelli, E., Morazzoni, P., Riva, A., & Mancuso, S. (2000). Clinical effects of a standardized soy extract in postmenopausal women: a pilot study. *Menopause, 7,* 105–111.

Schenck-Gustafsson, K. (1996). A European trial on secondary prevention of cardiovascular disease. In B.G. Wren (Ed.), *Progress in the management of the menopause,* pp. 80–82. New York: Parthenon.

Slemenda, C.W., & Johnston Jr., C.C. (1999). Epidemiology of osteoporosis. In R.A. Lobo (Ed.), *Treatment of the postmenopausal woman: basic and clinical aspects, 2nd ed.,* pp. 279–285. Philadelphia: Lippincott Williams & Wilkins.

Smith, H.O., Kammerer-Doak, D.N., Barbo, D.M., & Sarto, G.E. (1996). Hormone replacement therapy in the menopause: a pro opinion. *CA—A Cancer Journal for Clinicians, 46,* 343–363.

Soffa, V. (1996). Alternatives to hormone replacement for menopause. *Alternative Therapies, 2*(2), 34–39.

Sotelo, M.M., & Johnson, S.R. (1997). The effects of hormone replacement therapy on coronary heart disease. *Endocrinology and Metabolism Clinics of North America, 26,* 313–328.

Soules, M.R., Sherman, S., Parrott, E., Rebar, R., Santoro, N., Utian, W., & Woods, N. (2001). Executive summary: Stages of Reproductive Aging Workshop (STRAW), Park City, Utah, July 2001. *Menopause, 8,* 402–407.

Springhouse Corporation. (2002). *Nursing 2002 Drug Handbook.* Philadelphia: Author.

St Germain, A., Peterson, C.T., Robinson, J.G., & Alekel, D.L. (2001). Isoflavone-rich or isoflavone-poor soy protein does not reduce menopausal symptoms during 24 weeks of treatment. *Menopause, 8,* 17–26.

Stadberg, E., Mattsson, L.A., & Milsom, I. (2000). Factors associated with climacteric symptoms and the use of hormone replacement therapy. *Acta Obstetricia et Gynecologica Scandinavica, 79,* 286–292.

Stanford, J.L., Hartge, P., Brinton, L.A., Hoover, R.N., & Brookmeyer, R. (1987). Factors influencing the age at natural menopause. *Journal of Chronic Disease, 40,* 995–1002.

Stearns, V., Isaacs, C., Rowland, J., Crawford, J., Ellis, M.J., Kramer, R., Lawrence, W., Hanfelt, J.J., & Hayes, D.F. (2000). A pilot trial assessing the efficacy of paroxetine hydrochloride (Paxil®) in controlling hot flashes in breast cancer survivors. *Annals of Oncology, 11,* 17–22.

Sternfeld, B., Quesenberry, C.P. Jr., & Husson, G. (1999). Habitual physical activity and menopausal symptoms: a case-control study. *Journal of Women's Health, 8,* 115–123.

Stevenson, D.W., & Delprato, D.J. (1983). Multiple component self-control program for menopausal hot flashes. *Journal of Behavioral Therapy & Experimental Psychiatry, 14,* 137–140.

Subramanian, V.P., Raich, P.C., & Walker, B.K. (1991). Weight gain in breast cancer patients undergoing chemotherapy. *Breast Cancer Research and Treatment, 1,* 170.

Swain, S., Santen, R., Burger, H., & Pritchard, K. (1999a). Treatment of estrogen deficiency symptoms in women surviving breast cancer. Part 1: Defining the problem. *Oncology, 13,* 109–136.

Swain, S., Santen, R., Burger, H., & Pritchard, K. (1999b). Treatment of estrogen deficiency symptoms in women surviving breast cancer. Part 2: Hormone replacement therapy and breast cancer. *Oncology, 13,* 245–267.

Swain, S., Santen, R., Burger, H., & Pritchard, K. (1999c). Treatment of estrogen deficiency symptoms in women surviving breast cancer. Part 3: Prevention of osteoporosis and CV effects of estrogens and antiestrogens. *Oncology, 13,* 397–432.

Swain, S., Santen, R., Burger, H., & Pritchard, K. (1999d). Treatment of estrogen deficiency symptoms in women surviving breast cancer. Part 4: Urogenital atrophy, vasomotor instability, sleep disorders, and related symptoms. *Oncology, 13,* 551–575.

Swain, S., Santen, R., Burger, H., & Pritchard, K. (1999e). Treatment of estrogen deficiency symptoms in women surviving breast cancer. Part 5: Selective estrogen receptor modulators and hormone replacement therapy. *Oncology, 13,* 721–735.

Swain, S., Santen, R., Burger, H., & Pritchard, K. (1999f). Treatment of estrogen deficiency symptoms in women surviving breast cancer. Part 6: Executive summary and consensus statement. *Oncology, 13,* 859–875.

Tsai, M.E., Mehmi, I., Atlas, E., Oketch-Rabah, H.A., Kennelly, E., Nuntanakorn, P., Kronenberg, F., & Lupu, R. (2002, October). An herbal remedy, black cohosh, does not contain estrogenic-like activity. Abstract presented at the 13th Annual Meeting of the North American Menopause Society, Chicago, Illinois.

Twiss, J.J., Waltman, N., Ott, C.D., Gross, C.J., Lindsey, A.M., & Moore, T.E. (2001). Bone mineral density in postmenopausal breast cancer survivors. *Journal of the American Academy of Nurse Practitioners, 13,* 216–284.

Umland, E.M., & Boyce, E.G. (2001). Risedronate: a new oral bisphosphonate. *Clinical Therapeutics, 23,* 1409–1421.

Upmalis, D.H., Lobo, R., Bradley, L., Warren, M., Cone, F.L., & Lamia, C.A. (2000). Vasomotor symptom relief by soy isoflavone extract tablets in postmenopausal women: a multicenter, double-blind, randomized, placebo-controlled study. *Menopause, 7,* 236–242.

U.S. Bureau of the Census. (1996). *Population projections of the United States by age, sex, race, and Hispanic origin: 1995–2050.* Current Population Reports, Series P25-1130. Washington, D.C.: Population Division, U.S. Bureau of the Census.

Utian, W.H. (1990). The menopause in perspective. From potions to patches. *Annals of the New York Academy of Sciences, 592,* 1–7.

Van Kuijk, C., & Genant, H.K. (1999). Detection of osteopenia. In R.A. Lobo (Ed.), *Treatment of the postmenopausal woman: basic and clinical aspects, 2nd ed.,* pp. 287–303. Philadelphia: Lippincott Williams & Wilkins.

Van Patten, C.L., Olivotto, I.A., Chambers, G.K., Gelmon, K.A., Hislop, T.G., Templeton, E.,

Wattie, A., & Prior, J.C. (2002). Effect of soy phytoestrogens on hot flashes in postmenopausal women with breast cancer: a randomized, controlled clinical trial. *Journal of Clinical Oncology, 20,* 1449–1455.

Vega, V. (2001). Cardioprotective benefits of hormone replacement therapy. *Journal of the American Academy of Nurse Practitioners, 13*(2), 69–76.

Waldman, T.N. (1998). Menopause: when hormone replacement therapy is not an option. Part 2. *Journal of Women's Health, 7,* 673–683.

Watson, D., Clark, L.A., & Tellegen, A. (1998). Development and validation of brief measures of positive and negative affect: the PANAS scales. *Journal of Personality and Social Psychology, 54,* 1063–1070.

Wijma, K., Melin, A., Nedstrand, E., & Hammar, M. (1997). Treatment of menopausal symptoms with applied relaxation: a pilot study. *Journal of Behavior Therapy & Experimental Psychiatry, 28,* 251–261.

Wile, A.G., Opfell, R.W., & Margileth, D.A. (1993). Hormone replacement therapy in previously treated breast cancer patients. *The American Journal of Surgery, 165,* 372–375.

World Health Organization. (1981). *Research on menopause: Report of a WHO scientific group* (Technical Report Series 670). Geneva: Author.

World Health Organization. (1994). *Research on menopause in the 1990s: Report of a WHO scientific group* (Technical Report Series 866). Geneva: Author.

Chapter 17

LATE PHYSICAL EFFECTS OF CANCER TREATMENT

VICTORIA WOCHNA LOERZEL, RN, MSN, AOCN

INTRODUCTION

As a result of the tremendous advances in breast cancer treatment over the last decade, many women successfully complete their initial treatment and live cancer-free for many years after their diagnosis. As a result, however, many women may experience late effects of treatment that may have a long-lasting impact on their physical health and on their quality of life. Other late effects are seen in women who have undergone bone marrow transplantation (BMT). Late effects of treatment are a growing concern, but fortunately, many late effects are rare. Nurses must keep abreast of late side effects and educate patients who may be at risk for developing them in the future. This chapter aims to educate the nurse on the possible late side effects that can occur from treatment for breast cancer.

Late effects from chemotherapy and radiation are defined in this chapter as effects that occur several months to a year or more after treatment. These range from major organ toxicity to neurosensory deficits to secondary cancers. The major late effects that will be discussed include cardiac dysfunction, pulmonary dysfunction, impaired cognitive functioning, neurosensory effects, secondary cancers, and other late effects.

CARDIAC DYSFUNCTION

Cardiotoxicity is a dose-limiting toxicity. Causes of treatment-induced cardiac failure include radiation therapy to the left side, doxorubicin greater than 550 mg/m^2 total dose, combination chemotherapy with doxorubicin, advancing age, and preexisting cardiac abnormalities.

CHEMOTHERAPY-INDUCED CARDIOTOXICITY

Several chemotherapeutic agents that are highly effective in treating breast cancer at various stages are known to have serious cardiac effects. Doxorubicin, cyclophosphamide, paclitaxel, and trastuzumab have been implicated in cardiac dysfunction.

Doxorubicin. Doxorubicin can cause immediate electrocardiographic changes, as well as changes that can lead to congestive heart failure (CHF) or cardiomyopathy (Fristoe, 1998). Cardiac damage is thought to result from free radicals released during treatment causing cell damage to the myocardium. This damage leads to loss of contractility and eventual cell death (Speyer & Freedberg, 2000; Hochster *et al.*, 1995, Shan *et al.*, 1996). Von Hoff *et al.* (1979) state that the overall risk for cardiotoxicity is low at 2.2%.

Several factors increase the risk for cardiotoxicity with doxorubicin. These include age greater than 70 years, previous history of radiation to the chest and mediastinum, history of preexisting heart disease or hypertension, previous treatment with anthracyclines, or concomitant cyclophosphamide administration. The risk increases with cumulative doses of greater than 550 mg/ml. Allen (1992) adds that the schedule of administration may also increase the risk.

Cardiomyopathy most commonly occurs weeks to months after the last dose. However, cases have been reported 5 or more years after completing chemotherapy. Steinherz *et al.* (1991) examined cardiotoxicity in children that occurred 4 to 20 years after anthracycline therapy. The investigators noted that the incidence of compromised cardiac function increased the longer patients were followed, especially if they were treated with higher doses of doxorubicin. Even when there was no early evidence of cardiac damage, cardiac function declined. This data may correlate with incidence in adults. Allen (1992) believes that approximately 5% of patients who survive 10 years will experience new onset of symptoms. Late symptoms can occur in patients who have been asymptomatic, as well as those who developed CHF and subsequently recovered their cardiac function.

Cyclophosphamide. This alkylating agent may increase the risk of cardiac damage when given with doxorubicin. Cyclophosphamide is not associated with cardiotoxicity at standard doses. However, the risk of cardiotoxicity increases when it is given in high doses such as those seen with blood and stem cell transplant regimens. Unlike anthracycline toxicity, cardiotoxicity from cyclophosphamide is not cumulative (Allen, 1992). Risk increases with previous mediastinal radiation therapy, previous anthracycline therapy, and concomitant administration of chemotherapy drugs not normally associated with cardiac damage, such as carmustine (BCNU).

Taxanes. Taxanes are another group of drugs that have demonstrated effectiveness against breast cancer. Several studies have shown that combination regimens of doxorubicin and paclitaxel may increase the risk of CHF. Sparano (1999) and Valero *et al.* (2001) both concluded that patients receiving combination doxorubicin and paclitaxel developed a higher risk for anthracycline-induced cardiomyopathy. After reviewing the incidence of cardiotoxicity from early trials with doxorubicin and paclitaxel, Valero *et al.* (2001) concluded that there were several ways to minimize the risk of cardiotoxicity when using these drugs in combination, including administering individual doxorubicin doses at no more than 50 mg/m^2, keeping the cumulative dose below 360 mg/m^2, and separating the administration times of the drugs by 4 to 24 hours. Sparano (1999) concurred that the risk of CHF increased when using both drugs and a doxorubicin dose exceeding 360 mg/m^2.

Perez (2001) posited that paclitaxel decreases the clearance of doxorubicin when the two drugs are given close together. She also found that doxorubicin/paclitaxel could be given safely when the doxorubicin dose was limited to 340–380 mg/m^2. Interestingly, cardiotoxicity risk was not increased when doxorubicin was combined with docetaxel. High tumor response rates were noted without increased cardiotoxicity. Valero *et al.* (2001) presented studies that indicated that higher doses of doxorubicin could be given with docetaxel. Cardiac risk was similar using either the docetaxel/doxorubicin regimen or doxorubicin alone.

Trastuzumab. The monoclonal antibody trastuzumab, when combined with anthracycline therapy, increases the risk of cardiotoxicity in some patients (Tham *et al.*, 2002; Seidman *et al.*, 2002; Schneider *et al.*, 2002). Trastuzumab can have a direct effect on the myocardium, but these effects become apparent when the agent is combined with other known cardiotoxic agents such as doxorubicin (Schneider *et al.*, 2002). Trastuzumab may have a synergistic effect, and doxorubicin may prime the cardiac tissue.

Frankel (2000) reviewed several clinical trials with trastuzumab and found cardiac dysfunction to be the most clinically significant adverse event. Cardiac dysfunction could be CHF, cardiomyopathy, or decrease in ejection fraction. Those patients with the highest risk received anthracycline (approximately 360 mg/m^2) with cyclophosphamide. Data showed the following incidence of cardiac dysfunction:

- 7% when trastuzumab was used alone
- 11% when trastuzumab was combined with paclitaxel
- 28% when combined with an anthracycline and cyclophosphamide
- 1% when paclitaxel was used alone
- 7% when a combination of anthracycline and cyclophosphamide was used

Once cardiotoxicity is identified, trastuzumab is discontinued if patients are still receiving treatment. However, the benefits of therapy with trastuzumab may outweigh the risks of cardiotoxicity for women with aggressive disease.

Tamoxifen. Tamoxifen is now standard treatment in women with ER/PR-positive tumors. Although tamoxifen was originally thought to reduce the risk of cardiac events, Reis *et al.,* (2001) found that the risk of a cardiovascular event was not statistically different between women receiving tamoxifen and those receiving a placebo. Cushman *et al.* (2001), on the other hand, found that tamoxifen helps lower risk factors associated with cardiovascular disease, namely cholesterol and fibrinogen levels, supporting the idea of cardiac benefits. Further studies are needed in order to determine if there is a benefit for women taking tamoxifen.

CARDIAC SYMPTOMS

Symptoms of CHF in patients with cancer include dyspnea, cough, fatigue, decreased tolerance of exercise and activity, and signs of cardiac and pulmonary congestion. On clinical presentation in severe cases, Fristoe (1998) identified other symptoms, including dyspnea at rest with tachycardia, hypotension, and diaphoresis. Cardiac exam may show venous jugular distention, third and fourth heart sounds, peripheral edema, rales on auscultation, and peripheral edema. An echocardiogram may show nonspecific changes such as low voltage and left ventricular hypertrophy.

The use of multiple gated acquisition (MUGA) scans is a standard evaluation to determine baseline cardiac function and subsequent cardiac decline in patients receiving anthracycline therapy. Baseline studies must be done prior to receiving the anthracycline, because doxorubicin has been shown to damage myocytes in the days to weeks after the first dose (Allen, 1992). MUGA scans check for changes in wall motion as well as left ventricular ejection fraction (LVEF). Any changes may indicate myocardial damage resulting from chemotherapy. Further evaluation of damage can include repeated MUGA tests, as well as endomyocardial biopsy.

Despite the risk of cardiotoxicity, the anthracyclines remain one of the best categories of drugs available to fight breast cancer. Fortunately, there are ways to reduce the risk of toxicity. Limiting the cumulative dosage of doxorubicin to 450–550 mg/m^2 can help reduce the risk. Von Hoff et al. (1979) suggests smaller divided doses instead of large boluses, even when the cumulative dose is the same. Longer infusion times have been shown to reduce the risk of toxicity as well (Doroshow, 1991). Hortobagyi et al. (1989) showed a 75% decrease in congestive heart failure when doxorubicin, at doses greater than or equal to 450 mg/m^2, was administered as a continuous infusion rather than a bolus dose. They also concluded that longer infusions are safer and better tolerated than bolus infusions.

Fristoe (1998) and Allen (1992) further suggest that the treatment of doxorubicin-related CHF is much like that of other forms of CHF. This includes the use of digoxin to increase myocardial contractility and diuretics to decrease fluid overload and vasodilators. CHF can be managed and stabilized. Improvement can also occur, but unfortunately, like other forms of CHF, symptoms can also progress, eventually leading to death.

Acute cardiotoxicity, although manageable, may have an effect on future treatments. Women who have disease recurrence or need continued treatment because of incomplete remission may have their treatment options affected by previous cardiotoxicity. Because of this, it is important to recognize CHF early or use treatments that are less toxic to the cardiac system when future or prolonged treatments are predicted.

CARDIOPROTECTANTS

New agents are available that have shown success in reducing the risk of cardiotoxicity. These include Doxil® (ALZA Pharmaceuticals, Inc.) and dexrazoxane. Doxil® is doxorubicin hydrochloride encapsulated in long-circulating STEALTH® liposomes. These liposomes are microscopic vesicles composed of a phospholipid bilayer that are capable of encapsulating active drugs. The STEALTH® liposomes are formulated with surface-bound methoxypolyethylene glycol (MPEG), a process often referred to as pegylation, to protect liposomes from detection by the mononuclear phagocyte system (MPS) and to increase blood circulation time. Currently, experience with Doxil® is limited to establishing its effectiveness on the myocardium (Schwonzen et al., 2000). Further studies are needed to determine long-term effects.

Dexrazoxane is an agent used for prevention of cardiomyopathy associated with doxorubicin administration. It is thought to bind to free and bound iron, which reduces the formation of doxorubicin-iron complexes, thus preventing free radical formation. The free radicals are suspected to cause myocardial damage in anthracycline-based cardiotoxicity. The consensus among several investigators (Wiseman & Spencer, 1998; Hensley et al., 1999; Seymour et al., 1999) shows that dexrazoxane has a place in preventing anthracycline-induced cardiac damage. It is recommended for patients with metastatic, anthracycline-sensitive disease, not for patients receiving initial treatment. In the metastatic population, it is recommended for use when the cumulative dose of doxorubicin reaches 300 mg/m^2 or higher. Hochster et al. (1995) reported that they were able to treat women with FAC (5-fluorouracil, doxorubicin, and cyclophosphamide) and dexrazoxane up to a doxorubicin dose of 1000 mg/m^2 without any deterioration in cardiac function. Wiseman and Spencer (1998) believe that dexrazoxane can provide cardioprotection above standard doses, but they question the role that dexrazoxane may play in tumor protection and in long-term survival. Long-term studies are ongoing as to its definite role in preventing long-term cardiac damage.

RADIATION-INDUCED CARDIAC DYSFUNCTION

Pericarditis. Radiation-induced pericarditis can occur months to years after treatment with radiation therapy to the mediastinum. Pericarditis occurs when the radiation field includes the heart in left-sided breast cancer and in other cancers such as non-Hodgkin's lymphoma. Fristoe (1998) lists the risk factors as the volume of heart irradiated, the total dose of radiation delivered, and the dose per fraction of radiation. Pericardial and myocardial cells are sensitive to radiation and can be damaged, causing edema and rupture of the capillaries or small arteries located in the pericardium and myocardium. This leads to fibrosis of the tissue.

According to Fristoe (1998), radiation-induced pericarditis presents like other forms of pericarditis with fever, pleuritic chest pain, and friction rub. Treatment includes non-steroidal anti-inflammatory drugs, antipyretics for fever, and possibly corticosteroids. In rare instances, patients who are hemodynamically unstable may require pericardiocentesis.

Fortunately, radiation techniques can limit exposure of the heart to the radiation. Muren *et al.* (2002) reported that with three-dimensional conformal tangential irradiation (CTI), enough normal tissue can be spared from radiation, resulting in a reduction of cardiac mortality risk in left-sided cases. Gagliardi *et al.* (2001) further recommend that patients with left-sided breast cancer should have three-dimensional planning and treatment.

PULMONARY DYSFUNCTION

Both chemotherapy and radiation therapy can contribute to pulmonary toxicities. The majority of injuries are acute. However, acute injury can either evolve into chronic problems or become evident after treatment is completed without having an acute phase.

CHEMOTHERAPY-INDUCED PULMONARY TOXICITY

Chemotherapy-induced pulmonary toxicity is a result of specific chemotherapeutic agents, including cyclophosphamide, methotrexate, doxorubicin, paclitaxel, and tamoxifen. Bone marrow transplant regimens including BCNU, busulfan, and VP-16 also increase the risk of pulmonary toxicity. Combination treatment with any of these agents plus radiation therapy also increases the risk for toxicity. Taghian *et al.* (2001) urge caution when using taxanes and radiation therapy. Taxanes enhance effectiveness of radiation and may increase incidence of radiation pneumonitis.

Inflammatory Interstitial Pneumonitis. Inflammatory interstitial pneumonitis is a hypersensitivity reaction that can develop after the initial dose of chemotherapy or several months after completion of chemotherapy (Abid *et al.,* 2001). Pneumonitis begins with a nonproductive cough, progressive dyspnea, and occasionally low-grade fever. Chest X ray reveals scattered interstitial infiltrates with or without alveolar infiltrates. Lung biopsy results will include focal consolidation, bronchiolitis obliterans with organizing pneumonia (BOOP), and plasma cells, lymphocytes, and eosinophils in the interstitium. Usually, this syndrome resolves after the offending agent is stopped, but in severe cases, corticosteroids may be needed. Prognosis is good and lung function usually returns to pretreatment status.

Pulmonary Fibrosis. The most common chemotherapy-induced toxicity is pulmonary fibrosis. Late effects can occur from two months to several years after therapy (Abid *et al.,* 2001). Chemotherapy-induced pulmonary fibrosis can result from direct toxicity to the lung tissue, but hypersensitivity may also be involved. The immune response eventually leads to fibrosis of the lung tissue. Dyspnea will occur and is often accompanied by a nonproductive cough.

The most likely agents that cause pulmonary fibrosis are not seen in breast cancer therapy. Cyclophosphamide-induced pulmonary fibrosis is rare but has a mortality rate of

60% with the late onset form. Cyclophosphamide can also increase the risk of pulmonary toxicity when it is used with BCNU to prepare for bone marrow transplant. Busulfan and BCNU can also cause late pulmonary toxicity up to several years after bone marrow or stem cell transplant.

Chest X ray may be normal or show bibasilar reticular interstitial markings. Pulmonary function tests (PFTs) may show a restrictive pattern and decreased lung volumes. If the chest X ray is normal, Computed Tomographic (CT) or gallium scans showing increased lung uptake are very useful. Bronchoscopy may be used to rule out infections (Abid *et al.,* 2001).

Pulmonary toxicities are more apparent in patients with breast cancer who receive high-dose (HD) chemotherapy followed by autologous stem cell rescue. Wilczynski *et al.* (1998) noted a delayed pulmonary toxicity syndrome in women who received HD chemotherapy and autologous BMT. Their studies showed a high incidence of interstitial pneumonitis that required treatment with steroids. They were unable to determine risk factors for this syndrome.

Brockstein *et al.* (2000) sought to define risk factors of pulmonary toxicity for women with breast cancer and lymphoma undergoing autologous stem cell transplant and found that toxicity was most likely a result of busulfan used in the treatment regimen. Treatment for chemotherapy-induced toxicity includes stopping the agent and possibly utilizing steroids.

RADIATION-INDUCED PULMONARY TOXICITY

Radiation-induced pulmonary toxicity is a concern for women receiving radiation for their breast cancer. Toxicity is related to the volume of lung tissue irradiated, the total dose of radiation, the daily fractions given, and the quality of the radiation (Abid *et al.,* 2001). It appears that at least 10% of the lung must be irradiated to produce significant toxicity.

Radiation Pneumonitis. Radiation pneumonitis can occur 6 to 18 months after treatment with radiation. Fristoe (1998) and McDonald *et al.* (2000) describe damage resulting from an inflammation of the lung tissue. Age and underlying chronic pulmonary disease do not seem to be factors. With radiation pneumonitis, there is an infiltration of inflammatory products such as macrophages, lymphocytes, and mononuclear cells, as well as desquamation of epithelial cells from the alveolar wall. This impairs gas exchange, causing diffuse alveolar damage. Depending on how much of the lung has been damaged, these changes can become life threatening. Cells become unable to repair themselves because of extensive damage. Edema and thrombosis occur, leading to increased capillary permeability. Fluid-containing fibrin seeps into the alveolar spaces and begins to form hyaline membranes on the alveoli, which interferes with gas exchange. This may eventually progress to pulmonary fibrosis.

Patients may first complain of shortness of breath or fullness in the chest. They may also complain of a nonproductive cough or a cough that produces small amounts of pink sputum. This can be self-limiting or progress to severe respiratory distress (Abid *et al.,* 2001).

Diagnosis of pneumonitis includes ruling out other possibilities, including pulmonary metastasis or recurrence. On physical examination, pulmonary symptoms may be limited to moist rales, a pleural friction rub, or evidence of an effusion. Radiographically, abnormalities occur even when a patient may be asymptomatic.

Pulmonary Fibrosis. Pulmonary fibrosis is a late side effect that may follow radiation-induced pneumonitis or develop insidiously in the previously radiated field. It may take 6 months or longer for the injury to become apparent. Permanent changes may take 6 to 24 months to develop. In these cases, the alveoli collapse and are obliterated by connective tissue.

Fibrosis may be a natural progression of radiation-induced pneumonitis, or it may occur without an acute phase. Symptoms include dyspnea on exertion, decreased tolerance of exercise, orthopnea, cyanosis, chronic cor pulmonale, and finger clubbing. Symptoms of fibrosis are minimal if the damage is limited to less than 50% of one lung.

Diagnosis of fibrosis includes radiologic changes consistent with fibrosis (e.g., linear streaks radiating from the area of damage) and decrease in pulmonary function as evidenced by PFTs. The use of corticosteroids in pulmonary damage is uncertain (Abid *et al.*, 2001). Physicians may start the patient on prednisone 1 mg/kg/day, maintain the dose for several weeks, and then slowly taper it off. Supportive care is usually indicated with fibrosis, because this is damaged tissue that will not repair itself.

Prevention may be the best defense against treatment-induced pulmonary damage. Modification of drug dosages and newer radiation techniques may decrease the incidence of pulmonary toxicity. Attention to early complaints of dyspnea and a nonproductive cough may also facilitate early diagnosis and treatment.

Amifostine has been studied as a possible radioprotectant of the lungs. Wasserman (1999; Wasserman & Brizel, 2001) and Dorr (1998) believe that amifostine has been shown to protect normal tissue, such as lung tissue, from early and late radiation-induced toxicities without protecting the tumor. Vujaskovic *et al.* (2002) determined that use of amifostine during radiation showed a reduction in lung injury functionally and histologically, citing the reduction of macrophage activity and cytokine activity that is likely to induce the lung damage in the first place.

IMPAIRED COGNITIVE FUNCTIONING

Recently, cognitive dysfunction has received more attention and study than cardiac or pulmonary dysfunction. Nail (2001) found that patients report having difficulty with concentration, short-term memory, and problem solving, often stating they are experiencing "chemobrain." Olin (2001) found that deficits in attention spans and language skills have also been reported by women who have received chemotherapy. Cimprich (1992, 2001) describes attentional fatigue and suggests that older women may be more at risk for cognitive changes even if they have only received surgery. Factors that may contribute to changes in cognitive functioning include cranial irradiation as well as surgery, chemotherapy, and biological response modifiers. Emotional distress may contribute to cognitive deficits.

Wieneke and Dienst (1995) conducted a small study examining cognitive impairment after chemotherapy for breast cancer. In their sample of 28 patients, 75% scored in the range of having moderate impairment based on several neuropsychological tests. They concluded that even months after therapy is finished, patients with breast cancer may still have impaired cognitive functioning. Impairment may be related to chemotherapy toxicity. Other reasons for cognitive impairment may also include a preexisting condition that was not noted until chemotherapy or treatment-induced menopause and lack of estrogen.

Van Dam *et al.* (1998) studied cognitive dysfunction in women who received standard adjuvant chemotherapy and tamoxifen compared with high-dose treatment and tamoxifen. They found that women receiving high-dose therapy were most at risk when compared with women who received standard-dose treatment and control groups that received no chemotherapy. They also noted that the patients who complained of having problems were not necessarily the same patients who were identified with standard tests as having impaired cognitive function. This study also found that cognitive dysfunction was unlikely a result of a preexisting deficit, surgery, or radiation therapy. Hormone levels could not be ruled out as a contributing factor.

Schagen *et al.* (1999) conducted a study in the Netherlands comparing 39 women who received surgery, radiation, and adjuvant chemotherapy (CMF) with 34 women who received surgery and radiation but did not receive any chemotherapy. Standard cognitive tests and interviews were used. The study concluded that women treated with CMF had a significantly higher risk (28%) for cognitive impairments when compared to the control group (12%).

In another study, Schagen *et al.* (2001) looked at neurophysiological effects of adjuvant high-dose chemotherapy on cognitive function. Neuropsychological assessments included quantitative electroencephalography and a standard battery of neuropsychological tests. Of the group that received high-dose chemotherapy, 32% were found to have cognitive changes; 17% of the standard chemotherapy dose group and 9% of the control group had cognitive changes. The study found subtle neurophysiological changes. This lends support for cognitive function being a complication of high-dose systemic therapy in breast cancer. More studies with a larger population are warranted.

Ahles *et al.* (2002) also found that women treated with chemotherapy scored lower on neuropsychological standard tests when compared to those treated with local radiation, particularly with verbal memory and psychomotor functioning.

Bender *et al.* (2001) believe that the cognitive deficits reported by breast cancer patients are similar to those reported by women experiencing menopause. Estrogen has positive effects on the body, including the brain, and the natural loss of hormones has been shown to have an effect on cognitive function. Some of the changes may be a result of a decrease in hormones after chemotherapy treatment.

Paganini-Hill and Clark (2000) support this theory. They believe that tamoxifen may have a negative effect on cognitive changes. Women who used tamoxifen for four to five years reported seeing their doctors for more memory-related problems when compared to nonusers. However, there was little difference between these women and nonusers on several cognitive tests.

Cognitive dysfunction is a group of symptoms that may or may not improve over time. Patient concerns should be acknowledged, and researchers should be encouraged to study these changes further.

NEUROSENSORY EFFECTS

Peripheral neuropathy has been defined by Wilkes (1996) as inflammation, injury, or degeneration of the peripheral nerve fibers. Chemotherapy, radiation therapy, and direct effects of the tumor on peripheral nerves can cause injury leading to peripheral neuropathy.

CHEMOTHERAPY-INDUCED PERIPHERAL NEUROPATHY

Most neuropathies occur several days to weeks after administration of the offending drug, but some can occur months to years after treatment is complete. The peripheral nervous system is made up of sensory and motor nerves. Motor nerves control movement and muscle control. Sensory nerves communicate about pain, temperature, and touch (small fibers), as well as position and vibration (large fibers). Both types send messages to the central nervous system. The symptoms of peripheral neuropathy are dependent upon which nerves have undergone damage. Peripheral nerves that are damaged can regenerate themselves as long as the damage does not include the cell body and occurs outside the spinal cord.

The risk factors for developing peripheral neuropathy include high-dose chemotherapy or cumulative doses of neurotoxic drugs, combination chemotherapy with several neurotoxic drugs, age greater than 60 years, concurrent use of neurotoxic drugs, previous radiation to spinal fields that resulted in neurological damage, and preexisting neuropathy resulting from diabetes mellitus, HIV, or certain B-vitamin deficiencies (Sweeney, 2002; Wilkes, 1996).

Paclitaxel is associated with peripheral neuropathy in women receiving treatment for breast cancer. Damage occurs primarily to the small nerve fibers that affect pain, temperature, and touch. Large fibers are also affected, causing a loss of deep tendon reflexes, fine motor movement, and muscle strength. The first symptom is often a tingling, burning, or numb feeling in the hands and feet that takes on a "stocking–glove" pattern. Symptoms may also include alterations in position sensation, deep tendon reflexes, leg muscle weakness, and loss of fine motor control, making daily tasks such as walking up stairs and buttoning clothing challenging. Symptoms may appear hours to days after the dose of paclitaxel and may take months to disappear once treatment is stopped.

Docetaxel has also been implicated in peripheral neuropathy, but to a lesser degree than paclitaxel. Hilkens *et al.* (1997) state that neuropathy may occur after treatment with cumulative doses over 600 mg/m². Although most cases are mild, several cases were severe when treated above this dose. Again, most symptoms improve over a period of weeks after the drug is discontinued.

The best defense against peripheral neuropathy is early detection, discontinuing the causative agent, and monitoring the outcome. Patients need to be educated about the early signs of peripheral neuropathy. In severe cases, symptoms may only partially resolve after treatment is stopped. Treatment, according to Smith *et al.* (2002), is usually for pain associated with the neuropathy. Several different medications are available to treat pain. (See Chapter 14 for more information on pain management.)

RADIATION-INDUCED PERIPHERAL TOXICITY

Large doses of radiation can cause changes in or fibrosis of the nerves. Brachial plexopathy is rare and may be caused by direct tumor infiltration of the brachial plexus nerve group or by fibrosis caused by radiation to the axilla and supraclavicular regions. Those most at risk are women who were treated decades ago and had larger radiation fields. With today's radiation techniques, fewer individuals are at risk for developing brachial plexopathy.

The brachial plexus is a group of nerves that extends from the lower cervical nerves to the first dorsal nerves and extends from the lower lateral neck to the axilla and supplies the upper arm, forearm, and hand. Damage can be either progressive or transient. It begins much like chemotherapy-induced peripheral neuropathy, with tingling and numbness in the fingers and weakness in the hands and arms. This can progress to paralysis. Diagnosis can often be difficult, and disease recurrence must be considered as a cause of symptoms.

Salner *et al.* (1981) describe a low incidence of reversible brachial plexopathy. In this report, 8 of 565 patients developed symptoms at a median time of 4.5 months after radiation therapy. Paresthesias developed in all patients with some instances of weakness and pain. In most patients, these symptoms eventually resolved.

Much of the information on brachial plexopathy has been garnered from European studies. Studies by Johansson and colleagues (Johansson, Svensson, & Denekamp, 2000, 2002; Johansson, Svensson, Larsson, & Denekamp, 2000) evaluated women who received treatment up to 30 years earlier and found several cases of paralysis. The damage is probably a result of fibrosis around the nerve trunks. Large daily radiation fractions and overlapping hot spots during treatment have caused these severe problems by delivering a dose to the brachial plexus that was not prescribed. Olsen *et al.* (1990) noted that radiation-induced brachial plexopathy was more common in women who received radiation and chemotherapy than in those who received chemotherapy alone, but the difference was not statistically significant. However, chemotherapy may increase the effects that radiation has on the nerve tissue. Fathers *et al.* (2002) looked at the natural history of 33 women who had brachial plexopathy and noted that symptoms were always progressive in patients, sometimes taking years for women to completely lose function of their arm. Pain was also common in these patients.

Treatment is usually directed at relieving pain (McGrath, 1992). Today, with specific attention to overlapping radiation fields, late effects of treatment can be minimized.

OCULAR TOXICITY

Ocular toxicity has been reported with use of tamoxifen, but this complication is rare. Mayfield and Gorin (1996) reported that changes include crystalline retinal deposits, macular edema, and corneal changes, as well as retinal lesions and macular edema with tamoxifen. Tang *et al.* (1997) studied the incidence of retinal changes and found it to be 0.9% (3 of 274 patients). All 3 patients were asymptomatic. In contrast, Noureddin *et al.* (1999) reported that the incidence of ocular toxicity was 12% (8 of 65 patients). Most often, keratopathy in the form of subepithelial deposits, whorls, and linear opacities was reported, all of which were reversible when tamoxifen was discontinued. One patient developed bilateral optic neuritis that led to a decrease in vision. It is important that patients be reminded to receive clinical eye examinations yearly to assess for these changes and to treat them while they are still reversible.

SECONDARY CANCERS

Contralateral breast cancer is a concern for women who have undergone breast irradiation. According to Lavey (1990), the contralateral breast is exposed to 5–10% of the dose prescribed. However, women who received surgery alone were at the greatest risk for developing a contralateral breast cancer. Adjuvant chemotherapy with or without radiation therapy was seen to decrease the risk for developing another breast cancer in the first 10 years after initial treatment.

Boice *et al.* (1992) studied 41,109 women with breast cancer and reported a 2.7% risk of developing breast cancer in the contralateral breast in women who had received previous radiation. This risk was greatest in women surviving 10 years or more, especially in those women initially diagnosed at ages younger than 45 years.

Several studies have shown that there is a small risk for developing sarcoma. Yap *et al.* (2002) state that radiotherapy for breast cancer is associated with an increased risk for sarcoma, but the risk is small. The most common type is angiosarcoma. Five-year survival for women who developed sarcoma after breast cancer was 27–35%. Rustemeyer *et al.* (1997) reported a case of mesenchymoma of the chest wall, but indicate that radiation-induced sarcoma is a very rare complication of treatment.

Several studies have made interesting connections between breast cancer and subsequent cancers. In Sweden, Prochazka *et al.* (2002) looked at a cohort of 141,000 women treated for breast cancer from 1958 to 1997. In that group 613 lung cancers developed. The risk for developing lung cancer increased 5 years after treatment. Risk for developing lung cancer on the same side as breast cancer was seen more than 10 years after initial diagnosis. They concluded that women with breast cancer have a significantly increased risk of developing a subsequent primary lung cancer because of a possible interaction between radiotherapy and smoking.

Custer *et al.* (2002) suspect a link between breast cancer and meningioma. Women who have experienced breast cancer have an increased risk of developing a meningioma, and women who have had a meningioma also have an increased risk of developing breast cancer.

Scholl *et al.* (2001) in Switzerland investigated esophageal cancer after treatment for breast cancer with radiotherapy. This secondary cancer tended to appear at least 10 years after initial treatment, and mean survival time was 14.2 months.

In spite of the risk for a secondary malignant neoplasm, the benefits of chemotherapy and radiation therapy for the treatment of breast cancer outweigh the risks. Secondary cancers may also result from other factors and behaviors.

There has been a link between breast cancer and ovarian cancer in women who have mutations of the BRCA1 and BRCA2 genes. Several studies looked at the increased risk for developing ovarian cancer in women who had breast cancer. Bergfeldt *et al.* (2002) saw an increased risk of developing ovarian cancer in women who had been diagnosed with breast cancer before the age of 40 years and had a family history of either breast or ovarian cancer. This risk also increased when the woman had a relative who was diagnosed with breast or ovarian cancer before the age of 50 years. Overall, women with a family history of ovarian cancer had about a 10% risk of developing ovarian cancer themselves by the age of 70 years. The authors recommended that these women be closely monitored for signs of ovarian cancer.

Claus *et al.* (1996) also looked at women with a family history of breast and ovarian cancer. The proportion of women who had a family history of either breast or ovarian cancer had early onset disease. Of women diagnosed in their 20s, 33% had breast cancer attributable to gene mutations, compared to 2% of women diagnosed in their 70s. Of women diagnosed with ovarian cancer in their 30s, 14% could attribute their cancer to a genetic mutation, compared to 7% of women diagnosed in their 50s. This information may help screen women with a family history more thoroughly because of the increased risk of developing both of these cancers with a BRCA1 or BRCA2 mutation.

OTHER LATE EFFECTS

HEMORRHAGIC CYSTITIS

Until several years ago, autologous bone and stem cell transplant was frequently used to treat and possibly cure women with metastatic breast cancer. This would have exposed women to large amounts of cyclophosphamide and ifosfomide during their preparative regimens and their transplant protocols. This would increase their risk of developing hemorrhagic cystitis. However, hemorrhagic cystitis as a complication is not usually seen today.

RIB FRACTURES

Rib fractures are rare and occur in the radiated field in approximately 1% of patients (O'Rourke & Robinson, 1996). This complication results from the ribs becoming weakened under the treated breast. Fractures will most likely occur when the patient sustains a traumatic injury to the weakened area. In most cases, it may be asymptomatic, or women will experience only a mild discomfort in the area. Overgaard (1988) saw an incidence of 19% of spontaneous rib fracture on chest radiograph in women who had been treated with a large dose per fraction of radiation in the late 1970s and a 6% incidence in those treated with the standard dose per fraction of radiation. Treatment includes mild analgesics and anti-inflammatory agents for discomfort.

SKIN CHANGES

Late skin changes can occur weeks to years after radiation therapy (Sitton, 1997). Changes can include dry skin, skin atrophy and fibrosis, pigmentation changes, telangiectasia, and skin necrosis. Sebaceous gland loss or decrease in function contributes to an increase in dry skin. Dry skin, in turn, can cause itching. Scratching or rubbing the area can cause more irritation and itching. Caring for radiated skin includes preventing further drying; using mild soap, warm instead of hot water, and moisturizing agents, applied when the skin is moist, may help. Atrophy and fibrosis may result from changes in the dermal fibrocytes. Skin fibrosis can lead to skin induration, edema, and a thickening of the overlying dermis and subcutaneous tissue. These changes may cause functional limitations and limited movement in the affected area. Pigmentation changes can also occur. Hypopigmentation is related to skin atrophy and loss of melanocytes in the irradiated area and can occur several years after treatment. Hyperpigmentation is related to telangiectasia, which occurs when surface dermal capillaries, venules, and lymphatic channels become dilated. They appear as prominent red vessels on the surface of the skin approximately one to two years after radiation. This, in turn, reduces the blood flow to area tissues, causing atrophy.

PATIENT EDUCATION ABOUT LATE EFFECTS

Patient education is an integral part of cancer treatment. From the moment of diagnosis to the end of treatment, education has been known to answer questions, calm fears, and give factual information to patients. With education during treatment, patients are prepared for side effects and are equipped to manage them. After treatment, education can inform the patient of possible long-term side effects that may occur because of treatment. Early warning signs of cardiac complications, pulmonary complications, lymphedema, and brachial plexopathy can be recognized by patients, and interventions for these issues can begin earlier. It is important for nurses to become familiar with long-term side effects that can occur with treatment and to educate their patients who are disease free and are looking forward to a healthy, cancer-free life.

REFERENCES

Abid, S.H., Malhotra, V., & Perry, M.C. (2001). Radiation-induced and chemotherapy-induced pulmonary injury. *Current Opinion in Oncology, 13,* 242–248.

Ahles, T.A., Saykin, A.J., Furstenberg, C.T., Cole, B., Mott, L.A., Skalla, K., Whedon, M.B., Bivens, S., Mitchell, T., Greenberg, E.R., & Silberfarb, P.M. (2002). Neuropsychologic impact of standard-dose systemic chemotherapy in long-term survivors of breast cancer and lymphoma. *Journal of Clinical Oncology, 20*(2), 485–493.

Allen, A. (1992). The cardiotoxicity of chemotherapeutic drugs. *Seminars in Oncology, 19*(5), 529–542.

Bender, C.M., Paraska, K.K., Sereika, S.M., Ryan, C.M., & Berga, S.L. (2001). Cognitive function and reproductive hormones in adjuvant therapy for breast cancer: a critical review. *Journal of Pain Symptom Management, 21*(5), 407–424.

Bergfeldt, K., Rydh, B., Granath, F., Gronberg, H., Thalib, L., Adami, H.O., & Ha, P. (2002). Risk of ovarian cancer in breast-cancer patients with a family history of breast or ovarian cancer: a population-based cohort study. *Lancet, 360*(9337), 891–894.

Boice, J.D. Jr., Harvey, E.B., Blettner, M., Stovall, M., & Flannery, J.T. (1992). Cancer in the contralateral breast after radiotherapy for breast cancer. *New England Journal of Medicine, 326*(12), 781–785.

Brockstein, B.E., Smiley, C., Al-Sadir, J., & Williams, S.F. (2000). Cardiac and pulmonary toxicity in patients undergoing high-dose chemotherapy for lymphoma and breast cancer: prognostic factors. *Bone Marrow Transplant, 25*(8), 885–894.

Chung, C.T., Bogart, J.A., Adams, J.F., Sagerman, R.H., Numann, P.J., Tassiopoulos, A., & Duggan, D.B. (1997). Increased risk of breast cancer in splenectomized patients undergoing radiation therapy for Hodgkin's disease. *International Journal of Radiation Oncology, Biology, Physics, 37*(2), 405–409.

Cimprich, B. (1992). Attentional fatigue following breast cancer surgery. *Research in Nursing and Health, 15*(3), 199–207.

Cimprich, B. (2001). Attention and symptom distress in women with and without breast cancer. *Nursing Research, 50*(2), 86–94

Claus, E.B., Schildkraut, J.M., Thompson, W.D., & Risch, N.J. (1996). The genetic attributable risk of breast and ovarian cancer. *Cancer, 77*(11), 2318–2324.

Clemons, M., Loijens, L., & Goss, P. (2000). Breast cancer risk following irradiation for Hodgkin's disease. *Cancer Treatment Reviews, 26*(4), 291–302.

Cushman, M., Costantino, J.P., Tracy, R.P., Song, K., Buckley, L., Roberts, J.D., & Krag, D.N. (2001). Tamoxifen and cardiac risk factors in healthy women: suggestion of an anti-inflammatory effect. *Arteriosclerosis, Thrombosis, and Vascular Biology, 21*(2), 255–261.

Custer, B.S., Koepsell, T.D., & Mueller, B.A. (2002). The association between breast carcinoma and meningioma in women. *Cancer, 94*(6), 1626–1635.

de Jong, N., Coyrtens, A.M., Abu-Saad, H.H., & Schouten, H.C. (2002). Fatigue in patients with breast cancer receiving adjuvant chemotherapy: a review of the literature. *Cancer Nursing, 25*(4), 283–297.

Deutsch, M., Gerszten, K., Bloomer, W.D., & Avistar, E. (2001). Lumpectomy and breast irradiation for breast cancer arising after previous radiotherapy for Hodgkin's disease or lymphoma. *American Journal of Clinical Oncology, 24*(1), 33–34.

Diller, L., Medeiros Nancarrow C., Shaffer, K., Matulonis, U., Mauch, P., Neuberg, D., Tarbell, N.J., Litman, H., & Garber, J. (2002). Breast cancer screening in women previously treated for Hodgkin's disease: a prospective cohort study. *Journal of Clinical Oncology, 20*(8), 2085–2091.

Doroshow, J.H. (1991). Doxorubicin-induced cardiotoxicity. *New England Journal of Medicine, 324*(12), 343–345.

Dorr, R.T. (1998). Radioprotectants: pharmacology and clinical applications of amifostine. *Seminars in Radiation Oncology, 8*(4), 10–13.

Fathers, E., Thrush, D., Huson, S.M., & Norman, A. (2002). Radiation-induced brachial plexopathy in women treated for carcinoma of the breast. *Clinical Rehabilitation, 16*(2), 160–165.

Frankel, C. (2000). Development and clinical overview of trastuzumab (herceptin). *Seminars in Oncology Nursing, 16*(4), 13–17.

Fristoe, B. (1998). Long-term cardiac and pulmonary complications in cancer care. *Nurse Practitioner Forum, 9*(3), 177–184.

Gagliardi, G., Lax, I., & Rutqvist, L.E. (2001). Partial irradiation of the heart. *Seminars in Radiation Oncology, 11*(3), 224–233.

Hensley, M.L., Schuchter, L.M., Lindley, C., Meropol, N.J., Cohen, G.I., Broder, G., Gradishar, W.J., Green, D.M., Langdon, R.J. Jr., Mitchell, R.B., Negrin, R., Szatrowski, T.P., Thigpen, J.T., Von Hoff, D., Wasserman, T.H., Winer, E.P., & Pfister, D.G. (1999). American Society of Clinical Oncology clinical practice guidelines for the use of chemotherapy and radiotherapy protectants. *Journal of Clinical Oncology, 17*(10), 3333–3355.

Hilkens, P.H.E., Vecht, C.J., Stoter, G., & van den Bent, M.J. (1997). Clinical characteristics of severe peripheral neuropathy induced by docetaxel (Taxotere). *Annals of Oncology, 8,* 1–4.

Hochster, H., Wasserheit, C., & Speyer, J. (1995). Cardiotoxicity and cardioprotection during chemotherapy. *Current Opinion in Oncology, 7,* 304–309.

Hortobagyi, G.N., Frye, D., Buzdar, A.U., Ewer, M.S., Fraschini, G., Hug, V., Ames, F., Montague, E., Carrasco, C.H., & Mackay, B. (1989). Decreased cardiotoxicity of doxorubicin administered by continuous intravenous infusion in combination chemotherapy for metastatic breast carcinoma. *Cancer, 63*(1), 37–45.

Johansson, S., Svensson, H., & Denekamp, J. (2000). Timescale of evolution of late radiation injury after postoperative radiotherapy of breast cancer patients. *International Journal of Radiation Oncology, Biology, Physics, 48*(3), 745–750.

Johansson, S., Svensson, H., & Denekamp, J. (2002). Dose response and latency for radiation-induced fibrosis, edema, and neuropathy in breast cancer patients. *International Journal of Radiation Oncology, Biology, Physics, 52*(5), 1207–1219.

Johansson, S., Svensson, H., Larsson, L.G., & Denekamp, J. (2000). Brachial plexopathy after postoperative radiotherapy of breast cancer patients—a long-term follow-up. *Acta Oncologica, 39*(3), 373–382.

Lavey, R.S. (1990). Acute nonlymphocytic leukemia after radiation and MOPP chemotherapy for Hodgkin's disease. *Journal of Clinical Oncology, 8*(12), 2089–2090.

Mast, M.E. (1998). Correlates of fatigue in survivors of breast cancer. *Cancer Nursing, 21*(2), 136–142.

Mayfield, S.G., & Gorin, M.B. (1996). Tamoxifen-associated eye disease. A review. *Journal of Clinical Oncology, 14*(3), 1018–1026.

McDonald, S., Garrow, G.C., & Rubin, P. (2000). Pulmonary complications. In M.D. Abeloff, J.O. Armitage, A.S. Lichter, & J.E. Niederhuber (Eds.), *Clinical oncology,* pp. 1023–1046. New York: Churchill Livingstone.

McGrath, E.B. (1992). Myelopathy, brachial plexopathy and osteoradionecrosis. In K.H. Dow & L.J. Hilderley (Eds.), *Nursing care in radiation oncology,* pp. 334–341. Philadelphia: W.B. Saunders.

Muren, L.P., Maurstad, G., Hafslund, R., Anker, G., & Dahl, O. (2002). Cardiac and pulmonary doses and complication probabilities in standard and conformal tangential irradiation in conservative management of breast cancer. *Radiotherapy in Oncology, 62*(2), 173–183.

Nail, L. (2001). Long-term persistence of symptoms. *Seminars in Oncology Nursing, 17*(4), 249–254.

Noureddin, B.N., Seoud, M., Bashshur, Z., Salem, Z., Shamseddin, A., & Khalil, A. (1999). Ocular toxicity in low-dose tamoxifen: a prospective study. *Eye, 13*(Pt 6), 729–733.

Olin, J.J. (2001). Cognitive function after systemic therapy for breast cancer. *Oncology, 15*(5), 613–618.

Olsen, N.K., Pfeiffer, P., Mondrup, K., & Rose, C. (1990). Radiation-induced brachial plexus neuropathy in breast cancer patients. *Acta Oncologica, 29*(7), 885–890.

O'Rourke, N., & Robinson, L.M.P. (1996). Breast cancer and the role of radiation therapy. In K.H. Dow (Ed.), *Contemporary issues in breast cancer,* pp. 43–58. Sudbury, Mass.: Jones & Bartlett.

Overgaard, M. (1988). Spontaneous radiation-induced rib fractures in breast cancer patients treated with postmastectomy irradiation. A clinical radiobiological analysis of the influence of fraction size and dose-response relationships on late bone damage. *Acta Oncologica, 27*(2), 117–122.

Paganini-Hill, A., & Clark, L.J. (2000). Preliminary assessment of cognitive function in breast cancer patients treated with tamoxifen. *Breast Cancer Research and Treatment, 64*(2), 165–176.

Perez, E.A. (2001). Doxorubicin and paclitaxel in the treatment of advanced breast cancer: efficacy and cardiac considerations. *Cancer Investigation, 19*(2), 155–164.

Prochazka, M., Granath, F., Ekbom, A., Shields, P.G., & Hall, P. (2002). Lung cancer risks in women with previous breast cancer. *European Journal of Cancer, 38*(11), 1520–1525.

Reis, S.E., Costantino, J.P., Wickerham, D.L., Tan-Chiu, E., Wang, J., & Kavanah, M. (2001). Cardiovascular effects of tamoxifen in women with and without heart disease: breast cancer prevention trial. *Journal of the National Cancer Institute, 93,* 16–21.

Rustemeyer, P., Micke, O., Blasius, S., & Peters, S.E. (1997). Radiation-induced malignant mesenchymoma of the chest wall following treatment for breast cancer. *British Journal of Radiology, 70*(832) 424–426.

Salner, A.L., Botnick, L.E., Herzog, A.G., Goldstein, M.A., Harris, J.R., Levene, M.B., & Hellman, S. (1981). Reversible brachial plexopathy following primary radiation therapy for breast cancer. *Cancer Treatment Reports, 65*(9–10), 797–802.

Schagen, S.B., Hamburger, H.L., Muller, M.J., Boogerd, W., & van Dam, F.S. (2001). Neurophysiological evaluation of late effects of adjuvant high-dose chemotherapy on cognitive function. *Journal of Neurooncology, 51*(2), 159–165.

Schagen, S.B., van Dam, F.S., Muller, M.J., Boogerd, W., Lindeboom, J., & Bruning, P.F. (1999). Cognitive deficits after postoperative adjuvant chemotherapy for breast carcinoma. *Cancer, 85*(3), 640–650.

Schneider, J.W., Chang, A.Y., & Garratt, A. (2002). Trastuzumab cardiotoxicity: speculations regarding pathophysiology and targets for further study. *Seminars in Oncology, 29*(3 Suppl 11), 22–28.

Scholl, B., Reis, E.D., Zouhair, A., Chereshnev, I., Givel, J.C., & Gillet, M. (2001). Esophageal cancer as second primary tumor after breast cancer radiotherapy. *American Journal of Surgery, 182*(5), 476–480.

Schwonzen, M., Kurbacher, C.M., & Mallmann, P. (2000). Liposomal doxorubicin and weekly paclitaxel in the treatment of metastatic breast cancer. *Anticancer Drugs, 11*(9), 681–685.

Seidman, A., Hudis, C., Pierri, M.K., Shak, S., Paton, V., Ashby, M., Murphy, M., Stewart, S.J., & Keefe, D. (2002). Cardiac dysfunction in the trastuzumab clinical trials experience. *Journal of Clinical Oncology, 20*(5), 1215–1221.

Seymour, L., Bramwell, V., & Moran, L.A. (1999). Use of dexrazoxane as a cardioprotectant in patients receiving doxorubicin or epirubicin chemotherapy for the treatment of cancer. The Provincial Systemic Treatment Disease Site Group. *Cancer Prevention and Control, 3*(2), 145–159.

Shan, K., Lincoff, A.M., & Young, J.B. (1996). Anthracycline-induced cardiotoxicity. *Annals of Internal Medicine, 125*(1), 47–58.

Sitton, E. (1997). Managing side effects of skin changes and fatigue. In K.H. Dow., J.D. Bucholtz, R. Iwamoto, V. Fieler, & L. Hilderley (Eds.), *Nursing care in radiation oncology, 2nd Ed.,* pp. 79–100. Philadelphia: W.B. Saunders.

Smith, E.L., Whedon, M.B., & Bookbinder, M. (2002). Quality improvement of painful peripheral neuropathy. *Seminars in Oncology, 18*(1), 36–43.

Sparano, J.A. (1999). Doxorubicin/taxane combinations: cardiotoxicity and pharmacokinetics. *Seminars in Oncology, 26*(3 Suppl 9), 14–19.

Speyer, J.L., & Freedberg, R.S. (2000). Cardiac complications. In M.D. Abeloff, J.O. Armitage, A.S. Lichter, & J.E. Niederhuber (Eds.), *Clinical oncology,* pp. 1047–1060. New York: Churchill Livingstone.

Steinherz, L.J., Steinherz, P.G., Tan, C.T.C., Heller, G., & Murphy, L.M. (1991). Cardiac toxicity 4 to 20 years after completing anthracycline therapy. *Journal of the American Medical Association, 266*(12), 1670–1677.

Sweeney, C.W. (2002). Understanding peripheral neuropathy in patients with cancer: background and patient assessment. *Clinical Journal of Oncology Nursing, 6*(3), 163–166.

Taghian, A.G., Assaad, S.I., Niemierko, A., Kuter, I., Younger, J., Schoenthaler, R., Roche, M., & Powell, S.N. (2001). Risk of pneumonitis in breast cancer patients treated with radiation therapy and combination chemotherapy with paclitaxel. *Journal of the National Cancer Institute, 93*(23), 1806–1811.

Tang, R., Shields, J., Schiffman, J., Li, H., Locher, D., Hampton, J., Prager, T., & Pardo, G. (1997). Retinal changes associated with tamoxifen treatment for breast cancer. *Eye, 11*(Pt 3), 295–297.

Tham, Y.L., Verani, M.S., & Chang, J. (2002). Reversible and irreversible cardiac dysfunction associated with trastuzumab in breast cancer. *Breast Cancer Research and Treatment, 74*(2), 131–134.

Valero, V., Perez, E., & Dieras, V. (2001). Doxorubicin and taxane combination regimens for metastatic breast cancer: focus on cardiac effects. *Seminars in Oncology, 28*(4 Suppl 12), 15–23.

van Dam, F.S., Schagen, S.B., Muller, M.J., Boogerd, W., vd Wall, E., Droogleever Fortuyn, M.E., & Rodenhuis, S. (1998). Impairment of cognitive function in women receiving adjuvant treatment for high-risk breast cancer: high-dose versus standard-dose chemotherapy. *Journal of the National Cancer Institute, 90*(3), 210–218.

Von Hoff, D.D., Layard, M.W., Basa, P., Davis, H.L. Jr., Von Hoff, A.L., Rozencweig, M., & Muggia, F.M. (1979). Risk factors for doxorubicin-induced congestive heart failure. *Annals of Internal Medicine, 91*(5). 710–717.

Vujaskovic, Z., Feng, Q.F., Rabbani, Z.N., Anscher, M.S., Samulski, T.V., & Brizel, D.M. (2002). Radioprotection of lungs by amifostine is associated with reduction in profibrogenic cytokine activity. *Radiation Research, 157*(6), 656–660.

Wasserman T. (1999). Radioprotective effects of amifostine. *Seminars in Oncology, 26*(2 Suppl 7), 89–94.

Wasserman, T.H., & Brizel, D.M. (2001). The role of amifostine as a radioprotector. *Oncology, 15*(10), 1349–1354

Wieneke, M.H., & Dienst, E.R. (1995). Neuropsychological assessment of cognitive functioning following chemotherapy for breast cancer. *Psycho-Oncology, 4,* 61–66.

Wilczynski, S.W., Erasmus, J.J., Petros, W.P., Vredenburgh, J.J., & Folz, R.J. (1998). Delayed pulmonary toxicity syndrome following high-dose chemotherapy and bone marrow transplantation for breast cancer. *American Journal of Respiratory and Critical Care Medicine, 157*(2), 565–573.

Wilkes, G.M. (1996). Neurological disturbances. In S.L. Groenwald, M.H. Frogge, M. Goodman, & C.H. Yarbro (Eds.), *Cancer symptom management,* pp. 324–362. Sudbury, Mass.: Jones & Bartlett.

Wiseman, L.R., & Spencer, C.M. (1998). Dexrazoxane. A review of its use as a cardioprotective agent in patients receiving anthracycline-based chemotherapy. *Drugs, 56*(3), 385–403.

Yap, J., Chuba, P.J., Aref, A., Severson, L.D., & Hamre, M. (2002). Sarcoma as a second malignancy after treatment for breast cancer. *International Journal of Oncology, Biology, Physics, 52*(5), 1231–1237.

Section V

CULTURE AND ETHNICITY

Chapter 18

AFRICAN AMERICAN WOMEN AND BREAST CANCER

JANICE PHILLIPS, PHD, RN, FAAN
EVA SMITH, PHD, RN

INTRODUCTION

Despite the advancements in breast cancer detection and treatment, African American women are more likely to die from the disease. Similarly, African American women continue to show considerable disparity with regard to survival. Thus, this chapter provides an overview on breast cancer and African American women with a special emphasis on cultural and sociocultural determinants of breast cancer screening and detection. The chapter concludes with a discussion of future directions for improving the breast cancer profile for this population.

BREAST CANCER INCIDENCE

The number of new invasive cases of breast cancer that will be diagnosed in the United States in 2003 is projected to be 211,300, and the number of new in situ breast cancer cases that will be diagnosed is 55,700 (American Cancer Society [ACS], 2003). Overall, between 1992 and 1998, Caucasian women had the highest incidence rate of breast cancer, 115.5 cases per 100,000, among all ethnic groups (African American women = 101.5/100,000; Asian/Pacific Islander women = 78.1/100,000; Hispanic women = 68.5/100,000; and Native American women = 50.5/100,000). Between 1992 and 1998, epidemiologists report that incidence rates remained relatively stable among women of all racial and ethnic groups. For African American women, breast cancer is the most common cancer. Although the incidence rate for African American women is approximately 13% lower than the rate for white women (ACS, 2001), with the exception of African American women ages 20–24 years, African American women under age 40 years have a higher incidence of breast cancer when compared to whites (ACS, 2002).

BREAST CANCER MORTALITY

Although breast cancer is the second leading cause of cancer death in American women, it is the leading cancer for African American women. African American women have a 33% greater risk of dying from the disease than white women (Shinagawa, 2000). Epidemiologists estimate that in 2003, 40,200 deaths (39,800 women, 400 men) will be attributed to breast cancer (ACS, 2003). During 1992–1998, the highest age-adjusted mortality rate occurred among African American women (31.0 per 100,000 cases) followed by white women (24.3 per 100,000 cases), Hispanic women (14.8 per 100,000 cases), Native American women (12.4 per 100,000 cases), and Asian/Pacific Islander women (11.0 per 100,000 cases). The late 1980s and the 1990s witnessed reductions in breast cancer mortality, with the greatest declines seen among white women during the 1990s. The recent declines in breast cancer mortality are in part a result of improvements in breast cancer treatments and increased use of mammography screening (ACS, 2002). Although breast cancer death rates have declined in recent years, African American women continue to experience death rates that are approximately 28% higher than those of their white counterparts (ACS, 2001).

BREAST CANCER SURVIVAL

Similar to mortality rates, African American women continue to show considerable disparity in survival outcomes when compared with white women (Newman *et al.,* 2002). For example, African American women diagnosed with breast cancer are less likely than white women to survive for 5 years (73% vs. 87%, respectively). Currently, relative survival rates for women diagnosed with breast cancer are 86% at 5 years after diagnosis, 76% after 10 years, 58% after 15 years, and 53% after 20 years. When looking at 5-year relative survival rates, 81% of white women and 76% of African American women are expected to survive an additional 5 years. Similarly, 10 years after diagnosis, 87% of white women and 85% of African American women are expected to survive an additional 5 years (ACS, 2002b).

In the comprehensive study of the survival of African American and white women with breast cancer, Eley *et al.* (1994) examined the impact of sociodemographics, behavior, prognostics, health care access, and stage at diagnosis of breast cancer on the survival of 612 African American and 518 white women ages 20–79 years diagnosed with breast cancer. They concluded that 75% of the racial difference in survival between the two groups resulted from the stage at detection, tumor characteristics, and the presence of other illnesses and sociodemographic factors. These researchers found that approximately 30% of African American women presented with stage III or stage IV disease, compared to 18% of white women. An additional 15% of the variance resulted from histologic/pathologic differences. African American women were noted to have tumors that were poorly differentiated and estrogen receptor-negative, both of which are related to a poorer response to treatment.

Finally, an additional 18% of the difference in survival resulted from the extent of comorbid illnesses and a variety of sociodemographic factors. Compared to white women, African American women were found to have higher body mass indices, a higher rate of cigarette smoking, and a lower rate of available or adequate health insurance. Eley *et al.* (1994) concluded that the poor access to health care, often associated with low socioeconomic status, influenced the late stage of disease for African American women.

Similar findings were reported for younger African American women diagnosed with breast cancer. Surveillance Epidemiology and End Results (SEER) Program data were examined to assess the outcomes for African American and white breast cancer patients in metropolitan Detroit between 1990 and 1999 (Newman *et al.*, 2002). Data were specifically analyzed for stage of disease at presentation, primary tumor size, estrogen receptor status, progesterone status, and tumor histology in women diagnosed with breast cancer before age 40 years. Women younger that 40 years old were particularly selected because age 40 years represents the age interval characterized by the crossover in ethnicity-related variation in breast cancer. African American women younger than 40 years have a higher incidence of breast cancer when compared with white women (64 cases per 100,000 vs. 57 per 100,000, respectively).

Newman *et al.* (2002) found that African American patients had larger mean tumor sizes, lower rates of localized disease, higher rates of estrogen receptor negativity, and higher proportions of medullary tumors. African American women were noted to have significantly greater risk of death at every stage of diagnosis when compared with whites. The researchers highlighted the need for additional research to more clearly identify the influence of genetic, environmental, and hormonal factors on tumor biology in younger African American women.

Notably, women of low socioeconomic status have lower five-year relative survival rates than higher-income patients. Low-income African American women are three times more likely than higher-income African American women to be diagnosed with advanced stage breast cancer (ACS, 2002b). This is of significance given that African Americans are disproportionately represented among the socioeconomically disadvantaged. Data from the Census Bureau revealed that in 2000, the poverty rate for African American women was 22.1%, followed by 21.2% for Hispanics, 10.8% for Asian and Pacific Islanders, 9.4% for whites, and 7.5% for white non-Hispanics (Dalaker, 2001).

BREAST CANCER SCREENING AND DETECTION

Current efforts to reduce breast cancer mortality focus primarily on early detection. Numerous organizations and leading authorities support the use of one or more breast cancer screening measures: breast self-examination (BSE), clinical breast examination (CBE), and mammography. Specifically, the ACS recommends for women ages 20–39 years a monthly BSE examination and CBE every three years; at age 40 years and older the recommendation includes a monthly BSE and an annual CBE and mammogram (ACS, 2002a).

Recognizing the disparity in breast cancer outcomes among African American women, the landmark document *Healthy People 2000: National Promotion and Disease Prevention* identified explicit breast cancer screening targets for this population (Department of Health and Human Services [HHS], 1991). In the year 2000, the objective of increasing mammography screening to at least 60% of African American women age 50 years and older who had received a mammogram and CBE within the preceding two years was achieved. This represents an increase from the target goal of 43% in 1990, thus narrowing the gap in disparity for African Americans (National Center for Health Statistics, 2001). In 1998, 66% of African American women age 40 years and older received a mammogram within the two preceding years. The goal for 2010 is to increase the proportion of women age 40 years and older who have received a mammogram within the preceding two years to 70% (HHS, 2000).

Some of the progress in achieving the Healthy People 2000 objectives for breast cancer can be attributed, in part, to the success of the Centers for Disease Control and Prevention's National Breast and Cervical Cancer Early Detection Program (NBCCEDP) in increasing cancer screening rates among racial and ethnic minority women and the medically underserved. Established in 1990 in response to the Breast and Cervical Cancer Mortality Prevention Act, the NBCCEDP is devoted to improving the breast and cervical cancer outcomes of ethnic and racial minority and underserved women. This federally funded program provides screening and diagnostic services that include CBEs, mammograms, Pap tests, surgical consultations, and diagnostic testing for women with abnormal findings. Since its inception 12 years ago, the program is now available in 50 U.S. states, 6 U.S. territories, the District of Columbia, and 14 American and Alaska Native organizations. The NBCCEDP is responsible for screening over 15 million racial and ethnic minority and underserved women. Between 1991 and 1999, 17% of African American participants received a mammogram, compared to 52% of white, 20% of Hispanic, 6% of American and Alaska Native, and 3% of Asian and Pacific Islander women (National Center for Chronic Disease and Health Promotion, 2000).

SOCIOCULTURAL INFLUENCES ACROSS THE BREAST CANCER CONTINUUM

Although numerous studies and reports highlight the need for accessible and affordable breast cancer-related services in increasing breast cancer screening rates (Facione, 1999; Klassen *et al.,* 2002; Qureshi *et al.,* 2000), other investigators stress the importance of a number of sociocultural factors when addressing breast cancer screening behaviors and needs of African American women. Shi and Singh (2001) identified four categories of factors that affect health outcomes: (1) a person's genetic composition, (2) individual behaviors, (3) medical practices, and (4) the environment. Although all four factors are interrelated, this discussion will primarily focus on the sociocultural components of the environmental and individual factors that are documented as significantly impacting health outcomes.

Culture is viewed as a major factor that influences health outcomes. The concept of culture is a very expansive one and is sometimes used interchangeably with ethnicity. Culture represents a map that enables us to make sense of the unpredictability of life by giving us rules and directions for life. Cultural beliefs and values determine how health and illness are perceived and defined and how health care decisions are made (Buchwald *et al.,* 1994; Kagawa-Singer, 1987; Kagawa-Singer *et al.,* 1997). Although African American women are perceived as a unified group, many differences in beliefs and values exist among them. Cultural differences may be influenced by geographical residence, socioeconomic status, generational differences, acculturation, and assimilation (Iwamoto, 1994).

Culture-related attitudes frequently associated with African Americans and early detection practices are fear and fatalism (Phillips *et al.,* 1999; Powe, 1996; Powe & Johnson, 1995). Fatalism is defined by Powe (1996) as a complex psychological phenomenon that is characterized by perceptions of hopelessness, worthlessness, meaninglessness, powerlessness, and social despair. Powe states that cancer fatalism represents the uncompromising surrender of the human spirit to forces beyond oneself that destroy human personality, potential hope, and life. Because fatalism can immobilize a person, it is a barrier to cancer care (Phillips *et al.,* 1999; Powe & Johnson, 1995). Behaviors that affect breast cancer early detection in African American women are silence, "I won't claim it" or denial, and mistrust. Phillips *et al.,* (1999) state that silence is a barrier to breast cancer early detection because it inhibits women from sharing and seeking information valuable for decision-making. In our qualitative study (Smith *et al.,* 2000), professional African American women reported that although silence was a way of life, they nevertheless valued sharing of information. "I won't claim it" or denial is a tendency to think, "If I do not accept breast cancer as a disease, I will not contract breast cancer" (Phillips *et al.,* 1999). It becomes problematic when denial leads to decreased participation in early detection activities. Mistrust is an attitude that is increasingly being recognized as a factor that affects mammography screening practices (Gamble, 1993).

Many predictors of screening practices have been identified. Of the three early detection screening practices (BSE, CBE, and mammography screening), mammography screening is viewed as the most effective because it is the most sensitive and can detect a tumor or cancer at a much earlier stage than the other two methods can (Breen & Kessler, 1994; Moormeier, 1996; Shapiro *et al.,* 1982). Smith *et al.* (2001) grouped sociocultural predictors into three categories: (1) cultural beliefs and attitudes, (2) personal characteristics, and (3) health provider and system-related factors.

Cultural beliefs and attitudes and personal predictors of mammography screening behaviors include: attitudes and beliefs concerning breast cancer (Black *et al.,* 2001; Mandelblatt *et al.,* 1999; Dibbles *et al.,* 1997; Miller & Champion, 1997; Miller & Hailey, 1994; Sung *et al.,* 1997); knowledge (McDonald *et al.,* 1999; Price, 1994); previous mammography and/or BSE screening (Phillips *et al.,* 1998; Price, 1994; Bloom *et al.,* 1991; Holm *et al.,* 1999; Frazier *et al.,* 1996); regular source of care (McDonald *et al.,* 1999; Price, 1994); level of comfort (Dibbles *et al.,* 1997; McDonald *et al.,* 1999; Price, 1994);

perception of being at risk (Frazier *et al.*, 1996; Yancy & Walden, 1994; Hughes *et al.*, 1996); education (Phillips *et al.*, 1998; Miller & Champion, 1997); and age (Phillips *et al.*, 1998; Black *et al.*, 2001; Strzelczyk & Dignan, 2002).

System-related predictors include doctor recommendation (Miller & Hailey, 1994); convenience of screening time and location (Phillips *et al.*, 1998; Skinner *et al.*, 1995); income and/or insurance (Mandelblatt *et al.*, 1999; Phillips *et al.*, 1998; Miller & Champion, 1997; Miller & Hailey, 1994; Sung *et al.*, 1997); and access to care (Miller & Champion, 1997; Miller & Hailey, 1994; Sung *et al.*, 1997).

Wingood and Keltner (1999) underscored that in order to develop more effective prevention programs, sociocultural factors must be identified, understood, and appropriately incorporated when targeting racial and ethnic minority populations. When discussing the influence of culture on breast cancer screening and detection, Facione and Katapodi (2000) suggested that the influence of poverty and lack of education account for much of what is termed cultural. The maximum effect of screening practices results from adherence to recommended guidelines, such as those from the American Cancer Society (ACS, 2002b). Interventions identified as being effective in promoting mammography screening adherence among African American women are community-based; used innovative delivery methods; used natural helpers; were based on theory (Hiatt *et al.*, 2001; Mann *et al.*, 2000; Paskett *et al.*, 1996; Yabroff & Mandelblatt, 1999; Rakowski *et al.*, 1998); were tailored to the individual or group (Ryan *et al.*, 2001, Rakowski *et al.*, 1998; Campbell *et al.*, 2000; Champion & Huster, 1995); used multiple strategies (Campbell *et al.*, 2000); were interactive (Agre *et al.*, 2002); and were culturally sensitive (Erwin *et al.*, 1996; Paskett *et al.*, 1996).

The beauty shop is emerging as a community-based setting that is effective in promoting adherence to screening practices (Forte, 1995; Hendricks, 2000). The African American church has also emerged as an important setting for health promotion activities (Fox *et al.*, 1998; Smith *et al.*, 1997) and has been used successfully for breast cancer early detection interventions (Fox *et al.*, 1998).

Although research findings in this area have been mixed, increasingly researchers are beginning to explore the role of spirituality and religiosity when examining the breast cancer screening and detection behaviors of African American women. Research in this area is particularly important given that African American women often share a rich spiritual heritage. African American women frequently embrace their spirituality and/or religiosity when coping with the many demands of daily living. Spiritual and/or religious connectedness has traditionally been a major component of the health and well-being of the African American community. Although the terms are sometimes used interchangeably, a distinction between spirituality and religiosity is warranted.

Musgrove *et al.*, (2002) believe that a traditional definition of spirituality is more appropriate for women of color. More specifically, these authors define spirituality as one's acknowledgment of and relationship with a supreme being, a basic and inherent character in all humans. In contrast, religiosity can be viewed as one's behavior—one's religious practices or participation in religious activities. Thus, an individual can be spiritual without being religious and vice versa. Collectively or independently, these concepts provide an underpinning with which to cope with the world and with life.

To illustrate, in a phenomenological study of 23 low- and middle-income women, Phillips *et al.* (2001) reported that spiritual beliefs either increased or decreased one's breast cancer screening behaviors. In this study, spirituality emerged as a major concept in shaping participant's beliefs and practices. The belief that one's body is God's temple was viewed as a motivating factor in promoting breast cancer screening among some study participants. In contrast, other participants took less action, leaving their fate in the hands of God in the event that they would contract breast cancer.

In another study (Kinney *et al.*, 2002), the relationship between beliefs about God and adherence to breast cancer screening among high-risk African American women was examined. The authors used the God Locus of Health Control (GLHC) Scale to measure beliefs in God as a controlling agent over one's health. Findings indicated a negative association between GLHC and adherence to CBE and mammography. Thus, a strong belief in God as a controlling agent over one's health was negatively associated with breast cancer screening. The investigators emphasized the need to incorporate aspects related to spirituality in further assessments and educational and research endeavors targeting this population.

There are, however, some favorable results highlighting the role of spirituality in enhancing breast cancer screening. The Witness Project® is one example of a culturally sensitive community-based program that has successfully incorporated spirituality and faith in interventions targeting African American women (Erwin, 2002; Erwin *et al.*, 1999). A part of the Witness Project® was the successful partnering with the faith community and outreach activities of African American women with breast cancer. This project is credited with reaching over 1400 African American women nationwide over the past two decades. African American breast cancer survivors, referred to in the Witness Project® as role models, integrate aspects related to culture, spirituality, and faith when delivering breast and cervical cancer educational interventions to African American women age 40 years and older. In addition to partnering with the faith community, Witness Project® role models have successfully shared personal testimonies, experiences, knowledge, support, and resources when delivering health education messages. This program has positively influenced the breast cancer screening behaviors among rural and urban underserved African American women.

When evaluating the outcomes of the Witness Project® baseline, 6-month assessments were collected from 410 African American women (206 intervention, 204 control). Findings revealed that project participants significantly increased their practice of breast examination and mammography screening, compared with women in the control group. The researchers acknowledged that their educational intervention is time, resource, and labor intensive; however, they also emphasize the value of incorporating the faith community and cancer survivors as significant components for increasing the breast cancer screening behaviors of African American women (Erwin, 2002; Erwin *et al.*, 1999).

AFRICAN AMERICAN WOMEN AND BREAST CANCER SURVIVAL

The body of literature highlighting the influence of sociocultural factors on the breast cancer screening and detection behaviors of African American women has grown considerably during the last decade. In contrast, the body of literature related to breast cancer and survivorship experiences of African American women diagnosed with breast cancer is still in the infancy stage. Although an in-depth discussion of these findings is beyond the scope of this chapter, a brief discussion of selected research for these two areas is presented here. With governmental and private agencies emphasis on disparities in breast cancer outcomes, studies on survivorship and African American women are beginning to emerge in the literature. Data indicate the survival rates for African American women have remained rather constant (Shinagawa, 2000) or have increased (Brown, 2000) over the last 15 years; however, the number of African American women survivors is increasing. Two thirds of African American women diagnosed with breast cancer are expected to survive at least five years (Brown, 2000). Therefore, for a large population of African American women living with breast cancer, health care providers have little information about their issues and concerns and may not be providing appropriate interventions. There is a need to expand the studies on survivorship and African American women (Johnson & Smith, 2002; Aziz & Rowland, 2002). Studies conducted by Ashing-Giwa *et al.* (1999), Moore (2001), and Wilmoth and Sanders (2001) are among the few studies that address a holistic perspective on life after a diagnosis with breast cancer for African American women. Others (Moore & Spiegel, 2000) address how African American women are coping with a specific problem related to living with a diagnosis of breast cancer.

Ashing-Giwa *et al.,* (1999) used a mailed survey to explore the quality of life (QOL) of a sample of 278 middle-class women (117 African American and 161 white) who were cancer survivors. They concluded that women in their sample reported a "fairly good" QOL, with problems expressed only in the area of sexuality. With univariate analyses there were some differences between the two ethnic groups. However, with multivariate analyses no differences were found. Socioeconomics, life stress, comorbidity, and living situation were the most important influences on QOL. Compared to women with low QOL, women with the highest QOL had better discernment of health, lower life stress, a partner, higher incomes, higher educational achievement, and fewer comorbidities, and they did not live alone.

Wilmoth and Sanders (2001) conducted a focus group with 24 African American women diagnosed with breast cancer in order to identify personal issues and concerns of African American women who are breast cancer survivors. Five themes emerged: body appearance, social support, health activism, menopause, and learning to live with a chronic disease. In addition to femininity issues expressed by most breast cancer survivors, African American women stated concerns regarding losing total body hair, forming keloids after surgery, appearing unbalanced when dressed, and having difficulty finding prostheses to match their skin tones. The decision to have breast cancer reconstruction surgery was influenced by the fear of developing keloids. Unlike many white women, African American women, especially those from low-income groups, place great value on body hair, especially on the legs. For example, one participant in Wilmoth and Sanders's study stated, "… our hair is our crowning glory." (p. 877). Another body image treatment concern of African American women expressed by these women is discoloration of the skin, especially the palms of the hands, soles of the feet, and nails. Concerns about menopause were very similar to those of other cancer survivors—cessation of menses, vaginal dryness, hot flashes, loss of sleep, and changes in sexuality. The participants were especially concerned about health care providers not offering treatment or resources for menopausal symptoms, and the changes in their sexuality.

Some of the sociocultural themes for Wilmoth and Sanders's (2001) study (social support, health activism, and learning to live with a chronic illness) centered on the cultural heritage of African American women. Social support has been identified as a major coping strategy for all aspects of life for African American women. In Wilmoth and Sanders's study, there was a disintegration of the coping strategy for many women. For example, many of the women experienced loss of social contacts, including significant others, when they shared with them their diagnosis of breast cancer. Silence, as discussed earlier, presented a barrier to effective care. Family and friends had been conditioned not to talk about the "big C" and thus removed themselves from the relationship at a time when they were most needed. Stigma and fear played significant roles along with silence. Brown (2000) described how fear, shame, and lack of knowledge had impacted the coping and social support of the first two of five generations of breast cancer patients in the author's family. She states that it was her mother, the third generation, who broke the chain of transmitting fear, shame, embarrassment, ignorance, and social isolation, and eventually became a breast cancer activist. Brown's own activism was similar to that described by participants in Wilmoth and Sanders's (2001) study. Study participants expressed concerns regarding the inability to find support groups where African American women made up part or all of the participants.

The discussion related to the last theme of living with breast cancer reflected concerns about being different from white women. An implicit theme was coping with the loss of relationships. Concerns about the following consequences of living with a diagnosis of breast cancer were not discussed: family burden issues, fear of recurrence, emotional vulnerability, uncertainty, altered social roles, effect of a diagnosis of breast cancer on spirituality, employment and insurance discrimination, limited access to health and life insurance, excessive long-term care costs, and death (Johnson & Smith, 2002). Home-based computer interventions show much promise for African American women, who may be reluctant to engage in conversations in support groups soon after being diagnosed with breast cancer. Nurses, however, need to ensure that the divide between middle- and low-income women is bridged with interventions.

One intervention resource that has been effective for both African American and white women is the Comprehensive Health Enhancement Support System (CHESS) (*http://chess2.chsra.wisc.edu/chess*), a home-based computer system that provides information, decision-making, and emotional support for women diagnosed with breast cancer

(Gustafson *et al.*, 1999, 2001a, 2001b; McTavish *et al.*, 1995; Shaw *et al.*, 2000). CHESS was designed to assist breast cancer survivors and family members in making sense of breast cancer information, being more active and confident in their self-care, increasing social support, and maintaining a better quality of life. There are at least six sites using this resource in four different states—Wisconsin, Illinois, Indiana, and Michigan. Four of the six sites include African American women in their interventions. An evaluation of the outcomes of the home-based computer intervention with younger women, who were pro-filed as middle-income women, indicated that women of color (African Americans comprised 12.5% of the participants) used the intervention as frequently as white women but for fewer minutes at a time. The women of color used the group discussion board about 50% less frequently than white women, but they were more likely to use the decision-making and self-tracking services than white women.

To summarize, this section has provided a beginning overview on some of what is known about breast cancer in African American women, with a special emphasis on the socio-cultural determinants of screening and early detection. Although the incidence of breast cancer is generally lower for African American women, they continue to experience excess mortality and poorer survival when compared to white women. Interventions targeting this population that incorporate a variety of sociocultural factors show great promise with regard to increasing early detection rates and improving outcomes for this population. Information on African American breast cancer survivors is beginning to emerge; however, it is very limited at this time. Although data are too limited to generalize to all African American women living with breast cancer, current information can help to sensitize health care providers about the psychosocial needs of African American women. Continued and sustained efforts are sorely needed on all fronts (e.g., education, practice, research, policy) if we are to realize reductions in the disparities in breast cancer outcomes for African American women.

IMPLICATIONS FOR IMPROVING BREAST CANCER OUTCOMES

Although this chapter has provided an overview on breast cancer and African American women with a special emphasis on sociocultural factors, the content presented in this overview is limited to what is known about African American women and breast cancer. Thus, the current content is not generalizable to other black women or other women of color (e.g., Caribbeans, Africans, Haitians, and residents of non-Spanish-speaking Caribbean islands of African descent). Additional research is needed to identify and address issues related to other women of color. Similarly, because of the intracultural differences noted among African American women, findings related to low-income African American women are not applicable to middle-income women. It is important that we continue to tease out intracultural and socioeconomic differences so that we may successfully facilitate the earlier detection and prompt treatment of breast cancer.

The body of descriptive literature outlining the breast cancer beliefs and screening practices of African American women is well developed; however, intervention studies with sufficient rigor are needed to evaluate what really makes a difference in improving the breast cancer outcomes of African American women. Also, as more African American women are diagnosed at earlier and more treatable stages, survival rates for this population are expected to increase. Thus, more studies are needed to identify the psychosocial needs of African American women, their families, and their significant others.

Another implication relates to our aging population. Age is a risk factor for breast cancer; thus, we can expect to see an increase in the incidence of breast cancer among an aging population that is expected to have one or more chronic diseases along with breast cancer. Aging individuals may have very unique needs. This group may have experienced losses in their lives through death or retirement, or through declining health and functional status. Fear of being a burden on family and friends, inability to care for oneself, not being useful, and losing ability to manage financial affairs may impact their lives. To receive a diagnosis of breast cancer may be one more thing that adds to the burden of "living in the golden years." Nurses working with the aging population must assess the patient's socio-emotional status and connect the patient, not merely refer her, to the appropriate services at every level of care.

Women, regardless of background, should be supported in their efforts to manage their own breast health. Issues such as literacy, personal empowerment, navigating the health care system, and learning style preference should be assessed and addressed accordingly when targeting all women. Increasing access to and utilization of state-of-the-art cancer screening/detection and treatment services are critical to improving the breast cancer profile for African American women. Once resources are identified, educational efforts may need to focus on assisting women in developing skill and confidence in navigating the health care delivery system. This becomes particularly important when targeting low-income African American women.

The authors offer additional specific recommendations for future action in Table 18.1 and provide a list of resources in Table 18.2.

Table 18.1 Recommendations for Future Action

- Enhance outreach activities to increase the awareness of the disparities in breast cancer among African American women.
- Expand and evaluate activities that increase the awareness and utilization of breast cancer detection and treatment services for underserved African American women.
- Establish and sustain partnerships with members of the African American community when designing breast cancer interventions and policies targeting African American women.
- Develop focused strategies to increase the number of African American women enrolled in breast cancer clinical trials.
- Expand the current body of literature in breast cancer research to include topics such as cancer survivorship, long-term maintenance of screening behaviors, and family issues among African American women.
- Communicate and widely disseminate successful models designed to improve the breast cancer outcomes of African American women.

Table 18.2 Selected Resources

African American Breast Cancer Alliance
(612) 825-3675
www.geocities.com/aabcainc

American Cancer Society
(800) ACS-2345
http://www.cancer.org

Celebrating Life Foundation
(800) 207-0992
www.celebratinglife.org

Intercultural Cancer Council
(713) 798-3990
http://icc.bcm.tmc.edu

National Library of Medicine
"Multicultural Aspects of Breast Cancer Etiology"
www.nlm.nih.gov/pubs/resources.html

Office of Minority Health Resource Center
(800) 442-6472
www.omhrc.gov

Sisters Network
(713) 781-0255
www.sistersnetworkinc.org

Susan G. Komen Breast Cancer Foundation
(800) 462-9273
www.breastcancerinfo.com

SUMMARY

In summary, the disparities in health constitute a major focus for the 21st century. Successful models that assess and incorporate the psychosocial determinants of early detection and screening of breast cancer for African American women are sorely needed if we are to realize improvements in the breast cancer outcomes for this population. We must remain vigilant in our efforts to ensure equitable access to state-of-the-art cancer-related services, broaden traditional approaches to ensure the long-term maintenance of breast cancer screening behaviors, and hold our legislators accountable as stakeholders in the war against breast cancer. Then and only then will we begin to effectively reduce the disparities in breast cancer outcomes for African American women.

REFERENCES

Agre, P., Dougherty, J., & Pirone, J. (2002). Creating a CD-ROM program for cancer-related patient education. *Oncology Nursing Forum, 29,* 573–584.

American Cancer Society. (2001). *Cancer facts and figures for African Americans 2000–2001.* Atlanta, Ga.: Author.

American Cancer Society. (2002). *Breast cancer facts and figures.* Atlanta, Ga.: Author.

American Cancer Society. (2003). *Cancer facts and figures.* Atlanta, Ga.: Author.

Ashing-Giwa, K., Ganz, P.A., & Petersen, L. (1999). Quality of life of African-American and white long term breast carcinoma survivors. *Cancer, 85,* 418–426.

Aziz, N.M., & Rowland, J.H. (2002). Cancer survivorship research among ethnic minority and medically underserved groups. *Oncology Nursing Forum, 29,* 789–801.

Black, M., Stein, K., & Loveland-Cherry, C. (2001). Older women and mammography screening behavior: do possible selves contribute? *Health Education Behavior, 28*(2), 200–216.

Bloom, J.R., Grazier, K., Hodge, F., & Hayes, W.A. (1991). Factors affecting the use of screening mammography among African American women. *Cancer Epidemiology, Biomarkers & Prevention, 1,* 75–82.

Breen, N., & Kessler, L. (1994). Changes in the use of screening mammography: evidence from the 1987 and 1990 National Health Interview Surveys. *American Journal of Public Health, 84,* 62–67.

Brown, Z.K. (2000). Living in a high-risk family. *The Breast Journal, 6,* 288–290.

Buchwald D., Caralis P. V., Gany F., *et al.* (1994) Caring for patients in a multicultural society. *Patient Care, 28*(11):105–120.

Campbell, M.K., Tessaro, I., DeVellis, B., Benedict, S., Kelsey, K., Belton, L., & Henriquez-Roldan, C. (2000). Tailoring and targeting a worksite health promotion program to address multiple health behaviors among blue-collar women. *American Journal of Health Promotion, 14*(5), 306–313.

Champion, V., & Huster, G. (1995). Effect of interventions on stage of mammography adoption. *Journal of Behavioral Medicine, 18,* 169–187.

Dalaker, J. (2001). *Poverty in the United States: 2000.* U.S. Census Bureau, Current Population Reports, Series P 60-214. Washington, D.C.: U.S. Government Printing Office.

Department of Health and Human Services. (1991). *Healthy people 2000: national promotion and disease prevention objectives.* Washington, D.C.: Public Health Services.

Department of Health and Human Services. (2000). *Healthy People 2010, 2nd ed.* With *Understanding and Improving Health* and *Objectives for Improving Health* (Vol. 1). Washington, D.C.: U.S. Government Printing Office.

Dibbles, S.L., Vanoni, J.M., & Miaskowski, C. (1997). Women's attitudes toward breast cancer screening procedures: differences by ethnicity. *Women's Health Issues, 12,* 47–54.

Eley, J.W., Hill, H.A., Chen, V.W., Austin, D.F., Wesley, M.N., Muss, H.B., Greenberg, R.S., Coates, R.J., Correa, P., & Redmond, C.K. (1994). Racial differences in survival from breast cancer: results of the National Cancer Institute Black/White Cancer Survival Study. *Journal of the American Medical Association, 272,* 947–954.

Erwin, D.O. (2002). Cancer education takes on a spiritual focus for the African American faith community. *Journal of Cancer Education, 17,* 46–49.

Erwin, D.O., Spatz, T.S., Stotts, C., & Hollenberg, J.A. (1999). Increasing mammography practice by African American women. *Cancer Practice, 7*(2), 78–85.

Erwin, D.O., Spatz, T.S., Stotts, C.R.C., Hollenberg, J.A., & Deloney, L.A. (1996). Increasing mammography and breast self-examination in African American women: using the Witness Project™ model. *Journal of Cancer Education, 11,* 210–215.

Facione, N. (1999). Breast cancer screening in relation to access to health services. *Oncology Nursing Forum, 26*(4), 689–696.

Facione, N.C., & Katapodi, M. (2000). Culture as an influence on breast cancer screening and early detection. *Seminars in Oncology Nursing, 16*(3), 238–247.

Forte, D.A. (1995). Community-based breast cancer intervention program for older African American women in beauty salons. *Public Health Reports, 110,* 179–183.

Fox, S., Pitkin, K., Paul, C., Carson, S., & Duan, N. (1998). Breast cancer screening adherence: does church attendance matter? *Health Education & Behavior, 25*(6), 742–758.

Frazier, E., Jiles, R., & Mayberry, R. (1996). Use of screening mammography and clinical breast examinations among black, Hispanic and white women. *Preventive Medicine, 25,* 118–125.

Gamble, V.N. (1993). A legacy of distrust: African Americans and medical research. *American Journal of Preventive Medicine, 9,* 35–38.

Gustafson, D.H., Hawkins, R.P., Boberg, E.W., McTavish, F., Owens, B., Wise, M., Berhe, H., & Pingree, S. (2001a). CHESS: ten years of research and development in consumer health informatics for broad populations, including the underserved. *Medical Information, 10*(2), 1459–1563.

Gustafson, D.H., Hawkins, R., Pingree, S., McTavish, F., Arora, N.K., Mendenhall, J., Cella, D.F., Serlin, R.C., Apantaku, F.M., Stewart, J., & Salner, A. (2001b). Effect of computer support on younger women with breast cancer. *Journal of Internal Medicine, 16*(7), 435–445.

Gustafson, D.H., McTavish, F.M., Boberg, E., Owens, B.H., Sherbeck, C., Wise, M., Pingree, S., & Hawkins, R.P. (1999). Empowering patients using computer based health support systems. *Quality Health Care, 8*(1), 49–56.

Hendricks, C. (2000). Fostering healthy communities at hair care centers. *Association of Black Nursing Faculty. 11,* 69–70.

Hiatt, R.A., Pasick, R.J., Stewart, S., Bloom, J., Davis, P., Gardiner, P., Johnston, M., Luce, J., Schorr, K., Brunner, W., & Stroud, F. (2001). Community-based cancer screening for underserved women: design and baseline findings from the breast and cervical cancer intervention study. *Preventive Medicine, 33,* 190–203.

Holm, C.J., Frank, D.I., & Curtin, J. (1999). Health beliefs, health locus of control, and women's mammography behavior. *Cancer Nursing, 22,* 149–156.

Hughes, C., Lerman, C., & Lustbader, E. (1996). Ethnic differences in risk perception among women at increased risk for breast cancer. *Breast Cancer Research and Treatment, 40,* 23–35.

Iwamoto, R.R. (1994). Cultural influences on quality of life. In K.H. Dow & M.B. Whedon (Eds.), *Quality of life: a nursing challenge,* pp. 68–73. Philadelphia: Cerenex Pharmaceuticals.

Johnson, B.F., & Smith, E.D. (2002). Breast cancer survivorship: are African American women considered? a concept analysis. *Oncology Nursing Forum, 29,* 779–787.

Kagawa-Singer, M. (1987). Ethnic perspectives of cancer nursing: Hispanics and Japanese-Americans. *Oncology Nursing Forum, 14,* 59–65.

Kagawa-Singer, M., Wellisch, D., & Durvasula, R. (1997). Impact of breast cancer on Asian American and Anglo American women. *Culture, Medicine, and Psychiatry, 21,* 449–480.

Kinney, A.Y., Emery, G., Dudley, W.N., & Croyle, R. (2002). Screening behaviors among African American women at high risk for breast cancer: do beliefs about God matter? *Oncology Nursing Forum, 29*(5) 835–842.

Klassen, A.C., Smith, A.M., Meissner, H., Zaboar, J., Curow, B., & Mandelblatt, J. (2002). If we gave away mammograms, who would get them? A neighborhood evaluation of a no-cost breast cancer screening program. *Preventive Medicine, 34,* 13–21.

Mandelblatt, J.S., Gold, K., O'Malley, A.S., Taylor, K., Cagney, K., Hopkins, J.S., & Kerner, J. (1999). Breast and cervix cancer screening among multiethnic women: role of age, health, and source of care. *Preventive Medicine, 28,* 418–425.

Mann, B.D., Sherman, L., Clayton, C., Johnson, R.F., Keates, J., Kasenge, R., Streeter, K., Goldberg, L., & Nieman, L.Z. (2000). Screening to the converted: an educational intervention in African American churches. *Journal of Cancer Education, 15,* 46–50.

McDonald, P.A., Thorne, D.D., Pearson, J.C., & Adams-Campbell, L.L. (1999). Perceptions and knowledge of breast cancer among African-American women residing in public housing. *Ethnicity & Disease, 9,* 81–93.

McTavish, F.M., Gustafson, D.H., Owens, B.H., Hawkins, R.P., Pingree, S., Wise, M., Taylor, J.O., & Apantaku, F.M. (1995). CHESS: an interactive computer system for women with breast cancer piloted with an underserved population. *Journal of Ambulatory Care Management, 18*(3), 35–41.

Miller, A.M., & Champion, V.L. (1997). Attitudes about breast cancer and mammography: racial, income, and educational differences. *Women & Health, 26,* 41–62.

Miller, L., & Hailey, B.J. (1994). Cancer anxiety and breast cancer screening in African-American women: a preliminary study. *Women's Health Issues, 94*(4), 170–174.

Moore, R.J. (2001). African American women and breast cancer: notes from a study of narratives. *Cancer Nursing, 24,* 35–42.

Moore, R.J., & Spiegel, D. (2000). Uses of guided imagery for pain control by African-American and white women with metastatic breast cancer. *Integrative Medicine, 2*, 115–126.

Moormeier, J. (1996). Breast cancer in black women. *Annals of Internal Medicine, 124*, 897–905.

Musgrove, C.F., Easley Allen, C., & Allen, G.J. (2002). Spirituality and health for women of color. *American Journal of Public Health, 92*(4), 557–560.

National Center for Chronic Disease Prevention and Health Promotion. (2000). Improving national cancer control. *Chronic Disease Notes and Reports, 13*(3), 1, 4.

National Center for Health Statistics. (2001). *Healthy People 2000 final review.* Hyattsville, Md.: Public Health Service.

Newman, L.A., Bunner, S., Carolin, K., Bouwman, D., Kosir, M.A., White, M., & Schwartz, (2002). Ethnicity related differences in the survival of young carcinoma patients. *Cancer, 95*, 21–27.

Paskett, E.D., Tatum, C., Wilson, A., Dignan, M., & Velez, R. (1996). Use of photo essay to teach low-income African American women about mammography. *Journal of Cancer Education, 11*, 216–220.

Phillips, J.M., Cohen, M., & Moses, G. (1999). Breast cancer screening and African American women: fear, fatalism & silence. *Oncology Nursing Forum, 26*(3), 561–571.

Phillips, J.M., Cohen, M.Z., & Tarzian, A.J. (2001). African American women's experiences with breast cancer screening. *Journal of Nursing Scholarship, 33*(2), 135–140.

Phillips, K., Kerlikowske, K., Baker, L., Chang, S., & Brown, M. (1998). Factors associated with women's adherence to mammography screening guidelines. *Health Service Research, 33*(1), 29–53.

Powe, B.D. (1996). Cancer fatalism among African-Americans: a review of the literature. *Nursing Outlook, 44*(1), 18–21.

Powe, B.D., & Johnson, A. (1995). Fatalism as a barrier to cancer screening among African-Americans: philosophical perspectives. *Journal of Religion and Health, 34*(2), 119–125.

Price, J.H. (1994). Economically disadvantaged females: perceptions of breast cancer and breast cancer screening. *Journal of the National Medical Association, 86*, 899–905.

Qureshi, M., Thacker, H.L., Litaker, D.G., & Kippes, C. (2000). Differences in breast cancer screening rates: an issue of ethnicity or socioeconomics? *Journal of Women's Health and Gender-Based Medicine, 9*(9), 1025–1031.

Rakowski, W., Ehrich, B., Goldstein, M.G., Rimer, B.K., Pearlman, D.N., Clark, M.A., Velicer, W.F., & Woolverton. H. 3rd. (1998). Increasing mammography among women aged 40–74 by use of stage-matched, tailored intervention. *Preventive Medicine, 27*, 748–756.

Ryan, G., Skinner, C., Farrell, D., & Champion, V. (2001). Examining the boundaries of tailoring: the utility of tailoring versus targeting mammography interventions for two distinct populations. *Health Education Research, 16*(5), 555–566.

Shapiro, S., Venet, V., Strax, P., Venet, L., & Roeser, R. (1982). Ten- to fourteen-year effect of screening on breast cancer mortality. *Journal of the National Cancer Institute, 69*(2), 349–355.

Shaw, B.R., McTavish, F., Hawkins, R., Gustafson, D., & Pingree, S. (2000). Experiences of women with breast cancer: exchanging social support over the CHESS computer network. *Journal of Health Communication, 5*, 135–140.

Shi, L., & Singh, D.A. (2001). A distinctive system of health care delivery. In *Delivering health care in America: a systems approach*, pp. 1–27. Gaithersburg, Md.: Aspen.

Shinagawa, S.M. (2000). The excess burden of breast carcinoma in minority and medically underserved communities. *Cancer Supplement, 88*, 1217–1223.

Skinner, C.S., Zerr, A.D., & Damson, R.L. (1995). Incorporating mobile mammography units into primary care: focus group interviews among inner-city health center patients. *Health Education Research, 10*, 179–189.

Smith, E.D., Dancy, B., Dan, A., Jackson-Bacon, G., & Smith, P. (2000). An exploration of the early detection beliefs, attitude, and practices of middle-income African Americans. Unpublished report.

Smith, E., Merritt, S., & Patel, K. (1997). Church-based education: an outreach program for African Americans with hypertension. *Ethnicity & Health, 2*(3), 243–253.

Smith, E.D., Phillips, J.M., & Price, M.M. (2001). Screening and detection among racial and ethnic minority women. *Seminars in Oncology Nursing, 17*(3), 159–170.

Strzelczyk, J., & Dignan, M. (2002). Disparities in adherence to recommended followup on screening mammography: interaction of socioeconomic factors. *Ethnicity & Disease, 12*, 77–86.

Sung, J.F.C., Blumenthal, D.S., & Alema-Mensah, E. (1997). Knowledge, beliefs, attitudes, and cancer screening among inner-city African-American women. *Journal of the National Medical Association, 89,* 405–411.

Wilmoth, M.C., & Sanders, L.D. (2001). Accept me for myself: African American women's issues after breast cancer. *Oncology Nursing Forum, 28,* 875–879.

Wingood, G.M., & Keltner, B. (1999). Sociocultural factors and prevention programs affecting the health of ethnic minorities. In J.M. Raczynski & R.J. DiClemente (Eds.), *Handbook of health promotion and disease prevention,* pp. 561–577. New York: Kluwer Academic/Plenum Publishers.

Yabroff, K., & Mandelblatt, J. (1999). Interventions targeted toward patients to increase mammography use. *Cancer Epidemiology, Biomarkers, & Prevention, 8,* 749–757.

Yancy, A., & Walden, L. (1994). Stimulating cancer screening among Latinas and African American women. *Journal of Cancer Education, 9,* 46–52.

ASIAN WOMEN AND BREAST CANCER

Chapter 19

DIANNE ISHIDA, PHD, APRN, CMC

INTRODUCTION

The Asian American population in the United States is a diverse group covering 16 to 28 different Asian ethnicities (Paisano *et al.,* 1993). It is a fast-growing population, increasing from 6.9 million in 1990 to 11.9 million in 2000 (U.S. Census Bureau, 2002a), a growth rate of 72%. In comparison, the total U.S. population grew by 13%. Almost half of the Asians (49%) live in the western United States. About 45% live in the metropolitan areas of Los Angeles, San Francisco, or New York. Asian Americans comprise 26% of the country's foreign-born population. Although 2000 census data is not available, in 1990 nearly two thirds of Asian Americans spoke an Asian or Pacific Islander language at home (Paisano *et al.,* 1993). Asian Americans include a mix of very recent immigrants and some who have lived in the United States for more than six generations, such as some Chinese and Japanese Americans. The term "Asian" refers to people whose origins are from the Far East, Southeast Asia, or the Indian subcontinent. The six largest Asian groups in the U.S. are the Chinese, Filipinos, Asian Indians, Koreans, Japanese, and Vietnamese (U.S. Census Bureau, 2002a) (see Table 19.1). This chapter will concentrate on breast cancer among the populations from the Far East and Southeast Asia.

The diversity of the Asian American population in the United States, including recent immigrants and more acculturated groups, can give a deceiving impression when Asian Americans are grouped together. In income and education, they present a bimodal pattern. For instance, foreign-born Asians have the highest income of any foreign-born group, yet 13% live in poverty, compared to 11% of native-born Americans (U.S. Census Bureau, 2002b). When aggregate data of mean values are given, the complexity and diversity of the population is lost. Even within an ethnic group such as the Chinese, there is wide diversity, with different waves of immigrants from various geographical regions in

Table 19.1 Asian Population in the United States: 2000

Asian Group	Reported from One Asian Group
Asian Indian	1,678,765
Bangladeshi	41,280
Bhutanese	183
Burmese	13,159
Cambodian	171,937
Chinese, except Taiwanese	2,314,537
Filipino	1,850,314
Hmong	169,428
Indo Chinese	113
Indonesian	39,757
Iwo Jiman	15
Japanese	796,700
Korean	1,076,872
Laotian	168,707
Malaysian	10,690
Maldivian	27
Nepalese	7,858
Okinawan	3,513
Pakistani	153,533
Singaporean	1,437
Sri Lankan	20,145
Taiwanese	118,048
Thai	112,989
Vietnamese	1,122,528
Other Asian, not specified	146,870
Total	**10,019,405**

Source: U.S. Census Bureau, Census 2000.

China immigrating for many reasons and having a range of educational, occupational, and linguistic backgrounds. They may also have slightly different traditional foods, customs, beliefs, and practices. This diversity affects breast cancer risk, screening, and treatment, which increases the complexity of issues for health care providers.

BREAST CANCER RISK

The interest of researchers in acculturation or length of U.S. residency of Asian groups has a basis when determining cancer risk. Migration studies of various Asian immigrants demonstrate that certain cancers, particularly breast cancer, are more prevalent in Asian women living in Western countries than in Asian women living in the mother countries (Stanford *et al.*, 1995). Breast cancer risk increases with each decade of U.S. residency (Deapen *et al.*, 2002; Ziegler *et al.*, 1993; Grulich *et al.*, 1995; McCredie *et al.*, 1999; Mettlin, 1999). Age at the time of immigration may also affect breast cancer rates. Breast cancer rates are higher when women migrated early in life rather than later (Shimizu *et al.*, 1991). Although breast cancer risk had been considered lower for Asian Americans than for other groups, recent evidence suggests rising incidence rates.

In Los Angeles County, rates for Japanese American women are approaching and are predicted to surpass those of white women if the trend continues (Deapen *et al.*, 2002). The Japanese were the first Asian group to settle in Los Angeles and are considered more acculturated than other Asian groups. When compared to other Asian American groups, breast cancer risk for Japanese and Filipino women remains more than twice that of Chinese and Korean women (see Figure 19.1).

However, increased risk of breast cancer for Asian immigrants and residents does not necessarily mean poorer survival rates. In addition to ethnic differences, other factors appear to affect survival rates. Pineda *et al.* (2001) looked at the SEER (Surveillance, Epidemiology, and End Results) Program data from three regions and examined Japanese, Chinese, Filipino, and Caucasian women with primary invasive breast carcinoma. Although they found no significant difference in survival by place of birth within each Asian group after adjusting for demographic characteristics, stage of disease, and treatment, the researchers found that Japanese women had significantly better survival than all other races examined. Second-generation Japanese women had better survival rates than Japanese migrants. On the other hand, premenopausal Filipino women (age < 50 years) had significantly poorer survival rates compared with premenopausal Japanese women. Also, postmenopausal Japanese women (age > 51 years) had better survival than postmenopausal Caucasian women.

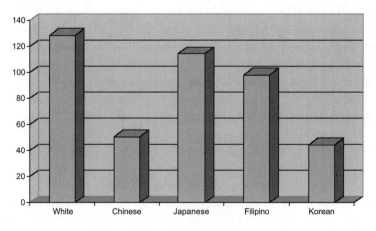

Rates per 100,000 population

Adapted from: Deapen, D., Liu, L., Perkins, C., Bernstein, L., & Ross, R.K., (2002). Rapidly rising breast cancer incidence among Asian-American women. *International Journal of Cancer, 99*, 747–750.

FIGURE 19.1   Los Angeles County, California, Invasive Breast Cancer Incidence, 1988–1997.

In several other studies (Meng *et al.*, 1997; Hsu *et al.*, 1997), Filipino women had poorer survival rates with localized breast cancer, suggesting that they had more aggressive tumors for the same cancer stage. The Hawaii study noted that Filipino women were three times more likely to die from breast cancer than were Japanese women (Meng *et al.*, 1997). Pineda *et al.* (2001) concluded that differences in tumor morphology and host response as well as environmental and lifestyle factors (such as diet and exercise) associated with acculturation can have an impact on breast cancer prognosis.

One study shows promise in survival for various ethnic groups. When insurance claim data from 1995 to 1998 were adjusted for stage, ethnic differences among Caucasian, Japanese, Hawaiian, Filipino, and Chinese women were drastically reduced by half compared to Tumor Registry data from the years 1989–1996 (Maskarinec *et al.*, 2002). This suggests that with treatment, survival differences between ethnicities can be negligible. However, cancer continues to be the leading cause of death for the Asian and Pacific Islander female (Chen, 1998).

BREAST CANCER SCREENING

Overall cancer screening rates for breast cancer in Asian and Pacific Islanders are lower than these of all ethnic groups and significantly lower than those recommended by Healthy People 2000 for white women (Kagawa-Singer & Pourat, 2000; Coughlin & Uhler, 2000). In the past 10 years, there have been numerous studies and efforts made to screen Asian American women for breast cancer. These include studies on Vietnamese (Nguyen *et al.*, 2001; Kagawa-Singer & Pourat, 2000, NCI, 1999; Phipps *et al.*, 1999; Jenkins *et al.*, 1999; McPhee *et al.*, 1997; Yi, 1995; Pham & McPhee, 1992), Chinese (M. Yu *et al.*, 2002; E.S. Yu *et al.*, 2001; Kagawa-Singer & Pourat, 2000; NCI, 1999), Koreans (Han *et al.*, 2000; Maxwell *et al.*, 2000; Juon *et al.*, 2000; Chen *et al.*, 1997; NCI, 1999; Kagawa-Singer & Pourat, 2000), Filipino (Kagawa-Singer & Pourat, 2000; Maxwell *et al.*, 2000), Japanese (Kagawa-Singer & Pourat, 2000), Cambodian (Tu *et al.*, 2000, 2002; Phipps *et al.*, 1999; Kelly *et al.*, 1996), and Hmong (Tanjasiri *et al.*, 2001). These studies point out the various reasons for the poor screening rates of Asian American women. The lack of knowledge about cancer screening is evident, especially in newer immigrant groups such as the Cambodians and Vietnamese (Phipps *et al.*, 1999; Kelly *et al.*, 1996; Pham & McPhee, 1992). Transportation, fear, cost, a preference not to know whether they have breast cancer, pain, family responsibilities, and embarrassment have also been cited as barriers (Bernstein *et al.*, 2000). Asian women who had insurance (Coughlin & Uhler, 2000; Kagawa-Singer & Pourat, 2000; McPhee *et al.*, 1997), were more acculturated (Tang *et al.*, 2000; McPhee *et al.*, 1997), and were younger (Juon *et al.*, 2000; McPhee *et al.*, 1997) were more likely to have had a mammogram.

Physician characteristics may affect screening of Asian women. In their studies of physician screening behavior for breast cancer among Cambodian Americans, Tu and colleagues (2000, 2002) found that Asian American and non-Asian American female physicians were more likely to provide screening than Asian American male physicians. Because of cultural values of modesty and sexuality, Asian women may be reluctant to give attention to their own breast health (Tang *et al.*, 1999; Mo, 1992). This reluctance may be communicated to the physician. If the Asian male physician feels uncomfortable broaching the topic in order to respect this modesty, an opportunity for screening is lost. The lack of or limited number of female health care providers from their ethnic group in different geographical areas may also preclude Asian women from seeing a primary care physician. A phenomenon that can occur is that Asian women use the emergency room as a substitute source for primary health care (Azevedo & Germano, 1999).

With lower screening rates, it is not surprising that Asian-born Asian American women have a greater proportion (79%) of tumors larger than 1 cm at diagnosis than U.S. white women (70%) (Hedeen *et al.*, 1999). U.S.-born Asian American women, however, did not differ significantly from U.S. white women (67%). In a study looking at abnormal first-round screenings, the percentages of abnormal mammograms ranged from 7.3% among black women to 9.3% among Asian and Pacific Islander women (May *et al.*, 2000). Ethnic differences in mammographic densities have also been noted. When comparing Caucasian, Native Hawaiian, Japanese, and Chinese women, the Asian women had smaller breasts but a 20% higher proportion of the breast occupied by dense tissue than Caucasian women (Maskarinec *et al.*, 2001). Breast cancer risk is postulated to relate to the absolute size of dense areas (Maskarinec, personal communication, October 1, 2002). When adjustment for risk factors was made in another study with similar ethnic groups (Maskarinec & Meng, 2000), the strength of the association was not statistically significant, although density levels varied by ethnicity.

A multiethnic study including Asian Americans noted that nonwhite women had a significantly longer median follow-up time (19 days) for an abnormal mammogram than white women (12 days) (Chang *et al.*, 1996). A variety of reasons for delay were postulated, such as anxiety, invalid names and addresses of providers given for notification of abnormal results, varying effectiveness of communication between provider and patient, access-to-care difficulties such as not having insurance or a regular health care provider, and difficulty maneuvering in public and private health care delivery systems. However, once these women started their diagnostic examination, there was no significant ethnic difference in time interval between the first and last diagnostic test.

BREAST CANCER TREATMENT

Although there is an abundance of literature on breast cancer screening of Asian American women, there appears to be a paucity of literature on treatment of Asian Americans. In looking at treatment options for stage I and II breast cancer, the National Institutes of Health Consensus Panel (NIH, 1990) recommended breast-conserving surgery (BCS) with radiation. It was determined that there was equivalent survival with modified radical mastectomy and BCS when followed by radiation. BCS was recommended because it preserved breast tissue and potentially improved the woman's quality of life. Despite this recommendation, Morris and colleagues (2000) found that Asian and Hispanic women received BCS at a statistically lower frequency than Caucasian women.

Lee *et al.* (2000) found similar findings, with Chinese women being less likely than African American and Caucasian women to receive BCS and reconstructive surgery after mastectomy. Vietnamese women who were younger at diagnosis than other ethnic groups were significantly more likely to have a mastectomy for in situ and localized tumors than other ethnicities (Lin *et al.*, 2002). A possible explanation for these results is that traditionally, Asian cultures place less attention on the breast than Western cultures. Thus, the self-concept of Asian women may be less affected by a mastectomy than that of Caucasian women (Kagawa-Singer *et al.*, 1997).

One study (Nold *et al.*, 2000) noted that women (no ethnicities cited) who chose BCS indicated that the surgeon, cosmetic results, and psychological aspects influenced their decision. These women as well as those who chose reconstruction after mastectomy were generally younger. For Asian women, like women in this study who chose mastectomy, fear may have influenced their mastectomy decision. They preferred to remove the worry about recurrence with a mastectomy (Kagawa-Singer *et al.*, 1997). A Hawaii study collaborates this finding. Japanese, Hawaiian, Filipino, Chinese, and white participants cited increasing survival as the most important factor affecting treatment decision (Gotay, 2002).

Interference with responsibilities can also affect choice of surgical treatment options (Kagawa-Singer *et al.*, 1997). With a modified radical mastectomy, Asian women with early-stage disease do not need the extended number of weeks usually required for daily radiation treatments. This would minimize the period of disability so that there would be less disruption of her obligations to family, friends, and employers. The question of access to a radiation facility can affect treatment decision. In Hawaii, Maskarinec *et al.* (2002) found that women with early-stage breast cancer on Oahu, where the major medical centers that have radiation facilities are located, were 70% more likely to receive BCS than women on the outer islands.

Although Kagawa-Singer and colleagues (1997) found that Japanese American and Chinese American women were significantly less likely to choose BCS than Anglo-Americans, they also noted that the use of adjuvant therapy (chemotherapy after surgery) was lower in the Asians (89%) than in white women (100%). Japanese, Chinese, Filipino, Hawaiian, and white women in Gotay's study (2002) mentioned the following factors affecting their decision making regarding treatment: drug side effects (57%), discomfort (48%), convenience (45%), avoiding nausea and vomiting (44%), and not losing hair (28%). Most of these factors are associated with chemotherapy treatment. Filipino women were more likely to rate these factors as important compared to other women. Chinese and Filipino women were also less positive about their chemotherapy experience. Lee *et al.* (2000) noted that fewer Chinese women had chemotherapy than Latino, white, or African American women.

CANCER TREATMENT EXPERIENCE

There are reported ethnic differences in cancer treatment. Using the various subscales of the Cancer Rehabilitation Evaluation System, Kagawa-Singer *et al.* (1997) found that Chinese American women scored significantly higher than Japanese and Anglo-American women on a scale measuring interactional difficulties with health care providers. The researchers noted that the Chinese women were younger and less acculturated, which may account for this result. Requests for help by Asian women tended to be for medical or physical issues, rather than the psychosocial, marital, or sexual issues of Anglo-American women. The nonexpression of emotions or not seeking psychosocial help common with Asian Americans did not mean they were not experiencing these emotions. In fact, the study showed that Asian American women experienced levels of emotional and psychological disruption similar to the Anglo-American women. Asian women tended to make these needs known in a manner different from the Anglo-American women through a more culturally acceptable way via physical or medical concerns (Marsella, 1993).

In a study of coping after breast cancer treatment among Caucasian, Japanese, Hawaiian, Chinese, Filipino, and mixed ethnicities, Bell (1994) found high self-esteem and a confrontive reaction to cancer associated with lower state of anxiety, lower depression scores, and better psychosocial adjustment. Though there were no significant ethnic differences in psychosocial adjustment, Asian women traditionally are nonconfrontational. The researcher did note that the mean state anxiety for her sample was significantly higher than the norm for all age groups, with Caucasian women reporting more than other groups. Posttreatment time was not a significant factor. Various approaches have been tried to assist women in coping with their disease and treatment, including support groups and one-on-one support as provided by the American Cancer Society's Reach to Recovery Program. Coping, quality of life, and survivorship are important issues for all women with breast cancer, including Asian American women, and are beyond the scope of this chapter. The reader is referred to other chapters on these topics in this text.

COMPLEMENTARY AND ALTERNATIVE MEDICINE

A topic that is receiving increasing attention is the use of complementary and alternative medicine (CAM) by cancer patients. About half of the 379 Latino, Caucasian, African American, and Chinese women with breast cancer contacted via telephone survey in San Francisco used at least one type of alternative therapy, with a third using two types (Lee *et al.*, 2000). Although the length of therapy was not long (generally three to six months after diagnosis), the choice of alternative therapies varied with ethnicity. African American women most often chose spiritual healing (36%), Chinese women most often chose herbal remedies (22%), and Latino women used dietary therapies (30%) and spiritual healing (26%). Caucasian women used dietary methods (35%) and physical methods (21%) such as massage and acupuncture. Chinese women were less likely to use dietary and mental therapies. Over 90% of the women found alternative therapies helpful and would recommend them to friends.

Another study of similar size (Gotay *et al.*, 1999) with patients having a variety of cancers found that slightly more than a third used alternative therapies. Caucasian, Filipino, Hawaiian, and Japanese participants reported that types of CAM use averaged 1.6 each. The ethnic breakdown was not significant (33.9% of the Caucasians compared to 38.9% of the Filipinos). The most frequent CAM was religious or spiritual therapy, followed by herbal medicine and lifestyle changes. CAM use was associated with younger age, being female, being Christian, and having a higher education.

A larger sample of the same ethnicities (Maskarinec *et al.*, 2000) found CAM use highest among Filipino and Caucasian patients and lowest for Japanese. CAM preferences varied with ethnicity, with Chinese using herbal medicines, Hawaiians using Hawaiian healing, and Filipinos using religious healing. The researchers noted that CAM users reported lower emotional functioning scores, higher symptom scores, and more financial difficulties than nonusers. A small multiethnic (Asian, Hawaiian, and Caucasian) study of cancer survivors who declined part or all of conventional therapy felt they wanted to avoid harm to their body (Shumay *et al.,* 2001). Most felt that conventional therapy would make no difference in disease outcome, and some perceived having unsatisfactory relationships with health care providers. Participants generally felt that CAM was an effective and less harmful alternative to conventional therapy. CAM therapy needs to be assessed on all Asian women in order to understand the cultural significance of these therapies and how they affect the woman's view of her situation.

ISSUES FACING ASIAN AMERICAN WOMEN

COMMUNICATION

There are many issues that permeate both screening and treatment of Asian American women. The most prevalent one is problems with communication. This includes more than the ability to converse in the English language. For the providers, it includes how to deliver a message, who best to communicate with, appropriate wording of the message, congruent nonverbal behavior, appropriate setting, and awareness of culturally appropriate messages for specific ages and genders. The success or lack of success of different screening programs with Asian Americans and other ethnic minorities may reflect how well these issues are considered.

For Asian Americans, communication depends on the degree of acculturation and language proficiency, knowledge of the American health care system, and the ability to navigate through it to get the kind of services they need when they need them. Perseverance and assertiveness are generally required to obtain good care. Because Asians traditionally prefer not to be assertive, they may not make their needs known clearly. They may trust health professionals whom they see as authority figures to look out for their best interest (Jenkins & Kagawa-Singer, 1994). If they become intimidated by the Western health care system or receive culturally inappropriate messages or care, they may choose not to repeat the experience. The availability of traditional health care practitioners and remedies may also affect if and when they access Western health care.

Community outreach is a necessary component for success in accessing Asian Americans, particularly first-generation immigrants. Various strategies have been proposed and may vary according to Asian group (Ishida, 2001; Bernstein *et al.,* 2000; Azevedo & Germano, 1999; Kelly *et al.,* 1996; Boyce, 1994). Having culturally appropriate materials helps, though literacy should first be assessed when using written materials. Asian immigrants may be too embarrassed to admit they cannot read, so subtlety is needed. An interpreter may be necessary. Conveying the concepts and explanations correctly is important because there may be no comparable word in their language to depict a specific anatomic part, diagnostic test, treatment, or complication. Likewise, the health practitioner needs to understand the meaning of the illness for the woman and her family.

CULTURE

Language proficiency does not guarantee understanding about the disease, adherence to appointments, or following screening and treatment recommendations. Cultural beliefs can influence how one views health and illness, when to seek care and from whom, what treatment to expect, the meaning and cause of cancer and its associated fears, how to behave when sick, expectations about how practitioners should behave, and how one responds to treatment and treatment options. Traditional health practices may not include prevention in the Western sense, or Western prevention and treatment practices may be unknown or misunderstood. Health care decision-making may involve more than the woman, including her husband, adult children, and possibly friends (Kagawa-Singer *et al.*, 1997). Common Asian cultural values present a contrasting picture to Anglo-American values (Lin-Fu, 1994). Values such as group and family orientation, indirectness, modesty, and suppressed emotions may be misunderstood or overlooked by Westerners as these are played out in the screening and treatment process.

SOCIOECONOMIC ISSUES

Other issues in the screening and treatment of Asian American women include socioeconomic factors, which influence the priority that health, prevention, and, thus, health screening and treatment receive. With newer immigrants, other priorities may take precedence over health. Competing priorities include those things necessary for economic survival and social adaptation, such as learning English, finding housing, and having stable employment (Asian American Health Forum, 1990). Immigrants who are working may hold several jobs but still not have health insurance. Taking time off for a clinic appointment may mean less income and thus may threaten survival. Asian immigrant women may have childcare responsibilities for their children or grandchildren so that other family members can work. This responsibility influences when they can make appointments and their ability to keep them (T. Imada, personal communication, September 28, 2002).

Socioeconomic issues can create access barriers. Kagawa-Singer and Pourat (2000) found that low income and lack of health insurance and/or a primary source of health care had a significant negative impact on screening of Asian and Pacific Islander women. This study, along with Coughlin and Uhler (2000), noted that Asian American women with health insurance were more likely to have been screened. However, even when screening is available free in a federally funded breast and cervical control screening program, qualified uninsured or underinsured Asian women may not access them without much encouragement and support from health care providers, family, or friends (T. Imada, personal communication, September 28, 2002).

SUMMARY

Many issues play a role in the breast cancer screening and treatment of Asian American women. The major issues are (1) increasing breast cancer risk with acculturation, which can potentially increase existing screening and treatment disparities; (2) communication problems, which pose hurdles for Asian American women faced with the Western health care system; (3) socioeconomic concerns, which pose barriers to access to screening and treatment choices; and (4) the interplay of culture, which influences all three of these factors and affects behavior. All of these issues must be addressed in order to not only eliminate health disparities, but to provide the same level of quality of care and choices that every woman should expect, whether it is at the primary, secondary, or tertiary level of prevention.

ACKNOWLEDGMENTS

The Author wished to acknowledge Terri Imada, A.P.R.N., A.N.P.-C., M.S.; Charlene Y.L. Bell, PSY.D.; Carolyn Cook Gotay, Ph.D.; and Gertraud Maskarinec, M.D., Ph.D.

REFERENCES

Asian American Health Forum. (1990). *Asian and Pacific Islander American population statistics* (Monograph Series 1). San Francisco: Author.

Azevedo, J.M., & Germano, C.D. (1999). Reducing treatment barriers for Asian Americans: primary care interventions in Shasta County, CA. *Asian American Pacific Islander Journal of Health, 7*, 48–57.

Bell, C.Y.L. (1994). Coping after the crisis: the psychosocial adjustment of multi-ethnic women after treatment for breast cancer. Unpublished doctoral dissertation, American Schools of Professional Psychology, Honolulu.

Bernstein, J., Mutschler, P., & Bernstein, E. (2000). Keeping mammography referral appointments: motivation, health beliefs, and access barriers experienced by older minority women. *Journal of Midwifery & Womens's Health, 45*, 308–313.

Boyce, C.A. (1994). The art of translation. *Asian American and Pacific Islander Journal of Health, 3*, 109–114.

Chang, W.W., Kerlikowske, K., Napoles-Springer, A., Posner, S.F., Sickles, E.A., & Perez-Stable, E.J. (1996). Racial differences in timeliness of follow-up after abnormal screening mammography. *Cancer, 78*, 1395–1402.

Chen, A.M., Wismer, B.A., Lew, R., Kang, S.H., Min, K., Moskowitz, J.M., & Tager, I.B. (1997). "Health is strength": a research collaboration involving Korean Americans in Alameda County. *American Journal of Preventive Medicine, 13*, 93–100.

Chen, M.S. (1998). Cancer prevention and control among Asian and Pacific Islander Americans: findings and recommendations. *Cancer Supplement, 83*, 1856–1864.

Coughlin, S.S., & Uhler, R.J. (2000). Breast and cervical cancer screening practices among Asian and Pacific Islander women in the United States, 1994–1997. *Cancer Epidemiology, Biomarkers & Prevention, 9*, 597–603.

Deapen, D., Liu, L., Perkins, C., Bernstein, L., & Ross, R.K. (2002). Rapidly rising breast cancer incidence rates among Asian-American women. *International Journal of Cancer, 5*, 747–750.

Gotay, C.C. (2002, September). Breast cancer treatment decision-making in Asians and Pacific Islanders. Paper presented at Asian and Pacific Islander Breast Cancer Survivorship Conference, Kailua, Hawaii.

Gotay, C.C., Hara, W., Issell, B.F., & Maskarinec, G. (1999). Use of complementary and alternative medicine in Hawaii cancer patients. *Hawaii Medical Journal, 58*(4) 94–98.

Grulich, A.E., McCredie, M., & Coates, M. (1995). Cancer incidence in Asian migrants to New South Wales, Australia. *British Journal of Cancer, 71*, 400–408.

Han, Y., Williams, R.D., & Harrison, R.A. (2000). Breast cancer screening knowledge, attitudes, and practices among Korean American women. *Oncology Nursing Forum, 27*, 1585–1591.

Hedeen, A.N., White, E., & Taylor, V. (1999). Ethnicity and birthplace in relation to tumor size and stage in Asian American women with breast cancer. *American Journal of Public Health, 89*, 1248–1252.

Hsu, J.L., Glaser, S.L., & West, D.W. (1997). Racial/ethnic differences in breast cancer survival among San Francisco Bay Area women. *Journal of the National Cancer Institute, 89*, 1311–1312.

Ishida, D.N. (2001). Making inroads on cancer prevention and control with Asian Americans. *Seminars in Oncology Nursing, 17*, 220–228.

Jenkins, C.N.H., & Kagawa-Singer, M. (1994). Cancer. In N.W.S. Zane, D.T. Takeuchi, & K.N.J. Young (Eds.), *Confronting critical health issues of Asian and Pacific Islander Americans,* pp. 105–147. Thousand Oaks, Calif.: Sage.

Jenkins, C.N., McPhee, S.J., Bird, J.A., Pham, G.Q., Nguyen, B.H., Nguyen, T., Lai, K.Q., Wong, C., & Davis, T.B. (1999). Effect of a media-led education campaign on breast and cervical cancer screening among Vietnamese-American women. *Prevention Medicine, 28,* 395–406.

Juon, H.S., Cho, Y., & Kim, M.T. (2000). Cancer screening behaviors among Korean-American women. *Cancer Detection and Prevention, 24,* 589–601.

Kagawa-Singer, M., & Pourat, N. (2000). Asian American and Pacific Islander breast and cervical carcinoma screening rates and Healthy People 2000 objectives. *Cancer, 89,* 696–705.

Kagawa-Singer, M., Wellisch, D.K., & Durvasula, R. (1997). Impact of breast cancer on Asian American and Anglo American women. *Culture, Medicine, and Psychiatry, 21,* 449–480.

Kelly, A.W., Fores Chacori, M., Wollan, P.C., Trapp, M.A., Weaver, A.L., Barrier, P.A., Franz, W.B. 3rd, & Kottke, T.E. (1996). A program to increase breast and cervical cancer screening for Cambodian women in a midwestern community. *Mayo Clinic Proceedings, 71,* 437–444.

Lee, M.M., Lin, S.S., Wrensch, M.R., Adler, S.R., & Eisenberg, D. (2000). Alternative therapies used by women with breast cancer in four ethnic populations. *Journal of the National Cancer Institute, 92,* 42–47.

Lin, S.S., Phan, J.C., & Lin, A.Y. (2002). Breast cancer characteristics of Vietnamese women in the Greater San Francisco Bay area. *Journal of Medicine, 176*(2), 91–92.

Lin-Fu, J.S. (1994). Ethnocultural barriers to health care: a major problem for Asian and Pacific Islander Americans. *Asian American and Pacific Islander Journal of Health, 2,* 290–298.

Marsella, A.J. (1993). Counseling and psychotherapy with Japanese Americans: cross-cultural considerations. *American Journal of Orthopsychiatry, 63,* 200–208.

Maskarinec, G., Dhakal, S., Yamashiro, G., & Issell, B.F. (2002). The use of breast conserving surgery: linking insurance claims with tumor registry data. *BMC Cancer, 2,* 3.

Maskarinec, G., & Meng, L. (2000). A case-control study of mammographic densities in Hawaii. *Breast Cancer Research and Treatment, 63,* 153–161.

Maskarinec, G., Meng, L., & Ursin, G. (2001). Ethnic differences in mammographic densities. *International Journal of Epidemiology, 30,* 959–965.

Maskarinec, G., Pagano, I., Yamashiro, G., & Issell, B.F. (in press). Influences of ethnicity, treatment, and comorbidity on breast cancer survival. *Journal of Clinical Epidemiology.*

Maskarinec, G., Shumay, D.M., Kakai, H., & Gotay, C.C. (2000). Ethnic differences in complementary and alternative medicine use among cancer patients. *Journal of Alternative and Complementary Medicine, 6,* 531–538.

Maxwell, A.E., Bastani, R., & Warda, U.S. (2000). Demographic predictors of cancer screening among Filipino and Korean immigrants in the United States. *American Journal of Preventive Medicine, 18,* 62–68.

May, D.S., Lee, N.C., Richardson, L.C., Giustozzi, A.G., & Bobo, J.K. (2000). Mammography and breast cancer detection by race and Hispanic ethnicity: results from a national program (United States). *Cancer Causes and Control, 11,* 697–705.

McCredie, M., Williams, S., & Coates, M. (1999). Cancer mortality in East and Southeast Asian migrants to New South Wales, Australia, 1975–1995. *British Journal of Cancer, 79,* 1277–1282.

McPhee, S.J., Stewart, S., Brock, K.C., Bird, J.A., Jenkins, C.N., & Pham, G.Q. (1997). Factors associated with breast and cervical cancer screening practices among Vietnamese American women. *Cancer Detection and Prevention, 21,* 510–521.

Meng, L., Maskarinec, G., & Wilkens, L. (1997). Ethnic differences and factors related to breast cancer survival in Hawaii. *International Journal of Epidemiology, 26*(6), 1151–1158.

Mettlin, C. (1999). Global breast cancer mortality statistics. *CA—A Cancer Journal for Clinicians, 49,* 138–144.

Mo, B. (1992). Modesty, sexuality, and breast health in Chinese-American women. *Western Journal of Medicine, 157,* 260–264.

Morris, C.R., Cohen, R., Schlag, R., & Wright, W.E. (2000). Increasing trends in the use of breast-conserving surgery in California. *American Journal of Public Health, 90,* 281–284.

National Cancer Institute. (1999). *Knowledge, attitudes, and behavior of immigrant Asian American women ages 40 and older regarding breast cancer and mammography screening: final report.* Bethesda, Md.: Author.

National Institutes of Health. (1990). Treatment of early-stage breast cancer. *NIH Consensus Statement.*

Retrieved September 28, 2002, from *http://consensus.nih.gov/cons/081/081/_statement.html.*

Nguyen, T., Vo, P.H., McPhee, S.J., & Jenkins, C.N. (2001). Promoting early detection of breast cancer among Vietnamese-American women: results of a controlled trial. *Cancer, 1*(S), 267–273.

Nold, R.J., Beamer, R.L., Helmer, S.D., & McBoyle, M.F. (2000). Factors influencing a woman's choice to undergo breast-conserving surgery versus modified radical mastectomy. *The American Journal of Surgery, 180,* 413–418.

Paisano, E.L., Carroll, D.L., Cowles, J.H., DeBarros, K.A., Robinson, A.J., & Miles, K.N. (1993). *We, the American Asians.* Washington, D.C., U.S. Department of Commerce, Government Printing Office.

Pham, C.T., & McPhee, S.J. (1992). Knowledge, attitudes, and practices of breast and cervical cancer screening among Vietnamese women. *Journal of Cancer Education, 7,* 305–310.

Phipps, E., Cohen, M.H., Sorn, R., & Braitman, L.E. (1999). A pilot study of cancer knowledge and screening behaviors of Vietnamese and Cambodian women. *Health Care for Women International, 20,* 195–207.

Pineda, M.D. White, E., Kristal, A.R., & Taylor, V. (2001). Asian breast cancer survival in the U.S.: a comparison between Asian immigrants, U.S.-born Asian Americans and Caucasians. *International Journal of Epidemiology, 30,* 976–982.

Shimizu, H., Ross, R.K., Bernstein, L., Yatani, R., Henderson, B.E., & Mack, T.M. (1991). Cancers of the prostate and breast among Japanese and white immigrants in Los Angeles County. *British Journal of Cancer, 63,* 963–966.

Shumay, D.M., Maskarinec, G., Kakai, H., & Gotay, C.C. (2001). Why some cancer patients choose complementary and alternative medicine instead of conventional treatment. *Journal of Family Practice, 50,* 1067.

Stanford, J.L., Herrinton, L.J., Schwartz, S.M., & Weiss, N.S. (1995). Breast cancer incidence in Asian migrants to the United States and their descendants. *Epidemiology, 6,* 181–183.

Tang, T.S., Solomon, L.J., & McCracken, L.M. (2000). Cultural barriers to mammography, clinical breast exam, and breast self-exam among Chinese-American women 60 and older. *Preventive Medicine, 31,* 575–583.

Tang, T.S., Solomon, L.J., Yeh, C.J., & Worden, J.K. (1999). The role of cultural variables in breast self-examination and cervical cancer screening behavior in young Asian women living in the United States. *Journal of Behavioral Medicine, 22,* 419–436.

Tanjasiri, S.P., Kagawa-Singer, M., Foo, M.A., Chao, M., Linayao-Putman, I., Lor, Y.C., Xiong, Y., Moua, M., Nguyen, J., & Vang, X. (2001). Breast cancer screening among Hmong women in California. *Journal of Cancer Education, 16,* 50–54.

Tu, S.P., Yasui, Y., Kuniyuki, A., Schwartz, S.M., Jackson, S.M., & Taylor, V.M. (2002). Breast cancer screening: stages of adoption among Cambodian American women. *Cancer Detection and Prevention, 26,* 33–41.

Tu, S.P., Yasui, Y., Kuniyuki, A., Thompson, B., Schwartz, S.M., Jackson, J.C., & Taylor, V.M. (2000). Breast cancer screening among Cambodian American women. *Cancer Detection and Prevention, 24,* 549–563.

U.S. Census Bureau. (2002a). *The Asian and Pacific Islander population in the United States: March 2000.* U.S. Department of Commerce. Retrieved August 29, 2002, from *http://www.census.gov/population/www/socdemo/race/api.html.*

U.S. Census Bureau. (2002b). *A profile of the nation's foreign-born population from Asia (2000 Update).* U.S. Department of Commerce. Retrieved August 29, 2002, from *http://www.census.gov/population/www/socdemo/race/api.html.*

Yi, J.K. (1995). Acculturation, access to care and use of preventive health services by Vietnamese women. *Asian American and Pacific Islander Journal of Health, 3,* 31–41.

Yu, E.S., Kim, K.K., Chen, E.H., & Brintnall, R.A. (2001). Breast and cervical cancer screening among Chinese American women. *Cancer Practice, 9,* 81–91.

Yu, M., Seetoo, A.D., & Qu, M. (2002). Challenges of identifying Asian women for breast cancer screening. *Oncology Nursing Forum, 29,* 585–587.

Ziegler, R.G., Hoover, R.N., Pike, M.C., Hildesheim, A., Nomura, A.M., West, D.W., Wu-Williams, A.H., Kolonel, L.N., Horn-Ross, P.L., Rosenthal, J.F., *et al.* (1993). Migration patterns and breast cancer risk in Asian-American women. *Journal of the National Cancer Institute, 85,* 1819–1827.

Section VI

SURVIVORSHIP AND END OF LIFE

Chapter 20

SUPPORT AND SURVIVORSHIP ISSUES

VICTORIA WOCHNA LOERZEL, RN, MSN, AOCN

INTRODUCTION

More than two million women are alive with a breast cancer history. Although many interventions are available for physical and psychosocial needs during treatment, assistance for the patient who has psychosocial needs after treatment may be lacking, leaving the patient unsure of how to deal with many situations. Cancer is not an individual experience; it is a family experience. Each patient may have preexisting stressors that may not be related to but are aggravated by a breast cancer diagnosis. Support or perceived support is a vital factor in helping the patient adjust to cancer. Unfortunately, sometimes a diagnosis of cancer alters a person's support system, and previously supportive people may be absent when the patient needs support the most. An individual's own fears about cancer may influence their ability to support a cancer patient and cause them to withhold or withdraw their support. Some people feel uncomfortable dealing with and talking about cancer and may avoid contact with the cancer patient (Fredette, 1995).

This chapter will describe some of the psychosocial concerns that breast cancer survivors, their partners, and their families have during the cancer experience. It will also discuss the importance of support and its relationship to adjustment to the diagnosis at various stages of disease, as well as the similarities and differences in the adjustment of different family members. Additionally, the chapter will examine support systems and what patients are doing to get the support and information that they need during this critical time in their lives.

PSYCHOSOCIAL CONCERNS

FEAR OF RECURRENCE

Several studies have shown that fear of recurrence is a major concern of breast cancer survivors, regardless of their stage at diagnosis (Ferrell *et al.*, 1995, 1996; Fredette, 1995; Woods *et al.*, 1989). Vickberg (2001) noted that the majority of women expressed moderate fears of recurrence rather than strong fears. Fears involving recurrence included the possibility of death, more treatment, pain, advancing disease, emotional concerns, and the suffering of their family members. Many women reported increased fear at certain times in their lives, particularly when hearing of other women who had recurrent cancer or when their own follow-up appointments or tests made them think about the possibility of a recurrence. Fears are also influenced by previous experience with breast cancer and other concurrent events in their lives at any given time. Social support was seen to be important for survivors; however, women identified that exposure to other women and hearing their concerns about recurrence also triggered fears.

Mellon and Northouse (2001) examined family survivorship and quality of life following a cancer diagnosis. Fear of recurrence was a major stressor for some families. The patient's own fear of recurrence affected how the family viewed the meaning of cancer in their family. Additionally, the family members' own fears of recurrence had an impact on overall family quality of life, especially if the family members kept these fears to themselves. Another factor that influenced family quality of life was social support. The more social support a family received, the higher they rated their quality of life. The investigators noted that social support was a continuous need for families during the survivorship period.

Many of the fears are similar for all family members. At times, some fears may be more prominent than others. Hoskins (2001) demonstrated differences in some fears between patients and spouses. For example, women experienced distress over treatment and the side effects, but their partners worried about taking on domestic chores such as managing the home and children. Although they were concerned about their wives' well-being, husbands seemed more distressed with day-to-day activities. Many of the concerns of the family will be outlined later in this chapter.

Vinokur *et al.* (1989) compared the physical and psychological functioning and adjustment to breast cancer among younger and older women. They found that older women faired better than younger women with regard to mental health and psychological functioning. Understandably, early-stage survivors experienced less physical and social dysfunction than those who were diagnosed with more advanced disease, when compared to the general population.

Ultimately, fear of recurrence is complex and may surface at any time. Oncology nurses need to assess this fear periodically or listen for cues that fears are a concern of their patients and family members. Once this fear is identified, oncology nurses can help them work through the fear.

CONCERNS RELATED TO RECURRENT CANCER

Several studies looked at the impact of recurrent cancer, which is often more distressing than the initial diagnosis of cancer (Mahon *et al.,* 1990). Hopes of cure are shattered when a cancer recurs and the future is again uncertain. Northouse *et al.* (1995) studied factors that affect a couple's adjustment to the diagnosis of recurrent breast cancer. Study results showed that both the patient and her partner sensed each other's support and emotional state, which in turn affected how the other adjusted to the recurrence. Levels of support, symptoms experienced, and feelings of hopelessness and uncertainty were integral to the level of adjustment of both patient and spouse. Ultimately, the higher the amount of perceived negative symptoms and emotions, the more difficult it was for women and their husbands to adjust to the recurrence. The findings from this study call for oncology nurses to find ways to support the caregiver as well as the patient and to include spouses in education and support programs.

SOCIAL SUPPORT

Hoskins (2001) found that emotional state could be predicted by support from the spouse and from other adults. Courtens *et al.* (1996) found that women who perceive low emotional support reported more symptoms and lower quality of life. Conversely, they noted that women with better emotional support had a better quality of life. They were unable to determine whether better quality of life resulted from more emotional support or whether a better quality of life led to more emotional support. Courtens *et al.* (1996) saw a loss of emotional support in some women who had an increase in their physical symptoms. Support from others waned when women needed it most, particularly when they were having more physical symptoms. The investigators posited that friends and family members may find it easier to deal with a patient who is getting better than with one who is becoming more ill. Also, some cancer patients become dependent on others and less able to give and support their friends at their own time of crisis. This may cause the relationship to suffer if friends perceive that they are not getting support in return. Physical limitations, such as mobility problems and other side effects, may cause social isolation from those people who act as a support for the survivor. However, friends and family may also be less attentive if they see that the patient physically looks better.

Lewis *et al.* (2001) explored social support, intrusive thoughts, and quality of life in long-term survivors. Social support was seen to have a positive effect balanced against long-term negative effects of cancer. Intrusive thoughts about cancer and the fear of recurrence were distressing to the patients. However, women who were able to talk to people about their disease and their feelings perceived fewer negative effects. Conversely, women who reported low perceived social support also reported having low quality of life, both mentally and physically.

SOCIAL SUPPORT FOR FAMILY

The cancer experience has a significant impact on the family. In a literature review, Woods *et al.* (1989) concluded that there were many different concerns among family members, depending on their specific role within the family. These concerns varied at different stages of diagnosis. Some concerns included a fear of cancer, disease progression, and possibility of recurrence. These were concerns of both patients and spouses dealing with early- and late-stage disease. Ability to bear children, emotional disturbance of the patient, and concerns about death were additional cited concerns. Each one was ranked differently by women and their spouses. As seen in other studies, women adjusted better to their diagnosis when family support was present.

Ferrell *et al.* (1995, 1996) identified family distress as a major concern of women undergoing cancer treatment and one that had great impact on their perceived quality of life. A diagnosis of cancer may be an additional burden on a family, making support for the family essential. Unfortunately, Ferrell *et al.* (1996) found that women felt that little support existed to help them and their families cope with breast cancer. In another study, women reported that support from friends and other people had a positive influence on their lives (Ferrell *et al.*, 1995). Women found that although they lacked support in professional situations, they found support through social contacts.

Another area of stress for the family is taking care of a chronically ill family member. As treatments improve and women live longer, they also run the risk of developing some debilitating long-term side effects, and they may lose some independence and functioning. Although family members may take on additional roles and responsibilities from the ill family member, it may cause a significant burden to the family and negatively affect their quality of life (Canam & Acorn, 1999).

Family support has an impact on the patient's quality of life. Mellon and Northouse (2001) saw a direct relationship between reported support and quality of life if this support continued into extended survivorship. Antonucci (1985) noted that patients expected their family to support them, and if they did not perceive support, they viewed the family negatively. However, when support came from an unexpected area such as friends, this support was perceived in a positive light. Alferi *et al.* (2001) explored family support in low-income Hispanic women. The investigators agreed that emotional support from family and friends decreased stress levels for patients. The study also showed that support may fade the longer the patient is away from diagnosis and treatment.

Although cancer was seen to have some positive influences on a family's quality of life, Mellon (2002) found that families had ongoing concerns about cancer in the family and how it may have an impact on them at a later time. These fears lasted for years after the initial diagnosis. Support was also discussed; one difference between family and patient was that family members saw their role as to support the patient instead of addressing their own needs for support. Because of this tendency, families may continue to have unmet emotional needs throughout the cancer experience, which may affect their quality of life.

CONCERNS OF THE SPOUSE

Several studies have looked at the specific needs of the spouse of the woman who has breast cancer. Petrie *et al.* (2001) reviewed the literature to determine the needs of the spouse of the breast cancer patient. Spouses feel many of the same emotions that their wives feel, including anxiety, fear, sadness, and uncertainty about the future. They also experience feelings of powerlessness; they feel uninformed and may experience difficulties at work and problems concentrating.

Samms (1999) interviewed several husbands and looked at their emotions and concerns related to their wives' breast cancer. The study found that their concerns seemed to evolve over time and focus on different issues. Initially, in the crisis phase, they reported feeling overwhelmed and were focused on immediate needs and on protecting their wives and themselves from their own feelings, instead of dealing with these feelings. They reported feeling left out and isolated during the initial diagnosis and treatment. During treatment, husbands were concerned with doing well by their wives, yet they felt that they were an inadequate support at times. Several spouses took on extra chores and responsibilities and felt overwhelmed by them. After treatment, husbands felt that they had trouble making the transition from treatment to recovery.

Samms (1999) also looked at what husbands felt would have helped them during the different phases of illness. They felt that education on the illness and guidance concerning how to help and support their wives would have been beneficial. Most felt left out of the whole experience, because health care professionals focused on the woman who had cancer. These feelings were stressful for husbands. They wanted more information on the disease, on what to expect for their wives, and on dealing with their wives' emotions, as well as an opportunity to talk about and deal with their own emotions.

Ultimately, the focus is on the patient who has been diagnosed with cancer. Spouses have many needs, as well, and they run the risk of feeling left out, both educationally and emotionally, of interventions that are focused on the patient (Hoskins, 2001). Health care professionals need to take a look at their treatment and inclusion of the spouse and family in their interventions to better prepare them to support the ill family member. Nurses can play a vital role in identifying issues and concerns of the family members and helping them to get the information and support they need.

CONCERNS OF CHILDREN

Not surprisingly, children of patients with cancer share many of the same concerns as their parents. However, they also have issues and concerns related to their own stage of growth and development. Psychosocial problems may occur in young children of cancer patients according to their age and the stage of their parent's disease (Germino & Funk, 1993; Nelson & While, 2002). Children may have difficulty adjusting to the diagnosis and subsequent treatment.

Nelson and While (2002) described how younger children may be at risk for adjustment problems if they are not informed about their parent's illness. They also noted that adolescents had a poorer time adjusting than younger children. In their interviews with children, the investigators determined that low self-esteem increased the risk for adjustment problems. Also, difficulty in the parent's adjustment to the diagnosis affected the child's adjustment, as well.

Germino and Funk (1993) interviewed the adult children of cancer patients who had recently been diagnosed. Adult children with parents having cancer are concerned with their parent's illness, treatment, and risk for recurrence. Additionally, they have concerns about the changing roles and relationships with their parents. For many adult children, this is a time of role changes. They are now a support to the person who has always supported them. They are caught in a role of both child and support person, which may be difficult for both parent and child to come to terms with. Additionally, adult children are also juggling the demands of their own families and careers. Adding in the responsibility of caring for a parent can often be exhausting. Several people in the study expressed difficulty in dealing with their parent's emotions, such as depression, because they were not emotions that they traditionally associated with their parent. As our population ages, more adults will experience a parent having cancer and would benefit from being included in educational interventions. They may also need emotional support, from both health care professionals and their own support systems.

WORKPLACE ISSUES

Employment is an important part of life for many cancer survivors. It gives them a sense of self, social support through interactions with other people (Maunsell *et al.*, 1999), and normalcy (Fredette, 1995). However, work can also be a significant source of stress. Many people may feel stigmatized at work because of their diagnosis of cancer, and they may worry about their coworkers' reactions. Fiore (1996) outlined several concerns of cancer patients related to their coworkers' reactions to their diagnoses. Patients fear the misperceptions of their coworkers, who may think that the cancer patient may not be able to do her job once she returns to work. Survivors fear that others will perceive them as being unhealthy and wonder if they will be able to do their fair share of the work. They may also fear insensitive comments from coworkers who may be uncomfortable with cancer because of their own experiences.

As more and more people return to work or even remain employed during their cancer treatment, cancer becomes an issue that is dealt with beyond the home and the doctor's office. On the whole, survivors can experience a seamless transition from the illness to the workplace, but a small minority report discrimination (Schultz *et al.*, 2002), which can have an impact on the survivor's quality of life. Many people fear discrimination, losing benefits, not being able to change jobs, and being stigmatized in the workplace because of their diagnosis of cancer (Dow, 1995). Privacy may also be an issue, as many people may not want to discuss the details of their disease and treatment and may be uncomfortable when coworkers inquire. Employers, too, may not understand the disease and the reasons for fatigue and cognitive deficits when a patient first returns to work.

Maunsell *et al.* (1999) reported on concerns of breast cancer survivors upon returning to work. These included demotions, job loss, being given different, unwanted tasks to perform, having problems with the employer and coworkers, and having an attitude change within themselves toward work and their own physical capabilities. This study also noted that the issues today are very similar to the issues women faced 20 years ago when they returned to work after a breast cancer diagnosis. Interestingly, this study did identify new areas of concern brought about by behaviors of health care workers. Coworkers may be more aware of the patient's diagnosis of cancer when a health care worker calls the patient during work hours to inform her of pathology and other test results. This may lead to a negative impression of the cancer patient if she becomes emotional as a result of being given poor test results over the phone.

Women may be unprepared for the physical challenges in returning to work. Many women felt that it took years to regain their previous feelings of good health and stamina (Maunsell *et al.,* 1999). Mock (1998) noted that fatigue in the workplace may linger for months after treatment has been completed. Individuals may need to be taught energy conservation techniques and health promotion activities in order to maintain and restore energy. Interestingly, even though work can help patients get their minds off of their illness and focus on something other than their disease, Mellon and Northouse (2001) noted that patients who were employed outside of the home or were homemakers reported lower quality of life than retired people.

SUPPORT RESOURCES

SUPPORT GROUPS

Both the patient and family members have a need for support during the illness and recovery period. Perceived support has an impact on adjustment to the illness and on quality of life for all members of the family. A good deal of the support on which patients rely is available from health care professionals in the form of written materials and support groups. For many, the doctor's office is the primary source of information for the patient and family. However, if the patient and family do not perceive this support to be readily available, they may try to obtain the information and support from outside sources. Perceived support from the oncology team can fluctuate over time. Patients may not feel comfortable asking for help in between doctor's appointments, especially if they have already completed treatment. Support groups may be at inconvenient times and places for many people to attend. Many times, patients and family members have to go outside the doctor's office in order to find the information they are seeking.

There are many resources available for patients with breast cancer, both in local communities and on the Internet. National organizations such as the American Cancer Society have a wealth of information for cancer patients. They also offer educational programs such as I Can Cope, which is designed to give patients and their families an overview of cancer. Peer support programs such as Reach to Recovery are also available in many communities. The Internet is an additional source of endless information for patients.

INTERNET SUPPORT

The Internet is increasingly used as a means of social support. Internet usage in women with breast cancer is on the rise (Pereira *et al.,* 2000). Typically, women who use the Internet for information are younger, better educated, and less satisfied with the amount of information given to them by their doctor's office than those women who did not look for information on the Internet. Internet users are looking for treatment-related information and options, information on alternative treatments, and general cancer information to supplement what they are being given by their health care providers. Some users were wary of information on the Internet and wondered about its credibility.

Clark and Gomez (2001) identified a variety of reasons that make the Internet appealing. The Internet is convenient for people; it gives them a sense of control during the illness, and they report being consistently satisfied with the information they receive. Not only can patients find information about their disease or illness, they also have access to support groups and chat rooms, which can increase their social support and decrease feelings of isolation.

Fogel *et al.* (2002) reported that 42% of the breast cancer patients interviewed used the Internet to obtain information concerning their breast cancer. They spent an average of 0.8 hours per week on the Internet. Fogel also found that use of the Internet for social support was associated with less loneliness than observed in women who used the Internet for other reasons. The Internet can also be a great source of frustration for patients because of the overwhelming amount of information, both credible and incredible, that is available.

Oncology nurses can help the patient and family find the credible information they are seeking and explain how to evaluate the credibility of Web sites. Patients should be informed about the variety of sites available and how to pick the best ones. Some of the keys include a Web site that is updated frequently. It should also have a link that discloses its funding sources. Privacy statements are important in order to keep personal information personal. Details about the provider of the Web site's information can also help patients decide if the site is credible. Ideally, the site should contain a section that gives information about a technical support person who can assist users with problems with the site. Table 20.1 lists common Web sites for women with breast cancer.

Table 20.1 Web Site Resources

American Cancer Society
http://www.cancer.org

Breast Cancer Education Network
http://www.healthtalk.com/bcen/index.html

Breast Cancer.Net
http://www.breastcancer.net

Breast Health Network
http://www.breasthealthnetwork.com/home

Table 20.1 (continued)

Cancer Information Network
http://www.cancerlinksusa.com/breast/index.asp

Gillette Women's Cancer Connection
http://www.gillettecancerconnect.org

National Coalition for Cancer Survivorship
http://www.canceradvocacy.org

National Institutes of Health
http://www.nci.nih.gov

Oncolink
http://cancer.med.upenn.edu

Phenomenal Women of the Web—Breast Cancer Awareness Network
http://www.phenomenalwomen.com/breast-cancer

Women's Information Network Against Breast Cancer
http://www.winabc.org

Women's Cancer Network
http://www.wcn.org

Y-Me National Breast Cancer Organization
http://www.y-me.org

REFERENCES

Alferi, S.M., Carver, C.S., Antoni, M.H., Weiss, S., & Durn, R.N. (2001). An exploratory study of social support, distress, and life disruption among low-income Hispanic women under treatment for early stage breast cancer. *Health Psychology, 20*(1), 41–46.

Antonucci, T.C. (1985). Social support: theoretical advances, recent findings and pressing issues. In I.G. Sarason & B.R. Sarason (Eds.), *Social support: theory, research and applications*, pp. 21–49. Boston: Martinus Nyhoff.

Canam, C., & Acorn, S. (1999). Quality of life for family caregivers of people with chronic health problems. *Rehabilitation Nursing, 24*(5), 192–196, 200.

Clark, P.M., & Gomez, E.G. (2001). Details on demand: consumers, cancer information, and the Internet. *Clinical Journal of Oncology Nursing, 5*(1), 19–24.

Courtens, A.M., Stevens, F.C.J., Crebolder, H.F.J.M., & Philipsen, H. (1996). Longitudinal study on quality of life and social support in cancer patients. *Cancer Nursing, 19*(3), 162–169.

Dow, K.H. (1995). A review of late effects of cancer in women. *Seminars in Oncology Nursing, 11*(2), 128–136.

Ferrell, B.R., Dow, K.H., Leigh, S., Ly, J., & Gulasekaram, P. (1995). Quality of life in long-term cancer survivors. *Oncology Nursing Forum, 22*(6), 915–922.

Ferrell, B.R., Grant, M., Funk, B., Garcia, N., Otis-Green, S., & Schaffner, M.L.J. (1996). Quality of life in breast cancer. *Cancer Practice, 4*(6), 331–340.

Fiore, N. (1996). Mind and body: harnessing your inner resources. In B. Hoffman (Ed.), *A cancer survivor's almanac*, pp. 91–113. New York: John Wiley & Sons.

Fogel, J., Albert, S.M., Schnabel, F., Ditkoff, B.A., & Neugut, A.I. (2002). Internet use and social support in women with breast cancer. *Health Psychology, 21*(4), 398–404.

Fredette, S.L. (1995). Breast cancer survivors: concerns and coping. *Cancer Nursing, 18*(1), 35–46.

Germino, B.B., & Funk, S.G. (1993). Impact of a parent's cancer on adult children: role and relationship issues. *Seminars in Oncology Nursing, 9*(2), 101–106.

Hoskins, C.N. (2001). Promoting adjustment among women with breast cancer and their partners: a program of research. *Journal of the New York State Nurses Association, 32*(2), 19–23.

Lewis, J.A., Manne, S.L., DuHamel, K.N., Vickburg, S.M.J., Bovbjerg, D.H., Currie, V., Winkel, G., & Redd, W.H. (2001). Social support, intrusive thoughts, and quality of life in breast cancer survivors. *Journal of Behavioral Medicine, 24*(3), 231–245.

Mahon, S.M., Cella, D.F., & Donovan, M.I. (1990). Psychosocial adjustment to recurrent cancer. *Oncology Nursing Forum, 17*(3 Suppl), 47–52.

Maunsell, E., Brisson, C., Dubois, L., Lauzier, S., & Fraser, A. (1999). Work problems after breast cancer: an exploratory qualitative study. *Psycho-Oncology, 8*(6), 467–473.

Mellon, S. (2002). Comparisons between cancer survivors and family members on meaning of the illness and family quality of life. *Oncology Nursing Forum, 29*(7), 1117–1125.

Mellon, S., & Northouse, L.L. (2001). Family survivorship and quality of life following a cancer diagnosis. *Research in Nursing and Health, 24*(6), 446–459.

Mock, V. (1998). Breast cancer and fatigue: issues for the workplace. *AAOHN Journal, 46*(9), 425–431.

Nelson, E., & While, D. (2002). Children's adjustment during the first year of a parent's cancer diagnosis. *Journal of Psychosocial Oncology, 20*(1), 15–36.

Northouse, L.L., Dorris, G., & Charron-Moore, C. (1995). Factors affecting couples' adjustment to recurrent breast cancer. *Social Science and Medicine, 41*(1), 69–76.

Pereira, J.L., Koski, S., Hanson, J., Bruera, E.D., & Mackey, J.R. (2000). Internet usage among women with breast cancer: an exploratory study. *Clinical Breast Cancer, 1*(2), 148–153.

Petrie, W., Logan, J., & DeGrasse, C. (2001). Research review of the supportive care needs of spouses of women with breast cancer. *Oncology Nursing Forum, 28*(10), 1601–1607.

Samms, M.C. (1999). The husband's untold account of his wife's breast cancer: a chronological analysis. *Oncology Nursing Forum, 26*(8), 1351–1358.

Schultz, P.N., Beck, M.L., Stava, C., & Sellin, R.V. (2002). Cancer survivors: work related issues. *AAOHN Journal, 50*(5), 220–226.

Sutton, L. (2001). The importance of social support in women with breast cancer—implications for nursing practice. *West Virginia Nurse, 5*(3), 18–19.

Vickberg, S.M.J. (2001). Fears about breast cancer recurrence: interviews with a diverse sample. *Cancer Practice, 9*(5), 237–243.

Vinokur, A.D., Threatt, B.A., Caplan, R.D., & Zimmerman, B.L. (1989). Physical and psychological functioning and adjustment to breast cancer. *Cancer, 63*, 394–405.

Voluntary Hospital Association. (1999, April 5). 43% of consumers turn to Internet for answers about their healthcare [Press release]. Retrieved November 21, 2001, from *https://www.vha.com/publicreleases/pagebuilder.asp?url=/publicreleases/990405.asp*

Woods, N.F., Lewis, F.M., & Ellison, E.S. (1989). Living with cancer: family experiences. *Cancer Nursing, 12*(1), 28–33.

Chapter 21

END OF LIFE AND PALLIATIVE CARE

KYLE-ANNE HOYER, RN, MSN, AOCN

INTRODUCTION

Of the 203,500 women diagnosed with breast cancer, an estimated 39,600 women will die from metastatic disease (Jemal *et al.,* 2002). Although great advances have been made in treating breast cancer and prolonging life, there has been no change in the natural course of the disease. In fact, many women will develop metastatic disease (Cha *et al.,* 1999; Georgoulias, 2001; Hortobagyi, 2001). Unfortunately, advanced breast cancer, which is characterized by local or distant metastases, is incurable and is responsible for death associated with the disease (Creagan, 1993). The situation is not hopeless, because the course of the disease can be controlled. The length of time for which the disease is controlled depends on individual patient characteristics, bone versus visceral metastases, and/or the presence of comorbidities (Rubens, 2001). Furthermore, the development of second- and third-line hormonal agents, monoclonal antibodies, and ongoing research in gene therapy and growth factors have provided hope to breast cancer patients and their families. One is cautioned, however, that these treatments do not offer substantial long-term survival results (Hortobagyi, 2001; Olin & Muss, 2000). This information could be debatable as older postmenopausal women have fairly long disease-free intervals (Cha *et al.,* 1999). Together, the patient and the health care team must find a balance between quality of life and palliation of symptoms.

When the patient with breast cancer presents with metastatic disease and the goal is no longer cure, the patient enters the palliative care trajectory. To palliate is defined in the *American Heritage Dictionary* as "to soothe without curing." This definition supports the delivery of palliative care along the disease continuum once advanced breast cancer is diagnosed. Palliative care becomes the standard of care for patients living with advanced breast cancer and plays a supportive role from diagnosis onward (Thompson & Reilly, 2002). The delivery of palliative care focuses more on quality of life and alleviation of distressing symptoms and less on aggressive interventions. Palliative care also offers psychosocial support to the patient, family, and friends to cope with death and bereavement (McHale, 2002). The purpose of this chapter is to describe the palliative care trajectory, apply the trajectory to advanced and metastatic breast cancer, describe the different types of metastases and treatments, discuss end-of-life symptom clusters, and consider communication and decision-making issues.

THE PALLIATIVE CARE TRAJECTORY

The palliative care trajectory as described by Brant (1998) and McHale (2002) involves three distinct phases. Each phase is characterized by the individual goals of the patient, life expectancy, and the presence and site of metastases. A palliative care trajectory can assist the health care team in identifying the physical and psychosocial needs of the patient and family and providing appropriate interventions to facilitate living life with meaning, dignity, and value. The first two phases are centered around treating the disease while the third phase focuses on comfort and end of life issues. Table 21.1 illustrates the palliative care trajectory and is provided as a guide. Throughout these phases runs the common theme of hope. Hope is always present in humans, but the perception of hope changes depending on age and life events. In the presence of a life-threatening illness such as advanced breast cancer, the goals and expectations of hope change (Nowotny, 1989). Each patient's perception of hope is unique.

In the first or active phase of the palliative care trajectory, the goal is control of the disease with the intent to prolong life. Quality of life is important at this phase, but the patient may be willing to tolerate some unpleasant side effects in exchange for a longer life. At this point, more aggressive therapies with second-line chemotherapy and/or hormonal treatment are reasonable considerations. Chemotherapeutic agents could be used alone or in combination, in addition to surgical and radiation therapy interventions. Cytotoxic chemotherapy can prolong life, improve or maintain quality of life, and provide a better response to the disease. These are reasonable goals for patients in the active

Table 21.1 Palliative Care Trajectory

Active phase	Symptomatic phase	Supportive phase
Halt disease progression	Slow or control disease	Treatment is for symptom management, not tumor effect
Aggressive treatment	Relief of tumor-related symptoms	management, not tumor effect
Tolerate toxicities	Less aggressive treatment	Goal: comfortable death
Goal: prolong life	Therapeutic index: balance between benefit and harm	
	Tolerate fewer toxicities	
	Goal: symptom relief/management	

phase when the goal is to receive treatment without evidence of disease progression (Seidman, 2001). A clinical example that illustrates this phase is a 63-year-old post-menopausal woman diagnosed 10 years earlier who received surgical intervention followed by systemic chemotherapy for hormone receptor-positive stage II breast cancer. Two years after her initial diagnosis, she presented with bone pain. Diagnostic workup revealed bone metastases secondary to her breast cancer. She was started on hormonal therapy and pamidronate, which has subsequently been changed to zolendronate.

In the second phase, or the symptomatic phase, the goal is control of the disease to relieve or palliate distressing symptoms. At this point, the cancer has progressed in spite of therapy but end of life is not imminent. The goal of treatment in this phase is to continue therapies, and the endpoint is relief of cancer-associated symptoms. The ultimate goal of therapy is to use a less active agent that demonstrates a moderate tumor/disease response rate, decreased toxicity, increased symptom relief, and better quality of life outcomes. Maintaining optimal functional status is important in this phase. There is no survival advantage in this phase, but treatment allows the patient to have acceptable quality of life (Seidman, 2001; Morris & Sherwood, 1987; Georgoulias, 2001). Chemotherapy given at this phase may help maintain a patient's sense of hope and decrease anxiety.

There are several factors that may influence decision-making in this phase. These factors are related to the disease, the treatment, or the patient (Grunfeld et al., 2001). Disease-related factors are sites of metastases, number of metastatic lesions, the pace at which the disease has progressed, the length of time from initial diagnosis to disease recurrence, and hormonal status of the tumor. Treatment-related factors include tumor response to previous treatment, dose-limiting toxicities, and the number of previous chemotherapy and/or radiation therapy options. Patient-related factors are chronologic age versus physiologic age, the presence of comorbidities, social support, and functional status. The needs and expectations of the patient and family should be clearly defined in this phase. Another clinical example that illustrates this phase is a 43-year-old woman diagnosed with HER2-positive, hormone receptor-negative stage II breast cancer three years ago. Two years ago she presented with visceral metastases and received systemic chemotherapy. She now presents with additional metastatic sites and will receive single-agent chemotherapy and trastuzumab.

Finally, the third phase, or supportive phase, focuses on the goal of comfort and not prolongation of life. Therapies or treatments are used to achieve a comfortable death. The patient is now making decisions to meet end-of-life goals. At this point, there may be increased psychosocial needs revolving around death and dying, grief, bereavement, and other fundamental spiritual and emotional issues. Bloch and Kissane (2000) observed that women with advanced-stage breast cancer have a greater need for emotional support than women with earlier-stage breast cancer because their loss experience will be greater. The implementation of psychosocial interventions and aggressive symptom management in this phase can positively influence quality of life outcomes (Creagan, 1993). One clinical example is a 73-year-old woman who presents with stage IV breast cancer. Her diagnostic evaluation reveals vertebral metastases from the lumbar (L5) to sacral (S1) spine with impending spinal cord collapse and multiple brain lesions. The patient is referred to hospice for pain and symptom management.

Palliative care can also be initiated once advanced breast cancer is diagnosed and continue throughout the palliative care trajectory as the patient's condition declines (Wrede-Seaman, 2001). Patient and family counseling with the health care team can facilitate the understanding of treatment goals, recognizing improvements in the control of metastatic disease, and accepting palliative treatment. Symptoms typically associated with the end of life are present at all points along the palliative care trajectory. It is important to note what the goals of treatment are so that the appropriate interventions can be implemented. The palliative care trajectory can serve as a framework in the decision-making process. The next section will attempt to illustrate the use of this framework in the presence of advanced breast cancer.

METASTATIC DISEASE

The realities of a diagnosis of cancer have an effect on how palliative care is delivered. One of these realities is the presence of local metastases, disease that is disseminated beyond regional lymph nodes, or distant metastases. In advanced breast cancer, the most common sites of metastases are the skin, the bones, the central nervous system (CNS), and visceral organs. The common sites of metastasis in breast cancer are listed in Table 21.2. The median survival for metastatic breast cancer is approximately two to three years. This statistic is dependent on the site of the metastases. Bone metastasis has the better prognosis at a median

Table 21.2 Metastatic Breast Cancer Sites

	Bone	Visceral	CNS
Signs and symptoms	Pain Pathologic fractures Hypercalcemia Nerve compression Decreased mobility	Depends on site Dyspnea Nausea Abdominal pain Anorexia Constipation	Changes in mental status Confusion Motor disturbances
Interventions	Pain medications Radiation Bisphosphonates Surgery Endocrine therapy Systemic chemotherapy	Systemic chemotherapy Endocrine therapy Symptom relief	Corticosteroids Cranial radiation Intrathecal chemotherapy

survival of three to five years, compared to CNS metastasis with a median survival of three to five months (Elomaa, 2000; Fokstuen *et al.,* 2000; Hillner, 2000; Olin & Muss, 2000). Other prognostic indicators include age, comorbidities, performance status, the length of time from initial diagnosis to disease recurrence, and the number of metastatic sites. Before a treatment plan can be implemented, each patient must be carefully screened for these variables. This section will discuss the impact of bone, visceral, and CNS metastases on the palliative care trajectory.

BONE METASTASIS

Bone metastasis is common in advanced breast cancer, occurring in approximately 65–75% of patients (Hillner, 2000; Sciuto *et al.,* 2001). The morbidity associated with bone metastasis and the frequency with which it occurs make it a significant clinical problem (Durr *et al.,* 2002). Skeletal metastases can result in pathologic fractures, vertebral collapse, spinal cord compression, impaired mobility, hypercalcemia, and bone marrow infiltration (Sciuto *et al.,* 2001; Bohm & Huber, 2002). If there is no visceral metastasis, bone disease from advanced breast cancer should be treated aggressively with chemotherapy, radiation therapy, and surgical interventions, as appropriate.

Advanced breast cancer in the postmenopausal woman typically follows an indolent course, and the survival rate of women having only bone metastases is favorable (Cha *et al.,* 1999; Groff *et al.,* 2001). For this reason, many women with bone metastases are in the active phase of the palliative care trajectory. Treatment goals are directed to control the disease and to decrease the morbidity associated with bone metastasis (Bohm & Huber, 2002). The patient's functional status and the biology of the breast cancer should guide the treatment planning for older women with bone metastases from breast cancer.

A long-term strategy to manage bone pain, control hypercalcemia, and prevent fractures that can occur as a result of bone metastases is the use of bisphosphonates (Mannix *et al.,* 2000). Bisphosphonates inhibit osteoclast activity, which increases in the presence of bone metastases in breast cancer. Once bisphosphonates are initiated, there is a decrease in bone pain and skeletal complications and an increase in mobility (Groff *et al.,* 2001; Rubens, 2001; Olin & Muss, 2000). Bisphosphonates currently used in the United States for the management of bone metastases in breast cancer are pamidronate, zolendronate, and a clinical trial with cladronate.

Other treatments for managing bone metastases include endocrine therapy, radiation therapy, and surgery. Endocrine therapy should be initiated immediately and can continue indefinitely in patients with hormone-responsive disease. External beam radiation is used to palliate the pain associated with bone lesions, but there is current research exploring the use of targeted radiation therapy and bone-seeking isotopes (Sciuto *et al.,* 2001). Bone metastasis in advanced breast cancer is a treatable disease and should not be considered a terminal event.

VISCERAL METASTASIS

The prognosis changes dramatically with the presentation of visceral metastases with or without bone metastases (Durr *et al.*, 2002; Olin & Muss, 2000). At the onset of visceral metastases, the patient enters the symptomatic phase of the palliative care trajectory. Death from visceral disease can occur rapidly if the course of the disease is not interrupted (Rubens, 2001). Although there is still promising antitumor activity and tolerability with endocrine agents in the presence of visceral metastases, the addition of systemic chemotherapy with or without trastuzumab is often considered. The patient and the health care team should collaborate to find a balance between relief of symptoms, toxicity of treatment, and prolongation of survival (Seidman, 1996, 2001; Olin & Muss, 2000). This balance is called the "therapeutic index." Patient characteristics that guide the choice of treatment with the intent to maximize the therapeutic index include age, performance status, organ function, site of metastatic disease, hormone receptor status, and the presence of comorbid disease. The most common sites for visceral metastases in breast cancer are the liver, pleura of the lung, and ascites from peritoneal metastases.

CNS METASTASIS

The development of CNS metastases heralds terminal disease (Rubens, 2001). CNS metastases occur in approximately 6% of women and when left untreated, patient survival is about six weeks. Treatment options are limited, and many women prepare to enter the supportive phase of the palliative care trajectory. Cranial radiation, corticosteroids, and/or intrathecal chemotherapy are viable treatment options and can prolong survival by four to seven months. The placement of an Ommaya reservoir is often considered in women having a high performance status and limited or no metastatic disease to other sites (Cha *et al.*, 1999; Fokstuen *et al.*, 2000).

Visceral disease that progresses in spite of treatment is considered terminal and the patient prepares for a comfortable death. The third and final phase of the palliative care trajectory is discussed in the next section.

END-OF-LIFE SYMPTOM CLUSTERS

There is a dramatic decline in quality of life and an acceleration of deterioration in performance function in women with end-stage disease in the last few weeks of life (Morris & Sherwood, 1987; Geels *et al.*, 2000). The goal at the end of life is to allow the woman to retain as much control over her disease as possible by maintaining the highest level of functional status. The key to achieving this goal is expert symptom management. Some reported symptoms experienced at this stage include pain, constipation, anorexia, cachexia, lethargy, fatigue, dyspnea, mental status changes, and insomnia. Because many of these symptoms have common themes and affect multiple body systems, these symptoms have been organized into symptom clusters. Table 21.3 lists the end-of-life symptom clusters.

Table 21.3 End-of-Life Symptom Clusters

Symptoms	Causes	Interventions
Pain	Bone metastases	Opioids/analgesics
	Nerve impingement	Adjuvant medications
	Tumor pressure	Physical therapy
	Organ obstruction	Complementary and alternative therapies
	Preexisting chronic pain	
	Depression	
Delirium	Confusion	Haloperidol
	Hallucinations	Chlorpromazine
	Sedation	Oxygen therapy
	Seizures	Terminal sedation
	Electrolyte imbalances	
	Medications	
	CNS metastases	
	Sleep disturbances	
Dyspnea	Visceral metastases	Oxygen therapy
	Anemia	Nebulizer
	Serous effusions	Diuretics
		Treatment of effusions
		Scopolamine patches
Anorexia/cachexia	Xerostomia	Mouth moisturizers/oral care
	Taste changes	Small, frequent meals
	Tumor effects	Laxatives
	Constipation	Antiemetic therapies
	Nausea	
	Bowel obstruction	
Depression	Social withdrawal	Antidepressants
	Sleep changes	Support groups
	Weight loss	Counseling or psychotherapy
	Suicidal ideation	
	Hopelessness	

PAIN

Although there are many vital factors that contribute to a comfortable death, pain relief is at the top of the list. In metastatic disease, women may experience somatic, visceral, and/or neuropathic pain syndromes. Somatic pain may result from bone metastases, skin metastases, and lymphedema. Visceral pain arises from liver metastases or complications associated with serous effusions. Neuropathic pain can be present in CNS metastases, spinal cord compression, or nerve damage to the brachial plexus. Pain management involves a careful ongoing assessment of the patient's pain and administration of the appropriate analgesics and adjuvant drugs. Managing the side effects of opioids segues into recognizing and intervening in the next symptom cluster, mental status changes.

DELIRIUM

One of the more distressing symptoms for families is the development of delirium. Delirium presents as disorientation, restlessness and agitation, change in sensorium, memory loss and attention deficit, changes in sleep patterns, confusion, and global impairment of mental function. In end-stage breast cancer, the development of delirium is an irreversible event (Lawlor *et al.*, 2000). Delirium can be caused by opioid use, CNS metastases, hepatic encephalopathy, and dyspnea. Identifying the source of the delirium and determining the imminence of death guides the choice of intervention. When the goal is reversal of delirium, an evaluation of the medication profile and assessment of oxygenation and hepatic encephalopathy should be done. Sometimes either the addition of medication or the elimination of other medications can provide relief from delirium. In end-stage breast cancer, regardless of etiology, the treatment for delirium is the same.

Haloperidol 0.5–2.0 mg every 4–6 hours as needed is the drug of choice. If haloperidol is not effective, chlorpromazine may be used. Newer medications are available, but they remain costly in the end-of-life setting. In extreme cases where terminal sedation may need to be considered, midazolam may be used (Smith, 2002).

PLEURAL EFFUSION

The presence of serous effusions in advanced breast cancer contributes to delirium and dyspnea. Pleural effusions are the most common, but pericardial and abdominal effusions can also be present (Rubens, 2001). Symptoms associated with effusions include dyspnea, fatigue, tachycardia, anorexia, confusion, restlessness, constipation, and early satiety. Symptom management includes the use of supplemental oxygen therapy, nebulizers, diuretics, opiates, and scopolamine patches to manage secretions. If death is not imminent, pleurodesis or percutaneous pericardiocentesis may be an option for pleural or pericardial effusions. A possible intervention for the management of ascites is the placement of a peritoneal catheter to facilitate drainage and promote comfort (Rubens, 2001). Complications associated with the use of a peritoneal catheter are shock or infection. Factors to consider before implementing invasive procedures are cost, life expectancy, functional status, and, in the case of the peritoneal catheter, the family's ability to manage at home.

ANOREXIA AND CACHEXIA

Anorexia and cachexia is another symptom cluster that contributes to patient and family distress at the end of life (Brant, 1998). This cluster of symptoms has been recognized in cancer patients for a long time, but the exact etiology is unknown. In women with metastatic breast cancer, some causes are mechanical obstruction from metastatic disease, constipation, nausea, taste changes from chemotherapy, fatigue, and pain. There is a decreased need for food and fluid when death is imminent, and it is helpful to remind the family that food and hydration may actually prolong suffering and decrease patient comfort (Brant, 1998; Dixon & Esper, 2002).

DEPRESSION

The final symptom cluster is depression, which affects not only the patient but also her entire support system. Many of the symptoms associated with depression in healthy people are also seen in women with advanced breast cancer. These symptoms are anorexia, fatigue, changes in sleep patterns, and withdrawn behavior. For these reasons, depression is often not diagnosed or treated appropriately at the end of life (Creagan, 1993). Unrecognized or poorly controlled depression can contribute to poor pain management, exacerbation of fatigue and anorexia, and difficulty in controlling other end-of-life symptoms.

Management of depression should include the appropriate use of antidepressants and counseling. The choice of antidepressants depends on the patient's medication profile and life expectancy (Kuebler, 2002). Psychosocial interventions such as counseling and support groups should include the family or caregivers (Lloyd-Williams & Friedman, 2001). Patient education is important to assist the patient in understanding the importance of treating depression. For example, a 48-year-old woman who has failed treatment and a stem cell transplant for her advanced breast cancer is prescribed antidepressants. She understands that she will die from her cancer, admits that her depression is situational, but states that taking antidepressants will not change the fact that she will die. After meeting with the oncology social worker, the woman decides to try antidepressants and continue with weekly trastuzumab infusions.

Patients initiate the use of complementary and alternative medicine (CAM) therapies throughout the disease and treatment trajectory. The increased use of CAM therapies at the end of life suggests that there is an increased awareness of the connectedness of the mind, body, and spirit (Thompson & Reilly, 2002). Using CAM therapies gives the woman more control over her symptoms in an otherwise uncontrollable situation. More research is needed to determine if the use of herbs and nutraceuticals is helpful in alleviating distressing symptoms and altering mood disturbances (Shen *et al.*, 2002). As more research becomes available, evidenced-based protocols using CAM therapies can be developed and implemented in the end-of-life setting for women with metastatic breast cancer.

COMMUNICATION AND DECISION-MAKING

Decision-making is a complex and difficult task for many patients when faced with the diagnosis of metastatic breast cancer. In spite of the difficulties associated with decision-making, the patient, family, and health care team should be involved (Koedoot *et al.*, 2001). This task becomes even more complex when the patient accepts that there is no cure and refuses further treatment, but the family wants to do everything possible to prolong life. O'Connor (1995) defines decisional conflict as a state of uncertainty about a course of action to be taken. This is especially significant to the woman with metastatic breast cancer where the choice involves uncertainty and when significant gains or losses are involved (Bloch & Kissane, 2000). The steps in making decisions regarding end-of-life care can be described as the path taken by a body moving under the action of given forces. This pathway is illustrated in Table 21.4.

CONCLUSION

Metastatic breast cancer is an incurable disease, and it is unfortunate that the only treatment is palliative in nature. In spite of this grim outcome, many options for treating and controlling the natural history of metastatic breast cancer are available. The palliative care trajectory can guide the selection of appropriate treatment goals and facilitate decision-making for the woman with metastatic breast cancer. The therapeutic index, the balance between the benefits of treatments with the toxicities, and a clear vision of the intended outcome are important issues to be evaluated before initiating therapy. Early interventions can decrease morbidity, especially in the presence of bone metastases, and prolong survival. When breast cancer progresses despite treatment, the goal of treatment becomes

Table 21.4 Palliative Care Trajectory Decision-Making Pathway

Decision to test	Voluntary (screening)
	Involuntary (palpable mass)
Timing of diagnosis	Career goals
	Family goals
	Personal goals
Assimilation of diagnosis	Expected (family history, presence of lump)
	Middle ground (fatalism)
	Shock
Presence of metastasis or disease recurrence	Bone metastasis
	Visceral metastasis
	CNS metastasis
	Multiple metastatic foci
Initiation of therapy	Active phase
	Symptomatic phase
	Supportive phase
Response to therapy	Disease controlled
	Disease progression
Changes in performance status	Changes in functional status
	Changes in body image and self-esteem
End points	Death
	Symptoms controlled
	Entry into hospice

comfort. The presence or onset of end-of-life symptom clusters can be distressing for the patient and the family. Managing these symptoms and maintaining an optimal performance status for as long as possible contributes to improved quality of life when the prognosis for the woman with breast cancer is terminal.

SUMMARY

A diagnosis of cancer is a life-altering experience for most people. When the diagnosis does not come with the hope of cure, then the goal of treatment becomes improving quality of life and alleviating the symptoms of the cancer. There are many treatments for advanced breast cancer that can prolong life and control symptoms for an extended period of time. Regardless of where a woman is on the palliative care trajectory, it is important to encourage her to live her life fully until she dies.

REFERENCES

American Heritage Dictionary (4th ed.). (2001). Boston, Mass.: Houghton Mifflin.

Bloch, S., & Kissane, D. (2000). Psychotherapies in psycho-oncology. *British Journal of Psychiatry, 177,* 112–116.

Bohm, P., & Huber, J. (2002). The surgical treatment of bony metastases of the spine and limbs. *The Journal of Bone and Joint Surgery, 84,* 521–529.

Brant, J.M. (1998). The art of palliative care: living with hope, dying with dignity. *Oncology Nursing Forum, 25,* 995–1004.

Cha, C.H., Kennedy, G.D., & Neiderhuber, J.E. (1999). Metastatic breast cancer. *Surgical Clinics of North America, 79,* 1117–1143.

Creagan, E.T. (1993). Psychosocial issues in oncologic practice. *Mayo Clinic Procedures, 68,* 161–167.

Dixon, S.W., & Esper, P. (2002). Anorexia, cachexia and nutritional support. In K. Kuebler & P. Esper (Eds.), *Palliative practices from A–Z,* pp. 13–22. Pittsburgh: Oncology Nursing Society.

Durr, H.R., Muller, P.E., Lenz, T., Baur, A., Jansson, V., & Refior, H.J. (2002, March). Surgical treatments of bone metastases in patients with advanced breast cancer. *Clinical Orthopaedics and Related Research,* 191–196.

Elomaa, I. (2000). The use of bisphosphonates in skeletal metastases. *Acta Oncologica, 39,* 445–454.

Fokstuen, T., Wilking, N., Rutqvist, L.E., Wolke, J., Liedberg, A., Signomklao, T., & Fernberg, J.O. (2000). Radiation therapy in the management of brain metastases from breast cancer. *Breast Cancer Research and Treatment, 62,* 211–216.

Geels, P., Eisenhauer, E., Bezjak, A., Zee, B., & Day, A. (2000). Palliative effect of chemotherapy: objective tumor response is associated with symptom improvement in patients with metastatic breast cancer. *Journal of Clinical Oncology, 18,* 2395–2405.

Georgoulias, V.A. (2001). Docetaxel/gemcitabine: salvage chemotherapy in anthracycline-pretreated patients with advanced breast cancer. *Oncology, 15,* 18–24.

Groff, L., Zecca, E., De Conno, F., Brunelli, C., Boffi, R., Panzeri, C., Cazzaniga, M., & Ripamonti, C. (2001). The role of disodium pamidronate in the management of bone pain due to malignancy. *Palliative Medicine, 15,* 297–307.

Grunfeld, E.A., Ramirez, A.J., Maher, E.J., Peach, D., Young, T., Albery, I.P., & Richards, M.A. (2001). Chemotherapy for advanced breast cancer: what influences oncology decision-making? *British Journal of Cancer, 84,* 1172–1178.

Hillner, B.E. (2000). The role of bisphosphonates in metastatic breast cancer. *Radiation Oncology, 10,* 250–253.

Hortobagyi, G.N. (2001). Treatment of advanced breast cancer with gemcitabine and vinorelbine. *Oncology, 15*(2), 15–17.

Jemal, A., Thomas, A., Murray, T., & Thun, M. (2002). Cancer statistics 2002. *CA—A Cancer Journal for Clinicians, 52,* 23–47.

Koedoot, N., Molenaar, S., Oostervald, P., Bakker, P., De Graeff, A., Nooy, M., Varekamp, I., & De Haes, H. (2001). The decisional conflict scale: further validation in two samples of Dutch oncology patients. *Patient Education and Counseling, 45,* 187–193.

Kuebler, K.K. (2002). Depression. In K. Kuebler, P. Berry, & D. Heidrich (Eds.), *End of life care: clinical guidelines,* pp. 269–279. Philadelphia: W.B. Saunders.

Lawlor, P.G., Fainsinger, R.L., & Bruera, E.D. (2000). Delirium at the end of life: critical issues in clinical practice and research. *Journal of the American Medical Association, 284,* 2427–2429.

Lloyd-Williams, M., & Friedman, T. (2001). Depression in palliative care patients: a prospective study. *European Journal of Cancer Care, 10,* 270–274.

Mannix, K., Ahmedzai, S.H., Anderson, H., Bennett, M., Lloyd-Williams, M., & Wilcock, A. (2000). Using bisphosphonates to control the pain of bone metastases: evidence-based guidelines for palliative care. *Palliative Medicine, 14,* 455–461.

McHale, H.K. (2002). Palliative care. In K. Kuebler & P. Esper (Eds.), *Palliative practices from A–Z,* pp. 193–197. Pittsburgh: Oncology Nursing Society.

Morris, J.N., & Sherwood, S. (1987). Quality of life of cancer patients at different stages in the disease trajectory. *Journal of Chronic Diseases, 40*(6), 545–556.

Nowotny, M.L. (1989). Assessment of hope in patients with cancer: development of an instrument. *Oncology Nursing Forum, 16,* 57–61.

O'Connor, A.M. (1995). Validation of a decisional conflict model. *Medical Decision Making, 5,* 25–30.

Olin, J.J., & Muss, H.B. (2000). New strategies for managing metastatic breast cancer. *Oncology, 14,* 629–641.

Rubens, R.D. (2001). Management of advanced breast cancer. *International Journal of Clinical Practice, 55,* 676–679.

Sciuto, R., Festad, A., Pasqualoni, R., Semprebene, A., Rea, S., Bergoni, S., & Maini, C. (2001). Metastatic bone pain palliation with 89-Sr and 186-Re-HEDP in breast cancer patients. *Breast Cancer Research and Treatment, 66,* 101–109.

Seidman, A.D. (1996). Chemotherapy for advanced breast cancer: a current perspective. *Seminars in Oncology, 23*(1 Suppl 2), 55–59.

Seidman, A.D. (2001). Gemcitabine as single-agent therapy in the management of advanced breast cancer. *Oncology, 15*(2 Suppl 3), 11–14.

Shen, J., Anderson, P., Albert, P.S., Wenger, N., Glaspy, J., Cole, M., & Shekelle, P. (2002). Use of complementary/alternative therapies by women with advanced-stage breast cancer. *BMC Complementary and Alternative Medicine, 2.* Retrieved from *http://www.biomedcentral.com/1472-6882/2/8.*

Smith, H. (2002). Delirium/acute confusion. In K. Kuebler & P. Esper (Eds.), *Palliative practices from A–Z,* pp. 81–83. Pittsburgh: Oncology Nursing Society.

Thompson, E.A., & Reilly, D. (2002). The homeopathic approach to symptom control in the cancer patient: a prospective observational study. *Palliative Medicine, 16,* 227–233.

Wrede-Seaman, L. (2001). Treatment options to manage pain at the end of life. *American Journal of Hospice and Palliative Care, 18,* 89–101.

Index